# PURITANS
# AT PLAY

*Also by Bruce C. Daniels*

CONNECTICUT'S FIRST FAMILY:
William Pitkin and His Connections

TOWN AND COUNTY:
Essays on the Structure of Local Government
in the American Colonies (*editor*)

THE CONNECTICUT TOWN:
Growth and Development, 1635-1790

DISSENT AND CONFORMITY ON
NARRAGANSETT BAY:
The Colonial Rhode Island Town

POWER AND STATUS:
Officeholding in Colonial America (*editor*)

THE FRAGMENTATION OF NEW ENGLAND:
Comparative Perspectives on Economic, Political,
and Social Divisions in the Eighteenth Century

# PURITANS AT PLAY

*Leisure and Recreation in Colonial New England*

Bruce C. Daniels

**St. Martin's Griffin**
New York

PURITANS AT PLAY

Copyright © 1995 by Bruce C. Daniels

All rights reserved. Printed in the United States of America. No part of this book may be used or reproduced in any manner whatsoever without written permission except in the case of brief quotations embodied in critical articles or reviews. For information, address St. Martin's Press, Scholarly and Reference Division, 175 Fifth Avenue, New York, N.Y. 10010

ISBN 0-312-16124-7 (paperback)

**Library of Congress Cataloging-in-Publication Data**

Daniels, Bruce Colin.
    Puritans at play : leisure and recreation in colonial New England / Bruce C. Daniels
        p.   cm.
    Includes bibliographical references and index.
    ISBN 0-312-112500-3 — ISBN 0-312-16124-7 (pbk.)
    1. Puritans — Recreation — New England — History — 17th Century.
    2. Puritans — Recreation — New England — History — 18th Century.
    3. Leisure — New England — History. I. Title.
GV54.A11D35    1995
709.1'9'08925074 — dc20                        94-37341
                                                  CIP

Book Design: Acme Art, Inc.

First published in hardcover in the United States of America in 1995
First St. Martin's Griffin Edition: September 1996

10 9 8 7 6 5 4 3 2 1

*For Hinton and Diana Bradbury*

# Table of Contents

Acknowledgments . . . . . . . . . . . . . . . . . . . . . . . . . . . . . . . ix

Introduction: Puritanism, Play, and American Culture . . . . . . . . . . . xi

### Section One  DID PURITANS LIKE FUN?

I. Sober Mirth and Pleasant Poisons: Historians, Puritan Ambivalence,
and the Concept of Pleasure in Early New England . . . . . . . . 3

### Section Two  INTELLECTUAL AND CULTURAL ENTERTAINMENT

II. Quiet Times: Reading for Pleasure and Profit . . . . . . . . . . . . 27
III. Music and Theater Struggle for Legitimacy . . . . . . . . . . . . . . 51

### Section Three  GATHERING TOGETHER

IV. Congregational Socializing: Gathering Together
at the Meetinghouse . . . . . . . . . . . . . . . . . . . . . . . . . 75
V. Civic Socializing: Parties for the Common Good . . . . . . . . . . . 93

### Section Four  MEN AND WOMEN FROLIC TOGETHER

VI. Frolics for Fun: Dances, Weddings, and Dinner Parties . . . . . . 109
VII. The Progress of Romance: Sex and Courtship . . . . . . . . . . . 125
VIII. Drinking and Socializing: Alcohol, Taverns,
and Alehouse Culture . . . . . . . . . . . . . . . . . . . . . . . . 141

### Section Five  SPECIAL OPPORTUNITIES AND BARRIERS

IX. Men Frolic by Themselves: Sport and Games in a Male Culture . . 163
X. The Fragmentation of Social Experience: Age, Gender, Location,
and Social Class . . . . . . . . . . . . . . . . . . . . . . . . . . . 185

**Section Six  PURITANS, REVOLUTIONARIES, AND AMERICANS**

XI.  The Puritan Legacy: The National Inheritance . . . . . . . . . . . . 215

Abbreviations Used in the Endnotes . . . . . . . . . . . . . . . . . . . . . 223

Endnotes . . . . . . . . . . . . . . . . . . . . . . . . . . . . . . . . . . . . . . . 225

Index . . . . . . . . . . . . . . . . . . . . . . . . . . . . . . . . . . . . . . . . . 265

# Acknowledgments

This book has taken eight years from start to finish. During this time my life as a person has gone on parallel to my life as a scholar. Many people and institutions have helped me write the book; many people have helped make me happy. A few stalwarts have done service on both sides of the parallel lines. I cannot repay any of these debts but I would like to acknowledge them.

The University of Winnipeg is a small, convivial school. Probably a third of the faculty have heard me speak on the subject of Puritanism either at a formal talk or over lunch. Some undoubtedly have heard more than they wanted to. Often faculty friends made substantive suggestions that have ended up in the final product. Within the history department I would like to thank Donald Bailey, Jennifer Brown, Sarah McKinnon, Daniel Stone, and Katherine Young for their help; special thanks to Robert Young, who has been an extraordinarily supportive colleague and friend. Outside the history department, John Coté, Richard Noble, William Rannie, and James Richtik deserve recognition, as do Deans Michael McIntyre and Donald Kerr. Among the staff I have benefited from the work and friendship of the history department's secretary, Linda Gladstone; Marilyn Cass; Judi Hanson; Heather Greene; Irma Kemp; Suzanne Martin; Bea Spearing; and Jackie Wong.

The generosity of fellow historians who gave freely of their time and expertise and then often thanked me for the opportunity never ceases to amaze. Some of the scholars listed below are close friends; some are acquaintances I see on professional occasions. Each has been my benefactor. I list them alphabetically and by institutional affiliation: James Axtell, Ann Gross, Robert Gross, Ronald Hoffman, and Michael McGiffert of the College of William and Mary; Richard D. Brown, Fred Cazel, Christopher Collier, and Albert E. Van Dusen of the University of Connecticut; Jack Greene of Johns Hopkins University; Evelyn Hinz and John Teunissen of the University of Manitoba; John Ifkovic of Westfield State College; Harry Stout of Yale University; David Thelen of the *Journal of American History;* and Bruce Tucker of the University of Windsor.

My debt to several institutions is less personal but more tangible. I wish to thank the Canada-U.S. Fulbright Program and Duke University, the Social Sciences and Humanities Research Council of Canada, and the University of Winnipeg Research Committee for their financial support. Parts of chapters I, V, and VIII appeared as articles in the *Journal of American Studies, American Studies,* and the *Historical Journal of Massachusetts;* these appear here with the editors' permission.

I thank the following people out of sheer gratitude for their presence in my life: my friends Arthur Allbee, Gail Bradbury, Dayle Everatt, Romeo and Wanda Fontaine, Judith Graham, Jack King, Gordon McKinnon, Fulton Niece, Carolina Springett, Lindsey Steek, and Kathryn Taylor; my sister and brother-in-law, Lea and Daniel Riccio; my mother, Willa Daniels; and my three daughters, Elizabeth, Abigail, and Nora. I dedicated my first book to my daughters when they were little girls; they are now young adults. I am as proud of them now as I was then.

Two university colleagues and golfing partners deserve my special thanks: Mark Baldwin and Hugh Grant. They are wonderful and talented friends who have read large portions of the manuscript and improved it greatly with their suggestions.

Finally, I wish to thank the two people whose names appear on the dedication page for friendship that is as strong as family.

# Introduction
## Puritanism, Play, and American Culture

Everyone plays; the need to do something for relaxation is built into the biology and psychology of human beings. The forms of play, however, are not universal but are a social construction shaped by specific physical circumstances, values, and history. Thus, a culture at play should tell much about itself. Patterns of leisure and recreation are manifestations of a society's core identity. Unfortunately, assaying the meaning of specific patterns of leisure and recreation is not easy. Though they often assert — virtually as a matter of faith — that pleasurable pastimes provide significant clues to a culture's inner workings, scholars then find the meaning of these clues puzzling and elusive.[1]

In particular, people have sought to understand the culture of the United States by analyzing how its citizens relax.[2] Americans at play, however, send ambiguous signals both to themselves and to the world at large. On the one hand, they pursue pleasure relentlessly, even wantonly. Licentious, narcissistic, hedonistic: all of these adjectives could be used to describe behavior that revolves around sexuality, individual gratification, and conspicuous consumption of everything. Much music and many films exaggerate reality and promote a picture of American decadence. Yet, on the other hand, many people, particularly foreigners, feel that Americans do not know how to play properly. According to this view, the seeming hedonism of Americans camouflages their true inability to relax. Coexisting with the American values of freedom of expression and behavior are deeper feelings that bespeak a repressive, censorious morality. Thus, bathtub gin can be explained as a product of abstemious temperance; sex on the movie screen reflects sophomoric insecurities; the frenetic chase for fun parallels the rat-race pace of work. Americans work too hard at play, a sure sign that they are not very good at it. They take their leisure and recreation just as they take their role in the world — too seriously.[3]

When foreign or American commentators search the past for clues to American identity, a number of explanatory factors surface with regularity. Among these, for example, are the frontier, abundance, immigration, and the short span of American history. Predictably, considerations of morality and pleasure begin with a short discussion about or diatribe against Puritanism. Something about Puritanism has fascinated—perhaps "fixated" is a more appropriate term—the historical imagination. The general story line of the popular analysis goes as follows. Political freedom, individualism, a fluid class structure, prosperity, geographical mobility—all of these factors (and others) fuel an American drive toward hedonism. But, lurking just beneath this surface gaiety, a cluster of attitudes derived from Puritan origins prevents Americans from truly enjoying themselves. Thus, popular pundits argue that despite their apparent carefree pursuit of pleasure, Americans have always been and still are chained to guilt, sanctimony, harsh judgments, and hypocrisy by their Puritan past. As the French paper *Le Monde* wrote recently in a front-page editorial on the Clarence Thomas/Anita Hill scandal, "since the arrival of the Pilgrim fathers, America has never truly settled its account with sin. The old Puritan heritage periodically surges forth from the collective memory."[4] Much of the popular culture shares this belief and associates Puritanism with dour prudery.

Contemporary historians have developed a view of Puritanism that is in opposition to this popularly held view. According to them, Puritans enjoyed sex, beer, and time free from work. New England's founders may have been harsh in judging sinners, but they were clear and fair-minded, not bigoted and hypocritical when they applied standards. Most professional historians attribute any ascetic, prudish qualities in American life to double standards created by Victorian Americans in the late nineteenth century. Puritans have been relieved of blame by scholars who have reassigned the historical burden of prudery to the more recent past. In an attempt to place Puritan attitudes in a more sophisticated context, historians have replaced the gloomy, religious fanatic with a relaxed moderate.[5]

I believe that both these historical figures—the gloomy fanatic of popular culture and the relaxed moderate of professional historians—are equally ahistorical and fail to personify the complexity of Puritan attitudes toward leisure and recreation. By this I do not mean that Puritans said one thing but did another. That was to be expected. Scholars know, as did Puritans, that a gap exists between ideals and practice in all societies; such a gap merely reflects the human condition. Recent social historians have done much to measure the distance between practice and preaching in New England by assessing criminality and deviance. It was within the preaching itself, however, that the real complexity existed. The Puritan ideal of leisure and recreation contained a profound ambivalence. Puritans had trouble articulating their ideal of appropriate leisure and recreation. This difficulty resulted in ambiguous messages to their own society and to future generations. Thus, many of the problems that strict moralists identified in the behavior of New England colonists resulted not from a failure to live up to ideals—frank deviance was always condemned—but rather from a failure to agree upon ideals and from an inability to agree upon the way ideals should translate into practice.

I have tried to make sense of the confusion and ambiguity that swirls around the Puritans' attitudes toward pleasure and relaxation by describing what New Englanders *said* and what they *did* between 1620 and 1790—to provide what the anthropologist Clifford Geertz called a "thick description" that distinguishes the meaningful from the meaningless, the general idiom from the idiosyncrasy.[6] I have also attempted to place these words and deeds in the context of an evolving, complex social structure. I believe that by examining the intersection of belief, practice, and social milieu, we can arrive at a truer understanding of New England culture than we would get through an isolated examination of either rhetoric or reality. I also believe that by following changes in belief and practice over the colonial and Revolutionary periods we can develop a better appreciation of what Puritanism bequeathed to American patterns of play. At the very least, a discussion of nearly two centuries of the evolution of leisure and recreation in New England should identify some of the beliefs and practices that survived to be part of the culture of the new nation.

I have shied away from providing definitions of the terms "leisure," "recreation," and "play"; the task defies precision. All three words sound prosaic but embody the poetic. At the heart of their meanings is another even more simple and more maddeningly elusive word—fun. Fun, as the Dutch historian Johan Huizinga wrote, is an "absolutely primary category of life, familiar to everyone at a glance right down to the animal level." Yet the essence of fun resists analysis. Theories abound: play is training for the serious purposes of life; play is a release of excess energy; play is an outlet for potentially harmful impulses. People intuitively feel that leisure and recreation have a serious function that is not play.[7] Fun, however, has adherents rather than theorists. And it is fun, in its many manifestations, that I have sought to describe in this book. Quiet fun, spiritual fun, family fun, civic fun, boisterous fun, deviant fun—the things that New Englanders did to enjoy themselves.

Apart from my admitted looseness in a few definitions, I have tried to stay safely within the bounds of professional historical standards. These standards need not be confining; besides, a book that wishes to add knowledge to subjects as important and complex as Puritanism and provincial New England should be careful and scholarly. A book about fun, however, should be fun. My goal throughout this work has been to do justice to both the richness of the historical material and to the inherent charm of the topic. I hope my efforts do not wander too much in either direction and become either ponderous or glib. I have consciously attempted to appeal to both professional and casual students of American history. Puritans believed that the ideal leisure activity was both productive and pleasurable. I share that belief. Writing this book has been instructive and fun; I hope reading it is.

Section One

# DID PURITANS
# LIKE FUN?

I

# Sober Mirth and Pleasant Poisons: Historians, Puritan Ambivalence, and the Concept of Pleasure in Early New England

For over four centuries "puritan" has been a synonym for the dour, the joyless, the repressed. Few historical concepts have proven so strong: from the literati of Elizabethan England through the critics of the Moral Majority in the 1980s, the image of the Puritan as killjoy has endured. Colonial Yorkers and Virginians, nineteenth-century novelists and historians, twentieth-century reformers and liberals—in fact, just about everyone else in American history—have thanked their lucky stars that they did not have to submit to the Puritans' iron regimen. A long list of iconoclasts have made a good intellectual living trying to outdo one another by debunking the Puritans and their inability to have fun. Contemporary wags such as Captain Thomas Morton, James Franklin, and the Reverend Samuel Peters, themselves self-described victims of Puritan censoriousness, and modern wits such as H. L. Mencken and Moses Coit Tyler were not unduly troubled by a strict sense of fairness or accuracy in creating quotable bon mots. Mencken's quip that Puritanism was "the haunting fear that someone, somewhere, may be happy" seems destined to live forever. Tyler's accusation that Puritans "cultivated the grim and the ugly" is an equally devastating indictment of their contempt for expressions of joy in beauty.[1] More honest literary figures, such as Nathaniel Hawthorne, Arthur Miller, and Robert Lowell, and scholars, such as James Truslow Adams and Vernon Parrington, have gone beyond the cheap shots of the Mencken-style wits and tried to extract a deeper meaning from the Puritan experience.[2] The Puritan who emerges from their analyses is no longer a guilt-ridden, hypocritical killjoy; though just as sober, just as serious, their Puritan is far more believable—with a far more sinister effect on subsequent American development. An antiliberal, antidemocratic, even totalitarian strain that courses through American history emanates from this Puritan—the joyless fanatic who shares the timeless qualities of the true believer with such historical figures as Cromwell, Robespierre, and Lenin. Both frivolous and serious critics of the Puritans have in common, however, the implicit belief that if only colonial New Englanders could have let down their hair a little, modern Americans might have been spared a host of problems ranging from silly prudery to the destructive force of McCarthyism.

Probably more than any other piece of literature, Hawthorne's *The Scarlet Letter* cemented the image of the joyless Puritan into the American mind. Not content to practice mere self-denial, Hawthorne's Puritans opposed happiness, leisure, and recreation anywhere they found them. Hawthorne, however, was transfixed by the idea that joy cannot be forever banished. Recreational impulses surfaced repeatedly and unexpectedly in all his characters. Puritan children "played" at going to church; Hester had occasional "sportive impulses"; Chillingsworth's "mock smile . . . played him false"; Dimmesdale felt a "strange joy" in Pearl's "game" of whispering in his ear; Pearl was a "plaything of the angels." Lurking just beneath the surface of *The Scarlet Letter*, and also in Hawthorne's less well-known "The Maypole of Merrymount," is his belief that the Puritans were trying to accomplish the impossible by restraining basic human instincts: joy and play were bound to emerge despite all efforts to banish them. Tyler, whose literary history of the colonies was profoundly influenced by Hawthorne, restated this theme in his appraisal of the Puritan's vain attempt to "eradicate poetry from his nature," where it "was planted . . . too deep even for his theological grub-hooks to root it out."[3]

## Intellectual History and the Creation of The Happy Puritan

Not until the 1930s did any serious body of work challenge the views of Hawthorne and the many historians who embedded his fictive anal-ysis in explicit historical narratives. Modern Puritan scholarship began with the publication in 1930 of Samuel Eliot Morison's *Builders of the Bay Colony* and received its most influential statement with the publication in 1939 of Perry Miller's *The New England Mind in the Seventeenth Century.*[4] Morison softened, warmed, and humanized the Puritans; Miller subjected their intellect and theology to one of the most extraordinarily rigorous and penetrating analyses ever attempted by any scholar of any discrete body of thought. In a series of biographical vignettes, Morison described individual Puritans enjoying life's pleasures. In his massive tome, Miller argued that joy, leisure, and recreation had a legitimate place in a Puritan cosmology that was far more complex than had hitherto been imagined. Miller's work greatly influenced an entire generation of historians. One scholar called it as persuasive and pervasive in American history as Copernican astronomy or Newtonian physics was in the world of science.[5] To call the colonist who emerged from the work of Morison and Miller a happy Puritan oversimplifies, but does not do an injustice to the essence of their conclusions. The "new" Puritans actively sought and experienced pleasure in their lives. Moreover, their pursuit of certain types of pleasure was not only sanctioned but actively encouraged by the ministerial elite.

Morison based his picture of the happy Puritan on a few essential facts that seemed to have eluded his predecessors. New England's Puritans were not strict Calvinists; the fire-and-brimstone sermons that earlier historians cited as examples of a terrifying religion were the product more of the mid-eighteenth than of the seventeenth century; the doggerel of Michael Wigglesworth (which was indeed joyless) was no more representative of Puritanism than was the sensual, loving poetry of Anne Bradstreet; and the Puritans did not prohibit alcohol as many people thought, but instead maintained taverns in almost every town. Morison's descriptive passages attached a great deal of importance to drink and the presence of taverns. This is not surprising when we remember that he was writing at the end of a decade of prohibition whose origins were often attributed to the allegedly abstemious Puritans. Nor, as he made clear, was the Puritan desire for drink indulged behind the backs of the authorities. "Beer, cider, even hard liquor were provided at town expense," according to Morison, "to attract unpaid helpers at [house-raisings] and to provide the necessary courage to walk out on a stringer or ridgepole." A parish providing poor relief for some of its members listed "malt and wine" as among the necessities of life. Morison's picture of a seventeenth-century New England small town sounds a little like one Norman Rockwell might have drawn except that

Morison added a few ribald panels. His picture of Boston is a larger, more urbane version of the same happy setting. Consider the following charming scene:

> The ordinary week-day scene in Boston of the sixteen-fifties was active and colourful enough to suit a Dutch painter. Holland, France, Spain, and Portugal coming hither for trade, shipping going on gallantly, taverns doing a roaring trade with foreign sailors and native citizens, boys and girls sporting up and down the streets, between houses gay with the fresh color of new wood and the red-painted trim; the high tide lapping into almost every backyard and garden; and Beacon Hill towering above all.[6]

Looking at this description closely, one sees that Morison does not say much: Boston had foreign trade, taverns, children, painted houses, tide, and a hill. But when the shipping is *gallant*, the taverns *roaring*, the children *sporting*, the houses *gay*, the high tide *lapping*, and the hill *towering*, all thoughts of Nathaniel Hawthorne's crabbed killjoys suddenly seem to vanish. Morison's evocative, compelling prose dressed up his substantive insights—which by themselves were important—in ways that any modern advertising executive would recognize as pure selling genius.

Few readers are likely to accuse Perry Miller of charming his way to dominance as the leading American intellectual historian of the twentieth century. His complex prose makes for very slow reading. Miller's influence lies in the strength of his analysis, which attempted to make a coherent whole out of a seemingly diverse body of religious, political, social, and moral thought that he identified as the "Puritan mind." Previous scholars, Miller believed, had misread Puritan ideals. When the Puritans failed to live according to these ideals—as they were mistakenly defined by scholars—the disappointed historians called the Puritans failures and hypocrites. The real failure, Miller argued, lay not within Puritan civilization but within the inability of subsequent scholars to penetrate its thought.

The most obvious discrepancy, according to most historians, lay between the ideal of piety and the practice of piety. The ideal should have sent the Puritans on "a solitary flight to the desert," according to their critics' expectations, and "attired them in their hair shirt of repentance." But the Puritans went not to the desert but to Massachusetts and Connecticut, and they wore comfortable cloaks and waistcoats of attractive colors. Consequently historians have thought that Puritans lacked the courage of their convictions—convictions, Miller writes, that the Puritans never had and would have considered absurd. Puritan piety never admired the extreme ascetic. Neither did it embrace a "gloomy, otherworldly, and tragic conception of life, which sought to forbid . . . relaxations." Puritans may have been tough minded in judging sinners, they may have been complacent about the superiority of their own beliefs, but they never argued that virtue had no room for "cakes and ale." To the Puritans, life in general could be grim; they seldom lost sight of the pain, unhappiness, and harsh circumstances of the world. Yet they believed that lives on earth should have, as the minister Samuel Willard wrote, "sometimes their exstasies." Similarly, the Puritans' emphasis on the next world did not cause them to reject the present world and worldly senses. Preparation for heaven did not mean that one should not try to bring the earthly "wilderness to blossom." In particular, Miller said, historians have so overstated the Puritans' emphasis on original sin as to cast a depressing pallor over their daily lives. Original sin was largely a "metaphysical convenience," according to Miller, which helped Puritans solve some pressing theological problems. Their body of thought about original sin did not inflict a sense of sin and tragedy on every occurrence.[7]

After discarding the picture of the Puritan as a failed ascetic, as a dark, brooding creature who carried Adam on his shoulders every waking hour, Miller created a new, much happier picture of the Puritan—as a religious person preparing for the next world, but also as a social person committed to enjoying moderate pleasures in the present one. "God has given us temporals to enjoy," Miller quotes the minister Joshua Moody; "we should therefore suck the sweet of them, and so slake our thirst with them, as not to be insatiably craving after more." Pleasure had a useful role in Puritan cosmology; never did Puritans believe that actions were sinful merely because they were enjoyable. Moderate pleasures, as Moody instructed his congregation, prevented one from pursuing immoderate ones. Eating, relaxing pastimes, and sexual gratification, the Puritan ministers argued, all gave refreshing pleasures that when practiced in moderation benefited the individual and hence the community. Gluttony, idleness, and lust, however, resulted when pleasure-seeking was carried to an extreme and became an end unto itself; these immoderate pleasures were a sin and should be punished. Thus, Moody wrote that enjoyable actions are never sinful if "they remain subordinate to their utility; they become reprehensible as soon as" they are practiced for their delectability alone. The people of God are free to use the things of this life . . . for their convenience and comfort; but yet he hath set bounds to this liberty, that it may not degenerate into licentiousness."[8]

In the half century since Miller published *The New England Mind in the Seventeenth Century,* critics have questioned a variety of the implications of his work and many of its nuances. Almost no one, however, has questioned the basic premise that Puritan ideology allowed for and encouraged a moderate amount of leisure and recreation, provided such pleasures remained subordinate to Scripture, the glorification of God, and the good of the community. The acceptance of a Puritan more at ease with joy and comfort has allowed scholars to produce hundreds of books and articles on New England culture with this new, more relaxed, and likable Puritan at the center of the story.

No historian has done more to chase Mencken's and Hawthorne's joyless Puritan out of New England than Edmund Morgan, one of Miller's first students. In his book on the Puritan family, probably the book on colonial history most frequently used in university classrooms, Morgan described the Puritan in terms one might use for the affable guy next door: "He liked good food, good drink, and homey comforts . . . he found it a real hardship to drink water when the beer gave out." Morgan, of course, wrote also of the genuine deep piety that suffused Puritan ideals and practice, but it is his emphasis on the idea that "God did not forbid innocent play" that has stayed with generations of students. Morgan's biography of John Winthrop, Massachusetts's first governor, made the stern leader into a tender, loving husband who controlled but enjoyed his passions; and his biography of Ezra Stiles, the president of Yale College in the eighteenth century, described the minister-educator as a "gentle Puritan" who delighted in good company and the refined pleasures of the intellect. Even more than these distinguished books, Morgan's article "The Puritans and Sex" etched the picture of the happy, well-adjusted Puritan into the modern historical consciousness. A repressed sexuality and a hatred of liquor had been frequently cited as the two most prominent examples of the antipleasure impulse in Puritanism. Morison and others had destroyed the utility of the latter example by establishing beyond the shadow of a doubt that Puritans enjoyed beer and other drink. Morgan attacked the accuracy of the former example by arguing that Puritans enjoyed sex, were told by their ministers and theology that sex in the proper channels should be enjoyed, and in general had as healthy an attitude toward sex as one could hope to find anywhere. Far from being squeamish, Morgan's Puritans treated sex in more matter-of-fact terms than twentieth-century Americans do.[9]

What was left to sustain the image of the dour, repressed killjoy? The Puritan who stopped off at the tavern for a glass of beer after work, made love that night, and went to church the next day with a clear conscience did not seem to be either an ascetic or hypocrite. The practical effect of the Morison-Miller-Morgan school of Puritan scholarship was to make the Puritans into real people—people who were religious and believed in a strict moral code; people who shared a harshness characteristic of most seventeenth-century society; but people with sex drives, appetites, a sense of humor, and an appreciation of the need for pleasure and joy in everyday life. "Sincerity," "consistency," "decency," "moderation"—these were the words attached to the Puritans' attitudes toward leisure, recreation, and morality, replacing words like "fanatic," "hypocrite," and "ascetic." Though not a boisterous person in anyone's estimation, the new, happy Puritan enjoyed "durable satisfactions," as Morison's summary put it.[10]

## The New Social History and the Complexity of Reality at the Local Level

Not until the 1960s did any major works question this new view of Puritans and pleasure or open any fresh lines of inquiry into New England society. In that decade, a group of scholars who called their work the "new social history" challenged the dominance of intellectual history and did indeed open new questions, which are still being considered. The new social historians rooted their work in large samples of quantifiable data and claimed to be much more empirical—much more *scientific*—than their predecessors, who dealt primarily with literary evidence. Much of this new work took the form of community studies that attempted to recreate the reality of everyday life for average people. The new social historians brought to their discipline a methodology long practiced by social scientists. When historians went to the local community to evaluate patterns of everyday life in relation to the ideology and values of society, they were, in effect, employing the methods that the anthropologists Bronislaw Malinowski and Franz Boas pioneered in their fieldwork in the early twentieth century.[11]

In "The Mirror of Puritan Authority," an article that truly deserves to be called seminal, Darrett Rutman put the challenge to the intellectual historians point-blank: "Was the ideal—so often expressed by the articulate few and commented upon by the intellectual historians—ever a reality in New England?" he asked, arguing: "Certainly, conditions in America were not conducive to it." How was the "abstract principle . . . toyed with by logicians" applied to the reality of the New England town and church? The questions Rutman asked were essentially those posed by the work of social historians for all fields of history. Was there a divergence between the rhetoric expressed in literary evidence, and the reality reflected in the daily living habits of the general public? Did the Puritan ideal impose itself upon behavior, or did behavior render the ideal irrelevant?[12] Questions such as these, of course, cannot be answered by intellectual historians. The questions are posed by social historians, and only social history can answer them. Moreover, crucial secondary questions arise from the general one about the practical effect on daily behavior of abstract principles. A majority of colonial New Englanders were not members of the church; did non–church members' attitudes toward pleasure differ from those of church members? New England had urban, rural, and frontier communities; did these have differing patterns of behavior and differing exposures to Puritan ideals? Did seacoast and backcountry differ? Did the colonies of Massachusetts, Connecticut, and Rhode Island? Did servants and the poor act and believe differently from freemen and the elite? Questions of this type, which have been asked repeatedly in the generation of the new social history, make it painfully clear that, in presenting a warm, human Puritan who sought pleasure in moderation, the intellectual historians painted their picture with a much sharper focus than the evidence warranted. We know what some Puritan leaders said about pleasure, but we do not know what most Puritans did. The ministerial elite may have written of the quiet, sensual joys of sex within marriage and the sinfulness of sex outside marriage. But to say is not necessarily to do. Puritans may have been guilt-ridden, repressed, and squeamish despite what their ministers told them; or they may have been lusty, ribald sexual sinners who carried on in spite of their ministers' ideology. As Rutman wrote in 1965, at the beginning of the social history generation, the answers to questions like these were not known.

The physical circumstances attendant upon the founding of New England certainly posed a challenge to the imposition of rigidly prescribed rules of conduct. Settlement in the New World, as Kenneth Lockridge has written, produced profound unsettlement in the social structure. Emigration; the frontier; the creation of new villages, churches, governments, and codes of laws; the sheer novelty of the colonial world—all combined to strain or destroy many traditional relationships. Family and community bonds were broken and had to be built anew. Geographical and economic mobility provided new opportunities for some people to experience more freedom from social restraint than ever before. Everywhere one looks in seventeenth-century New England, the physical details of life militated against a monolithic morality.[13]

## The New Intellectual History and the
## End of the New England Mind

At the same time that social historians began to identify some limits to the explanatory power of intellectual history, a new generation of intellectual historians began to challenge the work of Miller and others of his generation on its own terms. Debates have arisen over many specific propositions, but the details of these debates can be conveniently grouped around three main criticisms. First, the critics charge that the Miller school was so anxious to destroy the stereotype of the fanatical pleasure-hating Puritan that through gross overstatement it created a new, equally ahistorical stereotype of the Puritans as twentieth-century moderates in their views on pleasure. When scholars write "corrective" history of course this type of overstatement often occurs. Second, other historians argue that Miller and his generation of intellectual historians did not fully appreciate the diversity of New England thought. They paid lip service to the concept of diversity and wrote much about the outright dissent of Roger Williams and Anne Hutchinson; but in the final analysis, most scholars of the Miller school did believe that there was a "Puritan mind" and that it could be defined by a clear set of propositions to which most New Englanders would have acceded. Third, historians using insights and models from psychiatrists and psychologists suggest that the previous generation of intellectual historians failed to appreciate subconscious forces in the Puritan psyche and too readily accepted public statements at face value.[14]

When citing examples of overstatement and dubious interpretation of evidence, not surprisingly the critics often turn to the bugaboo longest associated with the Puritans — sex. Several recent historians have argued that the Puritan sermons extolling the pleasures of sex within the marriage bed were part of the rhetorical war Protestants had with Rome. Ministers liked to remind people that they were not celibates as were Catholic priests. Celibacy was not intrinsically bad, but it was a trap that inevitably led to the horrible sexual abuses that Puritans often associated with Catholics. As the Puritan minister Nicholas Noyes wrote, "Ye Popish dogs at marriage bark no more." The main reason (besides procreation) for recommending marital sex was to ward off worse temptations of "inexpressible uncleannesses." Puritans saw sexual snares everywhere, and in remarkably consistent language they associated "unrestrained sensuality" with paganism, atheism, idolatry, and blasphemy. And, this was as true for sex within marriage as for illicit sex: "intemperate adventures in bed" would

lead a husband to "play the adulterer with his own wife." Puritans treated
sexuality in all its forms with wariness—and at times even with horror,
seeing it as a lurking "invitation to damnation." It is true that some of Anne
Bradstreet's poems, and many letters from esteemed leaders such as John
Winthrop do suggest a tender, passionate sensuality within marriage. But
as much or more of the literature from the seventeenth century suggests
that sexuality held terror for many Puritans. Thomas Hooker, a minister
of towering influence, wrote in a vein similar to Bradstreet's poetry: "There
is wild love and joy enough in the world, as there is wild thyme and other
herbs but we would have garden love and garden joy." According to one
recent assessment of Puritan sexuality, however, the minister Samuel
Danforth's warning against excessive passion was probably more typical:
"Let thy lustful body be everlasting fuel for the unquenchable fire; let thy
lascivious soul be eternal food for the never-dying worm. Hell from
beneath is moved to meet thee."[15]

Although Danforth and Hooker gave sermons of contrasting emphases, both ministers operated within the limits of dissent allowed by Puritan
society. Other New England divines ventured outside these limits and
offered even greater intellectual alternatives. Roger Williams and Anne
Hutchinson are the most famous, but many other "radical spiritists"
rejected the essentials of Puritan theology and hence the essentials of
Puritan beliefs about pleasure. Diggers, Seekers, and Ranters—some of
the best-known radical dissenters in England—had adherents in New
England. Massachusetts's moderate Puritans were challenged by members
of these groups as well as by Familists, Anabaptists, Antinomians, and
Quakers. Important religious dissenters such as Williams, Hutchinson,
Benjamin Wheelwright, Samuel Gorton, John Clark, and William
Pynchon were not solitary figures; almost all of them had large groups of
followers and secret sympathizers. Because most of these pietistic dissenters rejected the doctrine of original sin, Puritans often thought them to be
near hedonists. Not being weighed down with the inevitability of sin gave
these dissenters a "faire and easie way to heaven," Puritan theologians
believed. Thomas Weld, a Puritan minister, explained the attractiveness
of antinomianism: "It pleaseth nature well to have heaven and their lusts
too." "Drunken dreams of the world" and "golden dreams of heaven,"
Thomas Shepard wrote in describing the theology of pietists, who thought
that if a believer had grace, salvation was inevitable. Nor was Shepard
wrong. The theology of most of these groups did make it possible to indulge
in behavior that was moral by their standards but that the respectable
moderate Puritan would have considered depraved.[16]

Eventually most of these groups became concentrated in Rhode Island, but they had sympathizers throughout New England and they provided a visible example of differing patterns of behavior and thought. When one considers that the dissenters did offer a "faire and easie way" to both heaven and life, and that many of the people of New England were not full members of the Puritan church, the popularity of the "radical spiritists" and the fear they inspired in the Puritan leadership are easy to understand.

The frequency of sexual references both negative and positive in Puritan literature suggests to many psychoanalytic historians that sex played heavily in Puritans' subconscious thoughts. Scholars now realize that in evaluating Puritan attitudes toward sexual (or any other) pleasure they must examine childhood, adolescence, child-rearing, and the developmental process by which a child was transformed into an adult Puritan. Puritans may have dwelled on sexuality in their published discussions of morality, but in practice parents were anything but matter-of-fact about sex; both in polite company and in the family, the subject was invariably avoided. Children received instructions about sex from the sermon literature, from examples of sexual crimes being punished, and from their peers. These sources, in general, do not seem conducive to imparting what psychologists would call "healthy attitudes" toward sexual pleasure. Among adolescents in seventeenth-century New England, sophomoric sexual talk was commonplace just as it is among many young people in twentieth-century America. The banter is delightful to them because it is shocking and regarded as wrong. But the sexual banter of the seventeenth century took place amid patterns of child-rearing strikingly different from those of the twentieth century.[17] The explicit attitudes toward pleasure of the adult Puritan world must be comprehended in the context of the personality occasioned by these patterns of child-rearing.

Pretending to a false certainty about the effects on the adult personality of Puritan child-rearing would be foolish. The best psychologists today disagree over the appropriate models of child development to use in historical analysis and the meaning that can be extracted from these models. Yet much can readily be agreed upon with respect to attitudes toward pleasure and people's ability to experience some kinds of pleasure. By almost any standard employed today, Puritan attitudes toward child-rearing were repressive. Heavy-handed practices were characteristic of most of the early modern world, but even judged by seventeenth-century standards, the Puritans were unusually harsh — we might even say psychologically brutal — in the way they prepared their children for adulthood. A

frequently cited child-rearing manual published in 1628 by the English
Puritan minister John Robinson stated: "There is in all children, though
not alike, a stubbornness, and stoutness of mind arising from their natural
pride, which must in the first place be broken and beaten down; that so
the foundation of their education being laid in humility and tractableness."
Original sin manifested itself without fail in the "spiritual diseases" that
children showed through acts of self-assertion. Children should not know,"
Robinson argued, "that they have a will of their own." In addition to
controlling children's wills, parents were enjoined to impress upon them
the full weight of their depravity. From the English Puritan background,
through the standard book used to teach literacy, *The New England Primer*,
through the writings of almost all the esteemed New England divines—
John Cotton, Thomas Shepard, and Increase and Cotton Mather—a
consistent message was heard. Puritans were closer to consensus on
child-rearing than on most matters.[18]

Determining precisely what injuries were inflicted on the psyches of
Puritan children is not easy. Nor is it entirely clear how successful parents
were in their efforts "to conceal their [own] . . . inordinate affections." At
one time historians believed that the weight of Puritan repression hung so
heavily that the young were almost completely deprived of childhood,
being expected to function as adults after the age of six. Clearly, this was
not the case; several stages of childhood, including the Sturm und Drang
of adolescence, did exist. Similarly, parents expressed far more love for
their children than an extreme application of theory would permit. Nevertheless, the philosophy and reality of child-rearing and the empirical
evidence from diaries, autobiographies, and other literary artifacts suggest
that much guilt, anxiety, and in particular, low self-esteem, were produced
before children reached the age of six. This, in turn, led children to attempt
to develop adult consciousnesses to control themselves—over manipula-
tion, psychologists today would call the process—which deepened their
sense of shame between the age of six and puberty. And then, at puberty,
the sum of all this guilt would create a series of taboos about the genitals
and other sources of pleasure. By almost any analysis, the pattern was
psychologically devastating and hostile to the development of a personality
that could be comfortable experiencing joy and sensuous gratification.
Thus, even if Puritan ideology and social thought explicitly told people to
pursue moderate leisure and recreation, the Puritan socialization process
made the pursuit at best ambivalent and conflicted.[19]

The most essential duty thrust upon Puritan children was to prepare
their souls for a religious conversion experience. In a psychological task

remarkably similar to the one Freud described, in which a boy has to conquer his lust for his mother—thus resolving the Oedipus complex—or face the terrifying punishment of castration by his father, the young Puritan had to conquer sinfulness and self-love or face eternal damnation. The only successful way to do this required a young person to subordinate self-love to love for God and to introject God's standards into what psychoanalysts call the superego. Thus, in psychoanalytic terms, Puritans had overdeveloped superegos with correspondingly compromised egos. People with dominant superegos tend to like external rules, order, structure, and stability; they tend to acquiesce easily to authority. They are not comfortable with individual assertions of behavior outside prescribed bounds, and they have a great deal of trouble being spontaneous, free-spirited, and lighthearted. They often master large bodies of knowledge, but tend not to be creative or playful with ideas. They have a great deal of self-loathing because, of course, they cannot completely conquer self-love and their inability to do so produces guilt and anxiety.[20]

The superego and ego, obviously, are not physically found anywhere in the mind or body; they are analytical tools—convenient fictions, some might say—to help explain certain patterns of child development and adult behavior that have been observed to recur in most societies. As analytical tools, however, they suggest not that Puritans believed pleasure to be wrong or inherently sinful, but that Puritanism as a collectivity had a psychological profile that made the pursuit of any self-enhancing or self-indulging pleasure a source of emotional conflict.

## Ambivalence in Theory

If we accept that neither their own psyches nor the values and ideology of their society provided Puritans with a clear, unambiguous guide to the role of pleasure in their lives, we may help explain the difficulty historians have had in agreeing upon Puritan attitudes toward leisure and recreation. The respectable Puritan mind—the body of thought sustained by the ministers and magistrates within the church's fold—clearly contained a diverse range of views on pleasure. The unrespectable Puritan mind—that belonging to New Englanders who exceeded the limits set by the clergy of Massachusetts and Connecticut—extended this range of views even further. Moreover, much rhetoric employed vague language, which permitted a great deal of subjectivity in definition and application.

Puritan thought on many crucial matters was inconsistent or contradictory. For a society remarkably consistent in its commitment to a primary purpose, early New England pursued its grand goal with a high degree of ambivalence over strategies, values, and secondary purposes. A series of conflicting impulses underlay much of this ambivalence: Puritans believed in conformity to doctrine but also in liberty of conscience; they worked for material prosperity but wanted to avoid worldly temptations; they prized social communalism but asserted economic individualism. Each of these pairs (among others) provided alternatives that competed for loyalty both within society as a whole and within the hearts and minds of individuals. The leadership usually pretended that no conflict existed, and tried to fit the divisions into a coherent whole. They argued, for example, that people should use their liberty of conscience to arrive at the same doctrine as the ministerial elite. Yet the contradictions did not go away in the seventeenth century; they resurfaced continually in both ideology and practice. In reality, they resurfaced because Puritans had neither the desire nor the ability to make these hard choices. So, rather than line up on either side of the alternatives for a showdown, they tried to make all the alternatives fit together comfortably. They could not; and Puritan society and individual Puritans were pulled in opposing directions by the strain of trying. As a result, Puritan society was profoundly ambivalent—partly because of divisions between individuals but even more because of unresolved conflicts *within* them. On many matters Puritans wanted to have things both ways, to have their cake and eat it, too.

Puritan attitudes toward leisure and recreation reflected this ambivalence. On the one hand, Puritans virtually unanimously stressed that all people needed relaxation to refresh their body and soul. As John Cotton, the most influential minister of the founding generation, wrote, "Life is not life, if it be overwhelmed with discouragements . . . wine it [is] to be drunken with a cheerful heart . . . thy wife beloved and she to be joyfully lived withal, all the days of thy vanity." Cotton was quick to add, however, that enjoyment of drink and love did not extend to "gluttony and drunkenness . . . swaggering and debaucht ruffians."[21] In these cautions we see the general Puritan ambivalence toward relaxation. Support of recreation and leisure in rhetoric was almost always accompanied by cautions against ungodly, unlawful, unreasonable, or unproductive activities. As if the very assertion threatened to open the floodgates to Hell, almost every endorsement of pleasure and fun was hedged with restrictions of its actual exercise. William Bradford, John Winthrop, Thomas Shepard, and Thomas Hooker, along with most other early leaders, took much care in their writings to identify the limits of lawful recreation and to cite many examples of fellow New Englanders who had exceeded these limits.

Winthrop's journal is not particularly dour, but it is full of references to divine judgments on those who abused their leisure time. Punishment was often immediate. One man who smoked too much was killed by gunpowder he had ignited seconds after telling a man who rebuked him that "he would take one more pipe [even] if the Devil should carry him away"—which, Winthrop believed, the Devil did, then and there. A wide variety of Sabbath-breakers, drunks, and miscreants were killed by lightning, falling trees, and other acts of God, according to Winthrop. A generation later, in 1684, Increase Mather echoed these sentiments when he wrote: "Lawful recreations . . . moderately and reasonably used are good and in some cases a duty." But people "often spend more time therein than God alloweth of. And, too many indulge themselves in sinful sports and pastimes. . . . The Scriptures commend unto Christians, gravity and sobriety in their carriage at all times; and condemn all levity," Mather concluded, with a blanket requirement that virtually negated everything he had said earlier in praise of recreation. He, too, identified an assortment of sinners whom God struck down.[22]

This tradition of moral rhetoric giving with one hand and taking away with the other continued into the eighteenth century. In 1707 the tradition received its most comprehensive statement in Benjamin Colman's 170-page tract, *The Government and Improvement of Mirth, According to the Laws of Christianity, in Three Sermons*.[23] Colman's tour de force is the only book-length study devoted exclusively to the subject of leisure and recreation published in colonial New England's history. Written at a time when the Puritan impulse seemed to be waning, *The Government and Improvement of Mirth* became the ideal text of its time. Its influence derived not just from its length but also from the care, judiciousness, and moderation Colman brought to his analysis, giving it an almost judicial quality of calm rationality.

As did John Cotton and Increase Mather before him, Colman extolled the virtues of leisure and recreation in the abstract. "I am far from inveighing against sober mirth," he wrote; "on the contrary, I justify, applaud, and recommend it. Let it be pure and grave, serious and devout, all which it may be and yet free and cheerful." The concept of "sober mirth," which Colman returned to continually, embodied in two words the ambivalence at the heart of Puritan attitudes toward fun. Almost no page passed without a reminder that "mirth may and generally does degenerate into sin: tis ordinarily the froth and noxious blast of a corrupt heart." Mirth is "graceful and charming so far as it is innocent," Colman admitted. But he felt compelled to add: "Tis pity that sin should mix with it to make it

nauseous and destructive and make it end in shame and sorrow." Yet,
continuing in this vein of giving and then taking, Colman reminded ascetics
that Christ himself neither scorned mirth on proper occasions nor censured
it in others; "we read of his tears but never of his laughing." Colman,
however, did not want readers to forget that above all, Jesus was "a man
of sorrow."[24]

In its overall thrust, Colman's work rehashed what must have been
a familiar message to New Englanders: Have fun, but not too much. Unlike
other Puritan moralists who freely gave advice on the pleasures/dangers
of recreation, however, Colman was systematic and precise in his attempt
to separate the joyful from the sinful. He was a list maker, and his lists of
rules provide a detailed guide to the rights and wrongs of sober mirth.
Colman's theoretical commitments to leisure and recreation were qualified
only by a few basic restrictions: they must be "innocent"; "do no injury to
God or our neighbour"; and "must not transgress sobriety, holiness, or
charity." If his analysis had ended with the above caveats, Colman's work
would stand as a monument to the happy, moderate Puritan. But after
rhetorically establishing his support for the principle of pursuing pleasure
in Sermon One, Colman examines the reality of the pursuit in Sermon
Two. Lurking within the innocent pastimes of "sober mirth," "virtuous
mirth," and "profitable mirth" are always their natural enemies, "carnal
and vicious mirths." Although these two types of mirth stood at opposing
poles of good and evil values, Colman argued that they were not far apart
in the realities of daily life. And herein lay the danger that was at the heart
of Puritan ambivalence toward leisure and recreation:

> [Once a] licentious manner of expressing our mirth takes over, all
> possibilities of innocence, neighborly love, or sobriety vanish. The
> pretence of restraint may be outwardly maintained but disdain is
> sneered from the eye and contempt is in the smile; tho indeed envy
> and spite are under the paint; the look is pleasing enough and gay but
> tis only disguise, a forced laugh while a man's galled and mad at the
> heart . . . a wretch cannot be overjoyed to see a friend but he must
> curse him and every cup of drink he gets he damns himself. . . . [T]he
> wanton man's mirth is ridiculous. He lays aside the man and the
> gravity of reason and acts the part of a frolic colt. He roars and frisks
> and leaps.[25]

Colman's list of licentious mirths — the attributes of the "frolic colt" —
was inclusive and more detailed than the list of acceptable sober mirths.

Among the commonplace practices that he found unacceptable: playing the part of the "merry drunkard"; "mirth ill-timed" on fast days, days of sorrow, or the Sabbath; "idle or impertinent mirth—a sport to a fool"; "making ourselves merry with sin"; "making religion and goodness the object of our mirth"; "making merry at the judgement of God." Also, mirth that "stops devotion, cramps industry and is big with idleness . . . [is] evil and unlawful." None of these "lewd practices" could be lawfully tolerated, argued Colman, because to allow them to exist, even if they were held in contempt, would expose the community to the dangers of contamination by one bad example: "Sensual lusts love company; men can't game and drink and be lewd and laugh alone. They provoke and spur on one another." Throughout the substantive heart of Sermon Two, one searches in vain for any specific nonreligious recreations that Colman found proper and lawful. (Undoubtedly there were some, but he left them unspecified.) In the final third of his book, Sermon Three, however, he described what he believed to be the greatest recreation of all: rejoicing in God. The worship of God was the source of true relaxation for a regenerate Christian.[26] Thus, for Colman, the apparently paradoxical phrase, "sober mirth," was more than a convenient literary device; it was a statement of an ideal—an ideal from which he was not prepared to condone much deviation in practice.

This idea of sober mirth animated the writings of most respectable moralists. A statement jointly written by twenty-two ministers in 1726, nearly two decades after Colman's tract appeared, is worth quoting at length to show the enduring quality of Puritan ambivalence. In *A Serious Address to Those Who Unnecessarily Frequent the Tavern* . . . , one of the last great Puritan manifestos on morality, a group of Boston-area ministers prefaced their diatribe against tavern and liquor abuse with a perfunctory endorsement of the need for leisure and relaxation: "We would not be misunderstood, as if we meant to insinuate that a due pursuit of religion is inconsistent with all manner of diversion. There are diversions, undoubtedly innocent, yet profitable and of use, to fit us for service." Then, however, they list some of the appropriate attributes of acceptable innocent diversion. "Harmless recreation," they argued, should "be governed by reason and virtue," be "convenient, sparing, prudent," "give place to business," "observe proper rules," "subserve religion," and "minister to the Glory of God." Not surprisingly, these ministers believed that few people satisfied these requirements for "sanctifying recreation" and for "resisting the temptations that mingle with their diversions." Most, instead, "drink down poison in their pleasant cups and perceive it not."[27]

### Erosion and Change

Determining how long these patterns of Puritan thought persisted is difficult. Attempts to define the chronological era of Puritanism have challenged the minds of the best historians, but so far no consensus on either dates or criteria has emerged. Nor is one likely to appear very soon. Nevertheless, some aspects of the evolution of the Puritan mind may be described with reasonable certitude.

Puritan thought did not end at any grand moment or event, but instead eroded over the entire colonial period. The erosion began when New England began, with the two primary settlements in 1620 and 1629, and was still going on in 1790, when the regional identity became submerged in a national polity. The first governors of Plymouth and Massachusetts Bay, William Bradford and John Winthrop, lived in societies whose practices sustained unusually high standards of moral conduct; yet both men complained of licentiousness and expressed fears that their colonies were backsliding into English degeneracy. On the other hand, in the 1790s, when moral conduct had significantly deteriorated by Puritan standards, the opponents of theater in Boston expressed their contempt with the same words used by their great-grandfathers of the early seventeenth century. Thus, despite a perceived fragility, despite being continually worn down, Puritan thought had an extraordinary tenacity and a very real influence long after any pretense of Puritan political and religious hegemony had ended.

Along this continuum, however, it is possible to identify a few periods of shifting emphasis, and also to identify a few of the agents of change. Tension between the forces of self-denial and those of self-gratification—between austerity and pleasure—characterized the whole colonial era. In the first generation, the forces of self-denial had the upper hand. In a collection of fifty-six letters (all those known to be extant) sent from Massachusetts to England in the 1630s, the subject of leisure and recreation rarely surfaced. Descriptions of land, climate, natives, and daily work, as well as news of self, family, and colony crowd the pages, but little mention is made of fun. Small talk abounds, but the only frequent reference to any form of relaxation comes in discussions of food and the joy of worship.[28] Without any conscious historical intent, the ordinary Puritans painted a somber picture of an austere Puritan milieu of ideology and practice.

This golden era of Puritanism ended about 1660. As students of the ministerial literature point out, a new type of sermon began to appear in the 1640s. The "jeremiad," a lament that extolled the virtues of the past and bewailed the vices of the present, castigated congregations for their declension—for their inability to maintain the purity and glorious intent of the founding generation. By 1660, almost all of that founding generation lay in the grave. The second generation seemed less sure of itself and more convinced that the moral leadership of the ministers was losing sway over average people. On the distant horizon, secular trends in Restoration England promoted what appeared to Puritans to be licentious, hedonistic behavior. Cards, dice, foppish clothes, idleness, theater, circuses, and ribald literature returned to England with renewed vigor when the Stuarts returned to the throne. Closer to home, the growth and dispersal of population in New England, the passing of the spirit of martyrdom among those who fled oppression by James I and Charles I, the pursuit of "God land and God trade" by the sons and daughters of pilgrims—all combined to create a world of alternatives and counterpoints to the stern morality of the early years. The plaintive cries of the jeremiads indicate that the second generation felt something was wrong but did not know how to fix it. Along with the increased shrillness of the warnings went an increase in prosecutions for crimes associated with the pursuit of pleasure: illegal sex, drunkenness, Sabbath-breaking, the wearing of vain clothes, and so forth.[29] Michael Wigglesworth's poem published in 1662, "God's Controversy with New England," is the most famous indictment of a New England grown "fat and comfortable" with success.[30]

From the 1660s to approximately the end of the 1720s, the second- and third-generation Puritan moralists struggled against what they regarded as the forces of laxity. Published sermons of the great ministers, always a barometer of their fears and insecurities but not a reliable guide to either popular thought or societal practices, repeatedly warned of the growth of sin and tried to maintain the proscriptions and prescriptions of the founding era. Several manifestos are of particular note. A Massachusetts church synod in 1679 issued a statement entitled "The Necessity of Reformation," which was a sort of official jeremiad in that it bore the moral authority not of one minister or congregation but of the churches of the entire colony. Among the recreational practices the authors found horrifying were "walking abroad and traveling on the Sabbath"; "having unsuitable discourses"; "sinful drinking"; "days of training and other public solemnities . . . abused"; "mixed dancing, light behavior and expressions"; "unlawful gaming"; and "an abundance of idleness."[31]

The father-son team of Increase and Cotton Mather, the two most respected and prolific moralists of the second and third generation, wrote sermon after sermon trying to stem the tide of licentiousness they perceived. But changing circumstances forced even the Mathers to make concessions to more relaxed standards. As they tried to resist laxity by excoriating what they regarded as the most horrible of practices, the Mathers and other members of the ministerial elite grudgingly softened their ideology to condone in the 1720s what would have been unacceptable in the 1690s.[32] This form of damage control received its last great statement in the 1726 collective jeremiad mentioned earlier in which twenty-two ministers combined their talents to blast the misuse of taverns. It was organized by Cotton Mather, who died two years later, and appended to it was a letter on the topic by Increase Mather, who had died three years earlier.

The deaths of the Mathers and the ending of this type of jeremiad symbolize the passing of the Puritan era.[33] Hereafter, important traces of the austere moralism survived, but only as fragments of an earlier unified ethos. Cautions against many practices continued into the mid-eighteenth century in New England; but in general, thought about the morality of leisure and recreation entered a new, more permissive phase in the 1730s. The moral arbiters, tired of waging a Sisyphean battle, began to make ideological concessions to reality. In the second quarter of the eighteenth century, New England was still relatively decorous, and certainly appeared "puritanical" compared to urbane New York or cavalier Virginia. But several recent analyses by social historians show that New England became less isolated and distinctive and more integrated into an Atlantic-Anglo world of culture and behavior.[33]

Many forces without and within New England created the shift in emphasis. Events near the end of the seventeenth century weakened Puritanism both politically and emotionally. Massachusetts's charter was revoked in 1684; when a new one was issued in 1691, it contained aspects of royal government, including a governor appointed by the crown. New Hampshire had an even stronger royal presence, and Connecticut and Rhode Island governments had to function with the knowledge that they also would lose their charters if they behaved too independently. The debacle of the Salem witch trials made the established church look foolish or antiquated in the eyes of many. And in general, religious, social, and economic trends militated against the maintenance of Puritan hegemony. By 1730, the Congregational church no longer had a monopoly on religion but had to compete with Anglicans, Baptists, and, in a few places, Quakers. The population had grown to approximately 120,000 persons in Massachusetts, 60,000 in Connecticut, 18,000 in Rhode Island, and 10,000 in New Hampshire; the vast majority of these people lived on isolated farmsteads whose locations ranged from the coastline to the White Mountains in the north and the Berkshires in the west. Over 250 incorporated towns existed, each with its own local government. And sophisticated urban centers began to emerge. Boston and Newport were preeminent among these, but Portsmouth, Newburyport, Salem, Springfield, Providence, New London, Norwich, New Haven, Middletown, and Hartford developed into secondary cities as their trade burgeoned and their social structures grew more varied by class and occupation. In short, the relative homogeneity of New England's churches, governments, and economy gave way as the clustered Puritan villages evolved into a bustling region.[34]

Not surprisingly, the morality of the Puritan village also gave way to more heterogeneous views and practices of leisure and recreation. Of course, some areas of New England, most notably the small settlements of Rhode Island, had departed from Puritan orthodoxy from the beginning. Conversely, some Puritan villages based on one church, one community, and one shared, restrictive vision of morality remained through the eighteenth century. And some vestiges of Puritan morality remained in all communities, including the cities. But overall, a new set of more permissive standards for leisure and recreation had become ensconced in New England by the fourth decade of the century.

This more secular, relaxed view of morality carried the region into and through the Revolutionary years. In the sixty years between 1730 and 1790, New England still felt the tension between self-denial and self-gratification—to some extent all societies do—but the best mirth was no longer defined as sober, virtuous, or profitable. In a wide range of activities—courtship, tavern life, social gatherings, holiday celebrations, music, the arts, games, and so forth—New Englanders pursued mirth actively, for the sheer sake of pleasure. The Great Awakening, the massive religious revival that lasted from 1740 to the early 1760s and convulsed all of the colonies, did little to alter these new liberal attitudes toward leisure and recreation. Ironically, the Revolutionary struggles from the mid-1760s through the 1780s may have posed a more explicit challenge to the new morality. When the political integrity of the colonies and new states was threatened, first by British oppression and then by internal disorder, some moralists identified the growth of vice as the underlying cause. Republican virtue might not survive, some Revolutionaries argued, unless the spirit of self-denial was reinvigorated. Both John and Samuel Adams, particularly the latter, shared and expressed some of that feeling. Puritan asceticism found a new voice in the guise of republican simplicity. This call for self-sacrifice had a certain appeal during the Revolutionary crisis, but no one seriously tried to translate the language into practice.[35] In reality, these new, secular jeremiads calling for a rededication to old-time virtue proved to be empty rhetoric, with no lasting impact as far as the pursuit of pleasure was concerned. They may have had an important role in rallying citizens to the causes of patriotism and good order, but they did not reinvigorate Puritan morality. The New England of 1790 continued to march along the path leading away from the ambivalent concept of sober mirth.

Section Two

# INTELLECTUAL AND CULTURAL ENTERTAINMENT

# II

# Quiet Times: Reading for Pleasure and Profit

John Cotton once wrote that for an evening snack, he "sweetened his mouth with a little Calvin" before going to bed. In a similar figure of speech, Increase Mather begged a fellow minister to loan him some books "out of pity to a famished man."[1] The metaphor employed by seventeenth-century New England's two leading clerics was apt: Puritans devoured reading material with a hunger unmatched among their contemporaries. Because they feared that migration to the New World threatened to cut them off from English culture, the Puritan leadership took strong measures to avoid literary starvation. Among the seed, grain, spices, and salted meat sent with the Winthrop expedition that founded the Massachusetts Bay Colony in 1630 was a library to sustain them in the first lean years. And, books continued to be highly sought-after imports. New Englanders who visited London in the 1630s often carried shopping lists of books to send back to friends and neighbors. Governor John Winthrop expressed a rare sense of joy at receiving a "box of books" from an English correspondent in 1636.

Despite the relative scarcity of books and the hardships of frontier life, New England was surprisingly literate, probably more so than any other region in the western world. Although one customarily thinks of England and Europe as being more culturally developed than the American colonies, in neither Elizabethan England nor Enlightenment Europe did reading play as important a role among the general public as it did in New England. In England and Europe, literary culture was essentially elite culture; in New England, it became democratized, part of popular culture. And all during the colonial period the literacy rate steadily increased. In the founding generation, approximately two thirds of New England's men and one third of its women could read; by the decade of the 1780s, nearly all men and 80 percent of the women could. Only Finland and Sweden came close to matching these statistics, and they did so only in urban areas.[2]

New England children learned to read through oral instruction at "reading schools," or "dame schools" as they were sometimes called. Usually private, but present in virtually every parish, these schools were taught by women using standardized techniques and materials. The first aid used, the hornbook, consisted of an alphabet written on a single page that was tacked to a paddle. Puritans imported hornbooks into New England along with primers, which showed how the alphabet could be combined into words. The first American primer, composed by the missionary John Eliot in 1669, was used to help convert Indians. Soon after, primers became a staple in American publishing. The most famous, the *New England Primer*, was the most successful and influential textbook in American educational history, with sales of about eight million from 1690, when it first appeared, until its last edition in 1830. The *New England Primer* used religious sayings to teach reading. The next text after the primer was the psalter (a book of psalms), editions of which were also printed in the colonies. The final text was the Bible. Teachers introduced all of these to students in one term; a winter's schooling produced sufficient literacy for students to progress through the hornbook, primer, psalter, and Bible. Although these schools also taught arithmetic, reading and writing received the primary emphasis and numeracy received shorter shrift.[3]

## Commitment to a Literary Culture

Puritans backed their commitment to a literary culture with money, institutions, and laws. In 1636, while still struggling to become self-sufficient in food, Massachusetts Bay founded Harvard College. Stephen and Matthew Day of Cambridge set up the first printing press in the English New World in 1640. The famous Massachusetts law of 1648 that enjoined all parents and masters to teach children to read was followed by similar laws in Connecticut and New Haven in 1650 and 1655. Dozens of towns passed bylaws to the same effect. Everywhere one looks in Puritan society, there abounds testimony to the importance of reading and writing.[4]

Unlike many Puritan values that eroded over the colonial span, belief in the virtues of the written word remained firm: material prosperity, improved technology, and population growth made it increasingly easier for New Englanders to indulge their penchant for reading and writing. Despite their heroic efforts, it was a struggle for early Puritans to sustain a literary culture. New England was, after all, a frontier—"a howling wilderness"—in terms of English amenities. Merchants moved as quickly as practicalities allowed, however, to meet the demand for reading materials. By the 1640s, important new books in England usually reached New England within two or three months of publication. By 1700, more than thirty bookstores had been in business in Boston at one time or another. An English wholesale book dealer visiting Boston to drum up some orders described some of the best-known retail book merchants at the turn of the century. Samuel Phillips, who operated a store from 1681 until his death in 1717, was regarded as "witty and the most beautiful man in the whole town"; Joseph Brunning was the most "compleat bookseller"; Duncan Campbell was "very rich and has got a great estate by bookselling."[5] These men occupied central positions in Boston society because they supplied goods that occupied central positions in Puritan society.

Boston always remained the center of bookselling and publishing in New England, but by the last quarter of the seventeenth century bookstores had opened in a dozen or so large towns. Throughout the eighteenth century, the number of stores selling books steadily increased, by the Revolution even remote villages usually had a general merchant who stocked a small supply. Urban stores also furnished books to a large hinterland sometimes extending more than a hundred miles into the interior and sold many related goods such as stationery supplies. Books were among the standard goods to bring home from an occasional visit to one of the cities. Jeremy Condy, pre-Revolutionary Boston's largest and most successful book dealer, sold books both wholesale and retail throughout New England. Condy's elaborate distribution system was created out of a network of Harvard graduates. Of his approximately 600 customers, more than 350 had been students at the college. Other customers both wholesale and retail were put in touch with Condy through his Harvard friends or through newspaper advertisements he placed strategically around the region. No one matched Condy in the scope of his distribution, but several other large-scale booksellers came close, and at least 200 stores in New England sold books by the end of the Revolutionary period.[6]

Thus, the emphasis Puritan New England placed on reading carried over to provincial and Revolutionary New England. Writing in the metaphorical idiom of her Puritan ancestors, the Revolutionary diarist Hannah Heaton referred to her "feast of reading" every night after the children went to bed. The content of what was read, written, and published, however, changed a great deal over the course of the colonial period. What a society reads may be the most instructive guide to its cultural landscape. Not surprisingly, Puritans' religious values suffused almost all of their thoughts on literature. The Bible was, of course, the most read book, but catechisms, primers, psalters, and even some racier literature—captivity tales, for example, of whites kidnaped by Indians—were meant to inculcate religious values as well as provide entertainment. Reading was the ideal form of quiet leisure for Puritans because it could educate, promote piety, and entertain at the same time.

In general, the English parent culture achieved its highest artistic expression in literature, not in architecture or painting. In this respect, the Puritans may be regarded as the most English of the English. The iconophobia that made most other forms of art difficult for Puritans to appreciate posed no ideological problem for written expression; if they could not make visual images of God, they could make literary ones. Puritans pictured their god in words, not in statues. The best-known defense of poetry in Elizabethan England was written by a devout Puritan, Philip Sidney, who argued that poetry provided wonderful entertainment because it could teach "What is good and true" to those who might otherwise not be inclined to hear the truth.[7]

## Religious Literature

It may strain twentieth-century secular credulity to think that a large percentage of society read the Bible to relax, but this, indeed, was the case. Puritans preferred the Geneva Bible of 1560 to all other editions. Much more detailed than the King James version used by Anglicans, the Geneva Bible contained textual notes in the margins, plus woodcuts, maps, headings, glossaries of names and events, and explanations of meanings. No other version of the Bible contained as many attractive diversions and learning aids. No other version made such an explicit appeal to popular culture in order to move Scripture from the few to the many.

And it worked. Individuals read the Scriptures daily. The most common form of family home entertainment was for one member to read aloud from the Bible to the rest. Certain passages would be read aloud again and again within certain families in the same ritualistic way that modern parents read some stories to small children so often that the children learn them by heart.[8] Reading aloud remained a commonplace activity throughout the entire colonial period. Parents read to children, children to parents. Courting young men and women often held reading parties. The method of teaching encouraged reading aloud. Students proved their competence to teachers not through analyses of content, but rather through oral demonstration.[9]

The majority of Puritan books written, published, and bought were meant to be read by the generality rather than by the elite. The most common seventeenth-century reading material after the Bible, the published sermon, was also a form of popular culture aimed at a mass audience. Few of these moral tracts—customarily twenty to thirty published pages, approximately an hour's reading—contained complex theological arguments. Most were talks given to a congregation and then reworked into published lessons. So the bulk of the books published in seventeenth-century New England employed rhetorical flourishes honed in oral delivery. Much like Protestant preaching today, they contained a lively and familiar litany of such words as "attend," "behold," "consider," and "rejoice." Sermons were meant to entertain as well as educate, and they did, both in their oral and written forms.[10]

The subject and style of Puritan writing enhanced its entertainment value. Ministers distinguished enough to warrant having a sermon published usually had the courage and the will to confront major moral issues. A certain luridness thus crept into many of these tracts. Since at least half of them were warnings against temptations, sin, and assorted evils, they often contained material that titillated as well as horrified the audience. Even a matter as potentially embarrassing as masturbation was the subject of many published sermons including one by Cotton Mather, *The Pure Nazarite. Advice to a Young Man, Concerning an Impiety and Impurity Not Easily to be Spoken of* (Boston, 1723). Mather's publisher, John Phillips, prefaced *The Pure Nazarite* with a defense of its printing in order to disarm some anticipated criticism. "I am told," Phillips wrote, "that it is an essay which there is more than a little occasion for. . . . I hope none will be so weak as to cavil against this publication that it may have a tendency to teach the vice which its intention is to warn against. We have many wholesome and holy books against fornication and yet nobody makes that cavil at them." Phillips also published ten editions of an English diatribe against masturbation—which, he proudly noted, sold over 15,000 copies in New England alone, an extraordinarily large number. It was one of the most popular— perhaps *the* most popular—pamphlet/books of the late seventeenth and early eighteenth centuries.[11]

As Phillips's apologia implicitly recognized, of course, explicit, widely circulated pamphlets on the evils of fornication, masturbation, and other sexual misconduct could be read with several purposes in mind. Certainly their description of practice could combine with a reader's anxiety and guilt to produce a trembling excitement. And Puritans' language, the "plain style" as they termed it, was indeed descriptive and explicit. By "plain style," Puritans did not mean simple language. Rather, they meant that they wrote with a simple, direct regard for the truth of their beliefs—religious truths. Truth and plainness—simplicity of purpose—suffused all Puritan writing from sermons to poems to history to personal diaries. John Cotton wrote that although the Puritan plain style was "not always so smooth and elegant . . . consider that God's altar needs not our polishings." Above all, Puritan authors always tried to avoid pretentiousness and the false sophistication they attributed to the flowing, ornate, baroque prose of many of their contemporaries. But just as the Bible resonates with metaphor and symbolism, so, too, did the Puritan plain style. Allusive but not usually elusive, Puritan language contained puffs of smoke, sudden storms, pieces of food laden with symbolic meanings; and it contained raw, direct, descriptive prose befitting people who prided themselves on having the courage to confront the world head-on with its own sinfulness. Anecdote, folklore, hearsay, and overstatement coursed through their writings. Imps, demons, witches, voices in the night, infernal trumpets blaring were among the parts of the invisible world that Puritan writers tried to make more visible to their readers. Amazing judgments on notorious sinners brought readers to the edge of their chairs and then gave them material for later conversations. Puritan authors also published stories of bizarre occurrences in nature that would have made latter-day showmen like P. T. Barnum envious: two-headed cows, twenty-five-pound babies, storms that blew boulders miles in the air. In a small, intimate village culture with few secrets or exotic qualities, these "stranger than fiction" items had the entertainment value of a good mystery or ghost story.[12]

As does the popular culture of any society, Puritan writing fused religion, entertainment, moral education, and views of science and history. The most prevalent metaphor used to compound the mixture was the concept of a pilgrimage. The Plymouth colonists have not been called Pilgrims mistakenly. Like all Puritans, they considered their entire lives to be a pilgrimage, and this became the theme or a sub-theme in most of their sermons as well as in other literature such as diaries, biographies, and histories. From sin to salvation—this was the standard journey of sinners who discovered their wickedness and their love of God. Warnings from criminals who discovered their faith too late to help themselves in their earthly existence constituted another variant on the pilgrimage theme. Other stock literary devices were descriptions of the shocking practices of Roman Catholics; of freaks of nature, which spoke of God's power and purposes; and of souls on their flight to heaven. All made for tantalizing reading as well as moral instruction.[13]

The authors of sermons used two literary techniques familiar to all Puritans: the jeremiad and argument by typology. The jeremiad, named after Jeremiah, the prophet of doom, reflected a set of beliefs held by some people in virtually all societies that the world is going downhill morally— "to hell in a handbasket," as the saying goes. Often Jeremiahs coexist with prophets of progress who believe in an ever-onward, ever-upward ethos. Among Puritan sermon authors between the 1660s and the 1720s, however, the Jeremiahs far outnumbered the believers in progress, and the jeremiad became the most characteristic stock-in-trade of popular literature. Invariably, the formulation was the same: the heroic generation of pilgrims who founded New England was being succeeded by children and grandchildren who failed to measure up to the early ideals. Declension; from virtue to apathy to vice; from self-sacrifice to self-indulgence; from eternal to worldly goals—this "then and now" principle was applied to dozens of subjects and analyses.[14]

Jeremiads are found in most societies; so, too, is some form of argument by typology. Typology embodied a form of scriptural analogy. Authors searched Scripture for examples of events that seemed to have parallels in their own lives. Ancient Israel was the model for behavior, and New England—the new Promised Land—should use the historical experiences of Israel, as revealed in Scripture, as a guide for its present behavior. Examples in the Bible were "types" for similar phenomena in New England. Once a type had been established, it provided a sure guide for present actions.[15]

The attractions of arguing by typology gave Puritan society an impetus to study history and biography. The classic piece of literature from the Puritan era, Governor William Bradford's *Of Plymouth Plantation,* is a history of the Pilgrim colony. Bradford's straightforward day-to-day account of life in Plymouth was (and still is) read for its charm and insight, for inspiration, and for historical detail. Its form is epic. Bradford begins with an account of Satan's opposition to saints, then tells the tale of the persecution of the saints in England and the Pilgrims' voyages to Holland and to America; then he describes life in the New World. Throughout *Of*

*Plymouth Plantation,* the same rhythmic struggles occur again and again. Man relies on his own strength, attempts to realize goals, and invariably fails. Failure brings success because it forces man to realize that only within God do real strength and success exist. All through Bradford's drama, the cycle is repeated in each new situation. The following is his account of the journey to Holland:[16]

> They neither saw sun, moon, nor stars, and were driven near the coast of Norway; the mariners themselves often despairing of life and once with shrieks and cries gave over all, as if the ship had been foundered in the sea . . . when the water ran into their mouths and ears and the mariners cried out, we sink, we sink . . . [the Pilgrims] cried, yet Lord thou canst save, yet Lord thou canst save with such other expressions as I will forbear. Upon which the ship not only did recover, but shortly after the violence of the storm began to abate, and the Lord filled their afflicted minds with such comforts as everyone cannot understand.[17]

*Of Plymouth Plantation* was not published during the colonial period; although manuscript copies circulated among some intellectuals, it had no direct role in providing entertainment or reading material to the public. Bradford's work stands, however, as the best-known example of a type of literature that abounded in the seventeenth century. Many epic histories were published and widely read, among them works by Nathaniel Morton, Governor Bradford's nephew; John Eliot, the most successful Puritan missionary to the Indians; and William Hubbard, a Puritan soldier in the Indian wars. The capstone to this tradition of epic, moral, personal history, Cotton Mather's *Magnalia Christi Americana, or the Ecclesiastical History of New England,* was finished near the end of the seventeenth century and published in London in 1702. Full of anecdotes, folklore, and gossip, *Magnalia Christi Americana* combined instruction and entertainment. Although Mather departed from the plain style and indulged in convoluted, pretentious, gratuitously polysyllabic prose, his epic was enormously successful and well-known to contemporaries.[18]

Another stock-in-trade was the treatise on the practicalities of leading a good Christian life. Invariably written and published in England, these moral guidebooks ranged over topics from choosing a vocation to maintaining a clear conscience to arranging daily personal devotions. Most literate seventeenth-century colonists and Englishmen read these advice manuals, but Puritans had more faith than others did in the concept of learning morality, proper manners, and good conduct from books. Henry Preacher's *The Complete Gentleman* (1622) became standard reading for all male New Englanders who aspired to gentry status.[19]

Handbooks on how to die were particularly popular. Dying played a more public role in seventeenth-century New England than it has in succeeding centuries. Funeral sermons and elegies constituted an important literary genre for the general public. Ministers did not give funeral sermons on the day of the burial, but instead incorporated them into the regularly scheduled Sunday or weekday lecture that followed. Elegies had an important role in each town because they usually involved a local stocktaking as the minister evaluated the deceased and his or her place in the life of the community. The forthcoming delivery of these assessments provoked much interest. Elegies for important leaders were often published as broadsides or as part of a larger sermon that used the occasion of a great person's death to make a point about general principles. Short didactic elegies, often using puns, wit, or figures of speech, were put on many gravestones. Anagrams were popular, as were poems for dead family members; the latter would be read at meals or devotions within private houses. And almost all diaries contained writing about the deaths of family and friends. Many diaries included long poems written in memory of deceased persons.[20]

The percentage of Puritans who kept a diary, spiritual autobiography, or some other form of personal memoir cannot be known precisely; but by any means of reckoning, it was high. Certainly, almost all leaders produced such works. Not one of the several hundred New England state governors since the end of the colonial period has written a diary or history matching the importance or literary worth of those of the first governors of Plymouth and Massachusetts Bay, William Bradford and John Winthrop. Neither man was thought of as particularly intellectual by the standards of his fellow Puritans. Yet both wrote long, carefully crafted diary-histories. And probably the majority of seventeenth-century New Englanders created at least a modest form of personal literature. Hundreds of these have been published; thousands survive in manuscript. Diaries, the most common item of this genre, ranged from the elaborate two-volume journal of John Winthrop to the bare-bones entries of occasional happenings recorded by a taciturn farmer. If people did something unusual—took a trip inland or went on a long voyage—they often kept a journal.

Spiritual autobiographies were explicitly concerned with the concept of grace. They customarily took the form of recounting temptations and then describing how the author did or did not overcome the snares prepared by Satan. This type of autobiography often read like a Puritan version of *Tom Jones*, as young men recorded the sins of their adolescence. John Dane, a young, unmarried Massachusetts man in the 1630s, trod a perilous course through a decade of trials; he found himself in bed nude by accident with a young woman who told him, "You are welcome to me"; he was stung in the finger by a wasp and nearly died the first Sunday he skipped religious services; and finally he realized that the parable of the Prodigal Son was God's way of calling him home to his parents. A low sense of self-esteem courses through these autobiographies; "shame," "evil," "weakness," "sinfulness," are recurring words. As did so much of Puritan literature, writing in spiritual autobiographies provided both therapy and entertainment to people, especially during the long, dark evenings of winter. Some people kept both diaries and spiritual autobiographies, either concurrently or consecutively. Most were private and meant only for the writer's own edification, but some, such as the famous trilogy of spiritual autobiographies kept by Richard, Increase, and Cotton Mather were intended for posterity and written with the expectation that they would be published. Others wrote spiritual autobiographies for their children and friends: John Winthrop's "Christian Experience"; Thomas Shepard's "My Birth and Life"; and Anne Bradstreet's "To My Dear Children" are well-known examples of these. After the person's death, family members would read them both silently and aloud in groups.[21]

Some major pieces of literature were produced by early Puritans, but, like Bradford's *Of Plymouth Plantation*, much of it remained unknown or seldom read by the general public of the time. The Puritan poet most admired by twentieth-century literary critics, Edward Taylor, was not "discovered" until Thomas Johnson read his manuscripts and communicated the findings in a scholarly article published in 1937. For nearly three centuries, Taylor's magnificent poetry remained in the realm of personal literature—part of his private diary. Anne Bradstreet, the gentle, loving poet of North Andover, Massachusetts, published her first volume of poetry in London in 1650. None of her work was published in New England until after her death; it remained unknown except to the "patrician peers" for whom she wrote.[22]

One writer of the founding generation who was well known to all of New England, the minister Nathaniel Ward, had an exuberant, witty, satirical, charming style that managed to please the public, Puritan moral guardians and subsequent literary critics. Ward's most famous piece of work, *The Simple Cobbler of Aggawam* (London, 1647), was called by a modern critic the "pleasantist [book] ever written by a Puritan." Ward's obscure cobbler looked up from his workbench to offer philosophical advice on religion, society, government, love, family, and nearly everything else. The cobbler, a widower of twelve years, used a steady stream of risqué sexual puns to make his points, many of which used women as the butt of their humor. Admittedly looking for a wife—a "yoke-fellow"—the cobbler had a difficult time finding one he could tolerate. "The world is full of care," he wrote, "much like unto a bubble; women and care and care and women, and women and care and trouble." Many Puritan divines had apprehensions about the near-ribald expressions of the cobbler, but Ward remained within the bounds of respectability because, in the final analysis, his message was profoundly conservative and Puritan. A severe critic of toleration, of licentiousness in any form, and of English religious practices, Ward was the son of a minister, the brother of two, and the father of three. By the time he arrived in America, he was already famous for his humor and his strict beliefs on church discipline. The cobbler was often tempted but never succumbed to vice. He admitted that after seeing attractive women, "I cannot clean my phancie of them for a month after"; yet he remained a model of chastity. A Puritan wit whose work presaged the homespun philosophy of Benjamin Franklin, the curmudgeonly quality of Oliver Wendell Holmes, and the biting satire of Samuel Clemens, Ward was singularly renowned for his humor. Increase Mather wrote that he knew of over a hundred witty speeches and sayings attributed to him. Mather often quoted his personal favorite from a Ward speech: "I have only two comforts to live upon: the one is in the perfection of Christ; the other is in the imperfection of Christians." Among the things Ward despised were women's fashions—he called one woman who inquired about the Queen's attire "the very gizzard of a trifle"; trendy language, or "new-quoddled words"; and Rhode Islanders who believed in "poly-piety, the greatest impiety in the world."[23]

Ward's popularity among both the ministerial elite and the general population makes it clear that Puritans liked humor in their reading as long as the humor did not detract from the serious business of religion. Ward was not alone in his efforts to harness humor in support of salvation. A few other respectable Puritan authors also published humorous work. Samuel Danforth, a Harvard graduate and minister; Thomas Wendle, a joint author of one of Puritanism's best-known religious tracts, *New England's First Fruits* (1643); and Hugh Peters, a prominent minister and government adviser, all wrote humorous poetry. Ward's nearest rival, however, would have been Edward Johnson, known in literary circles for his *History of New England* (London, 1654). Some witty poetry interspersed in Johnson's history suggests he was the author of Puritanism's famous ballad "New England Annoyances," which first appeared in 1643 and was quickly known to virtually every New Englander. It remained popular throughout the seventeenth century and appeared in new, updated forms during the Revolution. Sung to the English tune of "Derry Down," "Annoyances" was written to combat in satire the exaggerations sweeping England in the 1630s and 1640s about the superiority of New England. It showed a wonderful ability to poke fun at New England and the Puritan experiment. The sixteen verses of four lines each were organized around three basic complaints: the climate and geography; the lack of English amenities; and Puritan fastidiousness. Yet, for all of its criticisms, "Annoyances," like *The Simple Cobbler of Aggawam*, strongly affirmed the values of Puritanism and was humor from within the fold.[24] Consider the following three stanzas:

> From the end of November till three months are gone,
> the ground is all frozen as hard as a stone;
> our mountains and hills and valleys below
> being commonly covered with ice and with snow.

> Instead of pottage and puddings and custards and pies,
> our pumpkins and parsnips are common supplies;
> we have pumpkins at morning and pumpkins at noon,
> if it were not for pumpkins we should be undone.

> And we have a covenant one with another,
> which makes a division 'twixt brother and brother,
> for some are rejected and others made saints,
> of those that are equal in virtue and wants.[25]

Something of an "inside joke," "Annoyances" was written by a New England Puritan for a New England Puritan audience and took a gentle pride in the region's real or perceived deficiencies.

Little humor can be found in the work of Michael Wigglesworth, the poet whom Puritan New England accounted its greatest man of letters. His long poetic jeremiad, *The Day of Doom*, became the first runaway best-seller in American literary history. An astonishing number of copies—1800—were published at Cambridge, Massachusetts, in 1662 and sold out of stock the same year to a population of about 65,000 people in the New England colonies. Judged harshly by subsequent literary critics, Wigglesworth deliberately crafted *The Day of Doom* to appeal to popular taste. In doggerel, it told a traditional Christian tale of unsuspecting sinners suddenly ripped from earthly life to face judgment on the final day. So popular was *The Day of Doom* that virtually every New Englander read or heard it read aloud. Wigglesworth followed his first smash with a second, similar poem, *God's Controversy with New England*, which achieved a slightly higher level of artistic accomplishment and was somewhat less depressing than *The Day of Doom*.

Both poems, however, had a similar message and style. Both were emotionally charged anti-sin diatribes that fed on guilt in a manner resembling the evangelical crusades of the nineteenth and twentieth centuries.[26] Stanzas such as the following terrified yet titillated the less sophisticated among Puritan villagers.

> With iron bands they bind their hands
> and cursed feet together,
> and cast them all, both great and small,
> into that lake forever.
> Where day and night, without respite,
> they wail and cry and howl
> for torturing pain which they sustain
> in body and in soul.
>
> For day and night, in their despite,
> their torments smoke ascendeth,
> their pain and grief have no relief,
> their anguish never endeth.
> There must they lie and never die,
> though dying every day;
> there must the dying ever lie,
> and not consume away.

Popular pieces of literature such as Wigglesworth's were passed from person to person because even locally printed books cost a great deal in relation to most other goods. Perry Miller argued that the reason no copies of the 1662 printing of *The Day of Doom* survive is that they were "read to pieces." Approximately half of the seventeenth-century New Englanders had books listed in the probate inventories of their goods.

Schoolbooks constituted one of the largest categories of books available for sale and found in inventories in Puritan New England. A list for stock orders placed by Boston booksellers in 1685 shows the prominence of texts.

Religious books and school texts together represented over 80 percent of the stock, followed by manuals, history, and romance fiction. One sharp difference between the fare in London and Boston bookstores lay in the many fewer items of history and romance in the Boston stores. Puritans wrote and published many of their own histories, and they did not read much fiction. London bookstores were overrun with cheap, crude items—ballads, plays, tawdry romance; seventeenth-century New England stores were not.[27]

Bookstore owners used the phase "steady sellers" to identify books that remained popular year after year. The four most often cited in the second half of the seventeenth century were all religious. Two of these were imported from England: William Dyer's *Christ's Famous Titles* and Thomas Vincent's *God's Terrible Voice;* and two were published locally; Michael Wigglesworth's *The Day of Doom* and Thomas Shepard's *The Sincere Convert.*[28]

### Secular Trends in Literature

Some evidence suggests that an illicit book trade also existed that had its own steady sellers. The ribald *Aristotle's Masterpiece,* regarded as lewd by the authorities and hence not sold in respectable stores, was the best-known of these. Reading bawdy books was a popular pastime in Restoration England, and Puritan magistrates could not completely block their circulation in New England. Even some material that could be described as pornographic circulated in New England. The most salacious, a ninety-line poem entitled, "To Our Dreadfull and Most Sovereign Lord Heywood, High Cunstable [*sic*] . . . the Cunt Searcher," was referred to officially in the Suffolk County court records of 1664. This poem accused the constable of Concord of pursuing sexual offenders in order to satisfy his own prurient interests and "to scrape money out of cunts to pay." This type of raw language characterized a substantial body of bawdy, illicit literature circulating primarily among servants, sailors, and rebellious young people.[29]

Near the end of the seventeenth century, a new genre of popular literature emerged that provided the greatest number of steady sellers from the 1680s through the Revolutionary era. Captivity tales originated with the Spanish but all colonists and Europeans found them fascinating. Several short descriptions of captures and rescues were published in New England as parts of other books, but the first real Puritan captivity tale, Mary Rowlandson's autobiographical account of her capture during King Philip's War, was published in 1682 and caused an immediate sensation.

Within the year, printers released three more issues, which sold out. Over the course of the eighteenth century, New Englanders wrote and published several hundred of these tales. Most of them had a cluster of common traits that made them exciting, especially to people who themselves lived under constant threat of the very dangers about which they were reading. Raids, death of family members, seizures, forced marches, bizarre social practices, assimilation, adoption, and eventual rescue and repatriation were the topics of a standard story line. Threats of torture or of depraved sexuality either remained just beneath the surface or, occasionally, surfaced in lurid descriptions. Women often found it necessary to emphasize that although the threat might always have existed, they were never raped and did manage to maintain their virtue.[30]

Inasmuch as the stories were substantially true, were written by people known to many readers, and did indeed involve high drama, the popularity of captivity tales needs little explanation. Several aspects of the genre changed in the eighteenth century, however. The tales of the late seventeenth and early eighteenth centuries were very Puritan. The captured author, usually a woman, viewed her capture as a test of faith. Early tales had many of the characteristics of a spiritual autobiography: doubt, torment, faith, and delivery. The victim attributed her survival and rescue to God's will; having returned home, she invariably considered herself a better Christian for having been through the experience. The clergy approved of captivity tales because they provided yet another example of the triumph of faith. Many ministers ghost-wrote or helped in the publication of them. Among these, the ubiquitous Cotton Mather wrote the most famous of them all, Hannah Dustin's, which ended with a description of how Dustin tomahawked to death several of her sleeping captors before making her escape.

In the second quarter of the eighteenth century, captivity tales became more secular and sensational. As the Puritan spiritual-autobiography aspect of them diminished, the details of sexuality and torture became more graphic. And as they downplayed the religious quotient, the tales became even more popular and tantalizing. Old ones remained in demand, however; as late as 1773, a new edition of Mary Rowlandson's story was released.

Another type of horror literature, closely related to captivity tales, began in late seventeenth-century and flowered in eighteenth-century New England—the confessions of infamous criminals. Twenty-seven such confessionals were published in Boston between 1700 and 1740. They seldom departed from a standard formula: the criminal gave lurid details

of horrible deeds, experienced a miraculous conversion after being appre-
hended, and went to a serene death on the gallows, having made peace
with God. The story ended with the implication of possible redemption.
For New Englanders anxious about immortality and hungry for entertainment, these "sinner to saint" confessions combined much: excitement,
escapism, horror, a happy ending, and, of course, education in proper
moral values and theology. The most famous, that of Esther Rogers, who
was found guilty of murdering her two babies, described the astonishing
transition of Rogers from a vicious, lewd woman to a near saint who went
to her death with such composure that she was immediately "a candidate
for heaven."[31]

Confessional tales, like captivity tales, went from being primarily
religious tracts to being dramatic horror stories. In fact, the secular trends
of the eighteenth century affected every type of popular reading material.
Humorous writing grew, particularly satire, which was often used to
combat the shrill, near hysterical attacks of the learned clergy on what they
regarded as the shocking increase in sin, vanity, and excess. *The Origin of
the Whale-Bone Petticoat* (Boston, 1714) was perhaps the first genuinely
ribald piece of satire published legally in New England. The petticoat had
become a symbol of female vanity to many clerical moralists. An anonymous satirist pretended to join the ranks of its critics by examining the
origin of the petticoat, which, he argued, was invented by a French
prostitute named Belinda to conceal the fact that she was pregnant. Thus,
New England women were even worse than the ministers realized: not
only had they become slaves to vanity, they took their fashion cues from
foreign strumpets.[32]

James Franklin, Benjamin's elder brother, thought the essay on the
petticoat sufficiently important to warrant reprinting in slightly altered
form in 1722.[33] Franklin also published New England's first witty, satirical
paper, the *New England Courant*, which put out its maiden issue in 1720 and
its final one in 1726. Something like a cross between the modern *Harvard
Lampoon* and *National Enquirer*, the *Courant* treated New England to a new
diet of teasing, sarcastic reading fare. Based on the model of England's
leading satirical paper, the *Spectator*, the first issue of the *Courant* lamented
the dullness of Boston and promised a remedy. The second one invited
"some short pieces, serious, sarcastic, ludicrous or otherwise amusing."
Subsequent issues did indeed relieve the disease of dullness and did amuse
many as well as infuriate others, particularly the clergy who felt (correctly)
that the paper singled them out as special targets. Few were safe from the
sting of Franklin's pen. He reported that Cotton Mather's nephew spent

a night in bed with two women of ill repute. When a friend of Mather's, the Reverend Samuel Penhallow of Portsmouth, responded with a defense, Franklin attacked Penhallow in a thinly veiled spoof addressed to "Tom Penshallow."[34]

Eventually Franklin went too far for the thin-skinned sensibilities of official New England. He published an account of a man who allegedly castrated himself and thus enraged "the looser sort of the female tribe," who considered this a great loss. The *Courant* was finally shut down by the General Court of Massachusetts. Franklin fled to Rhode Island to avoid criminal prosecution, but not before releasing a masterpiece. His scathing final issue contended that he was forced out of Boston because he continually exposed sin, vice, evil, pomposity, and vanity but did not possess a Harvard degree and hence infringed on the moral territory of the ministers who did. For those who knew Boston's inner circle well, this valedictory contained a specific barb within the general one: Cotton Mather often used the pen name "John Harvard" to disguise his true identity in shrill letters he wrote to the paper complaining about its content.[35]

The *Courant* was dead, but satire lived; it grew into one of the great reading amusements of the century. And it rapidly gained legitimacy among all classes of New Englanders. As respectable a figure as Governor Roger Wolcott of Connecticut earned a reputation as a wag for his poetry, which lampooned high taxes, among other things. "I have a horse," Wolcott wrote, "but he's so thin, his bones appear most through his skin. Another calf I had last year, but where he's now, I cannot heare. Pray take this for a perfect [tax] list, for I think there's nothing mist." The genre reached its artistic height during the Revolutionary era in the work of John Trumbull, a poet, Yale tutor, and son of another Connecticut governor. Trumbull's *The Progress of Dullness*, published in 1773, achieved immense popularity with nearly all literate New Englanders. In the poem, Tom Brainless and Dick Hairbrain compete for the love of Harriet Simper. Brainless, a lazy lout, arrives at Yale with great references but proves to be an absolute dunce. Despite (or perhaps because of) his lack of character and ability, he does wonderfully well at Yale and goes on to become a minister. Hairbrain, a fop and dandy with even less character, has only slightly more ability than Brainless. Simper, an uncomplicated, shallow coquette, lives to be flattered and pampered. All told, Yale, the church, women, and New England culture came under ferocious attack. Satire often does not hold its appeal, but even in the twentieth century, *The Progress of Dullness* is very funny. Unlike Nathaniel Ward's *The Simple Cobbler of Aggawam*, which used satire and humor in a conservative way to bolster the seventeenth-century Puritan establishment, the satirists of the eighteenth century used their wit iconoclastically to attack the ruling elite, of which they were members, and the values of the established church.[36]

At approximately the same time that captivity tales, confessionals, and satire emerged as important components of the popular reading stock, journalists began producing two new items for the mass market: almanacs and newspapers. Foreign editions of both had been available in port towns sporadically, but in the early eighteenth century, New England began to publish its own.

Edward Holyoke, a Harvard graduate and future president of the college, compiled New England's first almanac in Boston in 1708. It caused a stir on two accounts. First, people were excited to see a homegrown variant and eagerly anticipated its release. Second, Holyoke alarmed the government because he did not seek the General Court's approval before publication. The governor and some members of the council seized the manuscript and deleted mention of such holidays as St. Valentine's Day, Easter, the Annunciation, and Christmas, and also of some political events, such as King Charles's execution. From this tenuous beginning, however, the almanac went on to become the most widely read body of printed material in New England. By the Revolution, the most popular almanac, published by Nicholas Ames, sold over 60,000 copies annually to a popu- lation of approximately 750,000 people. Several other almanacs were published in Boston, Connecticut, Rhode Island, New Hampshire, and other parts of Massachusetts. Overall, one almanac was sold in New England for approximately every three people; it seems likely that most people read several during the course of a year.

In form, almanacs tended to be similar. They included monthly schedules on tides, sunsets, sunrises, and other details of weather; anni- versaries of noteworthy events; short verses of original poetry; anecdotes; commentaries on current affairs; medical tips and cures; lists of public officials; recipes; tables of distances; compendia of unusual information; copies of important speeches; hundreds of aphorisms and proverbs; and short narratives often of historical nature. In short, almanacs were useful and entertaining, rather like modern magazines such as *Newsweek*, *Reader's Digest*, and the *Farmer's Almanac*. They were a ubiquitous part of the reading stock by the mid-eighteenth century, and their publishers strived con- sciously to broaden their entertainment value in order to get larger shares of a lucrative market. Consequently, almanacs tended to operate on the principle of least offense and were generally not controversial. During the Revolution, however, many abandoned their nonpartisan stance and openly embraced the Whig cause. Whether out of an impulse to increase sales or out of genuine patriotism, almanacs laced the leading body of popular reading culture with radical, revolutionary rhetoric.[37]

An astonishing number of newspapers had been started in New England by 1790: forty-six in Massachusetts; fourteen in Connecticut; twelve in New Hampshire; and eight in Rhode Island. Of these eighty papers, twenty-five were still in business in 1790. Like so many cultural and intellectual developments, newspaper publication started in Boston and slowly fanned out to the rest of New England. It remained an urban phenomenon throughout the colonial period. The first paper published, *The Boston Public Occurrences,* released its maiden issue in 1690 but was immediately shut down by the Massachusetts General Court because the editor had not received prior authorization. The first regular newspapers did not appear until the eighteenth century: the *Boston Newsletter* in 1704, the *Boston Gazette* in 1719, and the *New England Courant* in 1720. The first Rhode Island newspaper, the *Rhode Island Gazette,* appeared in Newport in 1732; the first Connecticut one, the *Connecticut Gazette,* in New Haven in 1755; and the first New Hampshire one, the *New Hampshire Gazette,* in Portsmouth in 1756. In the 1760s, the process of founding papers quickened as secondary centers such as Salem, Newburyport, Springfield, Norwich, Hartford, New London, Exeter, and Providence, among others, started them.[38]

Although modest when compared to modern newspapers, the colonial papers provided an entertainment feast for those who had access to them. The *Boston Newsletter* appeared weekly and for the first few issues consisted of but a single sheet with two columns of small print on each side. Subscribers saved them, however, often made marginal notes, and brought them to friends outside Boston when they traveled. Assessing the distribution of papers is difficult, but fragments of evidence suggest a wide circulation network. The elite of distant, secondary cities read the Boston papers. For one example, fifty-one people in Newport subscribed to the *Boston Chronicle* in 1767.

People made considerable effort to get papers. A loyalist captive sent to the remote town of Glocester, Rhode Island, noted with amazement that the farmer in charge of the prisoners sent his youngest son once a week to bring the Providence paper back from a nearby village and then "spent the whole forenoon perusing it . . . such is the fondness of people for news."

At first papers tended to include only news stories with little opinion or commentary; but after the appearance of Franklin's *New England Courant* in 1720, they became less wedded to hard news. As they spread throughout

New England in the 1760s and 1770s, papers became easily available in most of the region, contained more local news and opinion, and became lively and partisan due to the Revolutionary heating up of the political climate. Newspapers also became outlets for literary talent. In particular, poetry abounded. Virtually every issue of every paper from the 1760s onward contained poems, some written by local residents, some plagiarized. In the 1780s, immediately after the Revolution, the newspaper came of age and spread to dozens of smaller towns. Village library associations started stocking them, as did taverns, and they became part of most New Englanders' weekly reading fare.[39]

As newspapers, almanacs, small-town bookstores, and near universal literacy lessened the gap between urban and rural literary life, reading material became more specialized and aimed at certain groups or classes within society. Children's books became popular in the second half of the eighteenth century. Isaiah Thomas of Worcester made a specialty out of reprinting English children's books and the Boston booksellers, Cox and Berry specialized in "little books for the instruction and amusement of all good boys and girls." The most popular books, such as *Gafter Ginger* and *Goody Two Shoes*, imparted strong moral lessons and were regarded as both entertainment and education. Many editions of Mother Goose rhymes circulated, but these were controversial. So also were stories such as "Puss in Boots" or "Jack the Giant Killer," which some moral educators thought condoned or even endorsed cheating, lying, and stealing.[40]

The novel emerged in the middle of the eighteenth century and became a dominant form of literary entertainment for those outside the elite. In particular, romance novels appealed to women. In 1693, Increase Mather wrote a diatribe warning of the lure of this "vast mischief of false notions and images of things, particularly of love and honour." Had Mather lived another half-century, he might have found his fears coming true. *Tom Jones*, a genuinely ribald novel, was the steadiest seller from the 1740s through the rest of the century. The most popular novelist, however, was Samuel Richardson, whose three books, *Pamela* (1740), *Clarissa* (1748), and *Sir Charles Greenwood* (1754) were each major successes. Some men also read romance novels, but by and large these were regarded as women's reading.

Although moral arbiters continued to frown on all fiction, the records of booksellers and circulating libraries suggest that between 1750 and 1790, fiction went from approximately 5 percent to 33 percent of book sales. Ironically, this growth occurred partly because moral custodians encouraged women to read more at the very time that fiction was becoming popular with women in England. Reading was regarded as one of the safer leisure activities in a secular world full of immoral temptations. And women expanded their reading into other areas. Elite women read the classics, which in seventeenth-century New England were reserved by custom for men; and the percentage of women keeping journals and diaries increased. A new type of writing developed among eighteenth-century women, who sometimes kept little books of "sage counsel" or "pious instructions" to be read by their families after the author's death much as some spiritual autobiographies had been in the previous century.

This increase in reading and writing among women reflected three additional phenomena. First, for most of the colonial period, New England women had lower literacy rates than men did; in the Revolutionary era, rates for both sexes became closer as the region approached near universal literacy. Second, more acceptable alternative diversions opened up for men (and thus competed for their leisure time) than opened up for women. And third, a rapid growth in personal and free libraries in the second half of the eighteenth century vastly increased the supply of books and hence made them more available to people with little discretionary income. In particular, circulating libraries tended to make fiction more available, because many people who wanted to read it did not think fiction suffi-ciently useful to justify the economic investment of buying a book.[41]

New types of practical books targeted almost exclusively at men, however, did appear in the 1730s: building guides and handbooks on how to make various things. Like the moral guidebooks of the seventeenth century, the practical guides of the eighteenth tended to be published in London, but found a large market in the colonies. One of the first, Francis Price's *The British Carpenter* (London, 1733), is known to have been sold at twenty-seven locations in New England, and probably many more shops carried it. By the Revolution, a few manuals were being published in Boston and were tailored to the New England milieu, but most of the handyman books remained English. Guides were published to assist the would-be builder of every type of product: bridges, arches, chimneys, and furniture, as well as, of course, houses and barns. Over 147 such books were available at one time or another in the eighteenth-century colonies, and almost all of these could be bought in New England. Their titles have a surprisingly modern do-it-yourself sound to them, with such phrases as *The Practical Guide to Home Carpentry*, and *Every Man a Complete Builder*.[42]

The reading habits of the elite became increasingly different from those of "everyman" in late colonial New England. Well-educated men still read Scripture, history, and the classics, but they added to their reading

lists scientific publications (a wide range of scholarly periodicals to com-
municate new discoveries) and partisan political magazines such as the
*Spectator.* Among urbane men, periodicals such as *The Gentlemen's Magazine*
and *The London Magazine* were popular. Most of these types of reading
materials were not easily available to the average New Englander; they
were usually distributed through the clergy or through intellectual networks formed around Harvard and Yale graduates. Through these channels, elite, college-educated colonial New Englanders were exposed to the
same Enlightenment authors as their counterparts in England and Europe.
The most popular authors were Addison, Locke, Archbishop Tillotson,
Shaftesbury, Pope, Voltaire, Hume, Sidney, Trenchard, and Gordon.
Most of the New England elite followed the practice of their English
counterparts in carefully recording each author and piece of work they
read. Pope's *Essay on Man* was the most popular secular book among the
late eighteenth-century elite.[43]

## Reading in the Revolutionary Era

From the early seventeenth to the late eighteenth century, three important
changes in reading habits paralleled similar changes in New England
society. Foremost among these, as the Puritan village gave way to the New
England town, was the evolution of Puritan reading patterns into more
secular ones. The bulk of the literary material read and written by New
Englanders prior to the late seventeenth century related to religion. Even
the irreverent, satirical *Simple Cobbler of Aggawam* used his biting wit in
defense of the Puritan establishment. From the 1690s onward, however,
the religious content of the reading matter diminished and the secular
content increased. Even in genres, such as captivity tales and confessions
of criminals, that remained popular from the late seventeenth throughout
much of the eighteenth century, an internal shift in emphasis signaled this
decline in religious content.

Second, the idea of reading for entertainment became more explicit
in the eighteenth century than it had been in the seventeenth. Puritan
villagers in the founding years of New England read the Bible, sermons,
moral tracts, and so forth for entertainment; but they also read them for
religious instruction. The Puritan ethos embodied a holistic worldview in
which everything—religion, family, government, the economy and entertainment—was tied together in one bundle. People who refused to call
their place of worship a church because that suggested a separation
between religious services and daily life were certainly not willing to

separate entertainment and leisure from the central purpose of their lives. New Englanders of the eighteenth century found it progressively easier to do just that. They still read Scripture for entertainment and instruction in 1750; they read building manuals and textbooks for practical purposes; but they also read almanacs and romance novels for their appeal as leisure amusements.

And, finally, as the Puritan communal impulse fragmented into a world of competing classes and interest groups, so too did the reading habits of New Englanders splinter into differing patterns. Most New Englanders of the seventeenth century—men, women, children, the elite, yeomen, servants—were expected to and did read much the same material. Obviously, opportunity and ability produced some variations, but these were relatively minimal. As the eighteenth century developed, however, a variety of forces eroded the unity of the Puritan village. Divisions appeared between the clerical and merchant elites, between ports and remote towns, between members of the established church and dissenters. And obvious distinctions that had always been present—such as those to be made among men, women, and children, or farmers, tradesmen, and sailors—became more manifest. Secular forces at work in the western world, as well as the sheer growth in New England's population and economy, militated against the possibility of maintaining a unitary Puritan society. Those groups that emerged and competed for their place in the bustling world of the Atlantic trading economy and Revolutionary shakeup read different things because they had different interests.

What did not change, of course, between 1620 and 1790 was the commitment to reading. The intellectual intensity of the Puritan ethos may have waned, but the habit of reading did not. Revolutionary New England was one of the most literate places in the world because of its Puritan legacy. Both Puritan and Revolutionary New Englanders read for pleasure and educational profit; and they read with an unusual degree of intensity. Samuel Goodrich, the first author to achieve massive success writing children's books, wrote that his fellow New Englanders "approached a book with reverence . . . read respectfully," and took books as "grave matters demanding thought and attention."[44] Puritan authors such as William Bradford, Michael Wigglesworth, and Cotton Mather would undoubtedly have been troubled to see their grandchildren reading the antiestablishment satire of John Trumbull and the escapist romance of Henry Fielding; but it was the Puritan leaders of the founding generation who created the literary culture that made Tom Brainless and Tom Jones popular rascals in the Revolutionary era.

# III

# Music and Theater
# Struggle for Legitimacy

University students asked to describe Puritan society will offer up a wide variety of words and images. Typically, among the words mentioned will be "religion," "pilgrim," "witch-hunter," "pioneer," "bigot," and "founder." Typically, among the images described will be men and women in formal black clothes, ships sailing into harbor, and Indians and Englishmen sharing a Thanksgiving meal. Ask professional historians the same question and they furnish remarkably similar words and images. Neither students nor professionals are likely to use words or conjure up images associated with Puritans playing musical instruments, singing, or crowding into theaters. People tend not to identify Puritans as supporters of or participants in the performing arts. But neither do they tend to identify artistic cultural phenomena as the targets of Puritan narrow-mindedness. Sex and alcohol are cited much more often. Music and theater seldom merit mention in either the vernacular or the professional history of Puritanism.

The words and images of Revolutionary New England, however, tell a different story and paint a different picture. Yankee Doodle, church choirs, fiddlers, and military fife corps are but a few examples of musical culture etched into the popular iconography. Without straining definitions, the Boston Tea Party can easily be viewed as a form of political theater. The commonplace perception seems to be that patriots enjoyed these arts as much as Puritans ignored them. A circumspect religious worldview, in which music and theater played little part, gave way to a boisterous, secular worldview that celebrated its political independence in song and pageant. By and large this commonplace perception is accurate. Like most informal history narrated by vague words and illustrated by hazy images, it glosses over complexities and hence overstates the contrast; but between 1620 and 1790 New England changed its mind about music and theater. In its surface manifestation, the change ushered in a new set of possibilities for leisure; beneath the surface, it revealed profound alterations in definitions of human purpose. Puritans and patriots had differing views on music and theater that reflected differing views of their errand in the wilderness.

## Music: The Era of Psalmody

A variety of strands in their English and religious backgrounds gave New Englanders an array of alternatives from which to fashion their views on music. Many Elizabethans loved music. Among those, for example, were seventeenth-century England's two most famous Puritans: John Milton, whose father played the violin professionally, and Oliver Cromwell, who paid a musical staff. John Calvin, the theologian most closely associated with Puritanism's origins, did not on the surface seem hostile to music. He called it an "effective, divinely given" tool to help in the worship of God. Yet Milton and Cromwell were as exceptional in their enthusiasm for music as they were in their respective gifts for writing and waging war. And Calvin hedged his commitment to music with crippling caveats. He believed that only those songs God revealed in Scripture—that is, the psalms—should be used in worship. In keeping with the communal spirit of Christianity, he further argued that singing must be in unison. Moreover, singers must be unaccompanied because instruments were not sanctioned by any scriptural passages. In the theological war Calvin and other reformers waged against Rome, elaborate music, individual voices, and musical instruments in church became increasingly identified as examples of Papist idolatry and ritual. Calvin believed that music both inside and outside the church should "serve to edify rather than to amuse."[1] In other words, a religious purpose, not an artistic one, gave music its legitimacy.

New England's founding generation brought Calvin's mixed message with it to the New World. As in so many areas, the conflicting signals over music produced an ambivalence in Puritan culture and in attempts by historians to comprehend that culture. Amidst the ambiguities, however, some clear conclusions may be drawn.

New England's Puritans regularly incorporated music into their religious services. *The Bay Psalm Book* (Boston, 1640), compiled by three Puritan ministers, Richard Mather, Thomas Wilde, and John Eliot, was the first book published in the American colonies; it attests to the importance attached to the singing of psalms during worship. John Cotton, one of *The Bay Psalm Book*'s strongest supporters, shared Calvin's belief, however, that music should be judged not by the beauty of its sound but by the degree of spiritual arousal it occasioned in both singer and listener. Undue attention to artistry and other diversions such as instruments or choir directors not only smacked of Rome but distracted people from music's true purpose. Hence, Cotton argued (and virtually all New England Puritans agreed) church music should be completely confined to psalms sung without accompaniment and with little direction. A duly appointed person shouted out one line of a psalm, which the congregation would then repeat. Except for "lining out," as the process was called, no direction on tunes, notes, or cadence was given. Cotton made it clear, however, that the lack of formal leadership in the singing of psalms should not give rise to solo artistry or creative spontaneity; rather, a self-imposed discipline should be practiced by all in an attempt to blend individual voices with the entire community. In the absence of any rules or agreements, each individual was free to choose any tune he or she wished. Most people adapted the Psalms to the tunes of traditional English ballads with which they were familiar, and congregations tended to create their own idiosyncratic traditions of tunes. So, seventeenth-century New England developed an oral, nontechnical tradition that owed little to formal knowledge. Virtually no early New Englanders could read musical notes. Tune books, therefore, would have been of little aid.[2]

The Puritans' attitudes toward music paralleled their general attitude toward church government. As Congregationalists, New England's Puritans dispensed with many of the governing devices—bishops, synods, presbyteries—used by Rome and other parts of Christendom to bring order, structure, and uniformity to an inherently fractious world. Yet Puritans prized and sought stability and conformity. Congregational church government, however, did not have the coercive strength or structural wherewithal to provide order for a large and dispersed population. New England relied on voluntary submission and on the leadership of the clergy and of the civil authorities to knit each local congregation into a uniform whole. Puritan theologians believed that truth did exist and God's elect could come close to finding it without a pope, bishops, or other authoritarian bodies. In the main, time proved them wrong; New England existed amidst much religious bickering.[3]

So, too, did Puritan attitudes toward the practice of church music fail to produce a harmonious whole. Knowledge of music declined

throughout the seventeenth century: congregations forgot tunes; no training took place; and creativity was indulged only to the extent that each
singer anarchistically dealt with the psalms on his or her own terms. By
most accounts, the results were artistically dreadful. An obscure minister,
Thomas Walter, who became a critic of the system, wrote at the end of this
century of decline: "the tunes are now miserably tortured and twisted and
quavered, in some churches, into a medly of confused and disorderly
voices. Our tunes are left to the mercy of every unskillful throat to chop
and alter, to twist and change. . . . [N]o two men in the Congregation
quaver alike or together, it sounds in the ear of a good judge like five
hundred different tunes roared out at the same time with perpetual
interferings with one another." James Franklin claimed, in a nasty satire
published in the *New England Courant,* that he was "credibly informed that
a certain gentlewoman miscarried at the ungrateful and yelling noise of a
deacon" whom Franklin described as a "procurer of abortions."[4]

Walter and Franklin added two strident voices to a chorus of critics
pressing for reform in church music in the 1690s. For over sixty years,
New England's churches fought over the proposed changes. In the end,
reform succeeded and transformed religious music into an art form of both
beauty and entertainment. The 1698 edition of *The Bay Psalm Book,* the first
in New England's history to include tunes, provided the first hint of
change. This new edition supplied "some directions for ordering the voice"
that were designed to help people avoid "squeaking above or grumbling
below."[5] Since the book's authors were several prominent Boston-area
ministers, the suggested changes in singing methods did not occasion hot
debate at first and seemed destined to be a minor point of doctrine that
would be considered without haste or rancor.

In the 1720s, however, the proposed musical reforms became the
center of one of New England's most bitter debates. The controversy over
"singing by rote or note" — by the "old style" or by a "regular way" —
erupted because the proposed changes became attached to and symbolic
of a deeper struggle in Puritan society between a conservative, primarily
rural mentality and a newly emerging, urbane, liberal one centered in the
large towns. The urban clergy led the fight with a barrage of thirty-one
sermons published between 1721 and 1730 that provided doctrinal justi-
fication for singing by note as well as instructions for how to do so. In 1731,
a group of Boston ministers started "A Society for Promoting Regular
Singing in the Worship of God," which organized a series of "singing
lectures" — sermons on the proper singing of psalms. These clergy advocated reform for several reasons. They thought it had intrinsic merit:

organized, planned singing produced more pleasing music. Also, moral lessons could be found in the new style. "Tuneable voices," one wrote, distinguished man from the animals. Furthermore, another said, "God is not the author of confusion" and the old style made a virtue of musical disorder. Finally, and most importantly, the urban clergy saw singing reform as religious reform and thought that organizing music might help to restore religion to its earlier importance. Thus, many ministers thought they could use interest in music as a means of combating a perceived loss of religious zeal. Specifically, reformers argued that the new music was an act of devotion that pleased God; it was a "chariot" carrying prayers to heaven; it "soothed unhappy emotion"; it promoted a feeling of community; it helped resist Satan by "fixing the mind" on religious objects; and it helped prevent young people from giving in to "foolish, yea pernicious songs and ballads and . . . all such trash."[6]

The intellectual, urbane wing of the Puritan clergy promoted singing reform as part of a whole host of changes designed to combat laxity. Loosening of membership requirements and relaxed definitions of the conversion experience are some of the better-known departures from original Puritan precepts that characterized this reform. Not surprisingly, the urban clergy dominated the published literature in the singing controversy as well as in most areas of reform. Only one minister, Samuel Niles of Braintree, is known to have vigorously opposed the new style of singing and published a sermon against it. But a substantial proportion of the laity—probably a majority, and certainly a majority of the active church members—opposed what they regarded as a sacrifice in purity. Stigmatized as backward, stubborn, prejudiced "rustiks and country people," the opponents of the new style of singing countered with one basic but extraordinarily telling argument. They accused the musical reformers of bringing "superstitious ceremonies" into Puritan worship. This phrase had a rare and powerful effect because it was Puritan code for Catholicism. An anonymous letter to the *New England Courant* in 1723 put the matter bluntly: "If we begin to sing by rule, the next thing will be to pray by rule and preach by rule and then comes Popery."[7]

In congregation after congregation, the specter of creeping Popery haunted the debate. And, given the congregational structure of Puritanism, the reform had to be carried out on a parish-by-parish basis. In almost every parish, even the urban ones, some opposition arose. In general, by the 1740s the champions of reform had won the battle. Nevertheless, rearguard actions against reform continued in some parishes until the Revolutionary era. A Westfield, Massachusetts, minister, John Ballantine, who had a protracted battle with some parishioners over his support for "note" music, wrote with satisfaction in his diary entry for May 7, 1769: "Sung without reading for the last time." He then noted, without any apparent regrets, that a number of members "went out" (walked out) of services because they opposed the new music. The North Parish of Windsor, Connecticut, reversed itself twice in 1771 and 1772 over "singing by rule." Not until 1793 did Windsor put the fight to rest, when it voted to hire "a singing master to instruct in the rules and arts of singing Psalms so that singing may be performed decently and orderly." Local bitterness also produced occasional comic opera. A Glastonbury, Connecticut, parish voted to sing the old way half of the year and the new way in the other half. In many towns the opponents and proponents of the new style tried to drown each other out during worship.[8]

All told, the great singing controversy encapsulated the intellectual and practical dilemma of Puritan piety as it grappled with growth, modernity, and the flow of new ideas. Cotton Mather, ever a personal canvas for portraying Puritan ambivalence, tried to reconcile the forces of the old and new. Mather endorsed the new style of singing in the early years of the debate and further endorsed the concept of listening to music for pleasure and beauty. But he admonished his readers to avoid all styles of singing that might appear "sportive and wanton." As you sing psalms, Mather wrote, "let your outward carriage be grave and composed . . . let a sincere view to the Honor of God animate and regulate your endeavors." With rare pith and beauty, Mather concluded poetically that "the Christian and the musician must bear each other company. The one must not say to the other, I have no need of thee."[9]

Mather's liberalism on music did not extend beyond singing by rule. He implacably opposed the use of instruments in church and agreed with the conservatives that all instruments in worship, but especially organs, smacked of a return to Popery. If instrumental music breached the walls of the Puritan meetinghouse, "dancing as well as playing in the aisles" would inevitably follow. The hatred and fear that inspired so many ministerial diatribes against instrumental music in churches has led most historians to assume that Puritans loathed instrumental music in general. They did not. Once again, the problem for historians lies in their failure to appreciate the ability of the Puritan leadership to split doctrinal hairs.[10] On one hand, virtually all Puritans agreed that playing instruments during services distracted worshipers from their religious concentration and therefore should be proscribed. On the other hand, virtually all Puritans also agreed on the appropriateness of using instruments on ceremonial occasions; trumpets, fifes, drums, and bells were used at formal moments such as the arrival of important ships or personages, the installation of a governor, executions and whippings, the reading of proclamations, and so forth. Beyond the above, the probity of playing instruments inspired no unanimity. Many of the more austere Puritans allowed their contempt of instruments in the meetinghouse to color their views of instruments outside it. Having little theological basis, their hostility did not rise above personal reproof. Puritans who did play or enjoy listening to instruments usually did so in the privacy of their own homes, in the company of family or small gatherings of friends. As was the case with all forms of the pursuit of pleasure, if a Puritan lavished too much time or attention on musical instruments, he or she crossed the line between legitimate and illegitimate leisure. The lack of agreement over secular music in seventeenth-century New England, however, never sparked a lively debate. Foes of instruments disapproved quietly, and friends pursued their interest in peace and privacy.[11]

Probate-court inventories of personal goods left by decedents reveal a surprisingly large number and assortment of instruments; strings, such as citterns, lutes, and guitars; keyboards, such as virginals, harpsichords, spinets, and clavichords; horns, most prominent of which was the trumpet; several members of the viola family; and wind instruments, drums, and Jew's harps. Some instructive conclusions can be drawn about the ownership of these instruments. The founding settlers of Massachusetts and Connecticut—the Pilgrims of the golden age of Puritan piety—brought many instruments with them. Probably most of these were family possessions packed up in the normal course of moving. Owners of instruments did not tend to be overrepresented among Anglicans, deviants, or otherwise marginal New Englanders, but were just as likely to be respectable church members, prosperous or of average means. Instruments, after all, were valuable. Merchants constituted the largest group of owners, followed closely by ministers. No class or occupational group had a monopoly, however; farmers and craftsmen also owned musical instruments. Nor did urbanites have a monopoly on ownership. Although the proportion of owners was higher in the large towns, many of the less expensive instruments were found in rural areas. Thus, an appreciation of secular instrumental music was somewhat associated with the educated and sophisticated members of the urban gentry, but probably every Puritan in seventeenth-century New England had opportunities to listen to instrumental music if he or she wished.[12]

Certain instruments were associated with specific groups of people and activities. Most owners of the larger members of the viola family such as violas da gamba or bass viols had good educations; ministers, merchants, and schoolteachers predominated. They usually lived in large towns and often played in "consort" together in the evening. For the well-to-do, these large viols provided after-dinner entertainment. The ownership of small shoulder violins was more evenly spread across the social structure. Not surprisingly, a large number of tavern keepers owned them and used them for entertainment on the premises. Most prosecutions for lascivious dancing in taverns list the violin as the offending instrument that provided the tune. Virginals—small, plucked-string keyboard instruments of the harpsichord family—were widely used as accompaniment for singing in private homes. They produced a throaty, pretty sound that virtually everyone found pleasing. Virginals were also sophisticated, expensive, and difficult to master; their presence in large numbers implies a richness of musical culture. Except for Jew's harps, which were numerous and often owned by children, the cittern was the most common instrument in seventeenth-century New England. A noisy, cheerful cross between a banjo and a mandolin, the cittern had a flat back and vertical sides, and was strung with wire, not gut. Like the violin, the cittern was associated with lively celebrations and good times. Fifes, drums, and trumpets usually were owned by military men and government officials.[13]

## Music: The Golden Age

This modest tradition of secular instrument-playing constituted a secondary strand of musical experience in seventeenth-century New England that paralleled but never intersected the primary strand of psalmody. In the 1720s both sacred and secular music developed an enhanced artistry and new importance. And, of greater consequence, the two strands of experience began to intertwine to produce a musical culture that moved from the periphery to the center of leisure and recreational activities. With the rise of the regular-singing movement, music within the meetinghouse brought together beauty of expression and religious purposes. Outside of the meetinghouse, religious music became a major source of entertainment. Only a small minority of diehard conservatives continued to see a conflict between music as an art and music as a stimulus to religion.

In his influential sermon of 1721 that criticized the old way of singing, the Boston minister Thomas Walter explicitly justified the combination of the two traditions by recourse to historical metaphor. Walter described Christ as that "great musician singing at the last supper . . . that blessed man who was more than a man and who knew all the infinite varieties and even unsearchable melodies that lie hidden in the nature of sounds." Where an earlier generation would have condemned Walter's figure of speech as blasphemy, the religious leadership of the 1720s thought it both good history and good theology.[14] Walter joined forces with two of Boston's most distinguished ministers, Cotton Mather and John Tufts, and several prominent Bostonian laymen, among them Thomas Brattle, William Price, Thomas Johnston, Edward Enstone, Peter Pelham, and Stephen Deblois, to promote musical study and performance. Brattle, a devout Puritan and the treasurer of Harvard College, imported the first organ into New England in 1708; he played it in his home to the delight of many friends. At his death in 1713, Brattle willed the organ to the Brattle Square Church, the most liberal Congregational church in town. The church trustees faced a difficult choice—one that Thomas Brattle must have anticipated—and planned to force Puritans to rethink their position on the use of instruments in worship. Not surprisingly, the trustees compromised. "With all due respect," they wrote, "[we] do not think it proper to use the same [the organ] in the public worship of God." But they were indeed respectful— not scandalized—and they gave the organ to King's Chapel, one of the Anglican churches in Boston. Thus, through the good offices of a leading Puritan and of a Puritan board of church elders, organ music was introduced to religious worship. Brattle's remained the sole organ in New England for two decades, until an Anglican parish in Newport imported another in 1733. Shortly after, two more appeared in Boston, one each at the other two Anglican parishes, and then in rapid-fire succession a couple of dozen Anglican parishes elsewhere in Massachusetts and Connecticut bought and installed them. In the 1750s, organs began appearing among the household possessions of many merchants, dissenters and Congregationalists alike, and in 1770, the first Puritan church to allow one, the Congregational Church of Providence, installed an organ of two hundred pipes, a truly magnificent instrument for its time. Providence's Anglican church, piqued at being upstaged by the Congregationalists, immediately ordered one, which was installed the following year. The two Providence parishes engaged distinguished organists, Benjamin West being hired by the Congregationalists and Andrew Law by the Anglicans. The breakthrough became nearly complete when the Brattle Square Church, which had refused the first organ in New England, bought one in 1790.[15]

The growth of organ music in eighteenth-century New England was important for two reasons. First, nothing better symbolized the hated musical traditions of the Roman Catholic Church than the organ. To the founders of New England it represented an evil, one made all the more horrifying because of its outward charm and beauty—a snare to the soul of uncommon danger. During the English Civil War, Puritans destroyed many organs as examples of the worst Catholic excesses incorporated by the Anglicans into their weak-willed attempts to break away from Rome. The musical liberal Cotton Mather parted company with his reforming brethren on the matter of organ music in general and especially in worship.[16] Yet organ music gained respectability and legitimacy throughout the eighteenth century. Few rural Congregational churches would consider buying one in 1790, but probably every New Englander could hear one with no more than an hour's ride. And no one saw the Devil pulsing out of the organ's pipes.

Second, organ music lay at the center of a whole host of musical activities. Nothing else engendered as many artistic spinoffs. William Price and Thomas Johnston, the first two New Englanders to become proficient organ players—perhaps "professional" would be the right term—developed musical businesses. Price imported a wide range of instruments, which he offered for sale to the general public, and he gave lessons on all that he sold. Moreover, Price used his profits as entrepreneur and teacher to support music in many forms. In effect, he became a patron of the musical arts in the 1720s and 1730s. Johnston changed his religion from Congregationalism to Anglicanism so that he could worship at King's Chapel and indulge his love of the organ. He gave performances during which he sang to his own and Price's accompaniment. Johnston repaired the few organs in existence in New England in the 1730s and 1740s; then, when demand heightened in the 1750s, he began to build and sell them. In 1754 he finished his first one, ordered by the Anglicans of Salem, Massachusetts, and built several more in the next few years. Johnston also wrote, published and sold tunebooks, and gave money to support other musical activities.[17]

The presence of organ music provided the impetus for the creation of music and dance schools. In 1713, George Brownell, an organist, opened a school for "dancing, treble violin, flute, spinet, and stitchery." The following year, Edward Enstone emigrated to Boston from England to take a job as one of the organists at King's Chapel. Two years later, Enstone, an extremely well-trained musician, opened a "school of manners or dancing," a larger and more publicized undertaking than Brownell's. Much like charm schools of the twentieth century, Brownell's and Enstone's emphasized general cultural development. Both attracted primarily women as students and tried to produce graduates who could amuse others through private musical performances.[18]

In the 1720s, many similar schools opened (and closed—music and dance schools could be risky business) their doors in Boston. Slowly, the charm-school movement spread to other large towns in the 1730s and 1740s. These schools gave rise to public musical concerts. The first one was held in the evening of February 3, 1729, a Sunday, in the King Street Dancing School. After this breakthrough, Boston had at least three or four concerts during each of the next five years; all were held at dancing schools. In the late 1730s the number of concerts increased dramatically as they moved out of the relative intimacy of the dancing schools. Concerts were held outdoors—in the British Coffee House, King's Chapel, several taverns, and Faneuil Hall after it opened in 1742. A great moment in Boston's musical life occurred in 1754, with the opening of Concert Hall, built by the brothers Lewis and Gilbert Deblois, who were both organists at Anglican churches. Constructed specifically for musical performances, Concert Hall immediately became the musical center for Boston and, indeed, for all of New England. By mid-century, musical concerts became an established part of Boston's cultural and social life.[19]

Boston led the way in New England in the development of virtually all cultural and artistic activities; in no sphere was this more true than in music. Most of the first performers in Boston were English temporary sojourners or immigrants, persuaded to cross the Atlantic by one of the local masters of a dancing school. As the 1730s progressed and concerts became an established part of Boston's life, these musicians began to go on tour around New England. Because they supported themselves and had no patrons, performers usually limited their stops to fifteen or twenty of the large towns that had enough population to generate a reasonable number of ticket sales. The itinerant musicians fended for themselves, usually advertising in advance and planning programs to appeal to popular sensibilities. Almost always musicians gave individual lessons during the day before publicly performing at night.[20]

Concerts came to small-town and rural New England a couple of decades after they became part of urban culture, and they came in different form. As the new style of singing psalms gradually spread to every community, it spawned two new institutions that had a profound effect on secular music: church choirs and singing schools. Members of a congregation who showed interest in singing during worship often formed a special group in order to master the tune and lead the congregation in its performance. Initially, the minister or some other local person of talent provided instruction. During the 1740s, however, a few itinerant musicians called "singing masters" began offering classes to instruct choirs and local singers. The singing-school movement grew slowly for a decade but in the late 1750s surged suddenly in popularity. By the 1760s, the vast majority of parishes, even remote ones with no central village, had engaged a singing teacher to conduct a singing school. Terms occasionally were as short as one week, but three-month ones were average. Held variously at churches, schools, or taverns, singing schools were oversubscribed as soon as word went out that one was about to be held. Students paid tuition and met twice a week in the evening and sometimes again on Sunday. At the end of the term, the class put on a concert, a "singing lecture" as it was called, that would be directed and explained by the teacher and sometimes accompanied by a sermon preached by the minister on the joys and religious purposes of music.[21]

A singing-school mania characterized New England in the 1760s and 1770s. Recalcitrant parishes that had bitterly opposed changing their method of singing often hired a singing master within weeks of voting to sing according to the new style. When in session, singing schools injected energy and excitement into the local social life. They became known for fun and frivolity. One young man undoubtedly exaggerated but neverthe- less effectively conveyed his excitement when he wrote in his diary: "I have no inclination for anything for I am almost sick of the world and were it not for the hope of going to singing-meeting tonight and indulging myself in some of the carnal delights of the flesh, such as kissing, squeezing, etc., I should surely leave it now." Singing schools attracted students of all ages, but had a special appeal for teenagers and young adults, who constituted the majority of each class.[22]

Although singing schools usually taught and performed religious works, they had a far greater effect on secular patterns of leisure and social life than they did on formal religious worship in the meetinghouse. The broad demand for trained teachers and performers called forth hundreds of talented people who made music their vocation or an absorbing avoca- tion. The singing schools became the institution that not only legitimized music throughout New England, but also helped Americanize it. The elite masters of Boston and the urban areas previously had taught and per- formed English music that, at best, had been Americanized by a few hasty adaptations for marketing purposes. The urban music of the 1730s through 1750s furnished a classic example of the culture of colonialism: derivative, patronizing, and demonstrably below the standards of the mother country. The music generated by the singing schools in the 1760s and afterward may have originated from the same colonial impulses, but it developed along lines rooted in the soil of the New England countryside. Remote villagers and farmers were too poor, too unsophisticated, and too distant to pay for, care about, or have access to English high culture. Less Anglicized and more Puritan than their urban counterparts, country people embraced singing schools and choral music with a passion—and they created a vernacular American musical culture.[23]

The Revolution speeded up the process of Americanization. Time and distance had already made English icons, words, and tunes irrelevant to the countryside; now, the war with England made them foreign and unpatriotic. Historians of music refer to the period from the 1760s through the mid-1790s as the golden age of choral music in New England. The strength and hallmark of this vernacular music lay in the melodic writing in each of its parts. Individual singers "held" a good tune against several others. More of the music was performed a capella than would have been the case in England and Europe. The results, by almost all accounts, were aesthetically pleasing. John Adams, a young curmudgeon not known for rhapsodizing over the arts, gave the following description of a choir he chanced to hear in Connecticut in 1771: "The finest singing that I ever heard in my life; the front and side galleries were crowded with rows of lads and lasses, who performed all their parts in utmost perfection. I thought I was rapt up; a row of women all standing up and playing their parts with perfect skill and judgement, added a sweetness and sprightliness to the whole which absolutely charmed me."[24]

Foreign critics thought the sounds unorthodox, but by no means did they generally disapprove. Some may have, but many English musicians liked the New England sound and incorporated it into their own work. A number of English and European composers, most notably the English organist William Selby and the Danish musician Hans Gram, settled in Boston in the 1780s and wrote music for the singing-school style.[25]

New England furnished most of its own composers, however. William Billings of Boston, the most distinguished of these, deserves the recognition he received in his own lifetime and after by historians. Called the father of New England music, Billings stood head and shoulders above his contemporaries. In his short life (1746-1800), Billings wrote and published more than three hundred tunes, mostly set to psalms. A dynamic, gregarious person, he traveled to dozens of small towns and was the most sought-after singing-school master of the golden age. Billings also had an irrepressible ego and promoted both himself and music in general as divinely inspired. Billings obviously loved the sound and beauty of music, but he justified his work's importance in terms of religious piety. In addition to being a great composer and master, Billings became the teacher of teachers with the publication of his book, *The Singing Master's Assistant,* in 1778. It became the standard text used by his fellows for over a generation.[26]

Billings's greatness has obscured the careers of dozens of other composers of the same era. Most of these came from small towns; for some inexplicable reason, many more came from Connecticut than from Massachusetts. In particular, Connecticut composers created a special type of "fuging tone" that was immediately recognizable and the most original part of the New England genre. As they did for Billings, psalms and other religious topics furnished most of the words for these composers, but a significant amount of patriotic Revolutionary verse was also set to these new tunes. Several songs celebrated the Battle of Bunker Hill and several others the virtues of General George Washington.

The Revolution promoted music in additional ways. Although Bostonians hated the British troops stationed in town to maintain order after the Stamp Act riots, they loved the military music the regimental bands provided. The 64th Regiment of regulars had a particularly well-known band that gave frequent free concerts during the late 1760s and early 1770s. By 1775 the number of British regiments had increased to nine, eight of which had bands. Bostonians bitterly resented this coercive military presence, but they feasted on the music played at the changing of the guards, military parades, funerals, and so forth. All the regimental bands continued the 64th's tradition of giving free public concerts. After the outbreak of hostilities, the British regimental bands played less, and most colonists boycotted the occasions when they did play.[28]

New Englanders at war transferred their prewar love for British military music to their own patriotic regimental bands. Not by accident do so many pictures of battle feature fifers and drummers. Every regiment had them, and many had more extensive bands. The most famous band of the war, Colonel Crane's Band, had oboes, clarinets, bassoons, and horns in addition to the more commonplace fifes and drums. After the war, Crane's musicians regrouped in Boston in 1783 to form the Massachusetts Band, which gave frequent public concerts and was acknowledged to be the greatest American orchestra of its time.[29]

Music played a major role in developing camaraderie and esprit de corps among the common soldiers. Folklorists and musicologists have identified over three hundred of what John Adams called the liberty songs. New Englanders wrote a large percentage of these, including some by such well-known patriots as Joseph Warren and Mercy Otis Warren. Most of the songs were subliterary, meant to be sung by troops and not to be read or performed in concert. Laden with satire and scatological references, they often lampooned their own commanders and ridiculed the enemy. Troops adapted certain tunes over and over again to differing words; "Derry Down" and "Heart of Oak" were the two most popular. Some of the outrageously ribald songs would have horrified polite society. Dozens of them made metaphorical reference to England as a whore. Not until the 1960s, when rock and roll, folk music, and reform fused together in the student protest movement did balladry and vernacular music again play as important a role as they did during the Revolution.[30]

The ballads and ditties of the Revolutionary soldier were themselves a continuation of a tradition developing in New England after 1720 as a lesser part of the general expansion of musical culture. Unpublished ballads were frequently sung by young people at social gatherings to entertain and titillate. Often these told ribald tales. The most popular one in New England at mid-century was known by the title "Our Polly Is a Sad Slut." Secular musical broadsides, usually printed on a single piece of paper with writing on one side only, popularized many songs that offended contemporary good taste. Cheap to produce, the broadsides were nailed to tavern walls and reprinted in newspapers, chapbooks, and diaries. As early as 1713, Cotton Mather, the liberal promoter of the new style of singing, railed against musical broadsides by which "the minds and manners of many people . . . are much corrupted by foolish songs and ballads."

Mather's strictures notwithstanding, broadsides grew in number and ribaldry over the rest of the eighteenth century. The Revolution increased the growth rate geometrically, but previous wars also had quickened the pace. Nor did moral authorities condemn all of the broadsides. The fall of Louisbourg in 1745, one of the truly great triumphs for New England's military forces, inspired a host of broadside ballads. "New England Bravery," the best-known, was immensely popular. Entrepreneurs collected some of the more respectable unpublished ballads or broadside songs into books called songsters. Massachusetts publishers brought out six secular songbooks prior to 1776. During the Revolutionary era, 1776 to 1790, five more were published in Boston, three in Connecticut, and one in Rhode Island. Throughout the colonial and Revolutionary periods, Boston remained the unrivaled capital of music publishing not just of New England but of all the American colonies. Beginning in 1784, however, the printer Isaiah Thomas of Worcester started publishing music; in short order Worcester did rival Boston, solely because Thomas became the most prolific music publisher of the post-Revolutionary and early national periods.[31]

Some secular songbooks were specialized, some general. Boston's Masonic lodge published the first one in New England in 1750 as a part of its constitution. Another, *The Famous Tommy Thumb's Little Story-Book* (Boston, 1768), had songs as well as stories for young children. The most ambitious secular songbook, *The New Song Book, being Miss Ashmore's favourite collections of songs as sung in the theaters and public gardens in London and Dublin* (Boston, 1771), contained nearly three hundred songs, including many long and complex ones.[32]

Almost everywhere one looks in the second half of the eighteenth century, New Englanders were singing, listening, playing, and being entertained by music. The ambivalence that constrained seventeenth-century Puritanism's enjoyment of music had nearly disappeared. No greater symbol of music's cultural power and moral legitimacy could be found than in the Puritans' evolving views on the use of instruments during divine worship. Once taboo, instrumental music in the meetinghouse became first a matter of debate and then, gradually, an established practice. The first instruments used in meetinghouses, bass viols, were sometimes called the Lord's Fiddles or the church bass. By the Revolutionary era parishioners frequently played stringed instruments during worship and gave no scandal. Even organ music, which still conjured up the apparition of the Pope, appeared to be on the road to acceptance.[33] Reform within Puritanism, the growth of dissenting churches, secularization, Anglicanization, urbanization, immigration, prosperity, and even war all conspired to turn the isolated and awkward sounds of the seventeenth century into the ubiquitous melodies of New England's golden age of music.

## Theater: Toward Legitimacy and A Golden Era

Theater traveled a bumpier road and did not achieve legitimacy in New England until the last decade of the eighteenth century. Elizabethan and early New England Puritans felt no ambivalence towards theater: it was evil, pure and simple. "Plays," one cleric wrote, "were sucked out of the Devil's teats to nourish us in idolatrie, heathenrie, and sinne." Politics and circumstance mixed with theology to produce this unremitting hatred. At the same time as Puritanism emerged as an alternative to the Church of England, theater emerged as the center of Elizabethan entertainment. Because the stage lay at the heart of elite English cultural and literary life, Puritans associated it closely with the monarchy and Anglicanism. Thus, political and historical associations rendered theater odious to religious reformers.[34]

Beginning in the 1570s, however, Puritan theologians produced a litany of complaints that additionally condemned theater on doctrinal and moral grounds. These attacks reached their peak in the 1630s, the decade in which the major migration to New England took place. They received their strongest statement in 1633 in William Prynne's learned thousand-page diatribe, *Histriomastix*, which so infuriated Charles I that he had Prynne's ears cut off. Prynne went out of his way to ensure that no one thought him an ascetic who disapproved of all diversions and recreation. Among the activities he endorsed were "fishing, fowling, hawking, hunting, leaping, vaulting, wrestling, running, shooting, singing of Psalms and pious ditties, playing upon musical instruments, casting of the barre, tossing the pike, riding of the great horse, running at the ring, with a world of such like laudable, cheap, and harmless exercises." Prynne even approved of writing and reading plays. But, when actors staged a play, Prynne and virtually all Puritans recoiled in horror. Eight main reasons lay at the heart of this opposition.[35]

1. Theater did not fulfill the appropriate function of recreation because, unlike all legitimate forms of recreation, it did not allow one to return to work refreshed: staged plays exhausted both actors and audiences, leaving them dissipated.
2. Plays rendered men effete and effeminate, sapping their manhood. Often compared to the enervating disease of syphilis, theater originated in wanton impulses explicitly associated in English minds with French and Italian culture.
3. Theater deprived society of the labor of the actors who made their living out of the stage. This logic, of course, would allow amateurs or students to stage plays, but Prynne and others believed that amateur theater invariably produced professional aspirations.
4. In addition to mere effeminacy, theater also promoted homosexuality and unlawful sexuality. In England, as in most European societies, men played women's roles; this practice, Puritans said, violated specific biblical injunctions and encouraged sodomy. If women played women's roles, however, the stage would incite fornication or adultery. Either way, therefore, Prynne argued, theater led to sexual depravity with its "wanton gestures; amorous kisses; lascivious whorish actions; the beautiful faces; . . . the witty obscenities."
5. Theater encouraged treachery and hypocrisy. Acting was lying and actors were liars who were admired for their skill at deceit.

6. Theater was a rival of religious worship—a vicious rival of virtue. Viewed as an alternative way to learn morality through listening and observing speech and actions, theater functioned as "the church of infidelity" to those who flocked to it with regularity. The very popularity of theater in Elizabethan England helps explain why Puritans despised it. Many people found theater so compelling that it became the central focus of their nonwork life. Moreover, Sunday was the most popular day for performances.

7. Plays often presented doctrinal challenges to existing religious orthodoxies or questioned governmental actions. Thus, theater encouraged heresy, dissent, and sedition.

8. And, finally, critics associated a host of socially unacceptable activities with the theater. Thieves and pickpockets worked the audiences; fights broke out; the large crowds spread disease.

To some extent reality justified these criticisms. Sexual themes coursed through many plays and an easy sexuality, homosexual as well as heterosexual, often characterized the lives of actors and abounded in theater districts. Acting companies and actors took in large amounts of money for which they returned nothing more productive than performances. Large crowds did pose social problems. And actors and authors often questioned basic tenets of religion and government. Given all these very real circumstances, Puritan attitudes toward theater become more understandable—perhaps even reasonable. Many other moralists shared the Puritans' loathing and fear.

In the New World, all the English colonies, north and south, proscribed theater in the seventeenth century. For New England to pass laws against theater would have been gratuitous: public sentiment alone sufficed for a complete ban. Not until the mid-eighteenth century did professional theater appear in any of the colonies. In the Caribbean, southern, and middle colonies it was introduced by a professional English theater company headed by William Hallam, an actor, gentleman, and producer somewhat down on his luck, who came to the New World to reverse his declining fortunes. The American Company's first production, *The Merchant of Venice*, which Hallam put on in Virginia in 1752, was quickly followed by several others performed on tours throughout all of the colonies outside New England. Although some people in these areas still nurtured a suspicion of theater, Hallam encountered no real opposition and attracted sizable audiences. When Hallam died, his widow continued the company.[36]

After nine years of success, during which the American Company expanded its repertoire from Shakespeare and Greek tragedies to include sexually provocative comedies, Mrs. Hallam decided to bring her fare to New England. In 1761, armed with a letter of support from Governor Dinwiddie of Virginia, she arrived in Newport, and began rehearsing. Newport, a cosmopolitan city in liberal, non-Puritan Rhode Island, was an obvious strategic choice to attempt to breach the New England perimeter. But even in Newport opposition quickly arose; the town meeting voted to ban theater. Several wealthy Newporters, however, ignored the town meeting vote and persuaded the company to open its production, which it did on September 7, 1761. Between then and mid-November, the American Company put on twelve plays in Newport, attracted large audiences, and behaved with such decorum both onstage and off that hostility melted away. When the company returned in June 1762, it received virtually no opposition; it appeared as if theater might become established and respectable in Rhode Island.[37]

This turned out not to be the case. At the end of its second season in Newport, the American Company, emboldened by success, decided to extend its New England tour to Providence, Rhode Island's second-largest urban center. Providence society proved to be less tolerant. Sometime in either June or July 1762 the company opened its first production, which provoked extraordinary resistance. A town meeting voted not to allow the play to continue and to ask the Rhode Island General Assembly to pass a law forbidding theater. The company, mindful of its successful defiance of the Newport town meeting a year earlier, continued with the play in violation of the local bylaw. Despite the illegality, every performance was attended by large audiences including contingents of people who traveled forty or fifty miles from Massachusetts and Connecticut. Antitheater mobs formed and one night attacked the school where the play was staged. The militia had to be activated to restore peace and order. Petitions to the colony government by those opposed to theater echoed the contemptuous language of seventeenth-century Puritans. In August 1762, in order to avoid "the many mischiefs which arise from public stage plays," Rhode Island passed an extreme law providing prohibitive fines of £50 for anyone who allowed theater on his property, and £100 a performance for any actor. This effectively barred any professional or public amateur theater in Rhode Island until the 1790s.[38] The two seasons in Newport turned out to be the lone exception to the prohibition of theater in colonial and Revolutionary New England.

Massachusetts, Connecticut, and New Hampshire provided even tougher opposition. A couple of isolated instances of theatrical activity in Boston preceded the American Company's successful mid-century tours

of the other colonies. A three-act play written in 1732 vilified Massachusetts governor Jonathan Belcher for alleged greed in squeezing a large
salary increase out of the colonial legislature. The play was never published
and never performed; copies were circulated by hand. Dozens, perhaps
hundreds of Bostonians read it, and most knew of it: no one, however, had
the audacity to print it or stage it. In 1750, a Boston tavern allowed some
patrons to perform *Otway's Orphans*, a popular English comedy, but the
magistrates intervened and shut down the play within days. The next
known exceptions took place in the 1760s among small groups of Harvard
and Yale students, both while they attended college and after they returned
home. Nathaniel Ames, a physician from Dedham with a lifelong love of
theater confided in his diary that Harvard undergraduates secretly put on
some small-scale productions for their own amusement. After leaving
Harvard and beginning his medical practice, Ames helped arrange, direct,
and act in a few other plays put on in Boston and Dedham for small private
audiences. The amateur theater activities Ames described in the 1760s and
1770s were clandestine, but probably tolerated by the magistrates because
they were small and decorous, and tickets were not sold or given away to
the public. During the same period, college authorities disciplined Yale
students on several occasions for "acting a play." Punishments were
slight—public confessions and small fines.[39]

In 1767, as the activities described by Ames were taking place,
Massachusetts passed its first law officially outlawing theater. The Massachusetts authorities felt compelled to codify their opposition because
local magistrates needed help as theater achieved respectability in other
colonies and among some educated, urbane New Englanders. The law of
1767 proved remarkably effective. With the exception of a few private
entertainments such as those put on by Ames and his friends or by college
students, no theater activity took place in New England throughout the
entire Revolutionary era. Connecticut and New Hampshire felt no need
to put their opposition into law but continued to rely on the force of local
public opinion. Some New Englanders, particularly the young, did take
advantage of trips to New York to see theater. Isabella Bell, a young
Bostonian on a visit to New York, wrote to her friends back home of an
elaborate joke played on her after she went to see a play for the first time.
Her New York companions handed her a letter indicting her for immoral
conduct, for which they required a public confession.[40]

In New England, however, the custodians of morality thought theater no laughing matter. With the Revolutionary emergency over, the
debate over theater rekindled in the late 1780s. A small professional

company put on a play in Portsmouth, New Hampshire, in 1790 and returned to perform several more in 1791.[41] Then in 1792 a bitter debate took place in the Massachusetts General Assembly when Boston's delegates introduced a bill to repeal the antitheater law of 1767. In an anachronistic last gasp of asceticism, opponents of theater pulled out all the stops in the vain attempt to defeat repeal. The nasty debate pitted rural areas against urban ones, captured the attention of the entire New England region, and produced a remarkable pamphlet defending theater's moral legitimacy. John Gardiner's speech to the General Assembly was the most important and controversial moral statement published in late eighteenth-century New England. Gardiner's inflammatory peroration challenged beliefs, icons, and traditions that had survived unquestioned in public discourse since the founding generation. Sounding more like Voltaire than John Winthrop or Cotton Mather, Gardiner wrote: "[T]he bright sun of reason is rising upon us; the thick fogs of superstition must, necessarily be dispelled and vanish before the ascending luminary, and the dark gloomy bigot must soon go off the stage of life." The rest of the nation, according to Gardiner, regarded the New England ban on theater as absurd; nothing in Scriptures prohibited theater; some lessons in diction and stage manners might improve preaching; Harvard and Yale had curricula based on the classic civilization of Greece, where drama originated; and theater was "innocent and rational amusement," not worthy of all the anger and energy expended in stamping it out. Most important, Gardiner forced New England to confront its Puritan past. To answer the argument that New England's founders, the great Puritan divines, abhorred theater, Gardiner replied: "[S]ir, I really and truly venerate — I should rather say, I sincerely and almost enthusiastically admire — the many great and splendid virtues of our renowned Puritan ancestors *but still sir, they were only men, and like all other men were fallible — liable to frailties, to prejudices and to error. Some errors and some unjust prejudices they undoubtedly had"*[42] (italics added).

Gardiner's diatribe and the theater crisis of 1792 did not end the influence of the Puritan morality imported by New England's founders in the 1630s, but they did signal an end to its dominance. Many New Englanders, particularly rural residents, found both theater and Gardiner's assertions appalling; they maintained intact their austere vision of leisure and recreation. They, however, no longer carried the day. In short order, by the end of the first decade of the nineteenth century, amateur theater also entered a golden era and joined music as one of New England's most popular amusements.[43]

Section Three

# GATHERING TOGETHER

# IV

# Congregational Socializing: Gathering Together at the Meetinghouse

A s the leading proponents of Sabbatarianism in the modern Christian world, Puritan moralists unequivocally rejected the idea of Sunday as a day of leisure and recreation. A "Day of Joy," Puritans called the Sabbath, but no one in New England had any doubts about the otherworldly meaning of the word "joy." Sabbath laws forbade many practices regarded as proper and lawful on other days. Social custom proscribed sexual intercourse, unnecessary traveling, and any type of frivolity. Opportunities to hunt had to be forsworn even if food was scarce. Magistrates punished crimes regarded as minor, such as using profanity or stealing apples from a tree, with more severity if they were committed on a Sunday. Brandings and mutilations for crimes committed on the Sabbath were not unusual, and a few ministers and civil leaders believed the death penalty appropriate for Sabbath breaking. New Haven Colony provided fodder for generations of jests by punishing a husband and wife who kissed passionately on Sunday. And Michael Wigglesworth, the popular poet and a quintessential neurotic of historical anecdotes, added to his fame by agonizing over whether closing a stable door that was blowing in the wind constituted an act of work that profaned the Sabbath. New Haven and Wigglesworth, of course, marked one extreme of New England, being akin to the spirit that moved one English wag to charge a Puritan with the "[h]anging of his cat on Monday for killing a mouse on Sunday." But all of the region, with the exception of Rhode Island, embraced

Sabbatarianism with a ferocious sobriety.[1] Family prayers, a three-hour service in both the morning and afternoon, personal Bible study, acts of charity and public improvement, and evening meditations seemingly left little time for leisure. A good Christian spent the Sabbath re-creating his soul, not recreating his body.

## The Sabbath as A Day of Leisure

Every week, for twenty-four hours from sunset on Saturday to sunset on Sunday, Puritan New England became a quiet society of contemplation and worship, moving in slow motion compared to the efficient work regimen that characterized most of the other six days. Whether or not anyone ever articulated the fact, however, the New England Sabbath also was a day of relaxation. "Recreation" would be too strong a term to apply, if recreation is defined as sport or strenuous activity, but from the beginning the Sabbath was a day of leisure in many senses of the word. First and foremost, the Sabbath was a day of rest; only absolutely necessary work could be done. Second, the Sabbath broke the routine of a tightly structured week. Alterations from daily patterns are pleasurable to most people. Third, the two sets of religious services were meant to be intellectually stimulating, and usually were. Fourth, a wide range of social activities inevitably attended worship: meetings with friends, quiet conversation, even refreshments surrounded the formal aspects of the church service. And fifth, despite the religious demands placed on people, they had more discretionary time on days when they had no work responsibilities.

Sunday was the highlight of the week for most seventeenth-century New Englanders. Thomas Shepard, who mounted the greatest Puritan defense of the Sabbath in his *Theses Sabbaticae* (1649), argued that God needed "some magnificent day of state" but that this day must not be a "Dancing Sabbath" or "Everyday Sabbath." For New Englanders throughout the seventeenth and eighteenth centuries, Sunday remained this "magnificent day." As the colonial period unfolded, authorities relaxed their enforcement of the most severe Sabbath laws: Saturday night became detached from the solemnity of Sunday; more overt expressions of secular joy and pleasure became acceptable; travel for social purposes became commonplace; and public religious services became shorter and more voluntaristic.[2] But in 1790 Sunday remained for most New Englanders a quiet day of low-key activity that combined rest, sociability, and religious introspection. On Sunday, New England looked most like New England.

The physical simplicity of the first Puritan meetinghouses belied the complex social relationships that existed within. Although Puritans rejected any precise formula for services because they thought this smacked of a Catholic mass, their meetings did involve ritual. The morning meeting usually began at nine; a drum, bell, or conch shell called nearby villagers, and a volley of gunfire summoned those away from the town center. People began arriving fifteen or so minutes before the start of services and congregated at the front door. A few minutes before nine the men and women filed in separately and took seats on opposite sides of the aisle. Children entered after their parents. Boys were grouped together in one section, with an elder or two sitting among them to maintain order. In most meetinghouses girls sat with their mothers, although sometimes they, too, were seated in their own section. The more prominent families had pews in the front of the meetinghouse; servants sat in the rear. If a parish included blacks, they sat in their own pews. In general rigid segregation by gender, class, age, and race characterized the physical arrangements.

The minister and his wife entered either before or after all the others. If the minister entered first, he led what might appear to be almost a procession; if he entered last, the congregation stood as he escorted his wife to her pew and then mounted the pulpit. When services ended, the minister offered his arm to his wife and then walked her to the front steps, where the two of them greeted the parishioners one by one as they left. At two or three P.M., depending on the season, the worshipers repeated the process at their second service of the day.[3] For most of the colonial period, congregations also had a Thursday afternoon meeting.

Viewed in one way, these meetings may seem to be the last type of gathering one would attend for a leisurely time. The proceedings were formal, the atmosphere somber, the audience passive, the message long and complex, the meetinghouse unpainted, undecorated, and unheated. Convention tolerated no instrumental music, no talking, no shuffling about, not even any daydreaming. And despite the fact that magistrates occasionally prosecuted people for "rude and indecent behavior" or for "laughing in the meetinghouse," the services usually lived up to the community's expectations for good conduct.[4] We should not look for anachronistic Tom Sawyer behavior in Puritan boys or assume that the rest of the congregation secretly longed to be elsewhere.

Seriousness of purpose, however, does not preclude enjoyment. As an opportunity for conversation, as a spectator event, the entire milieu of the services had entertainment value. Virtually all of the community attended. After five or ten years, a majority of New England towns' faithful lived outside the town center and had to travel long distances to worship.[5] Poor roads made wagon use awkward. People more commonly rode on horseback, often two or three on one horse, or they walked. A great deal of quiet socializing took place on the trip into town, and of course, as people came closer to the meetinghouse, the number of travelers increased. People living at the farthest distances often stopped at neighbors' houses along the way and then walked or rode together with them. The crossing of rivers necessitated group arrangements. As rural parishioners streamed into the town center, villagers greeted them. Virtually everyone knew everyone else, and most people had relatives among their fellow parishioners. The segregated seating arrangements in the meetinghouse reflected the social interaction before and after services. Boys talked to boys, girls to girls, cousins to cousins, farmers to farmers, merchants to merchants, and so forth. But primarily, the community gathered together to worship, and in doing so its members came together to see and talk to one another.[6]

And despite the fact that a somber Sabbatarian atmosphere generally characterized all these proceedings, Puritans felt no hostility to the socializing and provided amenities to support it. In particular, the two or three hours between the Sunday morning and afternoon meetings afforded opportunities for refreshments and relaxed conversation. People visited in neighbors' homes during the break. In the first few years of a town's history, villagers often invited travelers from outside the town center to their homes between services; new towns had a majority of people living in the town center and a minority who lived in the countryside.[7] Within five or ten years, however, the ratio reversed and a majority of town residents were "outlivers." More formal arrangements had to be made for them and for their horses. By the end of the seventeenth century, most parishes had built a small hall or designated a school or even a tavern to accommodate their rural residents. Variously called noon houses, horse houses, or, most commonly, Sabbath houses, these buildings quickly became Sunday social centers. People drifted in and out, circulating among the public buildings and the homes of friends and relatives. Sabbath houses were expected to be quiet, befitting the serious nature of the occasion, but they were always heated in cold weather, and stoves were provided to warm the food families brought. Church members who seemed more interested in social chats than religious worship were often referred to as "horseshed Christians." People thrived on "the good fare of brown bread and the Gospel," a Stratford, Connecticut, man wrote of his Sabbath house.[8]

Between the founding of New England and the end of the colonial period, Sunday worship steadily became more social. Massachusetts and

Connecticut kept Sabbath laws on the books throughout the eighteenth century, but official interpretations gradually came to forbid only rowdy behavior, excessive drink, and hard work. Particularly in urban areas, quiet socialization lost its character as ancillary to worship and became a legitimate activity on its own. Judge Samuel Sewall of Boston, for example, was known in the early 1700s for his vigorous enforcement of Sabbath laws, yet Sewall entertained friends and frequently dined out himself on Sundays. In the first two decades of the eighteenth century, the dissenting churches of Anglicans, Baptists, and Quakers wrested a modicum of toleration from the Puritan magistrates, who reluctantly realized that under English law they could no longer insist on complete religious conformity. These dissenters, particularly the Anglicans, held less-strict Sabbatarian beliefs than did the Puritans. The larger towns of Puritan New England adopted the practices of Rhode Island, their dissenting neighbor on Narragansett Bay. Rhode Island had never enacted strict Sabbatarian laws based on Hebraic proscriptions, yet had created a body of local bylaws and customs that enjoined residents to enjoy a day of relaxing and socializing in quiet respectability.[9] Boisterous activities invited disapproval or even prosecution for disorderly conduct.

A variety of changes in detail attest to this overall change in attitude. Parishes began heating the meetinghouse, painting the pews, and making the rough, crude benches more comfortable; the separation of men and women ended; people became free to choose their seatmates, and even young, unmarried men and women could sit together. Almost all of these changes fueled local debate; usually change came to large towns first and to small, rural ones last. Opponents of change charged that the relaxation of rules of austerity would inevitably lead to abuse. In some measure, of course, they were right, but we need to keep the degree of disorder in perspective. Colonial New Englanders never abandoned respectability on Sunday, and in 1790 they still embraced much of the spirit that brought them to loggerheads with James I over the *Book of Sports*, which had attacked sabbatarianism so fiercely in the early seventeenth century.[10] A town as cosmopolitan as Newport, Rhode Island, the most urbane, heterogeneous community in New England, worried about the danger of Sunday licentiousness in the mid-eighteenth century. In response to numerous complaints, the town council ordered Newport's constables to:

> return the names of all tavern keepers and retailers whom you shall find selling strong drink . . . return the names of all persons whom you shall find drinking in taverns . . . sailing in boats, unnecessary

riding, swimming, fishing, gunning, or using any other diversions or recreations . . . disperse all noisy and disorderly gatherings . . . [and] prevent all unnecessary walking in the streets and fields upon the said day, especially during the time of divine services.[11]

Even in Rhode Island, Sunday socialization did not extend to Sunday sport.

Maintaining decorum on the other day of worship, Thursday, proved more difficult. Like Sunday services, the midweek afternoon meeting brought the community together. Thursday, however, entailed no Sabbatarian restrictions to keep excessive behavior in check. Among other problems, taverns were open at night. By the mid-eighteenth century, towns experienced problems, particularly among adolescents and young adults. Jacob Bailey described "lecture day" (as Thursday was called) in his small hometown of Rowley, Massachusetts, in 1741:

> You might see the fathers of families flocking from the house of devotion, with a becoming gravity in their countenances to the house of flip . . . the young sparks assemble in the evening to divert themselves, when after two or three horse-laughs at some passage in the sermon, they proceed to send for an old Negro, who presently makes his appearance with the parish fiddle . . . now the music begins which instantly inspires the youths, who lead out the willing fair to mingle in the dance. They hold this violent exercise till sweat and fatigue oblige them to desist. In this interval, one is dispatched to the tavern for a dram, which revives their spirits till midnight when they separate.[12]

The sermon itself continued to provide intellectual entertainment for many. Seldom has any one vehicle of mass communication been as central to a society as the sermon was to New England. Fusing religion, education, journalism, and entertainment, ministers gave over five million sermons in colonial New England to a society that regarded public speaking as its highest art form. An average churchgoer listened to approximately seven thousand in a lifetime—fifteen thousand hours of sermons.[13] Perhaps no one could match the interest of Elizabeth Phelps, who summarized in her diary every Sunday sermon she heard for fifty-seven years, but many New Englanders enjoyed listening to sermons and discussing them with friends in Sabbath houses and homes afterwards.

Dissenters from outside of the Congregational church after 1700, and then evangelical dissenters from within the church after 1740, added a provocative quality to church service as intellectual fare. Anglicans, Baptists, and Quakers delivered differing messages; Congregational evangelicals provided a differing delivery. The "New Light" preachers of the Great Awakening, as the evangelical revolt within Puritanism was called, rejected the dry, analytical, theological discourse of the earlier ministers and thundered simple messages in fiery rhetoric. Many itinerant preachers developed great reputations and spoke several times a week in different locations. A carnival atmosphere attended their performances. A young farmer, Nathan Cole, described a meeting near Middletown, Connecticut, where the most famous evangelist of the time, George Whitefield, preached to four thousand people. In the twelve miles he traveled, Cole wrote, "I saw no man at work in his field. The low rumblings, thunder of horses, and great clouds of dust" advertised the people coming from all over the region.[14]

Occasional sermons also afforded entertainment. Puritan society marked most formal ceremonies with a sermon delivered by a minister especially chosen for the event. Election and militia sermons were the two most important. The annual election sermon given in Boston, for example, was one of the highlights of the year in Massachusetts. It was both a great social occasion and an affair of state; a virtual national assembly of magistrates, deputies to the legislature, ministers, and other Massachusetts dignitaries gathered to hear the chosen speaker reflect on the political state of the colony. The annual sermons given to small-town voters and leaders or to militia companies may not have been delivered to such august assemblies as gathered in Boston; but from Newport to Hartford to hundreds of remote towns, excitement and anticipation ran through crowds as they listened to the local minister honored by the assignment.[15]

As the large towns grew in sophistication at the middle of the eighteenth century, competing ministers offered a cosmopolitan array of sermon types. Several dozen towns in New England had five or more parishes by the Revolution; each parish provided opportunities to hear ministers or guest preachers representing a variety of perspectives, techniques, and beliefs. As the number of college graduates increased in these large centers, sermons often explored matters of science, epistemology, and political relations as well as the more traditional subjects of theology and doctrine. Ministers had many functions in both the Puritan and dissenting churches—they were pastors, tutors, and civic advisers—but above all they were preachers: they prepared and delivered sermons that were meant to be moral and intellectual exercises, not dreary repetitive exhortations to faith.[16]

As in virtually all things cultural and intellectual, Boston led the way in providing pulpit entertainment. We can see in the diary of John Rowe, a young merchant who emigrated from England to Boston about 1736, how much enjoyment a cultured person might derive from taking advantage of local preaching. Not an overly devout man, Rowe was a communicant of Trinity Church and commented regularly on how much he liked his minister's sermons: "very clever," "very elegant," "most excellent," "delightful," "sensible," "serious," "very polite," "pathetic and moving," "metaphysical," and "well delivered." Rowe did not restrict his interest to Trinity Church, however, but attended other parishes several times a month for weddings, funerals, to hear visiting preachers, to hear local ministers speak on a topic advertised in advance, and so forth. Rowe also sought out the company and friendship of many ministers and sometimes "smoked a pipe" with one of them while discussing matters of intellect raised by a sermon. Although his diary contains none of the haunting introspection of seventeenth-century Puritans, and although he never examined his own faith or expressed any intensity over religious matters, Rowe centered his intellectual life on sermons and other church activities. In a quiet, scholarly, at times nearly secular way, Boston's churches were as important to this worldly Anglican merchant as they had been to the seventeenth-century pietists.[17]

### Ordination Ceremonies

In addition to holding services and providing sermons for special occasions, the church played a role in other social gatherings, such as funerals and days of thanksgiving. Of all of these types of events, the ordination ceremony was meant to be the most solemn; the evolution of its social function illustrates some remarkable changes in the attitude of New Englanders.

In the founding generation of New England, the gathering of a new church and the ordination of a new minister took place as part of a single process. Each would-be parish had to apply for an enabling act from the colony government, draw up a church covenant establishing rules and discipline, make appropriate financial arrangements, construct a meeting-house, select a minister, and then plan and hold a formal ceremony for the "gathering" of the church. A small group of eight or nine men who acted as the church's founding members undertook these activities. At the quickest of paces, the process took six months.

The gathering of a church constituted the most solemn moment in a Puritan community. Weeks of prayer, fasting, and study preceded the final day-long ceremony, which was attended by all of the parishioners, visiting ministers from nearby parishes, and many other distinguished citizens from outside the immediate locale. The gathering ceremony was exciting, of course, as is any great moment in history, but was celebrated as a fast—a day of "solemn humiliation." The next day, a thanksgiving service would be held followed by a quiet banquet. The ordination of the church's first minister usually took place a month or two after the church had been gathered and was accomplished in the same sober manner. After much preparation and prayer, the ordination took place on a day of fasting, again followed by a day of thanksgiving feasting.[18]

A church needed to be gathered only once, of course, but among Congregational Puritans, doctrine required that a minister had to be ordained every time he accepted a new charge. Thus, every change in the ministry required a new ordination ceremony. Until approximately the 1680s, an ordination remained a solemn day of humiliation planned and carried out by lay members of the community. In the last quarter of the century, however, the ordination ceremony began to emerge as a secular social event. By the end of the first quarter of the eighteenth century, ordinations had more of the character of modern presidential inaugurations—or great community parties—than of solemn humiliations.

The changing practices are easy to document, but more difficult to explain. In addition to the general lessening of the intense piety of Puritanism, the conduct of the clergy may have played an ironic role in the transformation. As the clergy became more professionalized, it tended to take formal charge of the ceremonies away from the laity. William Nile's 1672 ordination was the first one to reduce the role of the lay members. Thirteen years later, at Cotton Mather's ordination in 1685, the Boston ministers conducted the entire proceeding. The clergy relegated parishioners to observer status at the formal ceremony. The laity's sole function was to arrange refreshments and the social celebration to mark the occasion. They did this in ways that increasingly would have seemed horrifying—blasphemous—to New England's founders.[19]

Alcohol played an increasingly prominent part in most ordination celebrations from the 1680s onward. In 1681, a Boston parish brewed a special "ordination beer" for the occasion. Over the first half of the eighteenth century, this practice grew to the point where taverns sometimes served "ordination spirits" on the days before and after the event. Beginning with a few parishes in Connecticut's larger towns in the 1690s, dancing gradually became a regular part of the late afternoon and evening celebrations that took place after the formal laying-on of hands in the meetinghouse. By the 1720s, holding an "ordination ball" was commonplace. Ministers themselves did not dance, but of course they attended the balls, sat in places of honor, and received a stream of good wishes from the dancers.[20]

As they grew more complex and less decorous, ordination parties required more advance planning. The parishes or town usually elected a committee several months in advance of the ordination. The prospective minister played the central role in planning the clerical aspects of the ordination ceremony, but the secular committee usually consulted him only briefly about the social festivities. Ministers often recorded the details of their ordinations in diaries and, not surprisingly, emphasized the spiritual and downplayed the social aspects. Ebenezer Parkman provided a day-to-day chronicle of his month-long preparation to become Westborough, Massachusetts's, minister on October 28, 1724. He spent days in meditation and fasting, invited nearby clergy to play specific roles, agonized over a guest list, worked on his own ordination sermon, and the day after the actual event, characterized it as "truly the greatest day I ever yet saw." Parkman mentioned social arrangements only in passing, although the parish threw an elaborate ordination ball.[21]

Ordinations placed a strain on many small towns' budgets. The little community of Edgartown on Martha's Vineyard had to levy an emergency tax to "defray charges of entertainment" in 1747. Prosperous larger towns, however, could afford to and often did hold lavish parties. Henry Stiles's history of Wethersfield, Connecticut, describes fancy ordination balls in 1726 and 1727 that took place in two of the town's four parishes. The possible forms of celebration ranged from a late-night dance with fiddlers, many types of liquor, and mountains of food, to a convivial banquet with cakes, ale, and conversation. Whether quiet or raucous, however, ordinations were the occasion for a town party. Inasmuch as ministers had long tenures in office, ordinations took place infrequently in the normal course of events. Thus, a party that skirted on the edge of ribaldry was not likely to plunge a community into a pattern of licentiousness.[22]

Not surprisingly, given their importance and infrequency, ordination balls did sometimes get out of control. In 1759, the General Court of Massachusetts referred the problem to a council of ministers who issued some cautions against excess and some guidelines for appropriate celebrations. Their recommendations had little impact. The Reverend Jonathan Sewall, who chaired the ministerial council, himself came in for a barrage of criticism for an ordination party he hosted for a fellow Boston cleric two years later. Newspapers sometimes contained letters condemning overly boisterous ordinations. To some degree, of course, ribaldry, like beauty, was in the eye of the beholder. One rural Massachusetts minister proudly described his own party as "a jolly ordination. We lost all sight of decorum." The decorum lost, however, was less than at other balls, in which "mawdlin songs and much roisterous laughter," "pretty damsels," "scattering gravy, sauces and other divers things," and "inspiring Barbadoes drink" left a community red-faced and hung over after one of the most important days in its church's history.[23]

## Funerals

As with so much of their doctrine, Puritan beliefs about death stripped away the theological comforts of the Catholic church. Covenant theology allowed no certitude. Indeed, belief in one's own salvation served as a sign that a person labored under a false set of beliefs and hence was likely to be damned. Excruciating uncertainty lay at the heart of the Puritan adaptation of Calvinist thought. Thus, Puritans objected vociferously to the words that the Anglican Book of Common Prayer recommended be said at a decedent's graveside: "We therefore commend his body to the ground in sure and certain hope of resurrection to the eternal life." Nothing about the future could be "sure and certain" — not even hope.[24]

This uncertainty imparted a cruel ambivalence to Puritanism. Christian tradition prior to the Reformation emphasized death as a release of the soul from its earthly prison. People may have feared death as a practical matter, but intellectually most Christians died with the hope of salvation, believing that death began a new life of joy in paradise. Puritan ministers reminded their parishioners constantly of the falsity of this assurance. Death could release the soul to eternal happiness, but it could as easily cast it into eternal damnation. Since Puritans could never know the result in advance, death was as terrifying intellectually as it was practically.[25]

On another point of doctrine, Puritanism rejected a reassuring concept that developed among Catholic theologians in the late Middle Ages: Purgatory. Catholics believed that most people spent time in Purgatory, a stop midway between Heaven and Hell, on their way to salvation. The prayers, gifts, good deeds, and so forth offered by friends and relatives on behalf of the deceased could shorten his or her time in Purgatory and hasten the journey to Heaven. This cluster of beliefs surrounding Purgatory gave rise to elaborate funerals as part of a process by which the living aided the dead.[26]

Puritans rejected the concept of Purgatory even more strongly than they rejected false assurances of salvation. Nothing done on earth after mortal death could affect the future of a departed soul. The decision had already been made. Both the rejection of certitude and the rejection of the concept of Purgatory made Puritans in England contemptuous of funerals. Without assurance of salvation, mortal death should not be celebrated; and funeral rituals smacked of Popish idolatry. Most Protestants, but particularly Puritans, attacked the funeral ritual and treated death rites with few overt expressions of emotion or ceremony. In 1649, an anonymous French critic scathingly described the burial practices of the English Puritans in these terms: "[I]n many places, the dead [are] thrown into the ground like dogs, and not a word said."[27]

New England Puritans brought with them this hostility to funeral rituals. During the first twenty years of Massachusetts history, the dead were buried with a haste and unemotional matter-of-factness that shocked many contemporaries. A tolling bell summoned the neighbors, who gathered to carry the deceased to the cemetery and unceremoniously drop the corpse into a grave. Excessive mourning was frowned upon. Governor John Winthrop, a kind man capable of gentle expression, marked the death of his wife, Margaret, whom he loved tenderly, with two short sentences in his diary. He then moved on to other business of the day.[28]

With this set of Puritan beliefs in the background, it seems improbable that the funeral would become one of the central rituals and social events in colonial New England's history. But it did. Winthrop's own death in 1649 marked the beginning of the end of the no-funeral tradition. Massachusetts celebrated the governor's death as a civic holiday—as an affair of state that signaled the accomplishments of the man, who more than anyone else had ensured the successful rooting of Puritan society in New World soil. Among the tributes, a barrel and a half of powder was set off in a series of musket volleys by an artillery company that marched in his honor. Massachusetts celebrated itself by celebrating the life and death of its first great citizen.

In succeeding years, Puritan New England changed its funeral practices with surprising rapidity. Much of the ambivalence toward death remained, however, though in muted form, as did the fears of funeral idolatry. These lingering suspicions shaped the funeral as a religious and social event.[29]

The social aspects of the funeral developed more quickly than the religious ones. By the end of the 1650s large gatherings of people attended funerals and made their way back to the deceased's home for a ritual meal that included cakes and alcohol. The custom of wearing special "funeral gloves" developed at the same time. By the 1660s, the crowds had grown to include virtually everyone in the community, the meals became elaborate and were consumed with ceremonial eating utensils, and the special clothes—the "funeral finery"—often included scarves, ribbons, carved rings, and black feathers to decorate horse harnesses. Caskets of good wood and carved gravestones replaced the earlier shroud and unmarked gravesite. By the end of the third quarter of the century, standard funerals had become fancy affairs—combinations of mourning and celebration, but invariably big social occasions.[30]

The last of the earlier Puritan proscriptions tumbled in the 1680s. Until then, funerals had grown primarily as secular events: ministers had been present, but played no defined role. Certainly, they offered neither prayers at the graveside nor statements about the decedent's afterlife. Late in the century, however, some ministers began making simple graveside speeches. Soon these grew to include short prayers, communal recitations of psalms, and short eulogies. The hatred of idolatry proved sufficiently resilient to prevent some of the more better-known elements of Catholic ritual, such as kneeling and responsive reading, but within these slight limitations the Puritan funeral was transformed from a nonevent to a major social and religious occasion in a relatively short span of time.[31]

A few Puritan conservatives worried about the development of the funeral, but most did not. Cotton Mather, always foremost among those who feared change, expressed some misgivings; he thought the giving of carved rings excessive and fretted in general about the high cost of a funeral, which often took a sizable chunk of the decedent's estate. For Mather, however, a perennial worrier, these complaints were minimal. His own funeral was an elaborate event attended by fellow clergy from all over New England. And most ministers approved of the development of the funeral and of their own important role in the ceremony. One minister collected three thousand pairs of gloves in his thirty-year career and finally sold them to a Boston milliner. Mather justified accepting gloves and rings by making a self-conscious effort to think of the deceased every time he saw the gift.[32]

In the eighteenth century, funerals of important persons sometimes grew into pageants. Extraordinarily elaborate ones were held in all the large centers in 1761 to mark the death of George II.[33] John Rowe counted fifty-seven carriages in the cortège that carried Reverend Jonathan Mayhew's body to his Boston gravesite in 1766. A year later, when Grand Master Jeremiah Gridley, of the Masons' lodge in Boston died, the occasion surpassed any celebration previously held in New England. Rowe recorded it in detail.

The officers of his regiment marched in order first. Then the Brethren of St. Andrew's Lodge. Then the stewards of the Grand Lodge. Then the Brethren promiscuously two by two. Then the Warden's of the Master's Lodge. Then the three masters of the three several lodges. Then the past grand officers and the treasurer. Then the Grand Wardens, then myself as Deputy Grand master. Then the Tyler with the Grand Master's Jewels on a Black velvet Cushion . . . then followed the relations. After them the lawyers in their robes. Then the Gentlemen of the town and then a great many coaches, chariots, and chaises.[34]

Gridley was a distinguished lawyer and prominent citizen; his funeral occasioned a Boston civic holiday. Boston was too populous to take the day off to commemorate every citizen's death, but in many smaller towns each death did cause the entire community to put down its work tools and gather together. Funerals were the second most common social gathering in a community, surpassed only by regular church services. And funerals were less predictable and more varied in practice than regularly scheduled church services. This unknown, irregular quality made them interesting. Small-town funerals remained relatively simple compared to urban funerals or those of great personages, but their propensity to involve nearly all of the community gave them added meaning. And cakes, ale, rum, and funeral finery also became a standard part of small-town funerals.[35]

## Church Holidays

The church did not support all traditional Christian communal gatherings that engendered socializing. Puritans attacked regularly scheduled religious holidays with a ferocity that is partially responsible for their popular reputations as killjoys. The logic behind their vigorous affirmation of Sabbatarianism had as a corollary an equally vigorous denunciation of all other holy days celebrated by the Catholic church. Since the Fourth Commandment strictly forbade work and play on one day, Puritans argued, it implicitly sanctioned them on all others. Scripture commanded the Sabbath, but nothing more. Inasmuch as 165 days a year had at one time or another been given a special status by some part of Christendom, Puritans thought celebrating any one of them might open the door to idleness, a vice to be suppressed, not encouraged, by the church. Additionally, another implication arising from the concept of holy days offended Puritans: the designation of certain days as holy implied that other days were less so. With a smugness that infuriated both Anglicans and Catholics, Puritans argued that "they for whom all days are holy can have no holiday."[36]

Puritans saved their greatest contempt for Christmas. Throughout the seventeenth and eighteenth centuries, they successfully prevented any significant celebration of it. "Foolstide," as they called December 25, aroused their special ire for a variety of reasons. In addition to the fact that no holy days were sanctioned by Scripture, Puritans hated Christmas because it was an immensely popular holiday in both England and Europe and was almost always the occasion for excessive behavior. Cotton Mather argued that during the "Saturnalian jollities" of late December, "men dishonoured the Lord Jesus Christ more in the twelve days of Christmas" than in all the twelve months of the preceding year. Second, Christmas occupied a special place in the ideological religious warfare of Reformation Europe. Congregational and Presbyterian Puritans; most Anabaptists; Quakers; and several other groups loathed it as an abomination. But Anglicans, Dutch Reformed, and Lutherans, among others joined the Catholics in celebrating it. When the Church of England, after separating from Rome, promoted the Feast of the Nativity as a major religious holiday, the Puritans attacked it as one of the most egregious symbols of residual Papist idolatry—a "wanton Bacchanalian feast." Finally, Puritans argued that to select December 25 as Christ's birthday was ahistorical. It was far more likely that the true date was in September or October. Puritans believed that Christmas was celebrated on December 25 because the day had been a Roman holiday, which early Christians coopted. Hence, to celebrate Christmas was to pay tribute to pagan custom.[37]

The Pilgrims at Plymouth put this loathing into practice on the first December 25 they spent in the New World in 1620. They went to the fields and worked as they would have on any other day. Routine work served as an especially contemptuous way of showing that Christmas meant nothing. The following year, two small groups of people in Plymouth attempted Christmas celebrations. The first, a group of visiting non-Puritan seamen, were told by Governor William Bradford: "[Y]our conscience may not let you work on Christmas but my conscience cannot let you play while everybody else is out working." The second group, a few young Puritans, was punished by Bradford for the attempt. He noted years later that no one else had tried openly to celebrate Christmas since that second year.[38]

Massachusetts and Connecticut followed the example of Plymouth and refused to condone any observance of Christmas. When the Puritans came to power in England, Parliament enacted a law abolishing most holy days, including Christmas. New Englanders followed this with a series of laws that formally made Christmas celebrations illegal. The Massachusetts law of 1659 authorized a sizable fine of five shillings to punish anyone who celebrated Christmas day by "abstinence from labor, feasting, or in any other way." Restoration English officials forced the repeal of these laws in the 1680s, but respectable New Englanders continued to regard Christmas as an abomination throughout the colonial period and beyond. Eighteenth-century New England increasingly associated Christmas with royal officials, external interference in local affairs, and dissolute behavior; celebrations on December 25 had become a symbol of all the things that threatened New England's holy mission. Even Anglicans visiting in New England in the late colonial period, and even religious dissenters who showered contempt on Puritan values, tended not to make much of a display of any Christmas celebrations.

The Puritans' hatred of Christmas was one of the few ascetic traditions that did not erode over the course of the seventeenth and eighteenth centuries. Private journals and diaries often show that even within the confines of their house, most non-Puritans did not celebrate Christmas. Anna Winslow, an Anglican schoolgirl visiting in Boston in 1771, displayed a large capacity for social life; yet she wrote in her diary, "I kept Christmas at home this year and did a very good day's work." As late as the middle of the nineteenth century, New England children did not have the day free from school. Although celebrating Christmas was technically not illegal after the 1680s, magistrates forbid the "anticks," as decorations, parties, and gift-giving were called, and prosecuted celebrants for disturbing the peace.[39]

Similarly, Puritan thought condemned any celebration of Easter, All Saint's Day, and St. Valentine's Day, the other popular holy days of the Catholic church. None of these days, however, had the emotional and ideological charge of Christmas. The only exceptions Puritans made to this blanket proscription were for days of fasting and days of thanksgiving that they singled out for special observance. To Puritans, however, these were not exceptions: fasts and thanksgivings were not regularly scheduled and hence did not constitute idolatrous behavior. Puritans held fasts to mark lamentable occasions, natural disasters, fires, bad weather, loss of military battles, poor harvests, and so forth. They held thanksgivings to commemorate good happenings; the November day that has come to be known as Thanksgiving was merely the most famous. Even the fall thanksgiving was never regularly scheduled in colonial New England. If the harvest failed, a day of thanks would have been inappropriate. On both fast and thanksgiving days, people put aside normal work and gathered at the meeting-house for a special sermon on the specific reason for the observance of the day. Fast days were indeed fast days: no food was eaten from sundown to sundown. An occasion for group public humiliation, fast days provided a natural setting for the most famous type of Puritan sermon, the jeremiad. Ministers searched a community's history for signs of sloth, greed, pride, and sensuality to explain God's displeasure. They usually found what they looked for and enjoined the community to spend the rest of the day in conversation and reflection about the problems. Hardly a day of wild-eyed frolics, the fasts did have a holiday quality of a somber sort.[40]

Thanksgivings less ambiguously satisfy the modern criteria of a holiday: a day with no work and much socializing, food, and drink. They were, however, also meant to be somber days of conversation and reflection about the community's past and its state of moral health. A morning sermon at the meetinghouse marked the communal beginning of the celebration, after which the feasting began. The banquets seldom spawned bad behavior; to a remarkable degree, thanksgivings remained serious celebrations. Occasionally, to mark certain types of events, a day of fasting would be followed by a day of thanksgiving. At the end of King Philip's War in 1676, New England held a fast to commemorate the horror of the war and then a thanksgiving to rejoice in the triumph.[41]

Both fasts and thanksgivings were usually called by an act of the colony government and observed by all the communities of a colony. Sometimes several of the Puritan colonies of Plymouth, Massachusetts Bay, Connecticut, and New Haven would hold observances on the same day. Occasionally, local observances would be called by a town. For most of the seventeenth century, each colony averaged less than one day of fasting and one day of thanksgiving per year. Fast days and thanksgivings, however, were holidays primarily of the Puritan era. From the 1720s until the Revolution, few of either were called—perhaps one or two of each per decade. They stopped being a part of the yearly cycle, but were reinstituted briefly during the Revolution. Connecticut, for example, had only seven fast days and three days of thanksgiving between 1720 and 1770, but then had seven fasts and five thanksgivings during the early years of the war with England in the late 1770s.[42]

## Congregational Socializing

Puritans were communalists who grounded their social ideals upon groups: the family, the congregation, the town, the colony, and the way of life that knitted them together in New England. "Gathering together" was both metaphor and reality to New England's founders. Puritans visited one another a great deal, and much of their leisure and recreation derived from the informal give-and-take of everyday conversation. Being a covenanted people required of Puritans a sociability that sat easily upon pioneers and pilgrims removed by distance and dissent from many of England's familiar pleasures. Puritans filled their calendars with events revolving around the church that brought them together as a people who believed in sharing life's joys and hardships as well as in helping one another in the business of moral regeneration. This quiet sort of congregational leisure and recreation provided the truest relaxation most respectable Puritans experienced.

Throughout the colonial period, the Congregational church retained much of its social function. But in the eighteenth century, church activities lost their primacy as New England's most important social vehicle and metamorphosed into forms that would sometimes have shocked the seventeenth-century villagers who gathered at the meetinghouse for quiet conversation. As society became secularized and heterogeneous, so too, did patterns of leisure and recreation that emanated from the Congregational church meeting.

# V

# Civic Socializing:
# Parties for the Common Good

New Englanders gathered together inside the meetinghouse to worship and offer public testimony to their faith. Beyond all other occasions, these congregational meetings symbolized the Puritan way of life both to the church members and to posterity. New Englanders, however, also met outside the meetinghouse. They gathered together for nonreligious purposes: to work collectively, to perform civic duties, to affirm community values, and to celebrate patriotic events. These secular gatherings outside the meetinghouse had more in common with religious ones inside than might at first be apparent. Both kinds of gathering expressed the communal spirit of a covenanted people; both reflected the essence of the Puritan belief that the best recreation combined duty and enjoyment; and both had a serious purpose as well as a social function. These meetings constituted a type of gathering particularly congenial to colonial New England society: they were parties for the common good. In theory, duty ranked first at these gatherings, fun second. In reality, as the colonial period progressed, New Englanders shifted the relative weighting of the two components. Rather than gathering together to do their duty and have a little fun at the same time, they used duty as an opportunity—sometimes as a pretext—to justify having a good time. This change bespoke neither hypocrisy nor hedonism. Instead, it represented the emergence of more worldly, secular views of recreation. These views, however, remained embodied in forms based on Puritan ideals.

## The Productive Party

In a hazy way, almost all Americans have some notions of house-raisings and barn-raisings. Particularly associated with life on the nineteenth-century prairies, raising parties still go on today and have been much publicized in the 1980s and 1990s through Project Habitat, which puts up low-cost housing with voluntary labor. Although not prominent in the folklore about Puritanism, raisings were commonplace throughout colonial New England's history. In the seventeenth century, the frames for most buildings—personal homes, barns, shops, meetinghouses, mills—were constructed and hoisted into place at these communal parties. In the eighteenth century the custom became less prevalent in large towns as professional housewrights took over design and construction of ambitious buildings. Still, the practice continued to some extent in all communities, including Boston and Newport, and it remained commonplace in small towns and rural areas.[1]

Despite the hard work that had to be done, raisings were parties, replete with food, drink, frivolity, and some lighthearted ceremony. House-raisings customarily began with a woman—often a bride—driving in the first pin of the frame. The work part of the party ended when a selected local hero shimmied out on the ridgepole to hammer home the final beam. Spring months constituted the raising season, after the melting of snow in March but before planting time in late June. Raisings commonly took place in two stages, one of preparation, one of construction. The Westfield, Massachusetts, minister John Ballantine, wrote in his diary that in February 1761 twenty-five men came to hew and stockpile the timbers for his barn. In April, they returned with wives and families to build and raise the frame. The primary gathering was short and all work; Ballantine served no refreshments. For the second meeting, people brought a "plentiful supper . . . more provisions than was needed," and turned the construction into a real party. At this as at most raisings, the host supplied rum and other alcohol although virtually never did any problems of drunkenness or misconduct arise.[2] These were family parties with serious purposes.

Raisings were the most pure and poetic example of a particular genre of New England social life, the productive party. They fit perfectly the Puritan ideal of sober mirth—of useful recreation. The general principle of raisings could be and was applied to a wide range of activities. Community woodcuttings or harvestings, for example, were relatively common. Usually not done at the homes of average farmers, these types of parties were often held to benefit a local minister or a neighbor who was ill or experiencing hardship. Occasionally only men attended, but usually women also came to prepare refreshments and to provide company after work was over. A woodcutting might turn into a tea party after the men finished the splitting and stacking.[3]

The concept of communal productive parties owed much to a general collectivist economic impulse that carried over from medieval society to early modern England and parts of colonial America. Many—perhaps a majority—of the first generation of New England towns practiced a common-field system of agriculture under which individuals owned small strips or parcels of land that lay interspersed with those of their fellow townsmen in large common meadows. This type of land distribution combined aspects of the medieval commune with the emerging concept of individual land ownership, the fee simple. And it imparted a measure of fairness by minimizing differences in the quality of land assigned each townsman. This system of agriculture also meant that Puritan farmers usually worked side by side in the fields with their fellows, not alone in some isolated meadow. Additionally, early towns maintained common pastures, woodlots, and salt marshes.[4]

Common-field practices did not survive the seventeenth century, but a few other forms of communal work did. Throughout the colonial period, all able-bodied men owed the town several days work each year on town highways. A few discharged their obligations by paying money to hire someone, but most did the work themselves. Similarly, towns met other needs through work groups: the maintenance of fences around common town property, the creation and running of grist mills, and so forth.[5] Not surprisingly, the communal impulse that suffused Puritan society often carried over into work. Thus, for a people who worked in groups and relaxed in groups, a combination of the two activities in productive parties was more than desirable; it seemed virtually natural.

In the eighteenth century, as the Puritan ethos waned, many of the more urbane young adults found raisings and other productive parties too straitlaced and demure to be much fun. Nathaniel Ames, a Harvard graduate living in Dedham, a mid-sized town near Boston, thought them "very tedious scenes." Ames and others, however, regarded one type of productive party as an exception: the cornhusking. Probably because men could husk corn and socialize with women at the same time, cornhuskings became associated with great frivolity in the minds of adolescents and young adults. Indian corn was the last grain of the year to be gathered in New England, and huskings turned into noisy harvest celebrations and parties. Perhaps one could even search for sexual metaphors in the act of husking itself. Whatever the physical or symbolic reasons, huskings became immensely popular at mid-eighteenth century. Ames, the sophisticate bored with raisings, described one in the 1760s. "Made a husking entertainment," he wrote:

> possibly this leaf may last a century and fall into the hands of some inquisitive person for whose entertainment I will inform him that now there is a custom amongst us of making an entertainment at husking Indian corn whereto all the neighboring swains are invited and after the corn is finished they, like the Hottentots, give three cheers or huzzas, but cannot carry in the husks without a Rhum bottle. They feign great exertion, but do nothing until the Rhum enlivens them, when all is done in a thrice; then after a hearty meal about 10 at night, they go to their pastimes.[6]

Women also held an array of productive parties to provide benefit from their group labor. Quilting, spinning, and sewing parties, or "bees," were frequent. More tame—they customarily had no alcohol; smaller—usually attended by seven or eight women, who did not bring their husbands, these bees reflected an austere vision of recreation for women. In their traditional form they were prevalent among all classes and areas in the seventeenth century, but became increasingly associated with rural or small-town life in the eighteenth. The Revolutionary experience, however, made bees popular again among women from all classes and communities. Spinning bees in particular became a fixed part of a patriotic social life as women made cloth for men in the military.[7]

Bees were also capable of being adapted to more sophisticated circumstances. Ezra Stiles, a cosmopolitan minister in Newport and a future president of Yale College, described a pre-Revolutionary urban version of the spinning bee. No quiet, cooperative gathering of soft-spoken ladies, this "spinning match" was put on by "two Quakers, six Baptists, and twenty-nine of my own society . . . we dined sixty people. My people sent in 4 lb tea, 19 lb coffee, loaf sugar, about 3 quarters of veal, 1 11/2 dozen wine, gammons, flour, bread, rice, etc. etc. In the course of the day, the spinners were visited by I judge six hundred spectators." Quite a bash. Stiles's Newport congregation staged what an earlier generation of women or what rural contemporaries might have called a spinning frolic, a term that connotes much more frivolity and liveliness than its rural counterpart, the bee. The women staged the spinning match, however, for a traditional purpose: to produce all the cloth Stiles and his family were likely to need for a long time. They also made the match into a real party in order to have a good time—which they did. The women at the spinning match undoubtedly behaved themselves fairly well, but to the farmers' wives of small-town New England they might have appeared to be a raucous crowd.[8]

Teenage girls held quilting, spinning, and sewing bees similar to their mothers'. Often they helped each other ready things for their future life as married women. The most popular group activity for teenage girls in warm weather, however, was the berrying party. Usually consisting of from three to seven girls, berrying parties were possible for about two and a half months of the year, from early July to mid-September, and often were all-day affairs. Widely held everywhere in the seventeenth century, berrying parties, like bees, became more of a rural or small-town activity in the eighteenth century. Occasionally, however, a group of girls from a large town would take a trip out into the countryside to go berrying. Berrying parties were usually for girls; rarely did boys attend or hold their own. For girls, the attraction of the berrying party was simple. It was productive, fun, virtuous, and innocent of any negative connotations. Almost no one would be prohibited from attending on moral grounds. Berrying allowed young girls to be on their own for a brief time without the usual presence of adults. And, finally, young girls did not have many alternatives.[9]

## The Pleasures of Civic Duty

In general, men had more opportunities for socializing than women did; and in particular, rural men had opportunities that rural women did not. By the late seventeenth century, a clear double standard of conduct had emerged that judged men less harshly than women for abuse of a whole range of activities, cardplaying, drinking, and sex among them. Moreover, men could travel more readily, especially after dark, to take advantage of social opportunities that lay beyond the immediate neighborhood.[10] And men had military and political obligations that furnished opportunities for social gatherings. Society regarded these parties, too, as productive—as doing good for the commonweal.

Virtually all New England males between the ages of sixteen and sixty served in the militia. The number of militia-training days varied from time to time and among the differing colonies; threats to the peace usually occasioned more training days, times of tranquility occasioned fewer. But on average, in the 170 years between 1620 and 1790, local militiamen met six to eight times a year for drill exercises. Customarily held in April, May,

September, and October, militia-training days often supplied the opportunity for a "fine toot," as one seventeenth-century soldier wrote in his
diary. Obviously, if a military emergency lay at hand, the troops trained
with serious purpose. But if not, the formal aspects of training lasted only
a few hours from mid-morning to early afternoon. The rest of the day and
evening resembled aspects of a bachelor party.[11]

In the founding generation, this seems to have been less true. Puritan
militiamen from the 1620s through the 1680s regarded themselves as Christian soldiers doing battle for God. And bloody battle often needed to be done,
a fact that underscored the seriousness of the military meetings. Yet even in
these years, training days could be festive. An early historian of Stratford,
Connecticut, described an annual militia holiday the town celebrated beginning in 1654. The holiday was a family affair; the entire community—old men,
women, and children—gathered at eight A.M. to watch the troops conduct
exercises and parade in review. At midday, the women served a feast that
included a special dessert known as training cake. In the afternoon, athletic
contests of foot racing, wrestling, and "shooting at the mark" took place in
front of a large audience. This military parade cum town fair ended before
sunset, allowing both soldiers and their families to be home before dark. Little
untoward behavior happened, and training-day parties could be regarded as
part of the same wholesome genre of social gathering as barn-raising. On the
six or seven other days a year that Stratford's men trained, women and
children did not attend, but the men brought lunches and also held contests.[12]

Problems of undue revelry began to arise at the end of King Philip's
War in 1676, when for the first time much of southern New England felt
relatively free from Indian attack. In 1704, New England's wittiest and
most perspicacious social commentator, Sarah Kemble Knight, characterized militia training as the "Olympiack games" and wrote that training was
by far the biggest diversion in rural towns. Training days became the
occasion for heavy drinking after perfunctory drill. By the middle of the
afternoon, drunkenness and fighting often became problems. The soldiers
did not go home before dark and they developed the habit of firing guns
in the air as the meeting broke up. The problem of rambunctious militiamen
became serious enough to warrant much attention in ministers' sermons.
A collective jeremiad in 1719 accused the militia of making "war against
the soul" instead of against military enemies.[13]

The French replaced Indians as a threat to New England's security,
but training day did not return to its ideal as a community holiday fit for
the whole family or as a gathering of Christian warriors. Instead, it
continued to descend into more of a boys'-day-off party. During the wars

with New France, in particular those of the 1740s and 1750s, militia companies were often away from their home areas for months at a time. Invariably, troops not under the watchful eyes of family and friends behaved with a great deal less restraint than when at home. And extended military travel provoked a licentiousness that persisted after the troops returned; bad habits carried over to further exacerbate problems of wild behavior on training days. Parents complained about the ill effects the militia had on young men's character and conduct.[14]

In the 1750s a new social innovation made militia drill more of an explicit party: the training-day dance. Adding women to militia parties imparted greater respectability to the evening activities, but it also gave rise to a new set of possibilities for bad conduct. Not even the grim emergency of the Revolution and calls for a renewal of earlier virtue could turn the clock back to the Christian warrior of the mid-seventeenth century. In some of the tensest moments of the patriotic cause, a "fine parcel of ladies" made sure the troops were "splendidly entertained."[15]

Similarly, election days in each colony were the occasion for a civic holiday. Massachusetts and New Hampshire held colony-wide elections for deputies to the General Assembly once a year in the spring; Connecticut and Rhode Island each held them twice a year, in spring and fall. Much discussion preceded these elections, although virtually no electioneering did. The day itself took on a festive atmosphere. Men gathered all day outside the meetinghouse where the ballots were to be cast. In particular, elections provided diversion to rural freemen, who took the day off to travel to the town center to socialize, discuss politics, and vote. A British official, Thomas Vernon, imprisoned in the remote farming town of Glocester, Rhode Island, was amazed by the excitement election day generated. "This being the day for the choice of deputies," he wrote, "we are told that there is a very great resort of people of all kinds and that it is a day of great frolicking. Our landlord and his three sons are gone having rigged themselves out in the best manner. I must observe that a man on horseback passed by with a very large bag full of cakes which are to be sold to the people."[16]

Unlike militia-training drills, however, election days never became unruly and were never associated with an ancillary range of social activities. Rather like church-related gatherings at the meetinghouse, election days retained their seriousness of purpose throughout colonial history. Refreshments, including beer and punch, were always available, but rowdiness was not tolerated.[17]

In addition to colony-wide election days, each town held town meetings, which were local political holidays. In their founding years, towns met frequently, sometimes as often as once a month. Once the local population grew beyond several hundred people and once governing procedures became regularized, towns held fewer meetings; two or three per year was the norm for an established town in the eighteenth century. As they declined in number and increased in size, town meetings became more of a diversion from routine and took on more of the ambience of a civic holiday. This was especially true for the annual election meeting that chose town officers for the ensuing year. By the middle of the eighteenth century towns elected upwards of fifty people to office; some elected as many as two hundred. The sheer scope of the election meeting produced a social energy and hubbub of activity.[18]

Only men could vote on election day or in town meetings; women and children, of course, did not attend. As a rough rule of thumb, approximately 50 percent of adult males were admitted as freemen and entitled to vote although many fewer attended meetings. Nevertheless, New Englanders took governing seriously, and the decorum of the meeting reflected this. Freemen dressed formally, usually wearing what literally could be described as their Sunday-go-to-meeting clothes. Always adjourned at least an hour before dark, election meetings and town meetings offered occasions for quiet socializing of a conversational nature.[19] As young athletic men provided the spirit that sparked the ribaldry of training day, so did the wise fathers of the town provide the spirit that suffused election and town-meeting days with sobriety. They were a political parallel to the church meeting, but because they were fewer in number, elections and town meetings did convey more of the sense of a holiday. The Puritan ethos of duty and piety, though it failed to be strong enough to overcome the temptations of the training field, remained ensconced within the walls of the political and religious meeting hall. New Englanders were political creatures and found much to enjoy in the give-and-take of a long day discussing everything from local fences to colony taxes to imperial shipping regulations. But the election and town meetings never lost their essential Puritan purpose as civil versions of the Congregational church meeting.

## Public Punishments and Moral Theater

A grimmer type of civic gathering combined moral obligation and bizarre spectacle and included men, women, and children in a gruesome community ritual: the witnessing of criminal punishments. These ranged from noncorporal public humiliation, to whippings and mutilations, to executions. From the first days of Plymouth through the Revolutionary era, magistrates and moralists felt that justice was best served and crime most effectively deterred if the authorities carried out all punishments in full view of the community. The English had long held similar public punishments, but Puritan New England created much more of a ritual to surround the physical acts. In many ways the whole drama resembled a sort of moral theater. Sedate at first, punishments, in particular executions, took on a carnival atmosphere from the 1670s onward. Advertised well in advance, they attracted large crowds: drums played, the participants marched in procession, and ministers gave long sermons replete with details and graphic language. The criminals about to be punished for "black-mouthed oaths," "filthy drunkennesses," "vilest debauchery," and so forth were asked to play their part. Confessions provided the penultimate excitement before the final act took place.[20]

Executions often became the most talked-about event of the year and drew immense crowds. Both Governor William Bradford of Plymouth and Governor John Winthrop of Massachusetts thought John Billington's execution in 1630, the first one in New England's history, worthy of a long description in their journals. For James Morgan's execution in 1686, crowds began to gather in Boston a week ahead of the event. Some came at least fifty miles. On the Sunday before the hanging, two distinguished ministers preached sermons on the crime; and on the Thursday of the execution, Increase Mather preached a sermon to a crowd of five thousand, the largest theretofore ever gathered in New England. Vendors sold written broadsides, which, like theater programs, summarized the details of Morgan's crimes. Other particularly well-publicized executions included those of Esther Rogers in 1701, for murdering her children; the simultaneous executions of several pirates in Newport in 1723; and Hannah Ocuish's for murder in New London, Connecticut, in 1786. As a general rule, the more grisly the crime, the larger the crowd at the execution. Although a majority of those hanged were men, women's executions drew larger audiences.[21]

Complete figures have not been compiled for all the executions in New England, but the lowest of estimates would suggest they averaged at least one a year in the late seventeenth century and through all of the eighteenth. Prior to the 1670s, the number was lower. Estimates of crowd size range from three thousand to six thousand. And, unlike many of the harsher elements of early Puritanism, the spectacle of the public hanging did not fade in the late colonial period with the development of a more relaxed social ethos. In fact, executions increased in the years after 1750. Moreover, the rhetoric concerning criminality in the sermon literature of the late eighteenth century remained remarkably consistent with the language of the founding generation.[22] Public punishments as moral theater combined the frivolity of mid-eighteenth-century social gatherings with the more somber aspects of the congregational gathering of the founding era.

Lesser punishments produced lesser drama than executions, but these, too, attracted crowds. Being more numerous, humiliations, whippings, and mutilations were more a part of regular life. Diarists throughout the colonial and Revolutionary eras entered notations of seeing people "cropt and branded" or "whipped with rods." Authorities placed whipping posts, pillories, and stocks in prominent locations to facilitate public involvement. Students often went in groups to jeer criminals or pelt them with "every repulsive kind of garbage that could be collected." Nor did just rowdy young men take part. In the 1770s, eleven-year-old Anna Winslow, the daughter of refined and wealthy parents, made trips with her friends to Boston's whipping post to watch sentences being carried out. A young Marblehead apprentice described the fate of Jeremiah Dexter, "lately detected passing counterfeit dollars. . . . [He] stood in the pillory in the presence of a great many spectators, many of whom were very liberal in bestowing rotten eggs . . . particularly Dr. Seth Hudson."[23]

As the eighteenth century wore on, magistrates became less inclined to punish people for some offenses, such as idleness and fornication, for which earlier Puritans had meted out harsh sentences. But with a large increase in population, enough thievery, drunkenness, and general all-around bad behavior existed to furnish a growing cast for center stage. And, of course, the Revolutionary practice of tarring and feathering Loyalists or riding them on a rail continued this long-standing practice of combining punishment, deterrence, and entertainment.

### Patriotism as Political Carnival

Another type of public spectacle in the eighteenth century more explicitly fused morality and ribaldry into an outdoor festival: the celebration of great historical events. Something of a continuation of the Puritan tradition of thanksgivings, these political carnivals had none of the quiet, earnest sobriety associated with seventeenth-century feasting celebrations. Often they got out of control and ended in riot, fighting, and vandalism. The morning after, communities woke up with a hangover, sheepish faces, and a need to lay blame. Most associated with the larger towns and the lower ranks of the social structure, political carnivals took place in small towns as well and involved members of the elite, especially young ones.

New England celebrated only one of these festivals on a regular, annual basis—Guy Fawkes Day, on November 5. Held to commemorate the foiling of the so-called Gunpowder Plot, when Catholic terrorists tried to blow up Parliament in 1605, Guy Fawkes Day was celebrated in seventeenth-century towns with "bonfires, guns shot off and much revelry." By the beginning of the eighteenth century, Guy Fawkes Day took on the ambience of a twentieth-century Halloween. People wore costumes, built floats to pull in parades, and feasted during the day; at night the celebration often degenerated into vandalism. As early as 1709, the day filled Samuel Sewall with fears over safety and public disorder. Originally endorsed by magistrates and ministers because it affirmed New England's vigorous Protestantism, anti-Catholicism, and English patriotism, Guy Fawkes Day increasingly became the subject of discussion and debate. A particularly riotous "Pope's Day" celebration invariably provoked calls for a return to Puritan traditions of restraint and sobriety. But not until the Revolution did any towns make a serious attempt to end all observance of the day. These attempts succeeded because the Revolutionaries wanted to avoid offending their Catholic French allies. Moreover, celebrating the glories of the English Parliament did not seem as patriotic in the 1770s as it had earlier. After the war, however, celebrations of Guy Fawkes Day began anew.[24]

Boston's Pope's Day celebration became infamous in the 1750s and 1760s. Regular commerce and business ceased. Groups several thousand strong gathered in both the north and south end of the city and marched toward the center in the early afternoon, holding images of the Pope and Devil aloft. Much of the crowd had already consumed a considerable amount of alcohol before the march began. When the north-end and south-end crowds—now mobs—met, they tried to destroy each other's Popes. John Rowe, a merchant, described one of these scenes:

> In the afternoon, they got the north-end Pope pulled to pieces ... The south-end people brought out their Pope and went in triumph to the northward and at the Mill bridge a battle began between the people of both parts of the town. The north-end people having repaired their Pope but the south-end people got [won] the battle, many were hurt and bruised on both sides, and brought away the north-end Pope and burnt both of them at the gallows on the Neck. Several thousand people followed them, hallowing, etc.

This 1764 Guy Fawkes Day celebration provoked a particular outcry because a cart carrying the north-end Pope crushed and killed a young boy.[25]

Boston's riots, however, were only worse by degree than those in many other New England towns. In Salem, Massachusetts, Guy Fawkes celebrations in the 1760s were elaborate anti-Catholic productions replete with costumes, music, singing, symbols, and ritual. The town's first historian, Joseph Felt, described the large float that teenage boys towed to the center of town. "In the front was a place covered with paper for lights and several persons. In the rear, on the upper platform were effigies of the Pope, monks, friars, and offensive political characters. Behind these was the image of Satan, dressed with horns and other frightful appendages." The boys, accompanied by dancers, fiddlers, and a crowd of hundreds, stopped the float in front of the homes of noted gentlemen and demanded that the occupants come out to observe the procession. When the float reached the center of town, around midnight, after a four-hour journey, it was burned to the wild cheers of the crowd. Newport, Rhode Island, and New London, Connecticut, became known for unusually wild Guy Fawkes days; but smaller towns such as Newburyport and Marblehead, Massachusetts, and even a few rural areas experienced recurrent serious disorder. Virtually all of New England celebrated Pope's Day to some extent.[26]

Guy Fawkes Day was just the most raucous and regular of these political carnivals. From the 1680s, when a royal presence became apparent in New England, until the imperial crisis of the 1760s, the king's birthday was usually celebrated with toasts, parades, bonfires, fireworks, ox roasts, and general festivities. Special occasions also provided the moment for a good toot. When news reached Boston in September 1762 of a major naval victory in the French and Indian War, a day of thanksgiving was proclaimed. But, the party that ensued bore more resemblance to V-E Day in 1945 than to a Puritan thanksgiving. A diarist described it as follows: "[P]ublic rejoicing on account of the reduction of the Havannah. Sermon preached by Sewall, cadets mustered, bells rung, batteries fired, concerts of music, the town illuminated, bonfires, etc. Many loyal healths drunk, a vast quantity of liquor consumed, and General Winslow of Plymouth, so intoxicated as to jump on the table and break a great number of bowls, glasses, etc."[27]

In 1766, when the king's birthday began to lose its attractiveness as a public festival, another one began: the celebration of the fight against the Stamp Act. Although the act had been repealed in March, New England celebrated the event later, usually in May because the news had not reached the colonies until several weeks after the vote in Parliament. Throughout the Revolutionary era, most of New England held one of these political carnivals to celebrate the most glorious event in the pre-Revolutionary movement. Only gradually did July 4, Independence Day, overtake Stamp Act celebrations as a day of patriotic festivity. Boston celebrated August 14 as a great holiday for four successive years, 1766 through 1769. On that date in 1765 one thousand members of the newly formed Sons of Liberty had destroyed the house of Peter Oliver, the distributor of the hated tax stamps, in an effort to force him to resign his commission. For these four years, a gigantic parade of over three hundred chaises and coaches wended its way throughout the city in a day-long procession to commemorate the great Stamp Act riot-demonstration. This celebration, like all such carnivals, held the danger that the good times could get out of hand. When Connecticut held a celebration to commemorate the repeal of the Stamp Act, Hartford responded with a day of civic rioting that ended in tragedy when fireworks exploded prematurely and blew up a school.[28]

### Parties for The Common Good

On the surface, Guy Fawkes Day, public hangings, town meetings, militia drills, and house-raisings did not have much in common. Boisterous carnival, macabre spectacle, political convention, military exercise, and building party—they seem to run the gamut from the bloodthirsty to the bucolic. The differing surface manifestations, however, obscure a basic element common to all these activities: they were civic gatherings that produced something for the commonweal. All of them had a serious purpose; none was a mere party; none was an example of idle behavior whereby leisure or recreation became an end unto itself. All provided examples of how people could gather together to do good for the community and have fun at the same time. Some of these gatherings remained more of a serious business and less of a party than others did: house-raisings took sweat and work; town meetings maintained a sober sense of decorum. Some gatherings became wild parties; as often as not, militia drills and Guy Fawkes Days got out of hand. But house-raisings and town meetings had functions as parties; people looked forward to them as a chance to socialize and relax. And militia drill provided the community with needed security; Guy Fawkes Day affirmed New England's English and Protestant heritage. A day of patriotism, the wild and woolly Guy Fawkes celebration, despite all the problems it caused late in the colonial period, still satisfied Puritanism's basic test for appropriate leisure and recreation: it was useful.

Section Four

# MEN AND WOMEN FROLIC TOGETHER

# VI

# Frolics for Fun: Dances, Weddings, and Dinner Parties

Some party activities that developed in colonial New England less directly satisfied Puritanism's basic premise that leisure and recreation should be useful. Ordination balls and militia drills may have distorted the purpose of religious and civic gatherings, but—on the surface at least—they could be defended as dutiful activities. This was not the case with dances, wedding receptions, and dinner parties. These and variations on them were held for purely social reasons. One could, of course, defend dancing as physically healthy; wedding receptions as celebrations of the ideal of marriage; and dinner parties as opportunities to discuss matters of religious and civic consequence. But in none of these three cases did anyone seriously try to defend the activities as having a direct, palpable public good. They were parties held to have fun, and everyone understood that this was their purpose. The best thing that could be said for them from the standpoint of a strict interpretation of the Puritan code of morality was that nothing in Scripture unequivocally prohibited them.

## Dances

Dancing provided a puzzling challenge to New England's moral arbiters. No clear biblical proscriptions forbade it; it was immensely popular with all classes of Englishmen; distinguished Puritans ranging from John Milton to Oliver Cromwell enjoyed it; and, on the surface, dancing appeared innocent, did not consume great resources, and even provided healthy exercise. It should therefore have been high on the Puritan list of productive entertainments; it was not. Neither, however, was it directly condemned, as it was by some other Protestant denominations. Puritan moralists nurtured a nagging suspicion of dancing; the difficulty they had in identifying clear arguments against it increased rather than mitigated their wariness. The apparent goodness of dancing made it all the more dangerous. Lurking within what appeared to be a wholesome activity lay temptations that could—and often did—promote sin and sloth.[1]

No New England colony ever passed a general statute forbidding dancing, but colony and local laws hedged it about with extreme restrictions. A controversy over the probity of dancing surfaced in Salem in 1635. The congregation's young minister, Richard Levett, asked Boston's leading theologian, John Cotton, for guidance. Cotton replied that one should not automatically condemn all dancing. He cited a passage in Exodus that supported dance "[l]ending to the praise of . . . God." Cotton continued, however, that this did not include "[l]ascivious dancing to wanton ditties, and amorous gestures and wanton dalliances . . . [which] I would bear witness against as a great *flabella Libidinis*" (fanning of sexual desire). And herein lay the problem: at its worst, dancing was thought to incite adultery and fornication. Being particularly popular everywhere with women, dancing allegedly caused them to lower their guard against attacks on their chastity. Hence "lascivious dancing," which authorities defined as any dancing that allowed men and women to touch or hold each other, was forbidden, as was any association between alcohol and dancing. Often towns in the first half of the seventeenth century forbade dances themselves. Thus, dancing had to be informal and done either individually or in same-sex groups, not in couples of men and women. In fact, virtually no organized dances or mixed-sex dancing took place in the first generation of New England's settlement; dancing was spontaneous and done in the home, outdoors, or at celebrations.[2]

In 1684, Increase Mather published *An Arrow Against Profane and Promiscuous Dancing Drawn out of the Quiver of the Scriptures* in order to stop what he perceived to be an unsavory possibility: the opening of a dancing school in Boston. Indeed, schools had been opened in 1672 and 1681, but vigilant authorities had closed them immediately. The founder of the 1681 school, Henri Sheriot, was not only a teacher of idle and licentious behavior; worse yet, he was French, a condition that made him a priori a person of "ill fame." Mather penned his diatribe in the knowledge that a third school was being planned; it opened the following year in 1685 and suffered the others' fate of prosecution and closure.[3]

Mather's *Arrow* flew straight to the mark. Although he theoretically conceded John Cotton's point that "dancing or leaping is a natural expression of joy" if done "men with men" or "women with women," Mather felt that serious problems invariably emerged because innocent dancing led to "gynecandrical dancing or that which is commonly called mixt or promiscuous dancing, of men and women." "Vile, infamous, and abominable," he called it. Showing a remarkable willingness to elasticize meanings, Mather argued that the Seventh Commandment forbade the "Devil's Procession" of dancing because it condemned things that are evil in the sight of God. Not surprisingly, Mather believed mixed dancing was, indeed, evil in God's eyes. With equal inclusiveness, he argued that the Apostle Paul implicitly had dancing in mind when he condemned "rioting" in Romans 13:13. Similarly, God referred to dancing when in Isaiah 3:16 the Daughters of Sion were rebuked for "walking and mincing as they go and making a tinkling." Mather himself danced on a slippery theological floor when he adduced such vague and oblique references. The reality was that he feared the social consequences of dancing but felt compelled to buttress his position with scriptural endorsements. In presenting his case, Mather admitted that he was arguing against a half-century of a softer position on the part of New Englanders. "It is sad," he lamented, "that when in times of Reformation, children have been taught in their catechism that such dancing is against the commandment of God, that now in New England they should learn practically the contrary."[4]

When he moved from theological to social and historical reasons for outlawing dancing, Mather became nearly rabid. "Dancing is a regular madness," he wrote. "The Devil was the first inventor and the Gentiles who worshipped him the first practitioners." After that came "[a]postatizing, idolatrous, Israelites, Greeks who worshipped Bacchus," and others who thought "their Gods were adulterers." Among the evil historical men whom Mather identified as lovers of dancing were "Caligula, Nero, and such like atheists and epicures"; at present, "Popish causists justify it, as they do many other moral evils." In godly societies, dancing first appeared innocently, as at weddings or on days of thanksgiving, but inevitably it moved rapidly into a full expression of evil. To combat New England's existing practice of grudgingly allowing some dancing under decorous circumstances, Mather wrote that "it is an eternal truth that whenever any sin is forbidden, not only the highest acts of that sin, but all degrees thereof, and the occasions leading thereon are prohibited."[5]

On few matters did Increase Mather argue to less effect. After Massachusetts' transition from a private to a royal colony in 1692, dancers went on the offensive under the leadership of the first royal governor, Sir William Phips, who loved and sponsored formal balls. Dancing and dances became the delight of Boston's elite in the 1690s and showed signs of moving throughout the region and all strata of society.[6] The leadership of the opposition to this heightened danger fell to Increase's son, Cotton, who published *A Cloud of Witness Against Balls and Dances* in 1700 as a sequel to his father's *Arrow*. The change in tone between the father's and son's moral tracts tells much about the changes in attitudes and practices in the intervening sixteen years. Cotton Mather conceded much that his father had castigated earlier. Grudgingly, Cotton accepted mixed dancing, dances, and even the opening of dancing schools. "The Case before us is not whether people of quality may not employ a dancing master with due circumstances of modesty," the younger Mather wrote, but rather "whether the dancing humour as it now prevails and especially in balls or in circumstances that lead the young people of both sexes unto great liberties" should be tolerated. He also placed his opposition to extravagant balls and dancing parties in the larger context of Puritan fears of Anglicanism. Puritan young men and women attended Anglican parties because of the opportunity to dance they offered; late hours, immodest dress, vanity, lewdness, and, of course, eventual spiritual loss would inescapably result if one accepted these seemingly innocent invitations. Thus, whereas Increase had tried to roll back the clock to some imagined time in Reformation England when godly people prohibited all manner of dancing, Cotton tried to guard against excess and its accompanying vices.[7]

Cotton's *Cloud* proved little more successful than Increase's *Arrow*. The practice of holding dances spread throughout the region as the eighteenth century unfolded. Dances moved first to the large provincial centers, then to secondary towns, and finally to remote villages and rural areas in the immediate pre-Revolutionary years. The emphasis placed on dances in a given locale provided a barometer of its urbanity. Newport, Rhode Island, joined Boston as one of New England's two dance capitals; Hartford, New Haven, Norwich, Portsmouth, and Providence all proved anxious to emulate their sophistication.[8]

Worse than dances themselves, to recalcitrant moralists, were the dance schools that inevitably followed close on their heels. Boston, which had closed three of them in the late seventeenth century, had four competing dance schools in 1720 and eight by 1730. This nucleus of dance masters in Boston helped spread schools throughout New England. One opened in Salem in 1727; it was followed in 1739 by a second one, which also gave lessons in French. By 1790 towns such as Greenfield and Brookfield in western

Massachusetts or Durham in central Connecticut—three relatively small communities—had professional dancing schools. Even more horrifying to some diehards who had agreed with Cotton Mather about the specter of Anglicanism hanging over dance parties was the propensity of the dance schools to seek French dance masters, who were prized beyond almost all English ones for their "elegant deportment." French masters presided over several of Boston's mid-century schools. Newburyport, Massachusetts, and Portsmouth, New Hampshire, provincial towns with high social aspirations, vied with one another for two "French gentlemen of education and agreeable manner." Thus, Anglicanism became just the first dance step on a road leading to Popery and French degeneracy.[9]

The combination of making a profession of a recreation, Anglican and French influence, and fears of an enhanced sexuality in mixed dancing meant, of course, that some New Englanders remained suspicious of dancing even as it spread like wildfire in the second half of the century. John and Samuel Adams, the two dour Revolutionary cousins, who agreed on little, both thought dancing dissipated. John confided to his diary that he "never knew a good dancer good for anything else." He himself did not dance but admitted that he knew some men of "sense and learning" such as James Otis and Samuel Sewall who could and did; yet, neither of them "had the more sense or learning or virtue for it." Occasionally, people would put their opposition into action—one mid-eighteenth-century "besieging party of Puritans broke open the front door" and scattered some noisy dancers "like cattle jumping out of the window helter skelter"—but most people distrustful of dancing were, like John Adams, usually content to sniff the air in disdain and reprove with a mutter. Near the end of the eighteenth century, John Griffith, a dance master in Northampton, published a book to help dances and dance schools overcome the last pockets of small-town and rural opposition. It contained, among other things, a list of "ill manners to be avoided" for dances and schools lest they give offense.[10]

Although conservative Puritan sensibilities could not prevent the spread of dance, they could and did affect the nature of the dancing itself. More than the people of any other colonial region, New Englanders preferred "country dances" as the folk dances they imported from England were called. These resembled modern square or contra dances and were carefully described in John Playford's *The English Dance Master* (London, 1651), which was the most popular dance book in late seventeenth-century and early eighteenth-century New England. Country dances originated as folk dances in rural England but were given form and sophistication by

English and French dance masters in the seventeenth century. The French rechristened these folk dances "contredanses," which was just a false translation (a "borrowing") of the term "country dances." New Englanders tended to use the term "country" in the early eighteenth century but increasingly adopted "contra" as the century developed and the French influence on dance grew. By the Revolution, urbane dancers referred to "contra dance" almost exclusively, and "country" became known as a term used by rustics.[11]

Contra (country) dances were of three basic types: circles composed of large numbers of dancers, sometimes all those in attendance; sets for two, three, or four couples; and longways, two long lines that faced each other. In the eighteenth century longways became the most popular of the three. Most important, however, none of these dances placed a primary emphasis on couples. Dancers usually had partners, but little close or intimate physical contact took place between them. Thus the nature of the dances blunted one of the greatest criticisms raised by opponents. Little sensual or lewd conduct could be directly attributed to circles, sets, or lines of people performing routines to music. Moreover, the group nature of these dances fit smoothly into Puritan social thought, which emphasized communal activity.[12]

To date, scholars have identified about twenty separate contra-dance manuals published in eighteenth-century New England, most of them in the 1780s and 1790s. Several of these were published outside Boston, in cities such as Hartford, Portsmouth, and Providence, but a few were published in small towns such as Walpole, New Hampshire, and Stockbridge, Massachusetts. The books gave elaborate instructions on how to perform the various dances and included local favorites or variations on well-known dances. Some zealous dancers took notes and kept personal dance commonplace books detailing specific steps and maneuvers, which they shared with other enthusiasts. Altogether, 212 dances were described in these manuals, all but three of which were longways. Dance names often memorialized creators, events, places, or prominent dance masters; the names originated in New England even though the dances themselves were derivative of English and French ones, were done to English tunes, and repeated familiar steps. "Nancy Dawson," "Sukey Bids Me," "Rickett's Ride," "Mr. Turner's Academy Cotillion," "Money in Both Pockets," and "Balance a Straw" were some of the colorful names. The tunes, often borrowed from military music or well-known songs, were meant to be catchy, easy to play, and hard to forget. Manuals did not specify the instruments to provide music; people danced to whatever was available. Only at great balls were several instruments likely to be used. Fiddles were most popular, and often a lone one sufficed; sometimes a flute, horn, or drum, or a combination of them, was used. Occasionally, if no instruments were available, dancers made do with an unaccompanied singer or "caller."[13]

New Englanders tried a few other types of dances, although none proved very popular. Some kinds of coupled dancing took place in urban areas and among the elite, who were more Anglicized and anxious to copy the fashionable styles of England and France. Most of the couple dances had French names: minuet, gavotte, rigadoun, and bourrée. The most popular of these, the minuet, was often used to begin formal balls in mid-eighteenth-century high society; but even in New England's most cosmopolitan areas, it did not enjoy the popularity it did in New York and the South. The minuet offended some New Englanders who otherwise thought dancing acceptable, and its popularity declined even among the urban elite in the Revolutionary era. The nineteenth century revived the minuet but modified it into a contra dance done in sets.

Hornpipe jigs also skirted the edges of acceptability in New England. If the minuet challenged the Puritan legacy by smacking of Anglicanism and the nobility, jigs posed challenges from the other direction. Usually done solo, jigs were aggressive dances associated with drunken sailors trying to outdo each other in boastful competition. Always regarded as unsavory by New Englanders, at their least jigs engendered vanity and excessive pride; at their worst they provoked fights and brawls. When men started dancing dueling jigs it was usually a sign that a wedding reception, dance, or waterfront party had gotten out of control. The ribald, aggressive jig fit no more comfortably with eighteenth-century New England's notion of ideal behavior than the excessively polite minuet did.[14]

By the second half of the eighteenth century, even though dancing could still raise the eyebrows of some New Englanders, it was the most widespread recreation of the youthful and was popular with all ages. Young adults filled diaries with memories of dances past and dreams of dances future. Special shoes were often worn; dress styles for parties became less restrictive and cooler. Dancing opportunities abounded in a wide range of formal balls, wedding receptions, organized dances, impromptu get-togethers, and so forth. Just about every kind of activity was sometimes celebrated by dancing. A French visitor to New Haven, expecting a drab social landscape, was shocked when he attended a ball with "a hundred charming girls with bright rosy cheeks," and even more shocked to see another such "enchanting spectacle" in the small nearby town of

Wethersfield. Twelve-year-old Anna Winslow of Boston had a few girlfriends drop by one day and they "made four couples at country dancing." In the evening, an adult house guest, "hearing of my assembly, put his flute in his pocket and played tunes to which we danced mighty cleverly," the exhausted but happy little girl wrote later that night.[15]

Although dancing became a ubiquitous pastime in New England, it reached its height in the capitals and urban centers. Boston's elite held regular winter dances once every two weeks from January through April in the 1760s and 1770s. Attendance ranged from one hundred to two hundred, and guests invariably included the governor of Massachusetts, other important royal officials, military officers, and great merchants. At these the usual fiddler and piper of small dances were replaced by five to ten musicians led by a conductor. Often the governor sent out formal invitations to select individuals; prominent visitors to Boston were honored guests. About ten other New England cities emulated these balls, which often became items of conversation and subjects of gossip.

A few people became renowned for their dancing ability or for their love of dancing. John Adams wrote that an acquaintance of his, Zab Howard of Weymouth, "had the reputation for at least fifteen years of the best dancer in the world. Several attempted but none could equal him, in nimbleness of heel." One young man's grandmother lamented—surely with overstatement—that he wore out "12 pairs of shoes a year." In the family papers of Sukey Heath Goddard, a young woman from Brookline, Massachusetts, and her husband, Dr. John Goddard, a Harvard graduate and physician, one can find evidence of the role dancing played in the life of a young, successful couple and the way in which dance culture spread. The Goddards moved from Boston to Portsmouth, New Hampshire, in order for Dr. Goddard to set up his medical practice. Portsmouth, obviously inferior to Boston in sophistication, nevertheless had a lively social whirl of dances and dance parties, which the Goddards joined upon arrival. Their love of dance thus eased the young Goddards's transition from Boston to Portsmouth, lessened any hardships they felt, and provided them with new friends and social opportunities. The Goddards, in turn, added to Portsmouth's growing reputation as a cosmopolitan city. As the dancing twig was bent, so grew the trees: the Goddards's young children grew up as part of Portsmouth's elite society, filling their own diaries with stories about "dancing til two o'clock."[16]

Only a small fraction of New Englanders enjoyed the social status of the Goddards or lived in an urban area. Most residents of Boston, Portsmouth, or other cities did not receive invitations to lavish balls, nor could they afford the costs of going to them. Moreover, most New Englanders lived in relatively small towns and had to find their dancing pleasures in modest circumstances—usually private homes during the winter, or the outdoors during the summer. Barn dances, so much a part of the present folk-cultural view of early American dancing, belong to a later era; most barns were too small, crowded, and otherwise inhospitable for socializing in the eighteenth century. Neither were meetinghouses physically well set up to accommodate dances. The pews were close together and fastened in place; moreover, to hold a dance in a meeting-house offended some people's sense of good taste. Nevertheless, despite the drawbacks, dances—particularly ordination balls—did occasionally take place in meetinghouses and in the adjacent Sabbath houses or horse houses. Some towns had school buildings that were used. Communities developed differing traditions about where to hold dances outside of private homes. For much of the colonial period, authorities permitted no dancing in taverns. Alcohol and dance seemed too combustible a mixture, virtually guaranteed to promote unacceptable behavior between the sexes. But because taverns were ideal for both spontaneous and organized dances the proscription against mixing alcohol and dancing proved difficult to enforce. In the second half of the eighteenth century a few taverns in large towns began permitting mixed dancing; during the Revolution the floodgates opened, and dancing and dances became regular parts of New England tavern life. After this taboo receded, few, if any, barriers to dance remained. In 1790 many New Englanders shared Increase Mather's sentiments of a century earlier but, unlike Mather, they nursed their suspicions quietly—not pleased, but aware that they were out of step with the times.[17]

## Wedding Receptions

The kind of party at which eighteenth-century New Englanders most frequently danced was the wedding reception; it became central to the social life of every type of community. At mid-seventeenth century, one would not have guessed that this would likely become the case. Puritans, who regarded the family as a political and religious institution as well as a social and economic one, believed marriage was far too serious to permit ribald or even slightly frivolous festivities. Puritans did celebrate marriage with two social activities, an espousal ceremony and the wedding itself. On both occasions neighbors and family marked the event by feasting much in the manner of a day of thanksgiving. Espousals took place a week or two before the wedding itself. Both were joyful but quiet, sedate gatherings that traditionally took place in the bride's home. At espousals, the bride's minister gave an espousal sermon in which he instructed the couple in the proper way to prepare for marriage; at the wedding he gave a parallel sermon on the duties and obligations of husbands and wives.[18]

Until 1686, when the Dominion of New England imposed a code of law based on Anglican practices, in neither Massachusetts nor Connecticut could ministers perform the marriage ceremony; magistrates did. Using a secular justice signaled the civil importance of marriage to a well-ordered society; it was also a sign of the Puritans' theological quarrel with Catholics, who made marriage a sacrament, something Puritans thought Scripture did not justify. After 1686, the couple could choose to have either a minister or magistrate conduct the ceremony, a choice that had been available all along in Rhode Island. For a generation after the Dominion of New England, weddings remained generally sedate and continued to be celebrated primarily by feasting. "I was married to Elizabeth Garrish," a rural minister, Joseph Green, wrote in his diary in 1699—"a virgin." Nothing else about the day or his bride's status seemed remarkable enough to cause more comment. Three of New England's most best-known diarists of this period, Michael Wigglesworth, Cotton Mather, and Samuel Sewall, describe many weddings—including their own—in much the same matter-of-fact terms. "Had a good supper and cake," "had our cake and sack-posset," Sewall wrote of wedding celebrations: the most extravagant reception he went to, that of the wealthy Bostonian Colonel Fitch Joy, consisted of "good bride-cake, good wine, Burgundy and canary, good beer." Mather worried about ways to impress upon celebrants "maxims of piety, I may with brevity, but pungency let fall on the people."[19]

The quiet feasting era of wedding celebrations began to end in the 1730s and 1740s; by mid-century, the boisterous and lavish reception had emerged. The conservative rural minister John Ballantine, of Westfield, described his own wedding in 1743 as a "two-day feast" in Dedham that ended with a triumphant open-carriage ride to nearby Boston. The wedding reception of Nicholas Gardiner's daughter in South Kingston, Rhode Island, in 1751 was New England's social event of the year. Over six hundred guests drank, danced, and feasted for three days at Gardiner's expense. In 1753, Jacob Bailey, a Harvard student, traveled from Cambridge to remote Rowley, Massachusetts, to celebrate a friend's wedding to the local minister's daughter. Inasmuch as it involved a clergyman's daughter and took place in a small town, the wedding was a decorous affair by prevailing standards. Nevertheless, the hosts threw a three-day party.

"About the coming of the evening," Bailey wrote, "the younger sort, to the number of about fifty, repaired to the western chamber, where we spent the evening in singing, dancing, and wooing the widow" (a game similar to spin the bottle). The next day "having saluted the bride, we spent our time, some in dancing, the other in playing cards . . . after dinner, we young people repaired to our chamber where we spent the day, in play such as singing, dancing, wooing the widow, playing cards, box, etc."[20]

By the eve of the Revolution, weddings, even rural ones, could take on extravagant, ribald dimensions and still be regarded as respectable. Elihu Ashley described one he attended in Greenfield, Massachusetts, in 1774 that took four days to celebrate; it involved a procession of twenty-six couples in wagons, several dinner and breakfast feasts, three dances, and vast quantities of wine and beer. On the way home to neighboring Deerfield, where he lived, Ashley confessed that he and his girlfriend, Polly, "were very dull" from lack of sleep and overindulgence. A few months after this wedding bash in the upper Connecticut River Valley, a diarist described a fancier one in Windsor, Connecticut, a day's ride downstream. Wethersfield's young minister, John Marsh, married Anne Grant, the daughter of East Windsor's leading citizen, Ebenezer Grant. Guests came from all over New England and celebrated with two days of food, wine, and dancing. Reverend Marsh and his bride did not dance themselves but did not think it unseemly to be escorted to their new home by an honor guard of twenty whooping horsemen.[21]

High jinks more often than not characterized weddings in the late colonial period. A joke so commonplace as to become a ritual involved the groom running away to be caught and "dragged back to duty" by the other men at the wedding. Cutting the reins on the groom's horse or bobbing his horse's tail was another particular wedding joke, somewhat akin to tying tin cans to a car today. Men who had "dragged back" the groom before the wedding sometimes would "steal the bride" in the middle of the reception. Friends of the new couple rushed the house where the reception was being held to spirit the bride away to a nearby tavern or a second party. Custom required people attending the primary reception to rescue the bride from her "kidnapers." Usually the two parties amalgamated during the rescue attempt and ate and danced together in a truce. One wonderful story from Windsor told of a kidnaped bride who turned out to be a decoy—a man dressed as a bride.[22]

Weddings convulsed entire areas of towns with party activities, people coming and going at all hours of the night, sounds and shouts of music and dancing, all of which lasted at least a weekend. Things could get out of hand. The Reverend John Ballantine fumed at the "sons of Belial" whose "riotous behavior" was an "outrageous insult to a newly married couple. What incivility, what rudeness, nay, of what barbarity you were guilty of that night," he preached to some of the penitent revelers the day after their unspecified offense. The fact that the outrages took place at Ballantine's own daughter's wedding undoubtedly added insult to injury. Receptions became a place for toasts, sometimes risqué ones. When one of Boston's legendary femmes fatales, Polly Smith, married in 1770, the best man, drinking the bride's health, read a poem that would have shocked an earlier generation: "At length gay Polly you have paid for all your triumphs past, the scene is changed and you are made a vassal at the last." The maid of honor added her own mocking bons mots concerning her sister, the headstrong bride: "In wedlock women all must say that horrible frightful word *obey;* then Polly no uncommon fate will have for every married women is a slave."[23]

## Dinner Parties

Eating and talking—these are the essence of the dinner party, a kind of social gathering that has been and still is popular with people in most societies. The Sabbath dinner, the thanksgiving, the dance, the wedding reception: each had some of the trappings of a dinner party, but each had other explicit purposes or activities as well. The explicit purpose of a dinner party is to enjoy one another's company while eating and drinking.

Throughout colonial and Revolutionary New England history, food and conversation played a major role in virtually everyone's social life. People seldom ate alone or even in intimate groups; few meals were eaten on the run. Regular breakfasts, dinners, and suppers were invariably social occasions with at least seven or eight people at the table. Although they rhetorically worried about the sin of gluttony, Puritans had few reservations about unabashedly enjoying food. The ambivalences that characterized most of their attitudes toward pleasure failed to diminish their zest for the dinner table. Diarists placed an inordinate emphasis on food. Partly this was because the colonists encountered so many new and seemingly exotic foods, which were exciting to note; partly it was because food was so abundant after the first few years of settlement. But mainly it was because the Puritans liked recreational eating and saw few dangers lurking beside the "family altar," as the fireplace was called by one wag. When people who kept diaries went out to dinner, they usually noted in detail what they ate. John Winthrop's journal is spare in references to all pleasures except food; here he waxed eloquent about the joys of "fat hogs, kids, venison, poultry, geese," "fine strawberries," "good beer," and "rich pastry."[24]

Food played a similar role for all classes of New Englanders, as it did not in England and Europe, where distinctive patterns of consumption characterized differing classes. In medieval and early modern England, two culinary traditions existed, that of the court and that of the peasant. The court eating of the well-off emphasized meats, sauces, and other high-fat items; the peasant tradition centered on the three staples, bread, cheese, and beer. In seventeenth-century England the distinctions between the two strands of eating culture began to blur as the nobility and gentry became aware that their diet lacked healthfulness and tried to include more fruit and vegetables in it. In turn, the farm and urban workers of the peasant tradition began to aspire to more of the rich foods of the upper classes. Puritan New Englanders did not transplant these two traditions. Instead, everyone ate "above their station." Laws in Massachusetts and Connecticut prohibited people from dressing above their social rank or using titles to which they were not socially entitled, but everyone tried to eat as well as he or she could. And the colonists usually ate very well; servants as well as the "better sort" had much meat, cake, and fruit in their regular diet.[25]

No dramatic change occurred in recreational eating habits over the course of the colonial period; the eighteenth century elaborated on the patterns of the seventeenth. Dinner parties outside the family existed from the first settlements; in the eighteenth century they were inclined to be larger, more frequent, more formal, and more extravagant. The "art of cookery" as one author called it, began to be developed along sophisticated lines. Bookstores started stocking cookbooks and a few were published in Boston. At mid-eighteenth century, a series of innovations in preparation and storage techniques substantially reduced the seasonal nature of the food supply and foods that had been served only at certain times of the year became available for longer periods. An increase in animal husbandry and a corresponding decrease in hunting as a source for meat added to this process. Mutton, turtle, salmon, and veal, the luxury meats and seafoods of the early modern era, became commoner treats at special family meals or dinner parties in the eighteenth century. By mid-century, New England's two dozen newspapers carried innumerable advertisements for specialty foods often identified by place of origin: East Indies Bohea and Hyson tea, coffee, chocolate; West Indies fruit and rum; Irish pork and butter; Philadelphia flour; Dorchester ale. Spices, too, received big play;

cloves, mace, nutmeg, pimiento, ginger, cinnamon, aniseed, and allspice among them. Vegetables abounded. In 1764 the *New Hampshire Gazette* carried an advertisement for a Portsmouth merchant who had "just imported from London, Black-eyed non-pareil and Essex reading beans; early bush and pale beans of all sorts; early Dutch, Yorkshire Battorica; sugarloaf, May, Red, turnip and winter cabbage; green, curled and yellow savoy; early and late cauliflower; broccoli, summer, winter, and mountain spinach; Spanish and silver onion; orange and horn carrot; swelling and Dutch turnip; Redith; white mustard; Asparagus; white and green Gofs; cabbage and seletia lettuce; early cucumber."[26]

The *Gazette* undoubtedly targeted its advertisement for the above food, drink, spices, and vegetables to the nearby urban elite. Dinner parties became an avocation with many of its members. John Rowe, a merchant in pre-Revolutionary Boston, attended or hosted private dinner parties with from four to forty people at least once a week on average. As John Winthrop had at his more staid parties in the 1630s and 1640s, Rowe usually listed the foods he ate while dining out and appraised their quality. Among the 150 or so dinner companions Rowe identified in his diary were most of the Revolutionary luminaries: John Adams, Samuel Adams, John Hancock, James Otis, Thomas Barnard, Thomas Hutchinson, Robert Treat Paine—even Captain William Preston of Boston Massacre notoriety—were guests at his house. Rowe also attended over a dozen large banquets each year, most of which were held at the Concert Hall or Faneuil Hall. Private groups such as the Masons or merchant associations sponsored these. If Rowe had visitors from afar—a sea captain from Halifax or a business associate from New York—he assembled a dinner party to introduce and entertain them. And at times he dispensed with formalities; Rowe and his wife often joined a circle of friends in the warm weather for a "barbekue."[27]

Neither the elite nor the people of Boston, of course, enjoyed a monopoly on dinner parties. Most extant diaries that provide details of day-to-day living describe them. A few types of dinner parties, often seasonal, became known by name and by the customs associated with them. The most famous (or infamous?), the turtle frolic, took place in port towns—sometimes in a waterfront tavern, sometimes outdoors—and could be counted on to be loud, rollicking, and well attended. A huge sea turtle, preferably over two hundred pounds, served as the centerpiece and guest of honor. If the turtle had been towed back alive from the Caribbean by a sociable captain, as was usually the case, its arrival in town would be known several days ahead of the frolic, and plans made accordingly. Much rum, punch, and other food preceded the ceremonial cooking of the turtle, which the captain or some other specially trained chef supervised to the cheers of the other guests. Some Newport merchants placed standing orders for turtles with West Indian suppliers. A Rhode Island slave, "Cuffee-Cockroach," achieved fame in the 1750s as the best turtle cook in New England. Commonly attended by young adults and visiting seamen, turtle frolics also attracted respectable people—even some couples—out for a good time. Dr. Edward Holyoke and his wife, Mary, eminent members of Salem's social elite, attended three turtle frolics in the summer of 1759.[28]

Oysterbakes were less dramatic but more frequent. These, too, usually took place in summer or early fall and were held on the waterfront or as barbecues. Strict moralists associated oysterbakes with revelry much as they did turtle frolics. They were not wrong. In the 1780s, Providence briefly prohibited serving open oysters outdoors at night because the practice occasioned so many disturbances.[29]

At the other end of the spectrum, in landlocked rural areas winter tea parties became popular at mid-eighteenth century. The high cost of tea, coffee, and chocolate gave these nonalcoholic drinks a special status as a treat for middle-class and poor people and for small-town residents who customarily drank fruit juices or alcoholic beverages. Although much more sedate than plunging a turtle into a huge kettle, the serving of tea at a party also took on a form as the central ritual of a party. Elizabeth Phelps, then a newly married woman, described tea parties in Hadley, Massachusetts, in the 1770s. Invited guests received formal written invitations a week or so in advance; usually ten to fifteen couples attended. Because the parties were customarily held in winter, people fretted about the possibility of bad weather. About an hour after everyone had arrived, the hostess served the tea by "sending it round," which meant passing it cup by cup in a circle made by the guests. When everyone had tea, someone would be asked to say a blessing after which "the hum renewed" and biscuits and cakes made similar rounds. After the first cups of tea were drunk, the circle broke up into smaller groups for chatting. About half an hour before the party was to end, the hostess circulated with nuts and apples as a dessert treat and a signal that the party was almost over. Tea parties lasted from about six to nine P.M. and were most often held on Friday nights. The men went outside before the women to ready the horses and wagons or the sleighs if snow permitted. New Englanders loved sleighs and considered it a wonderful ending to take one home after a party.[30]

### Frolics for Fun

Wholesome, pious, quiet—Hadley's tea parties were a far cry from John Rowe's elegant dinners for visiting merchants or from a boisterous turtle frolic in Providence. But, of course, young couples in Boston and Providence had tea parties also; and people in western rural Massachusetts kicked up their heels at parties lasting all night. The location, size, and class structure of a community obviously conditioned the opportunities its residents had for socializing; but the diverse experience of prosperous eighteenth-century New England suggests that inventive and energetic colonists could seek out the social life they wanted. Far from being drab and somber, late colonial New England hummed with a constant variety of parties.

Many of the dances, wedding receptions, and dinners would have offended New England's first generation of Puritans. But none of them would have been or was categorically rejected by the founders. Even dancing had some proponents in the first generation and had not been condemned out of hand, only so limited as to be made nearly impossible. A relatively austere world of quiet Puritan group celebrations and fellowship evolved into the lively whirl of parties that characterized the late colonial period. But the new social world did not overturn the old one; it grew incrementally out of it. And the opportunities New Englanders developed for a very active—even ribald—social life should not obscure two crucial points: most of these party activities stayed within respectable limits that at least paid lip service to biblical guidelines; and many people continued to live by standards closer to the austere habits of their grandparents than to the less restrained conduct of some contemporaries. As it did in many matters, the late colonial and Revolutionary period offered New Englanders choices in how to get together to have a good time. Virtually all these choices could be comfortably fit within a widening range of appropriate conduct defined by the equally widening visions New Englanders had of Christian virtue.

# VII

# The Progress of Romance: Sex and Courtship

Practiced with moderation, sex within marriage met all the Puritan requirements for appropriate relaxation: it was sanctioned by Scripture; it did not squander undue time or resources; it refreshed body and spirit; and it was productive. Although theologians did not dwell on the recreational qualities of sexual intercourse, they did regard it as a pleasurable duty wives and husbands owed each other. Failure to perform the marital act was evidence of the failure of the marriage and one of the permissible grounds for divorce. "God was of another mind," John Cotton wrote, than to believe in "the excellence of virginity."[1]

## Sex and Courtship in The Founding Era

The above notwithstanding, one should not assume that Puritan married couples believed in or practiced a robust, anything-goes-with-consent sexuality. Although they neither condemned the sexual function nor embraced the theoretical position of the Stoics that passion inevitably led to sin, Puritans manifested a vague discomfort with sexual activities of any kind. Like many Christians, they believed that man was half angel and half animal, and that sexuality derived from the animal side. They also believed that original sin made the passions unruly and excessive. As the strongest of the passions, sexuality could most easily lead humans astray. Thus, sexual activity did not invariably lead to sin, but it did incline man toward bad behavior. Even married couples could "play the adulterer in bed" if they allowed their animal sides or passions too much sway. Moralists regarded oral sex and anal intercourse, for example, as abominations.[2]

Outside of marriage, recreational sex of any sort, from passionate kissing, fondling, and masturbation to the more serious crimes of fornication, adultery, sodomy, and bestiality, was proscribed and punished as a crime against soul, state, and church. From its inception onward each Puritan colony put its opposition into laws, which magistrates strictly enforced. The little colony of Pilgrims at Plymouth experienced enough problems with sexual misconduct to trouble its aged governor, William Bradford, deeply. In 1642 Bradford speculated on the cause of "sundrie notorious sins, especially drunkenness and uncleanness, not only incontinence between persons unmarried . . . but that which is worse, even sodomie and bugerie (things fearful to name) that have broak forth in this land." The immediate cause of Bradford's soul-searching was the conduct of an otherwise pious young man, Thomas Granger, aged seventeen, who pleaded guilty to "buggery with a mare, a cow, two goats, five sheep, two calves, and a turkey." Plymouth executed Granger for his heinous crimes, and also killed the animals, which were "cast into a great and large pit that was digged of purpose for them and no use made of any part of them." The governor's final analysis attributed Plymouth's problems with illicit sexuality to three causes. First, the Devil worked unusually hard to snare sinners from among God's chosen people because he knew what a great victory it was to do so; second, "as it is with waters when their streams are stopped or dammed up, when they get passage they flow with more violence"; and third, Plymouth was very good at detecting criminality. All three of Bradford's reasons, of course, reflected positively on the general state of Plymouth's morality and gave solace to his troubled mind.[3]

Sexual crimes also beset New England's other small Puritan colony, New Haven, which had the strictest laws governing interaction between the sexes. Here, too, some of the crimes were sensational and attracted much publicity then, as they have since among historians. In the two most famous, authorities accused George Spencer and Thoms Hogg of having sex with sows, both of which produced offspring that looked like the alleged fathers. When the court made Hogg caress the sow she became so excited that she exhibited a "working of lust . . . [and] poured out seed." Despite the improbability of the above evidence, New Haven convicted and executed Spencer and Hogg. And herein lies one of the problems historians have created in assessing Puritan sexual conduct. Sensational, bizarre examples are repeated endlessly to the neglect of more mundane ones. Other reliable proof, including eyewitness testimony and confessions, indicates that both Spencer and Hogg were indeed guilty. In general, Puritan courts did not jump to smug, self-righteous conclusions but required a substantial body of evidence to sustain a conviction. People were presumed innocent until proven guilty, and magistrates carefully weighed witnesses' veracity as well as circumstantial and physical evidence.[4]

To a degree, Governor Bradford's assessment of the reasons for illegal sexual conduct in Plymouth was accurate for all of New England and has colored the interpretations historians have placed on Puritans and sex. Puritan ideals held illicit sex in such contempt that when it occurred it was newsworthy; fewer outlets for sexual energy existed in New England than in most other places; and society was indeed zealous in detecting and prosecuting breaches of propriety. Obviously, inappropriate sexual activity took place in Puritan society—the real news would be if it did not—but all comparative data suggest that in the first generation of New England, rates of deviant sex, fornication, and adultery were far lower than they were in England. Sex provided pleasure for most Puritans within marriage and for a few outside, but in both cases the degree of activity has been overstated by the revisionist historians of the mid-twentieth century who tried to rescue the Puritans from their earlier image as repressed prudes. Excessive passion, deviant sex, fornication, and even masturbation constituted acts of such profound rebellion against deeply held beliefs of the church and community that pious persons could not embrace any of these sins without deeply troubling their souls.[5]

The restrictions on sexual conduct, however, did not mean that courtship, romance, and male-female interaction did not offer possibilities for recreation among adolescents, young adults, and the widowed. First marriages usually took place between young adults in their mid-twenties and late twenties and were preceded by discussions and agreements between the parents of the couple. Intended to ensure the personal suitability and financial security of the bride and groom, these arrangements were rationally planned, much as a business deal would be, to promote the well-being and profit of both partners. But these marriages were not mere accommodations in which romantic attraction played no role. Parents usually entered into negotiations after their children had expressed an interest in each other. Aging bachelors or widowers frequently made a decision to get married and then began a search for an appropriate partner. Marriages required a rational underpinning but they often resulted from brief courtships based on romantic attraction that might include some mild flirtation. Not surprisingly, the nature of a courtship and the level of

romantic influence varied by individuals, gender, and social class. Young
women in particular seemed susceptible to romantic notions of love.
Servants living together under the same roof developed a reputation for
risque sexual banter. One young man told friends that a woman servant
made his heart leap; she replied that "she made his heart leap in his
britches." Even the most demure young woman could find herself the
target of a flirt. Fifteen-year-old Hety Shepard, a pious teenager, confessed
to being secretly pleased when a boy passing refreshments after a church
meeting teased her that he would "rather serve me than the elders." No
less an ascetic than Michael Wigglesworth, the Puritan minister who
exemplified the dour, judgmental, abstemious killjoy, wrote a widow he
wished to marry that after their first meeting, "my thoughts and heart have
been toward you ever since." Wigglesworth went on to assure his prospective bride, however, that he subjected this shallow attraction to "serious,
earnest, and frequent seeking of God for guidance . . . [and] my thoughts
have still been determined unto and fixed upon yourself as the most
suitable person." The example of Wigglesworth, who was an atypical
Puritan in many respects, nevertheless typifies the combination of business
deal with romance that characterized Puritan marriage. Courtship per se
involved no dating and no clear rituals involving calling hours and prescribed activities. Physical interaction such as kissing or holding hands,
was not accepted as appropriate. Children could not marry contrary to
their parents' wishes. But in a relatively closed society that met frequently
for a variety of religious and social reasons, where people had often known
their likely marital prospects most of their lives, where many unrelated
people lived together as servants under the same roof, an informal courtship process developed. Attended by glances, banter, and clear expressions
of personal and physical attraction, unspoken courtship activities were
woven into the fabric of the Puritan communal world.[6]

### Virtue Under Siege

In the late seventeenth century, courting began to change from an informal
process to an acknowledged practice; at the same time, authorities lessened
penalties for illicit sexual conduct. The two phenomena were closely
related: young men and women spent more time together under circumstances that fostered opportunities for romance and sex. Fitz-John Winthrop, the grandson of Governor John Winthrop and himself the governor
of Connecticut, wrote in 1707 that it has "been the way and custom of the
country for young folks to choose, and when there is no visible exception,

everybody approves it." Winthrop's statement does not herald a complete departure from past practice but suggests instead a change in degree that placed more emphasis on the couple's initiative and less on the parents'. Nor did change proceed evenly across the New England landscape. That acute social critic Sarah Kemble Knight wrote at the turn of the century that rural justices of the peace maintain the old "zeal, very rigid . . . even to a harmless kiss or innocent merriment among young people." By the 1720s two young future leaders of New England could write about the dangers of courtship. In his diary, Ebenezer Parkman listed among his blessings his chastity that he had maintained until marriage despite "so many temptations as those passed in the time of courtship." Parkman counted himself among a minority. Roger Wolcott, a future governor of Connecticut and already a poet of note, warned the young women of his colony to beware "the subtle intrigues that a young man lays, in his sly courtship of an harmless maid." He entitled another diatribe against courtship practices "Who Can Find a Virtuous Woman, for Her Price is Far Above Rubies."[7]

Court records and patterns of conception both confirm that premarital sex increased in the late seventeenth and early eighteenth centuries. Punishment for fornication between people who subsequently married became mild—a censure or small fine. As the eighteenth century progressed prosecutions became infrequent; by 1720 they were rare. Authorities turned from the criminal courts to moral suasion to enforce codes of sexual conduct. In the sermon literature, a good guide to social concerns, New England's moralists identified an increase in masturbation as one of their greatest fears and the sexual snare most likely to draw young men into a life of sin. A recent scholarly analysis of young men's diaries confirms the fears were well founded. Many young men agonized over their inability to refrain from "self-pollution." Among these was Cotton Mather, who as an adult railed so strongly against the sin; as a young man he described "Satan buffeting me with unclean temptations" to such a degree that he wanted to "pluck out my right eye and cut off my right hand." Mather would fast, overcome the temptation, gain back his strength and health, and then succumb all over again. He spent a horrible adolescence trying to cope with the guilt his sexuality imposed on him. Mather's problem seems to have been chronic among boys and young men of his era. They lived at a time of increased temptation and flirtatious interactions, but sexual activity outside of marriage still challenged society's basic values.[8]

The adult Mather used his considerable talents as a writer, his reputation as a minister and scientist, and presumably his firsthand knowledge gained from personal tribulations to warn others about the dangers of sexual licentiousness in general and masturbation in particular. Some of Mather's scorching sermons sound like jokes to the modern ear, but they were not humorous to his own audience nor were they intended to be. As early as 1690, Mather warned against "abominable self-pollutions" that might be dismissed as "easy peccadillos." In a frank, detailed essay, *The Pure Nazarite,* published in 1723, Mather, by now known not only as a theologian but also as a distinguished medical scientist, identified a variety of the terrifying consequences of this "unnatural prostitution . . . defended by such filthy dogs as Diogenes." Spiritually, no ambiguity existed: unrepentant masturbators lost eternal salvation. Medically, "the perpetrators of this impiety bring such a destruction upon their health as to render themselves a sort of self-murderers." Mather described a patient he had treated: "a wretch putrifying and emaciated with the arrest of that fool design . . . reduced into a woeful consumption, his visage pale and lean, and stomach depraved, and his blood filled with acid and acrid particles which do at the same time further provoke the venereal appetites." Moreover, the destruction went beyond the offender's moral and physical health. A masturbator who married would usually be unable to produce children, or if he did, they would be mentally handicapped. In another sermon, "Onania," originally published in London and then reprinted in Boston in 1726, an anonymous author even more graphically outlined the physical consequences: "ulcers especially if managed by raw, unskilled people," "priapism and other disorders of the penis and testes," "fainting fits and epilepsies," and a "distemper [which] often proves fatal." If the guilty were lucky enough not to die, masturbation "so forces and weakens the tender vessel that when they come to manhood, it renders them ridiculous to women."[9]

The lurid language of these scare-mongering tracts was new to the eighteenth century and reached its height in the 1720s. Changes in courtship patterns and in relations between the sexes frightened some conservative moralists; they in turn tried to frighten the potential sinners they envisioned among their parishioners. Masturbation became a target because it was perceived to be a widespread type of sexual misconduct, could be easily concealed, and might even appear to some to be innocent—a victimless crime. Moreover, in addition to its own horrors and evil consequences, masturbation, it was argued, inevitably led to greater and more dehabilitating sins. *The Pure Nazarite* used the same logic and tactics as *Reefer Madness: Tell Your Children,* the famous antimarijuana movie of 1936. Masturbation, it was claimed, like marijuana, destroyed people in and of itself, but in addition both allegedly led to more vicious habits: fornication, adultery, or bestiality in one case, heroin or opium in the other.[10]

No one, of course, publicly characterized masturbation as proper sexual conduct or an appropriate form of recreation. But another activity that conservatives also thought would open the gates to Hell was defended briefly by some members of polite society. Although regarded as quaint by twentieth-century American culture, bundling's rich potential for sexual sin is celebrated in centuries of jokes, the most recent genre of which involves traveling salesmen and farmers' daughters. Webster's early nineteenth-century dictionary defined two types of bundling that took place in colonial New England. The first, "an expedient practiced in America on a scarcity of beds, where on such occasions, husbands and parents frequently permitted travelers to bundle with themselves, their wives, and daughters." The second was quite different. Men and women in advanced stages of courtship, but not yet married, bundled together in the same bed. In both cases, the bundlers remained fully clothed. Practicality lay behind the practice of traveler bundling just as it often forced guests in inns to share beds. In the case of courting bundlers, practicality also played a role. Often a young man would call on a woman miles away from his own home and not be able to return safely to his own bed that night. But a recreational defense gradually became added to the expedient one; some respectable people defended bundling between courting young adults as an appropriate form of amusement and a good way for the couple to get to know each other well — too good a way and too much amusement thought many other shocked conservatives.[11]

New Englanders did not invent courtship bundling. The Swiss and Dutch had done it for centuries — "queesting," it was called in Holland. The English, too, had bundled in the latter Middle Ages but by the sixteenth century the practice had been discredited everywhere in the British Isles except in Wales, where it was continued into the seventeenth and eighteenth centuries. New Englanders borrowed the custom from the Welsh, although precisely how and why is not clear. The English and the rest of the colonial world poked fun at bundling in the Puritan colonies and implied always that it was far from innocent and a hypocritical consequence of overzealous prudery. Washington Irving's *History of New York* ascribed the "marvelous fecundity" of New England to "this singular custom prevalent among them."[12]

Originally, bundling was confined almost exclusively to the lower classes, the winter season, and remote areas without inns. In the 1730s, however, bundling made some slight inroads into the middle class and began to show signs of gaining respectability as a form of entertainment as well as an expedient. Before this time bundling was known primarily as something other people somewhere else did. Few households or regions admitted to doing it, especially for fun. Bostonians, for example, associated it with backcountry Massachusetts rustics and Rhode Islanders. By the Great Awakening of the 1740s, however, bundling became—or was perceived as—a sufficient problem throughout New England to provoke a sustained attack by the clergy.[13]

Among the attackers was Jonathan Edwards, the great revivalist, who lived in rural western Massachusetts, a likely locale for bundling to occur. Edwards called the practice one of the main causes of the "growth of uncleanness in the land." Added to bundling's inherent propensity to "stir up lusts" was a further danger: parents thought that if children were properly counseled they could resist the temptation to go beyond the innocent companionship allowed. "Peter was very confident that he would not deny Christ," Edwards wrote, "but how dreadfully otherwise was the event. The most self-confident are most in danger." Edwards seemed more shocked that some people defended bundling than that it took place. Sin was ever present in society, but that good people were "ready to laugh at its being condemned" seemed inexplicable to him.[14]

At mid-century the elite of Boston, Newport, and Salem mounted crusades against what they believed to be an outrageous invitation to sin although there is scant evidence that bundling ever became widespread in those towns or any others in New England. The English minister Andrew Burnaby, who traveled through the region in 1759 and 1760 delighting in everything he could find to make colonists look like licentious boors, believed that bundling only occurred among "the lower people" and then only for one night in which they were supposed to hammer out the details of their future wedding plans. "Tarrying," Burnaby said it was called, and if an agreement was not forthcoming the couple usually did not get a second chance to try under these circumstances. Burnaby also dismissed charges of sexual misconduct during bundling as "an accident that seldom happens." The bitter, caustic Loyalist historian, the Reverend Samuel Peters, who even more than Burnaby searched New England's past for evidence of moral decay and hypocrisy, thought bundling sounded worse than it really was. "The sofa in summer," he argued, "was more dangerous than the bed in winter."[15]

In retrospect, bundling was much less prevalent and more innocent than conservative moralists of the eighteenth century and snickering antiquarians of the nineteenth and twentieth centuries believed. It did, however, ignite a debate at mid-century that did not end until the late 1780s, when any claims bundling had to respectability as a courtship activity were abandoned. The anti-bundlers won, and bundling vanished into the illicit subculture and then, as a curiosity, into history. Three ballads published within a year of one another provided the last major salvo of the bundling war.[16] "A New Bundling Song" appeared in a Boston almanac in 1785 as a "reproof to those young country women who follow that reproachful practice and to their mothers for upholding them therein." Stanza after stanza of doggerel told of artful pretense, always with the same result. In one of them,

A bundling couple went to bed
with all their clothes from foot to head
that the defense might seem complete
each one was wrapped in a sheet
But O! this bundlings such a witch
the man of her did catch the itch
and so provoked was the wretch
that she of him a bastard catch'd

The anonymous author summed up bundling as "a vulgar custom this, I own, admired by many a slut and clown."

Within a few months, "A New Song in Favor of Courting," less humorous and much longer, defended the integrity of bundling by providing numerous examples of other opportunities for illicit sex outside the bundling bed. The final epic in the battle of the bundling ballads, "The Whore on the Snow Crest," forswore any pretense of subtlety. The essential point was that made by "A New Song in Favor of Courting": if people want to sin they will find a way. "Whores will be whores" captures the ballad's essence. The most outstanding example of this principle was "one whorish dame" who conceived a child "on the snow when sol was low."

The remarkable part of the bundling debate—which lasted fifty years, from the 1740s through the 1780s—was not the details or the fact that bundlers eventually lost; it was that the debate ever took place in a society that just a few decades earlier had tried to prevent men and women from dancing together. Increase and Cotton Mather had feared that young adults would be unable to resist the temptations posed by holding each other in public on the dance floor. Thirty years later, Jonathan Edwards was forced to argue that a young couple would be unable to resist the temptations posed by lying in bed together all night.

## Flirting Legitimized

The bundling controversy symbolized a shift in courtship patterns and in society's views of appropriate conduct between young men and women. All forms of sex outside marriage remained proscribed, but opportunities for young men and women to meet and socialize expanded geometrically as New England grew increasingly tolerant of romantic interplay between the sexes.

Urban areas led the change. Descriptions of social life among the youth of Newport in the 1720s and 1730s have an idyllic, modern quality. Unmarried young men and women took evening walks together, went on Saturday afternoon picnics in the countryside, and enjoyed romantic canoe rides on nearby lakes. Outings for couples, as well as mixed dances and parties, became not just acceptable but commonplace. A tavern outside the city became known as a favorite place for courting sweethearts to go for dinner.[17]

Dr. Andrew Hamilton, a physician from Maryland who toured New England in 1744, described the social whirl of Boston's young men and women in much the same way. Boston, too, had a romantic tavern famed as a "rendezvous of . . . both sexes who make an evening's promenade in the summer time." A handsome, charming man and an accomplished physician, Hamilton found himself pursued by women of that "illustrious class of the sex commonly called coquettes." When he spurned these overtures, he found himself importuned by a mother on behalf of her daughters, "two pretty ladies, gay and airy," whom he also rejected. Hamilton was sufficiently surprised by the ongoing lighthearted banter laden with romantic innuendo that he recorded much of it in his diary. Inasmuch as this talk flattered Hamilton, he may have embellished it, but even allowing for exaggeration, some of the women were extraordinarily forward. One approached a companion with whom Hamilton was walking and asked in a stage whisper: "Lord what strange mortal is that?" "'Tis the flower of the Maryland beaux, Dr. Hamilton," the friend boasted, to which the woman replied that she would like to be his patient.[18]

Change came to small towns also. One example of it can be seen in the decision made by town after town to end sexual segregation in seating at the meetinghouse. Before the 1720s unmarried men and women sat separately; by the 1760s virtually every town seated them together. Kissing at parties and the possibility of a "good-night kiss" between a couple that had been on an outing became accepted parts of social life. Jonathan Edwards described the changes he saw in western Massachusetts in the

1740s with horror. "A loose, vain, and irreligious generation," he called the "young people of both sexes who get together in companies for mirth . . . spending the time til late in the night in their jollity." "Where frolicking is carried out," Edwards warned, "there are the most frequent breaking out of gross sins, fornication in particular."[19]

New England's most ardent evangelist exaggerated what he perceived to be the symptoms of a hedonistic society, but he was right about the fundamental change that occurred by mid-century. The diaries of three young men—a cad, a flirt, and a confirmed bachelor—suggest the range of socialization possible in the pre-Revolutionary period.

Elihu Ashley, a twenty-four-year-old unmarried man, kept a diary for 1774, the year he studied medicine and lived with Dr. William Williams in the remote western town of Deerfield, Massachusetts. A charming, superficially upstanding future citizen, Ashley lived a roguish life at the center of which was a sexual relationship with Polly, a respectable young woman who lived next door. The most interesting part of this was not the relationship itself, or the fact that Ashley deceived Polly by seeing other women, but that the young medical student could entertain his girlfriend alone night after night in his chambers with the knowledge of the doctor and of Polly's family. The couple often sat in the kitchen drinking tea and talking; Ashley would try to persuade Polly to "come to my garret." She usually resisted at first but relented after the extortionate Ashley would threaten to break off the relationship or cajole her with professions of love. The emotional dynamics of the situation may be timeless, but the physical opportunity for a young, unmarried couple to spend so much time unsupervised together represented a dramatic change from the past. Predictably the story had an unhappy ending: Ashley refused to marry Polly and left after completing his studies.[20]

William Gregory, a visiting Scot and polished gentleman about thirty years old, cut a wide swath through the young women of New England on a two-week trip from New Haven to Boston in 1771. Gregory's indisputably insincere flirting and lechery are not the point of greatest interest, any more than Elihu Ashley's character defects were. But the ease with which Gregory could meet and spend time with women is positively astounding. Consider the following synopsis of his exploits.[21]

> September 18 and 19: he met five women—two widows, one married woman, and two young girls—with whom he traveled for two days from Springfield to Worcester before leaving them after he decided "they would only be a bill of costs and no advantages."

September 20: he and a friend, "a widower with a fine daughter," spent the evening with "several agreeable ladies" in Watertown.

September 23: while in Boston, he "spent the evening with some Salem ladies."

September 25 and 26: also in Boston, his landlord introduced him to "twelve ladies, four of whom were married women, the other eight— good God! How can I express it—were such divine creatures." The same landlord later said: "Gregory, you was as happy a dog as any in Boston." He saw two of them, "Miss Gray and Miss Greenlees the adorable," again the next day.

September 27: on his way to Providence, Gregory stopped in a tavern and met "two fine handsome girls," with whom he passed the after-noon.

September 28: he "fell in company with a young lady on horseback bound on my way so that I came along the last four miles very merrily."

September 29: he went on a tour of Providence in the afternoon with a friend's daughter and another friend's wife, "an accomplished lady of great humour and affability." He was persuaded to stay one additional night in town because his tavern was having "dust kicked up" where he would "have the pleasure of seeing the young ladies [a dance]."

September 30: at the dance, his partner, "the finest lady in the room, was Miss Polly Brown, an excellent dancer . . . we were happy enough this night, broke up the dance at one O'clock, saw my partner home."

October 1: "this day passed very agreeably paying visits to the ladies [he had met at the dance]."

October 2: before leaving, Gregory "did some small errands about town such as goodbye my sweetheart."

October 3: in Newport, he "drank tea at Turner's [a coffeehouse] with a couple of fine ladies."

October 4: Gregory left Newport by ferry; his "fellow passengers [were] two ladies with whom I was quite agreeable."

October 7: after experiencing some problems with his horse for two days, Gregory went to a Killingworth, Connecticut, tavern where he danced with a "couple of fine hale lassies." He left this party for another "where there was finer girls than we left."

Gregory arrived back in New Haven the next day, presumably a tired but happy man. It appears that at no time in his trip did he engage in any sexual activity beyond kissing, but the two weeks reveal an endless stream of meeting and chitchat with local women and female travelers. They also reveal that both he and "the ladies" lived in a society that indulged flirtatious banter and made a game of it.

Nathaniel Ames, a Harvard-educated physician, had more substance and character than either Ashley or Gregory. After graduating from college in 1761, he returned to his Dedham home to study medicine with his father. He also took advantage of Dedham's location near Boston, his network of friends from Harvard, and his own high social status to pursue an active social life much of which consisted of traveling to nearby towns to call on young women. For over a decade Ames's leisure time consisted of an ongoing round of dances, parties, and meetings with ladies none of whom he courted in the strict sense of the word. His outings were more like modern dates than preliminaries to a marriage proposal. In all of this he behaved with decency and apparent decorum. After his parents died, however, Ames, now in his early thirties, began to reflect on his "solitary situation." The peripatetic social life as one of the area's most eligible bachelors appeared less attractive, and he made a conscious decision to seek a wife. Shortly afterward, at age thirty-four, he was married.[22]

Not only young adults wrote of flirtation and the charms of the opposite sex. Fourteen-year-old John Boyle of Marblehead came to Boston to be apprenticed to a printer; he filled his diary with appraisals of women "whose qualifications are better conceived than experienced" or who were "well qualified to make their husbands happy" or "made a splendid appearance." Precocious ten-year-old Anna Winslow gossiped salaciously in letters to friends and family. "Dear Mama," she wrote: "I suppose that you would be glad to hear that Betty Smith who has given you so much trouble is well and behaved . . . but the truth is, no sooner was the 29 Regiment encamped upon the common but Miss Betty took herself among them (as the Irish say) and there she stayed with Bill Pinchion." Esther Edwards Burr, the third child of Jonathan Edwards and an intensely pious woman, was not abashed to engage in teasing wordplay that would undoubtedly have shocked her father. Kidding a friend who had just become engaged, Burr wrote: "So madame, you are about business I see . . . but, stay, *did you use to like widowers?* This is a new doctrine to me."[23]

It is difficult to look at many diaries in the second half of the eighteenth century without finding either examples of courtship becoming a recreation or examples of people condemning it as such. Men were more inclined to write about it than women, but the new views of courtship may have been of greater importance to women and signaled a change in their status. Historians of women's culture have recently argued that the ideal woman of seventeenth-century New England sought God at an early age, prayed and fasted, kept a journal of pious instructions, nursed the ill, submitted her will to man's, and conversed primarily on spiritual or family matters. In the early eighteenth century a new ideal began to emerge. The "genteel lady" of refinement did not necessarily replace the submissive woman of piety; rather, she added another set of virtues to the old ones to create a new, composite ideal. The new lady could charm at dinner-table conversation as well as minister to the family's needs and souls. Feminine charm, graciousness, ease, softness, sensitivity, and so forth began being added to definitions of the virtuous woman. One sees this most clearly stated in funeral sermons eulogizing beloved women. Ideal women, of course, still should be pious, but they should additionally have these new graces, and nowhere could such graces be better displayed than in social situations. The ideal woman emerging in the eighteenth century was expected to charm as well as to help men.[24]

Religious thinkers of the eighteenth century also laid less stress on Eve's sin, making of her more a friend, a soft, loving partner—a victim herself—and less a temptress. In this they were following the work of John Milton, from whom they liberally quoted; Milton had been one of the few Puritans to soften Eve's image and find virtue in her. A 1792 poem entitled "Female Character" suggests how far from a Calvinist definition some New England romantics were prepared to go.[25] In particular, the word choice is revealing:

> Queen of every gentle passion,
> tender sympathy and love,
> perfect work of Heavenly fashion
> miniatures of charms above.

Seventeenth-century Puritan thinkers would have been horrified by the concepts of "perfect work" and "miniatures of charms above" being applied to any human; "gentle passions" would have been regarded as an oxymoron.

## The Triumph of Romance

As changes in the definition of the ideal woman became more woven into daily life in the second half of the eighteenth century, marriage, too, underwent alterations in meaning and perception. In general, eighteenth-century theorists became more inclined than their seventeenth-century predecessors had been to emphasize love and downplay fear as an appropriate force to bind society together. This imparted a new tenderness, a new dynamic to the relationships between men and women—and especially to courtship and marriage. By the Revolutionary era, a body of thought described marriage as an institution designed for pleasure, recreation, and happiness: Puritan theologians had argued that joy in marriage came primarily from fulfilling one's duties. An essay published in a 1774 issue of a Boston magazine stated the new concept in terms that rejected the businesslike realism of a Puritan marital contract. A married person "by giving pleasure . . . receives it back again with increase. By this enduring intercourse of friendship and communication of pleasure, the tender feeling and soft passions of the soul are awakened." It is hard to imagine these terms being used to describe an ideal New England marriage a century earlier. Puritans would have regarded the language as an invitation to indolence and as placing an unacceptable emphasis on worldly emotions. The absence of cautions, warnings, and statements of duty would have been equally alarming. In other eighteenth-century literature, wives appeared as companions and as pleasure-givers, and marriage was more like "the school of affection," as one commentator wrote, rather than a mere sensible partnership. Affection and pleasure, of course, did not mean vice, luxury, and dissipation but instead deeper, nurturing feelings based on friendship and virtue.[26]

Changing ideas about women and marriage had a symbiotic relationship with changing patterns of courtship. The seeking of a soft, tender, charming companion required a different process than selecting a partner for the arduous duties of managing a family. Physical beauty, wit, and personality matched piety and social rank as appropriate qualities men sought. Women who had a good supply of looks and charm could use them to great advantage in the rituals of romantic courtship. Nowhere was this revealed more than in a curious type of literature that emerged in Revolutionary America. Ballads, poems, and essays celebrated the virtues of beautiful women who used their desirability to reward heroic, brave young men and even more so to punish Loyalists and cowards. One young woman poet wrote that marriage with someone not sufficiently patriotic would "propagate a race of slaves." With no apparent embarrassment, she refused (in the poem) to take a man to "my virgin bed [until] freedom's foes are dead." Some young women went so far as to take group oaths not to accept the attentions of men who were not anxious to fight for and defend their rights.[27] Real or apocryphal, these stories reflect a cavalier brand of courtship that has more in common with romantic images of Revolutionary

Virginia or the pre–Civil War South than with the seventeenth-century Puritan world.

Quantitative and demographic data add more support to the conclusion that romantic courtship grew steadily after 1720 and became the norm by the second half of the eighteenth century. Parents exercised less and less control over marital arrangements as the century progressed. By the Revolutionary era young people chose their future partners; the approval they asked for was more a blessing or endorsement than a parental decision. Women increasingly married out of rank order: younger sisters did not wait for their parents to arrange the marriages of elder sisters. Men and women also showed a greater willingness to marry into social classes above or below their own than they had earlier, when parents had found it appropriate to bargain with social equals. Rates of premarital conception, which had increased steadily but slowly over the seventeenth and early eighteenth centuries, shot up sharply after 1730, reaching a peak of 30 percent, the highest of any period in American history including all decades of the twentieth century. Moreover, these high rates characterized all social classes and age groups in the childbearing years—unlike rates in modern America, which are disproportionately higher for poor people and teenagers. One recent scholar argues that with premarital sex so prevalent, the late eighteenth century may have been the most "free" period of sexuality in American history. In the early nineteenth century, rates of premarital conception dropped to near their seventeenth-century lows under the influence of religious revivals and a new standard of purity that Victorian Americans created for the ideal woman.[28]

To paint a picture of a scarlet Revolutionary New England awash in sexual sin would distort historical reality as much as do the dreary grays used to drape Puritan New England in joyless hypocrisy. Revolutionary and Puritan men and women alike found much pleasure in their interaction with the opposite sex, believed in a Christian ideal of morality, and frequently failed to live up to their own professed standards. Nevertheless, though "red" and "gray" overstate the contrast, a change of extraordinary proportion did take place in the way in which men and women conducted themselves toward one another. Romantic courtship, and all that it entails—choice and dating, banter and flirting, kissing and sex, love and treachery, heartbreak and joy—became one of the leading recreations among young people in the second half of the eighteenth century; its effects reverberated throughout society.

# VIII

# Drinking and Socializing: Alcohol, Taverns, and Alehouse Culture

Puritans had a straightforward attitude toward alcohol: moderate use was good; immoderate use was evil. Most of their European contemporaries shared this view in the seventeenth century, and most of the western world still does today. Thus, in abstract terms, the morality concerning the consumption of alcohol posed no problems to Puritan ideology. Used in an appropriate manner alcohol was socially beneficial, relaxing, sanctioned by Scripture, even healthy. Used in an inappropriate manner, it destroyed body and soul, ravaged the family and community, and was an abomination in the eyes of God and the commonwealth.[1]

When Puritan thinkers moved from theory to reality, however, simplicity of principle gave way to complexity of practice. How to prevent moderate drinking from becoming immoderate posed challenges to both moralists and magistrates. When and why did beneficial social drinking cross the line to turn into the scourge of drunkenness? Inevitably it did for some people. Consequently, society had to be vigilant in devising structures and rules to minimize the number of those who crossed the line and to detect and punish them. Thus, New England's laws and traditions about alcohol were created by men who loved a glass of beer but abhorred a drunkard. This thought contained no logical contradictions, but it did contain the seed of many problems.

## Consumption of Alcohol

Respectable people from all groups in early New England society consumed alcohol, children, women, and ministers among them. Alcohol was served at virtually all occasions, including ordinations, funerals, and regular Sabbath meals. Puritans, like most Englishmen, harbored doubts about the safety of drinking water and considered it an unappealing alternative. "Drink no longer water," the Apostle Paul had admonished in his first Epistle to Timothy, "but use a little wine for thy stomach's sake and thine oft infirmities." Recent experience in England also taught the Puritans that water could be hazardous to good health. On the other hand, alcohol—particularly beer and fermented juices—was thought to be helpful in warding off certain diseases, such as scurvy and dysentery. The Plymouth Pilgrims stocked the *Mayflower* with an ample supply of beer—which, the captain feared, would be consumed entirely by the passengers and crew on the way to America, leaving none for the seamen on the return trip. Governor Bradford himself yearned for a "small can of beer" after falling ill upon landing. John Pond, a servant to Governor Winthrop during the first year of Massachusetts Bay's settlement, wrote his English father asking for three things he could not buy in his new home: butter, a certain type of cloth, and a "hoggshead of malt unground for we drink nothing but water." Pond did not have to suffer long; within two years of the founding of Boston, settlers brewed beer in most towns.

Throughout colonial New England's history, beer remained a popular beverage, but by the middle of the seventeenth century fermented cider overtook it and became the most popular drink for the remainder of the century. Cider was easier to press than beer was to brew; New Englanders also preferred its taste and thought that it was healthier, particularly for women and children. Neither cider nor wheat was commonly distilled; instead, local millers fermented them as they did the juices from almost every fruit that could be grown or picked wild in the countryside. Perry, the drink made from pears, was the third most popular. Fermented drinks usually had a low alcohol content compared to distilled spirits, so relatively large amounts could be consumed without causing noticeable ill effects on behavior or judgment. At meals, family members drank pressed juices, which often had undergone some degree of fermentation and contained at least a small amount of alcohol. Beer, less ubiquitous at meals and usually higher in alcohol content, was consumed by children and women in small amounts.[2]

Distilled alcohol and wine fit into a different category and played a lesser role in daily family life. Regarded as more masculine drinks, they were considered to pose a greater danger to public safety. Rum enjoyed the greatest popularity by far among New Englanders who drank spirits. West Indian rum was being produced in the Leeward Islands and Jamaica by the 1640s and was exported to New England, where it was prized above all others. Most regions of New England distilled their own rum by the middle of the century and also produced local brandies from apples, peaches, and cherries. Englishmen on both sides of the Atlantic believed that distilled liquor, particularly rum and brandy, was good medicine for people who were chilled and that men working in cold weather should take a dram before going outdoors. At mid-seventeenth century, New England produced a small amount of wine, primarily from currants, but imported the majority of its wine from Portugal. Wine consumption remained relatively low in the seventeenth century compared to drinking of beer, cider, perry, rum, and brandy.[3]

## The Puritan Ordinary

Settlers drank alcohol at home as a regular part of meals, but from the beginning they also consumed some in taverns. Boston's first tavern, or "ordinary," as most of the seventeenth-century ones were called, opened in 1631 with a license to sell beer; by 1638, a second one sold beer and a third was authorized to sell spirits and wine in addition. By 1648, five ordinaries could sell beer, wine, and hard liquors, and eight others could sell beer and fermented drinks, for a total of thirteen places where the public could legally gather to drink alcohol in a town of approximately three thousand people. During the 1630s and 1640s, as ordinaries were being opened in Boston, Cambridge, Salem, and other Massachusetts towns, the General Court passed a series of laws regulating conduct in them; dancing, singing, bowls, and shuffleboard were prohibited, strangers frequenting ordinaries had to be reported to the magistrate, and prices for food, drink, and lodging were set by the General Court and had to be prominently displayed. The court, of course, outlawed drunkenness and made both the tipsy patron and the ordinary-keeper who served him liable to prosecution. Local residents could not spend more than half an hour a day in an ordinary; travelers could exceed this limit since they lodged on the premises for the night.[4]

Connecticut, New Haven Colony, and Rhode Island soon followed Massachusetts' lead. In 1644, the Connecticut government ordered each of the first three towns, Hartford, Windsor, and Wethersfield, to keep an ordinary for "strangers and passengers that upon occasion have recourse to these towns and are straightened for want of entertainment." As part of this order, the court provided penalties for bad behavior or excessive "tippling." All three towns complied with the court's directive within two years. Ann Scott, a widow, opened Hartford's first ordinary in 1644, and a second one opened the following year. In 1645 New Haven passed a similar law requiring towns to have and regulate ordinaries. Two years later in 1647 Rhode Island passed its first large body of laws regulating in detail how ordinaries should be run. "No tavern, alehouse or victualling house should be kept without license," the colony government decreed. But, in keeping with its decentralized structure, Rhode Island gave its four towns the authority to issue licenses at the local level. Tavern-keepers, however, had to post sureties that they would "keep good order" and not allow "unlawful games such as carding, dicing, slide . . . and not to suffer any townsmen to remain tippling therein for one hour's space" (thus doubling the time Massachusetts allowed its residents). The court also wrote with a directness and pith that required no amplification: "drunkenness is forbidden throughout this whole colony."[5]

Thus, by mid-century, New England's colonies had each enacted bodies of laws that licensed and regulated ordinaries, or "public houses," as they also were frequently termed. The authorities' interest in requiring them stemmed as much from a need to provide lodging and food for travelers as from the desire to provide centers for relaxation where townsmen and strangers could imbibe alcohol. Yet all ordinaries did have licenses to sell beer and/or liquor; and they were all open to local residents. They need not have been if the needs of travelers were the only concern. Ordinaries were indeed *public houses*. Most of the early ones were quite small—a couple of rooms set aside in a large house—and most maintained a quiet and decorous atmosphere. Few court cases arose from disturbances in them. Favorite locations were in town centers near the meetinghouse, on docks along the harbor, on intertown highways at strategic spots, and at ferry slips.[6] In retrospect, the ordinary served as a fitting symbol of Puritanism's ideal of appropriate leisure: modest, moderate, peaceful, and useful.

## Provincial Taverns

Beginning in the 1660s, however, ordinaries increased rapidly in number and began to change character. Several factors lay behind the growth and changes: population increase and dispersal, safer and easier overland travel, and a loosening of some of the strict regulations governing the sale of liquor. Entrepreneurs started most of the new taverns, but in a few cases either the colony or the local government commissioned people to open them. For example, by 1665 a string of six taverns—about one every eight miles—lay on Massachusetts' most important highway south, the "Bay Path" to Cape Cod. At the end of the Path in Falmouth, however, no tavern existed at Ferry Point where travelers had to wait for the ferry to Martha's Vineyard. The General Court ordered the ferry-keeper to open an ordinary to provide food and drink and gave him some financial support to do so.

Ordinaries dotted all the important highways connecting regions and major towns. A New York almanac listed the taverns between New York City and Boston in 1697: twenty-six of them lay on the 274-mile Boston Post Road, which stretched south from Boston through Rhode Island and west along the Connecticut shoreline. Distances between taverns ranged from four miles to two thirsty gaps of twenty and twenty-four miles. Roughly every ten miles one could expect refreshments and lodging. By 1725 the most-traveled highway in western New England, which ran fifty-four miles from Springfield through the Connecticut River Valley to Hartford and then south to New Haven, had twelve taverns.[7]

Coastal fishing villages and urban towns joined those on major highways in having the largest number of taverns. In particular, seaports had many; in the 1670s, Marblehead and Salem, for example, with populations of fewer than four hundred people had eight and fourteen taverns respectively. As early as 1675, Cotton Mather complained about an undue proliferation of ordinaries; so did the Reverend Nathaniel Saltonstall of Haverhill, who called them "pest houses and places of enticement" in a bitter complaint to the Salem town court. By 1714, Boston's population of ten thousand could choose from among thirty-four taverns, which served liquor and offered lodging, and forty-one additional places that retailed liquor to take out. Thus, seventy-five businesses sold or served alcohol. Colonial Boston seemed to have reached a maximum threshold of taverns in the early eighteenth century: from 1714 through the end of the century, the number of taverns stayed virtually constant, hovering at about thirty-five despite a doubling of the population between 1714 and 1776. This was about a third of the number in New York and Philadelphia in the second half of the eighteenth century. But if Boston had fewer taverns than comparable cities in other regions, it still had enough for Governor Thomas Pownall to complain that "every other house [was] a tavern."[8]

Although the number of taverns leveled off in Boston early in the century, it did not do so in other towns, which lagged behind Boston in urbanity but began to catch up in some areas, among them the opportunity to drink liquor. Newport had twenty taverns in 1723 but by 1774 had thirty-four, thus pulling even with Boston despite having only half as many inhabitants. Hartford, one of Connecticut's co-capitals, had twenty-four taverns by mid-century. Average-sized towns usually had one tavern in their first couple of decades, two to four in the next couple of decades, and several more by the time they were a half-century old. Table I shows the number of taverns in twenty-two towns for which data are readily available in the second half of the eighteenth century. Although the number varied considerably, every town had at least three taverns, and most had several more. Towns with large transient populations—ports, capitals and county seats, villages on highways—tended to have more; but some landlocked, isolated farming communities such as Farmington, Connecticut, or Princeton, Massachusetts, had many. There was approximately one tavern for every three hundred residents; if this ratio is projected to all of New England in 1790, it yields an estimate of nearly three thousand taverns for the region.[9]

Numbers by themselves, however, can be misleading. The word "tavern" varied in meaning from town to town and even within towns. In general, the terms "ordinary" and "public house" became less used in the late seventeenth century and were seldom used in the eighteenth. "Inn" and "tavern" replaced them. Inns in the eighteenth century (and also today) were thought of as places where people could spend the night as well as eat and drink. Taverns then (and also now) were thought of rather as places for social drinking, conversation, and relaxation. The terms thus had differing connotations in the eighteenth century but were used loosely both by towns issuing licenses and by patrons. Undoubtedly, a percentage of those three thousand taverns and inns would not have been thought of by contemporaries as gregarious centers of revelry. Many of them were small, a room or two set aside in a house where the proprietor lived with his or her family. Owners of places such as these made their primary income from another source—farming, retailing, and so forth. Running the tavern combined part-time work with public service.[10]

However, by the late decades of the seventeenth century enough taverns of the other sort existed to arouse notice and opposition. Drunkenness was always perceived as a danger and a sin that should be punished as both a civil crime and a church offense. One of Governor John Winthrop's famous decisions as a magistrate in Massachusetts required a notorious offender, Robert Coles, often punished for drunkenness, "to wear a red D about his neck for a year." Cole's scarlet "D," however, was unusual, befitting the worst recidivist in early Massachusetts. Courts customarily fined drunkards five shillings for the first offense and ten for

## TABLE I
### Number of Taverns in New England Towns
### in the Second Half of the Eighteenth Century[*]

| Town | Year | Taverns | Population |
|------|------|---------|------------|
| Boston | 1752 | 36 | 16,000 |
|  | 1769 | 32 | 18,000 |
| Hartford, Ct. | 1756 | 24 | 3,027 |
| Londonderry, N.H. | 1758 | 5 | 2,100 |
| Windham, Ct. | 1760 | 12 | 2,800 |
| Greenwich, Ct. | 1761 | 7 | 2,200 |
| Lyme, Ct. | 1768 | 19 | 3,400 |
| Nantucket, Mass. | 1772 | 13 | 4,412 |
| Newport, R.I. | 1774 | 34 | 9,208 |
| Coventry, Ct. | 1774 | 7 | 2,800 |
| Princeton, Mass. | 1775 | 5 | 701 |
| Weston, Mass. | 1776 | 6 | 1,027 |
| Great Barrington, Mass. | 1776 | 4 | 961 |
| York, Mass. | 1776 | 8 | 2,742 |
| Bolton, Ct. | 1776 | 4 | 1,000 |
| Danbury, Ct. | 1776 | 5 | 2,600 |
| Wethersfield, Ct. | 1776 | 8 | 3,500 |
| Winchester, Ct. | 1783 | 5 | 600 |
| Glastonbury, Ct. | 1790 | 8 | 2,732 |
| Kent, Ct. | 1790 | 7 | 1,318 |
| North Brookfield, Mass. | 1790 | 3 | 1,100 |
| Farmington, Ct. | 1790 | 13 | 2,696 |
| Wallingford, Ct. | 1790 | 8 | 3,373 |

[*] See note 9 for the sources for this table.

a second; they gave a public whipping to go along with a fine for the third. Fines and whippings were not to be taken lightly, but by and large, drunkenness in the first thirty years of New England's history, although one of the more frequently committed crimes, was not regarded with the same horror as were fornication, thievery, contempt of authority, and contempt of religion. Magistrates saw more danger in crimes associated with drunkenness than in drunkenness per se. Thus, intoxicated men who abused their wives or children were dealt with harshly by the courts. And herein lay the real danger perceived: abuse of alcohol invited abuses of a more vile nature. Mere drunkards could be readily forgiven if they reformed. Thus, when the infamous Coles, convicted over a half-dozen times of the same crime, managed to stay sober for two months, the court allowed him to remove the red "D" despite the fact that the original sentence had not expired.[11]

Church discipline could be as embarrassing or consequential as punishment by civil authorities. Churches admonished drunkards publicly and often expelled them from fellowship. Yet ministers and congregations were inclined to be forgiving if presented with evidence of real reform. The Reverend John Fiske of Wenham, Massachusetts, kept a detailed notebook describing the cases that came before his church for discipline. Drunkenness ranked high on the list, particularly if it involved collateral sin. Thus, Fiske was more inclined to expel a communicant who drank spirits on fast days or drank to excess on the Sabbath than he was to excommunicate a person whose sole offense was to be frequently found drunk. Fiske also viewed some of the excuses for drunkenness he received with a mixture of horror, skepticism, and amusement. He listened patiently to Edward Kemp's explanation that he had only drunk rum on a fast day to keep company with a desperately ill man who needed nourishment but would not eat alone. The starving man could not be found. Kemp's act of alleged altruism was detected when he "found himself much overcome with wind" and made loud noises shortly before vomiting in public. But the church received a reformed (and presumably quieter) Kemp back into Christian fellowship later in the year.

Ministers themselves could fall victim to the temptations of drink. The Reverend Samuel Stone of Wethersfield, the son of the distinguished, revered Hartford minister of the same name, became a scandalous drunkard shortly after his ordination in 1666. Despite his well-known problem, Stone served as Wethersfield's assistant pastor until he died in a fall while allegedly drunk in 1693.[12]

Before the 1660s, drunkenness was not a major problem in New England. A few people drank to excess, they were accordingly punished, and if they showed signs of reformation they could regain respectability. Ministers tended not to spend much energy denouncing alcohol abuse; they had bigger concerns. In the 1660s, however, drunkenness became a more serious problem and received more attention from moralists. Three groups gave particular offense: adolescents, visiting sailors, and servants. Young people posed the greatest problem since they were most numerous and could not be identified as outsiders but were the children of the present and the leaders of the future. Court records became choked with stories of minor crimes associated with adolescent drinking: fighting, disturbing the peace, fornication, and vandalism went hand-in-hand with alcohol abuse. Sailors—particularly those visiting from England—were less numerous but more ill-behaved and violent. In the summer of 1687, two major riots broke out in Salem when drunken English sailors and local residents brawled in the streets. Coastal towns had three times as many alcohol-related crimes as landlocked ones. Servants also sometimes had a footloose quality that made them more likely to drink too much without being too mindful of the consequences. All the New England colonies forbade servants from drinking in taverns without their master's approval, but enforcement of these laws proved difficult.[13]

Not surprisingly, Increase Mather led the rhetorical charge against alcohol abuse. In 1673 he published: *Wo To Drunkards, Two sermons Testifying Against the Sin of Drunkenness: Wherein the Wofulness of that Evil and the Misery of all that are Addicted to it is discovered from the Word of God* (Boston). "Wine is from God," Mather wrote, "but the Drunkard is from the Devil." He defined drunkenness for his fellows as a state in which a person "is so overcome with wine as that he can neither speak nor act like a rational creature . . . when neither the head nor hand can do their offices aright." In a sequel published three years after *Wo To Drunkards*, Mather placed alcohol abuse in the standard form of a jeremiad: "When our fathers were *patterns of sobriety*," he preached, "They would not drink a cup of wine nor strong drink more than should suffice nature, and conduce to their health; men of later time could transact no business, nor hardly engage in any discourses, but it must be over a pint of wine or a pot of beer, yea so that drunkenness in the sight of man is become a common sin." In his private diary, Mather dwelled on drunkenness as much as he did in his public preaching. He noted examples of the ways in which the "unobservable Providence" punished notorious drunkards by accidents seemingly unrelated to their vice. In one instance an entire town was punished: "God shot an arrow into the midst of this town to testify to his displeasure against the sins of drunkenness and of multiplying alehouses." Stonington, Connecticut, the community in question, was a port with many taverns and a virulent smallpox epidemic.[14]

Other Puritan writers—most notably Benjamin Colman, in his opus on mirth, and Increase Mather's son Cotton—continued the attack on excessive drinking. "Above all deliver me from the drunken club who belch out noisy revelry," Colman pleaded, "nothing is so noxious as a merry drunkard." In 1726 Cotton Mather and twenty-two other Massachusetts ministers published the capstone to a half-century of writing about the ills of tavern-haunting: *A Serious Address to Those who Unnecessarily Frequent the*

*Tavern* (Boston). The ministers described the insidious process by which tavern-haunting stole one's soul. "Don't you run the hazard," they rhetorically asked their readers, "of being drawn on, before you are aware, from a mere transient chat over the glass, to a tarrying long at the wine, from taking a sip to swallowing down a draught, and from one draught to another, until at the last, it bites like a serpent and stings like an adder?" This question laid bare the problem Puritan moralists saw: moderate, healthy drinking inevitably seemed to be luring more and more New Englanders into immoderate, sinful drinking, and the taverns served as the most frequent venue for men and sometimes whole communities to be "brought into this snare."[15]

When Mather et al. penned their warnings, well over a thousand such snares existed in New England. Throughout the colonial period, political leaders created a vast body of legislation to regulate taverns and to minimize alcohol abuse. When problems did not go away but continued to grow, new laws would be added to the old ones. Seldom were old laws repealed: ineffectual ones stayed on the books, surviving as historical curiosities long after they stopped being enforced.

Many people were barred from spending time in taverns or buying liquor retail, among them all Indians, known alcohol abusers, servants without their masters, and children without their parents. Known drunks would have their names "posted," which meant that a selectman or justice of the peace required local taverns to display a public list of people not to be served. At first in both Massachusetts and Connecticut the colony government issued liquor licenses, but within a few years the two orthodox Puritan colonies adopted Rhode Island's practice of assigning the licensing power to the towns, which were expected to revoke any taverner's permit if he or she did not behave responsibly. And responsible behavior did not mean merely maintaining surface order: Massachusetts, Connecticut, and Rhode Island each passed laws stipulating how long local residents could spend in a tavern and how much they could drink. Constables could and did visit taverns to enforce compliance. Tavern-keepers themselves were virtually deputy constables by dint of their responsibility for keeping good order. They had to report troublemakers—"those who carry themselves uncivilly"; frequent patrons—those who spend "their time and estate by drinking and tipling"; and, of course, any "common drunkard." At times tavern keepers and magistrates disagreed on the meaning of "drunkard." After one troubling case in which a man appeared drunk but had consumed only a small amount of liquor, Massachusetts considered passing a law defining drunkenness but then decided not to. More courageous and probably less practical, Plymouth Colony did codify the term. In 1660, its General Court wrote: "By drunkenness is understood a person that either lisps or falters in his speech by reason of overmuch drink or that staggers in his going or that vomits by reason of excessive drinking, or cannot follow his calling."[16]

In the eighteenth century, the New England colonies continued to tinker with the laws regulating taverns. Magistrates increased fines to keep pace with inflation and occasionally put drunks in jail for short terms; licenses remained subject to revocation; and constables continued to drop in on taverns for inspections. By 1750, however, they stopped whipping offenders or placing them in stocks. They also set regular opening and closing hours to replace the previous laws restricting individual consumption, and proper decorum became more loosely defined. Community standards, especially in urban areas and on busy travel routes, created a more permissive atmosphere in taverns. Yet in the 1780s all the New England colonies still passed new legislation dealing with tavern regulation and drunkenness. And of course, for nearly the next two centuries—until the late 1960s—drunkenness was the number one crime for which men and women were jailed in New England.[17]

Despite ministerial misgivings, elaborate legislation, and public contempt for drunkenness, the tavern grew to be one of the primary institutions for socializing in eighteenth-century New England, rivaling home and church. As a symbol of the changes that overtook the sober Puritan ordinary, eighteenth-century taverns usually had colorful, evocative names borrowed from the boisterous tavern life of secular Whig London. The Bag of Nails, Cat and Wheel, Goat and Compass, Pig and Carrot, Bull and Mouth, White Lion, Bull's Head, and Bunch of Grapes were all found in mid-century Boston or the surrounding area. Taverns in smaller towns copied the practice. Urban taverns tended to cater to a specialized clientele; both rural and urban establishments varied greatly in atmosphere and quality.[18]

## Alehouse Culture

Newport, Rhode Island, New England's second-largest city, developed the region's first sophisticated tavern culture. More secular and cosmopolitan at its inception than Boston, Newport traveled the road from a pietistic, communal village to a bustling entrepôt a decade or two ahead of the other capitals and large towns in New England. By the mid-1720s Newport, with a population of about four thousand, had twenty taverns, many of which had an ambience not found elsewhere in New England. The King's Arms catered to prominent merchants; Sarah Bright's Exchange Tavern was regarded as the social center of the town; the town council used Mary Nicol's inn as their informal meeting place. Newport had several social organizations—the Tuesday Club, the Convivial Club, and the Philosophical Club among them—each of which regularly met at a tavern with which it was associated. A few taverns were known to allow illegal gaming and most had a wide assortment of games that had once been forbidden but were now tolerated: bowling, shuffleboard, cards, backgammon, chess, billiards, and darts. Taverns stockpiled newspapers left by visitors. Patrons gossiped at length, and virtually no restrictions were placed on the number of hours they could spend sitting, talking, and drinking. In general, a ribald, raucous atmosphere prevailed in many taverns, particularly the larger ones. When a stranger walked into a few of the wilder places, the "bumper men," as regulars were known, called him over to buy them drinks and give them news. The bumper men would drink a toast to the stranger's health in return and welcome him to their tavern society.[19]

Rowdiness, drunkenness, and overall bad behavior became problems for Newporters. Sober-minded members of the elite complained about rudeness and a lack of decorum, but to little avail. Bawdy talk and puns became standard tavern language. Drinking prowess became a matter of pride to many patrons. One wag offered a definition of drunkenness that differed sharply from Increase Mather's and Plymouth Colony's: "Not drunk is he who from the floor can rise again and still drink more. But drunk is he who prostrate lies without the power to drink or rise." Newport's night watch, formed in the seventeenth century to stand guard against hostile Indians, pirates, and military attack, devoted its energies primarily to dealing with disorderly taverns. Sailors and local residents often brawled; beating up the watchmen became a sport for some visiting seamen.[20]

In general, Newport's taverns became centers of amusement in the early eighteenth century. Many of them hired professional entertainment or allowed patrons to put on their own shows either formally or informally. One keeper bought a trained baboon who did tricks for customers. Another employed a magician, who for a fee displayed "his art of lergerder-maine [*sic*] or subtle craft." One of the more respectable taverns had flute and violin concerts. Another had a singer "who sang with such a trumpet note" that one patron feared the walls would collapse from the vibrations. Shows in taverns ranged from animal imitations to discourses on mathematics and science. Patrons often were prevailed upon to do tricks or give "Jack Pudding speeches" about humorous subjects. Practical jokes abounded; strangers and locals alike found themselves the butt of tricksters. Even more unsavory than illegal gamblers, some prostitutes began to use taverns to transact business. One visitor to Newport described a ferryboat operator "with a tongue much faster than his oar" who informed him of opportunities to meet prostitutes in certain taverns.[21]

Newport's taverns played an extraordinary role in the city's social life. Although disparate classes and people mixed in the taproom, most Newporters frequented taverns that catered to their own social identities; they were able to select the atmosphere they wanted from a broad range of possibilities. In the 1730s and 1740s much of the rest of New England began to catch up to Newport. Taverns were ubiquitous in urban, small-town, and rural New England; but their position on the continuum that stretched from quiet inn to robust alehouse was primarily a function of the urbanity of their location. However, New England men and women from all classes and of all types gathered at taverns to have fun. Two rural Masssachusetts ministers, Ebenezer Parkman and John Ballantine, arch-conservatives on most matters of morality, frequented local taverns without a thought that the practice could compromise their respectability. As a serious, sober-minded young candidate for a clerical position in the 1720s, Parkman stopped in "sundry taverns" without worrying that this could effect his chances of getting a ministerial position. As a middle-aged pastor, he similarly saw no problem with having a bit to drink before church. "Having taken brandy and drunk some beer without staying to dine," he wrote matter-of-factly in his diary, "I went to meeting and preached sermon." John Ballantine saw nothing incongruous about excoriating some unnamed "minister from Billerica discovered to be guilty of intemperate drinking . . . how [such ministers] wound religion," and recording a few days later details of his own ample rum consumption in a tavern.[22]

Women travelers had no choice but to frequent taverns for food and lodging; in increasing numbers they also joined their male counterparts in using local taverns for purely social reasons. Certainly, women patronized taverns less often than men, but in the second half of the eighteenth century, as taverns expanded their functions to include some dancing and cultural entertainment, women could and did stop in for a drink without automatically being regarded as morally deficient. A local woman visiting a tavern would, however, almost always be accompanied by a man. A substantial number of tavern-keepers were women; male proprietors of small taverns often worked somewhere else in addition and left the part-time work of serving food and drink to the female members of their families. Widows of tavern-keepers frequently applied for and received the license that had been issued to their deceased husbands. Approximately a fourth of the tavern licenses issued by the Boston town meeting in the eighteenth century went to women. During war the percentage was higher. In 1776, twenty-three of Boston's thirty-five taverns were operated by women. Owners of large taverns quickly learned the value of having charming, friendly serving women to attract customers. Not uncommonly, travelers rated the attractiveness of waitresses in their diaries along with the quality of the food and atmosphere. Dr. Alexander Hamilton, a gentleman reputedly of great courtesy and charm, was a true boor in his diary entries about women he met while traveling. On a three-day trip he described women in five different taverns: "Betty, a jolly buxom girl," in Dedham; "a fat Irish girl, very pert and very forward," in Wrentham; "several young girls, the daughters of the women of the house . . . as simple and awkward as sheep," in Newport; again in Newport, "a handsome girl . . . most unaffected and best behaved country girl I had met"; and, on the way out of Newport, "Thankful, [another] jolly, buxom girl, the landlady's daughter."

Throughout the colonial period, taverns continued to be dominated by males but most would have some women present. Hamilton also described some women customers in taverns: "an old maid whom they called Miss Katy, being a great fat woman with a red face"; "a young, modest looking lady"; and "a walnut-coloured thin woman, sluttishly dressed and very hard favoured." It would not arouse any undue attention to find an elderly female proprietor, serving girls, a minister's wife having dinner with her husband, an elegant lady on a journey, and a twenty-five-year-old fun-seeking woman in the company of a male friend all sitting in the same tavern room.[23]

Drink itself changed in response to an expanded, diverse, and more sophisticated clientele. In the eighteenth century beer and ale regained their popularity in urban centers, and cider came to be regarded as a drink for rural people. In addition to these three staples, rum cocktails and Madeira wines became part of the standard fare available. Several rum drinks waxed and waned in popularity: bogus was unsweetened rum added to beer; mimbo or mim mixed rum, beer, and sugar; toddy and grog were heated rum combined with sugar and butter; and black-strap mixed rum and molasses. Flip became New England's most popular mixed drink in the eighteenth century. Flip was two-thirds beer, sweetened with sugar, molasses, dried pumpkin, and a measure of rum. Some taverns used cider instead of beer or included other ingredients, such as cream, eggs, nutmeg, or ginger. Exotic recipes were sometimes called fancy flip. The crucial part of flip making, however, came after mixing the drink: a red-hot chunk of iron shaped like a poker was plunged into the large flipmug, giving the drink a burned, bitter taste. Taverns kept the flip poker heated in the fireplace. Immensely popular, flip was served in huge glasses that could hold as much as two quarts. New Englanders also drank much punch; the name came from the Hindi word *panch*, meaning five, because of its five ingredients: tea, arrack, sugar, lemon, and water. Other fruit juices could be added, orange, lime, and pineapple among them. Alcohol, usually rum, liqueurs, or whiskey, was added to the five ingredients. Some taverns, people, and even towns became known for their special punches.[24]

Beers varied more than twentieth-century ones customarily do. Spruce, birch, sassafras, molasses, maple syrup, and apple parings were regularly used to flavor beer, and almost every plausible additive was tried occasionally. Similarly, brewers experimented with various grains. "Oh we can make liquor to sweeten our lips, of pumpkins, of parsnips, of walnut-tree chips," a tavern poet wrote proudly. There were more than ten types of apples, and consequently a similar variety of ciders. Other popular drinks included mead, made from fermented honey, herbs, and water; switchell made from rum, vinegar, and water; and ebulum, a combination of elder and juniper berries and whiskey or rum. Most wines were sweet and came from Madeira, Portugal, or the Canary Islands. Sack was a popular light-colored member of the sherry family; increasingly in the eighteenth century the term came to describe all sweet wines. Celebrants used "sack-posset" to toast the bride at weddings. Wines drunk in taverns were often mulled, which meant they had added ingredients and were served hot.

Eighteenth-century taverns varied physically as much as their liquor offerings did, but some general features characterized many of them. They had one main area, the taproom, for drinking and eating. Customarily, taprooms had a large fireplace, many chairs and tables, a bar, and a desk for making out bills. They usually had several signs with prices, other information, or cute sayings many of which dealt with the extension of credit: "[M]y liquors good, my measure just, but honest sirs I will not trust" was a popular one. "I've trusted many to my sorrow," another read, "pay today, I'll trust tomorrow."

Large taverns often had a dining room, adjacent to the taproom, in which full meals were served at specified times. Diners sat together, paid a set rate, and passed dishes communally among themselves as if they were members of a family. People eating at other times or wanting a snack, ordered and ate in the taproom. Large taverns also had adjacent rooms set aside for use by groups or special parties. Sleeping chambers were on the second and third floors of the taverns; there might be one room or a dozen. In the middle and late eighteenth century, many large urban houses were converted into taverns. Tavern-keepers usually were substantial citizens of prosperous means; a well-located, commodious tavern produced a sizable income.[25]

Sleeping in a tavern held the possibility of adventure. In a small seventeenth-century ordinary, travelers often slept either in the same room as the proprietor, in a room with members of his household, or in the public rooms after dinner and drinks were no longer being served. In a few eighteenth-century taverns this was still the case; usually, however, eighteenth-century lodgers shared private rooms with other guests, often people they had not previously met. Sometimes people had to share beds if the tavern was crowded. Guests of high social rank received preference for private rooms and for their own beds. People complained much about their roommates, bedmates, or neighbors. Sarah Kemble Knight, a woman of refinement who wrote one of the period's most charming travelogues about her trip in 1704 from Boston to New York, found herself unable to sleep one night because of a group of drunken revelers in the room next to her. She amused herself by composing a poem:

> I ask thy aid, O potent rum
> to charm these wrangling topers dum
> thou has their giddy brains possest
> the man confounded with the beast
> and, I, poor I, can get no rest.
> Intoxicate them with they fumes:
> O still their tongues till morning comes.

Few travelers did not have occasion at some point to complain of "roaring fellows . . . inspired by the great God, Bacchus," as one sleepless guest wrote. A traveling Englishman, William Gregory, was told that his bed had recently been slept in by the great evangelical preacher George Whitefield. That night he was awakened by an unanticipated stranger crawling in with him. "I bawled out," Gregory later wrote, "thinking old Whitefield had come from New York that night to disturb me on account of my pretended sanctity." Fortunately, his bedmate turned out to be a drunken sailor on his way back to ship from a husking frolic. "I hailed my unknown friend with, 'what cheer brother?'" to which the sailor replied "[D]amned good cheer" and then passed out. Gregory contrasted the sailor's behavior to that of his bedmate the previous night, "who came to bed to me and got up before me so that I know not who he was."[26]

A vain, arrogant dandy touring New England in 1771, Gregory penned one of the most ribald accounts recorded of tavern life in Massachusetts, Connecticut, and Rhode Island. On an eighteen-day trip through the region, he consumed an extraordinary amount of alcohol, often drinking to excess at every meal including breakfast. He continually joined others he met in the taproom, on the road, or in his evening chamber. One morning he and a large party of men had a roaring breakfast "refreshing themselves with gin." Later in the day in another tavern, he "got very intimate with a Scot from Jamaica after drinking plentifully of punch, toddy, and wine." That night in yet a third tavern he drank and played backgammon with a new set of companions. In the space of eighteen nights, he attended three dances in taverns and played his own violin one night to amuse others. Another night he called a rival violinist of limited talent "the string tormentor." Gregory complained about many things—food seldom met his superior standards—but often praised the women with whom he inevitably flirted. He hated the New England practice of tipping the various personnel: "[A]fter paying my landlord's bill and after satisfying the shoe boy, house maid, and all the rest of the fraternity of tavern biegles, I mounted Dick" (his horse). He also hated the practice of charging for additional services such as paying to "oat Dick" by putting the horse in a pasture for the night. Money matters angered Gregory most, particularly the fact that tavern-keepers did not seem to trust their patrons and would not extend credit even during one's stay. He noted with contempt one of the signs near the accounting desk in a tavern named the Rose: "He's a friend to the Rose who pays as he goes." The same day, Gregory refused to stay in another tavern whose keeper required payment in advance.[27]

Gregory invariably puffed a pipe as he drank and socialized. Although originally banned in taverns, smoking became commonplace in them by the eighteenth century. Men smoked pigtails of cut, dried tobacco in red clay pipes or corncobs. All classes of men smoked, including some ministers, but sailors enjoyed a particular reputation for being devotees of the "noxious weed." Respectable women did not smoke; if a woman was seen smoking it reflected very negatively on her character. Tobacco smoke hung heavy enough in eighteenth-century taverns to prompt many complaints and to inspire a satirical poem by James Franklin about the "nasty black pipe . . . [and] poisonous weed that crept in here."[28] Complaints about food matched those about the hardships of sleeping and enduring tobacco smoke. Consider Sarah Knight's reviews of her three tavern meals on her first trip outside of Boston. Her first night she was served a "dish of pork and cabbage, I suppose the remains of dinner. The sauce was a deep purple, which I thought was boiled in her dye kettle, I being hungry got a little down . . . what cabbage I swallowed serv'd me for a cudd the whole day after." Knight wrote a poem to describe her second night's meal: "May all that dread the cruel fiend of night keep on and not at this curs'd mansion light—tis hell, tis hell, and Devills do here dwell." Her third night, fortunately, was spent happily with friends; but her fourth evening meal matched the first two. "We called at an inn to bait," she wrote: "our landlady come in, with her hair about her ears, and hands at full pay scratching. She told us she had some mutton which she would broil . . . but I supposed forgot to wash her scratches: in a little time she brought it in; but it being pickled and my guide said it smelt strong of head sauce, we left it and paid."[29]

New Englanders seemed to love to complain about tavern food, rowdiness, bad beds, and rude staff; yet, these problems notwithstanding, they spent a lot of time in taverns and had fun doing so. Not only did drinking, eating, smoking, fighting, gaming, and joking go on; so, too, did dancing, concerts, and lectures. Traveling acrobats and magicians used taverns as a place to do tricks. A tavern owner in Salem, a colonial precursor to P. T. Barnum, had a series of "monstrous sights" on his premises, among them a walrus, a camel, a leopard, and a moose, a pig that did tricks, and several "deformed beasts." Merchants transacted business in taverns; local governments used them to draw lotteries; speculators auctioned lots in new town sites in them; town selectmen and councilors met in them; they were primary centers of communication and for the spread of knowledge; insurance was sold and sometimes goods were exchanged in them. A culture of "alehouse tales" produced an oral literature that held sway in the tavern. "Thieving lawyers" and "cuckolded husbands" provided the best subjects, as people gathered to swap stories and sing ditties.[30]

To romanticize the tavern culture that had developed in New England by the late colonial period would be easy. "Charming," "gregarious," "quaint," "democratic"—these are all terms that accurately describe the places where New Englanders went to drink, eat, sleep, and socialize. But as some New Englanders saw it, the fears of earlier Puritan moralists had come to be realized: as the ordinary gave way to the tavern, serious problems of drunkenness, loitering, neglect of duty, violence, and wastefulness did emerge. Some latter-day purists disapproved of alehouse culture almost as completely as Increase and Cotton Mather had. John Adams, a young old fogy who searched for opportunities to be a stick-in-the-mud, described Thayer's Tavern in Weymouth, where he went to meet some friends in 1760. "Every room, kitchen, chamber was crowded with people. Negroes with a fiddle, young fellows and girls dancing in the chamber as if they would kick the floor thru . . . fiddling and dancing of both sexes and all ages, in the lower room, singing, dancing, fiddling, drinking flip and toddy, and drams — this is the riot and revelling of taverns and of Thayer's frolics."[31] Adams did not approve of what he saw; but, he was there. And his description could serve beautifully as an advertisement for Thayer's as well as for all the taverns of the era. Undoubtedly, many New Englanders shared Adams's misgivings about alehouse culture. Yet they, too, were often there. The tavern became the new meetinghouse — a central social institution — where eighteenth-century New Englanders gathered to hear and spread not the Word, but the news; a place where food, drink, conversation, and entertainment ameliorated the stresses of daily living; and a community where individuals and families, neighbors and strangers, joined together in fellowship.

Section Five

# SPECIAL
# OPPORTUNITIES
# AND BARRIERS

# Men Frolic by Themselves: Sport and Games in a Male Culture

Societies express some of their most basic impulses through their attitudes toward sport and games. Like many cultural phenomena that may appear to be irrelevant diversions, sport and games provide a guide to beliefs and values buried beneath surface behavior. As recreational activities they can be a safety valve to let off collective steam, an avenue of escape from everyday reality, a ritual of community bonding, or a form of exploitation and social control; but sport and games cannot be detached from the specific intellectual and material milieu in which they exist.[1]

## English Sporting Precedents

The Elizabethan traditions in sport that supplied examples to the colonial world had their origins in the thirteenth and fourteenth centuries, the latter years of the Middle Ages. Medieval sports tended to be dominated by military considerations, as was most of feudal society. In the thirteenth century the wild mêlée of open-field mock battles, which had the nasty habit of turning into serious fights during the course of play, gave way to jousting tournaments held in small confined spaces. Attended by a large audience, these martial contests had the trappings of modern spectator sports: costumes for the participants; women cheerleaders, who supported specific contestants; partisan, cheering fans; clearly stated regulations; and promoters, such as monarchs or local nobles, who arranged and sponsored the events. Part theater, as is all modern sport, jousting tournaments took place between members of a secondary elite, the knight class, in front of a lower-class crowd made up of a mixture of yeomen and landless peasants. Tournaments took on herculean proportions. A fourteenth-century event allegedly involved forty thousand knights; another held in 1520 between partisans of the rival kings of England and France lasted three weeks. Over the course of the fifteenth and sixteenth centuries, individual battles between two rivals gradually replaced the large-scale mock combat. The battles frequently led to serious injury or death among participants and engendered rowdy behavior or rioting that could make being a spectator as dangerous as being a contestant. A perfect symbol of feudal values, jousting reflected the harsh realities of military life.[2]

England's second most important sporting activities, hunting and fishing, were also woven into its medieval history. Before the Norman Conquest, freemen hunted as they wished. The Conqueror, eager to extend his royal prerogative, set aside large areas as the "King's Forest," where game could be taken only with his permission. Eventually this area amounted to a fourth of England and included most of the best land. Previously, Englishmen from all orders — nobility, clergy, and commons — had loved hunting. But between the Conquest and the Elizabethan era, successive monarchs imposed an elaborate array of restrictions. Punishments for infractions included castration, dismemberment, and death. By the eve of colonization opportunities for hunting and fishing had virtually ceased to exist for anyone ranking beneath the gentry in the social hierarchy. Few bodies of law produced more anger among the peasantry than these regulating the King's Forest.[3]

A third category of sport in Elizabethan England, ball games, did not become commonplace until the late fourteenth century; before that ball games were associated with women and children. Among the French, however, ball games became popular in the late Middle Ages; Paris alone had 250 tennis courts at the end of the sixteenth century. Ball sports spread from France to much of western Europe, including England. As with martial sports and hunting, opportunities to participate varied according to social class. Tennis, handball, and bowling became extremely popular among the nobility, clergy, gentry, and wealthy merchants. Royal decrees forbade all others from playing them because they supposedly encouraged indolence. In any case, tennis and handball required expensive courts, which prevented anyone outside the elite from playing them. But bowling needed neither elaborate courts nor equipment and could easily be played in any open space. Hence, despite the royal restrictions, people from all classes often bowled, and justices of the peace tended not to enforce the prohibition against it.

Football became the ball sport of the English peasantry; by the fifteenth century it was associated exclusively with the lower classes. Villages challenged neighboring villages on festive occasions or several neighboring teams met in tournaments. Football required little equipment and rules could be adjusted to accommodate need. At times upwards of several hundred men competed under riotous conditions on mile-long playing fields that might stretch from one village to another and include all the territory in between. "Rough and tumble" would understate the nature of these games, which as a matter of course produced disabling injuries and great property damage.[4]

An even more violent Elizabethan pastime, the blood sports, or "butcherly sports," pitted humans against animals, animals against animals, or humans against humans in contests with the explicit object of inflicting pain, injury, or death. They involved outright cruelty or even torture; in bearbaiting and bullbaiting, for example, people teased and then killed the animals in front of cheering crowds. Men boxed with each other until one was seriously injured and could not continue; or they fought with cudgels and "broke heads." Cockfighting and dogfighting to the death were popular spectator sports, as was horse racing, by far the most benign of the animal competitions and the only one that did not truly deserve the name "butcherly."[5]

## Sports, Puritan Thought, and New England Practice

Thus, a wide variety of sporting practices characterized England in the late sixteenth century as the Puritan movement began to formulate attitudes about morals and behavior. Jousting tournaments had recently disappeared, metamorphosing into other martial competitions such as marksmanship, wrestling, and foot racing; these had some of the trappings of modern track-and-field events but provided less theater than the medieval jousts. Hunting and fishing retained their appeal but were more and more restricted. Ball sports remained rigidly segregated by class. And the blood sports appealed to all types of people—Elizabeth I loved bearbaiting—but especially to the lower classes.

By the end of the century, Puritans had become implacably opposed to ball and blood sports. They condemned them with the vehemence usually reserved for special evils such as theater or organ music. Puritans denounced these activities so heatedly and so often that the word "sport" to them came to mean ball games and bloody contests. Hunting, fishing, and martial competitions, of which they did approve, were defined out of the term. Hence, Puritan rhetoric seemed to condemn all sport, though in fact it did not.

Puritans' opposition to sport was grounded on at least seven propositions: sport was frivolous and wasted time; sport did not refresh the body as good recreation should, but tired people instead; much sporting activity was designed deliberately to inflict pain or injury; sporting contests usually led to gambling; more sport took place on Sunday than on any other day, so, sport encouraged people to defile the Sabbath; sport was noisy and disrupted others, sometimes entire communities; and many sports had either pagan or "Popish" origins.[6] Thus, Puritans based their contempt for sport (as they defined it) on sociological, humanitarian, and historical grounds as well as their belief that it failed their basic test for all recreations of being moderate and useful.

Additionally, sports became entangled in the political battles the Puritans waged as religious reformers against the Anglican church and as political reformers against the crown. To the Puritans, the greatest symbol of royal repression became the *Book of Sports*, issued in 1618 by James I and reissued in 1633 by his son Charles I. Read to the congregation from every Anglican pulpit, the *Book of Sports*, which attacked the cherished Puritan commitment to Sabbatarianism, stated that "no lawful recreation shall be barred to our good people." Regarded as an endorsement of sin, this royal support identified sports in the Puritan mind with both the Anglican apostasy and overweening political power. In particular, tennis and handball became associated with the idle nobility and the established church; football with pagan ritual and low-class criminality; and anything involving spectators with theater.[7]

New England's Puritans brought this intemperate hatred of ball and blood sports with them. Virtually no such sports took place in the founding generation, and surprisingly few in the next hundred years. Puritan conservative moralists were more successful in opposing relaxed standards for sport than they were for any other recreational activity with the exception of theater. At the end of the Revolutionary era in 1790, ball games, for example, were just beginning to lose their unsavory reputation and still had the capacity to call forth ascetic attitudes that had long since withered in other areas. The cultural historian Ralph Gabriel accurately summed up the progress of New England sport when he wrote that it grew "like a flower in a macadam prison yard."

Blood sports so obviously offend modern sensibilities that we have little difficulty understanding the Puritans' horror of them. Ball sports, however, are another matter. In the twentieth century, they appear innocent, even healthy, so the contempt they engendered in the seventeenth century is difficult to comprehend. It derived, however, not from the intrinsic activity of playing with a ball itself, but from what were regarded as the inevitable ancillary evils that accompanied ball playing and from the historical evils associated with it in England.

Colonies did not pass laws against ball and blood sports; public contempt sufficed to bar them. Persons playing in a ball game might not have been prosecuted unless they did so on the Sabbath or made enough noise to disturb the peace. But the activities were regarded as so abominable that they seldom took place. Their absence from diaries, letters, and journals of everyday routine speaks volumes. Even at places like Harvard, even during the militia gatherings that offered the greatest opportunities for young men to indulge in disreputable behavior, one does not find accounts of ball games occurring. In one of the few mentions of them, Governor William Bradford of Plymouth wrote about some workmen who were caught celebrating Christmas and committed a double offense by "openly pitching the barr and some at stoole-ball and such like sports . . . since which time nothing hath been attempted that way, at least openly." Bradford's counterpart Governor John Winthrop of Massachusetts enjoyed many recreational pleasures as a young man in England, but drew the line at ball games.[9]

However, the other two categories of English sport, fishing and hunting and martial contests, fared better in the move across the Atlantic. Both sets of activities fit comfortably into Puritan ideology: productive, useful, despoiling no one, they were a natural part of life. Fishing and hunting produced food, and martial contests improved military skills. Fishing and hunting took place without spectators; at martial contests the spectators were other soldiers.

The physical setting of the New World added to the popularity of these sports. Repeatedly, New Englanders used the phrase "howling wilderness" to describe their new environment. The seemingly endless forests and myriad of streams that vanished into the uncharted woods filled them with terror in both spiritual and practical senses. The Devil lurked in the wilderness, they believed, figuratively and literally. The savagery they associated with the woods provided a Satanic sanctuary, a home for the anti-Christ. Puritans pictured the woods as symbols of spiritual darkness and perceived the Indians as "men transformed into beasts," in the words of Reverend John White. Although intending no direct harm to the Indians, Puritans had no illusions about the need for constant vigilance. New England existed in a continual state of readiness for war.[10]

Military preparedness required men who could fight hand to hand, march and run, and shoot accurately, and who were in good health. Puritans marveled at the physical condition of the Indians, who all seemed to be beautifully muscled and able to perform extraordinary deeds of strength, endurance, and agility. With only a few exceptions, all New England men between the ages of sixteen and sixty met for military training on a regular basis, and martial sports constituted a crucial part of the training. In the morning, soldiers practiced and honed requisite skills. In the afternoon, officers held contests among the men. These involved competitions and rivalries far beyond the immediate needs of military training. Wrestling generated the most excitement. It had the drama of a genuine battle between men, but lacked the dreadful consequences of blood sports such as boxing or cudgel fighting. Wrestling's respectability can be seen in the fact that two of New England's best-known seventeenth-century wrestlers were respected ministers. One of the founding clergy of Connecticut, Reverend Henry Smith of Wethersfield, famed for his piety, was as well known to soldiers for his "delight in sports of strength." A brilliant preacher persecuted by the Anglican church hierarchy, Smith had a "merrie eye and sweet smiling mouth" at wrestling matches, even as an old man. Another minister, John Trumbull of Waterbury, Connecticut, frustrated by his militiamen's losses to the trainbands of another town, disguised himself and wrestled in an evening's match with a champion from the nearby town of Westbury. Trumbull won after a long contest that became legendary in the retelling.[11]

The wilderness and perceived savagery of the environment also had a positive side. Puritans freed from the welter of royal regulations that limited their fishing and hunting in England found themselves in an outdoor sportsman's paradise. From John Smith's exaggerated description in 1616 onward, Puritans celebrated the abundance of the environment. Paradoxically, "the Promised Land" was nearly as ubiquitous a phrase as "howling wilderness."[12]

Fishing immediately became—and remained through the seventeenth and eighteenth centuries—New England's most popular sporting pastime. Commercial fishing, of course, was one of the region's major industries. Few things could recommend a recreational activity more than the fact that godly men also pursued it as a respectable calling. The first generation of Puritans filled their letters and diaries with accounts of the pleasures and rewards of fishing. Near the end of the voyage over from England, Richard Mather, Increase's father, viewed the fish jumping in Cape Cod Bay as "marvellous merry sport" and a "delightful recreation to our bodies." A companion on the ship, Francis Higginson, described "an abundance of sea fish . . . almost beyond believing." Many echoed these sentiments, including critics such as Thomas Dudley, the deputy governor of Massachusetts, who thought the soil and climate overrated but the fish supply rich beyond expectations.[13]

All males seem to have fished in seventeenth-century New England. Two sober-minded deacons of the church, Thomas Minor of Salem, Massachusetts, and his son Manasseh, of New London, Connecticut, both near ascetic in most matters, delighted so much in fishing that they went all year round, including the frigid months of January and February. Samuel Sewall, an urbane curmudgeon if ever there was one, loved fishing from boyhood throughout his life. Harvard College did not officially allow much time for its students to indulge in leisure or recreation; the president and fellows customarily issued orders designed to restrict these activities. But they explicitly approved of "fishing and fowling" for Harvard students.[14]

Theoretically, sport fishing could offend moral sensibilities if men pursued it immoderately. Nothing in the sermon literature, however, suggests that any congregation was ever warned against excessive fishing or thought to be guilty of it. Commercial fishing posed spiritual dangers and created moral problems, as did all sailing trips because they removed crews for long periods from the restraints imposed by normal society. But sport fishing was the ideal pastime for men and boys. Unlike in England, it remained virtually unregulated. An early Massachusetts law guaranteed every resident "free fishing and fowling" except for restrictions that might be imposed by town governments. The only restraint on this blanket permission came later in the century, when limits were placed on catches of certain species during spawning season.[15]

The growth in population and in urbanity in the eighteenth century did not diminish fishing's popularity. New Englanders of all stripes continued to love the sport. Cotton Mather used examples from fishing to instruct his children on moral matters. Although decidedly no enthusiast, Mather himself fished occasionally when in the company of people who enjoyed it. Many travelers took fishing equipment with them and asked local residents for advice on locations and techniques. A young, nervous Harvard graduate, Ebenezer Parkman, who would go on to a sixty-year career as one of Massachusetts' most conservative ministers, described his first interview for a clerical position. "Prayers and breakfast ended," he wrote, "Mr. Winthrop and Mr. Flagg and I walked to a fine brook and fished. We caught salmon, trout, etc. These were well taken and we din'd richly on them." Winthrop and Flagg, the two deacons assigned by the congregation to host the minister-to-be, took the earnest young man fishing to get to know him and to entertain him. What may well have been New England's first sports association, the Shad and Salmon Club of Hartford, was organized in the 1780s to promote outings and a series of fishing contests.[16]

In Revolutionary Massachusetts, John Rowe, a major Boston merchant who made his fortune trading fish cargoes, provided posterity with a fitting symbol of the commercial fishing industry when he successfully introduced a resolution to hang a representation of the codfish in the state House of Representatives. Rowe's interest in fish, however, went beyond account books and politics. As a young man he was a near fanatical sport fisherman who usually recorded more than twenty fishing outings a summer. Rowe fished regularly with three or four cronies and meticulously recorded the type, size, and number of his catch each time. He also went on weekend fishing parties with several friends and their wives. Consider the following convivial trip:

> July 26, 1773. Went with Mrs. Rowe to Salem. We stopped at Newalls in Lynne from thence to Flex Pond. I fished there. I had very good sport. We reach'd Salem. We dined at Goodhew's tavern. July 27, 1773. Went with Mr. Inman and Duncan to Flex Pond. When we came there we found James Perkins and Sam Calef. [Later] we were joined by Mrs. Inman, Mrs. Rowe, the Rev. Mr. Nicholls, Jack Rowe, Jack Coffin, and Lewis Deblois. We were merry there. The men fished while the women dined under the trees.[17]

Although many men loved to trek through woods in search of game, hunting never rivaled fishing as a pastime among New Englanders. Neither did it enjoy the popularity it knew among England's elite. New England's forests abounded with game; few regulations limited access; and, of course, hunting could be productive and put food on the table. But two problems lessened hunting's appeal: the first was historical, the second technological.

To wealthy Englishmen, the word "sport" at times seemed nearly synonymous with hunting. The nobility hunted continually and had a vast assortment of props to help them: horses, dogs, hawks, falcons, gamekeepers, and so forth. Hunting was the subject of private letters, public discussions, and political disputes. Expert hunters wrote treatises and guides—even etiquette books—on it; hunters appear in virtually all of the literature of England. By contrast, fishing was seldom mentioned in literature or public discussions; the first English book on fishing was not published until Izaak Walton's *The Compleat Angler* in 1653. Hunting thus had a sense of mystique about it, but it also had an unsavory reputation as a wasteful sport of the rich, vain, and idle. Many of the more sober-minded businessmen and members of the gentry—the type of people who inclined toward Puritanism—saw that hunting was a consuming passion, one that people seldom pursued with moderation.[18]

Hunting also was a bad investment both in England and New England. Quite simply, it consumed more resources than it produced. The elaborate paraphernalia of English hunting made it too costly to yield a profit. In New England the expensive rituals of English hunting were not reenacted. But the muskets and skills of the settlers proved inadequate in most cases to make hunting a successful business proposition. One might assume that large animals such as deer and bears, which would yield a supply of meat, would be attractive targets for hunters, but big game was elusive and difficult to bring down. Birds proved a better bet and became more popular objects of prey. Wild turkeys, pigeons, partridges, and grouse were plentiful and easily killed with guns or trapped with nets and snares. New Englanders also hunted a host of varmints that afflicted crops, animals, or man. Wolves, rattlesnakes, groundhogs, crows, blue jays, woodpeckers, and blackbirds were among the pests on which small bounties were often placed. Young boys frequently hunted some of the more easily killed nuisances. In particular, New Englanders despised snakes and took pleasure in killing them. One large town, Norwich, Connecticut, paid out bounty on the extraordinary number of sixty-eight rattlesnakes in one year.[19]

In addition to some unsavory associations and its relatively low productivity, hunting could be dangerous. People occasionally got lost; accidents were not uncommon. Nevertheless, a large number of men, including many ministers, hunted for pleasure and profit throughout the seventeenth and eighteenth centuries. With the growth of white settlement, however, the animal population declined in most areas and the sport became even less productive. Sometimes this was welcome. Wolves all but disappeared from populous areas by the middle of the eighteenth century. In 1786, Norwich, which had so actively encouraged its residents to hunt rattlesnakes, paid a bounty for the first time in years; the victim was entered in the records as the last rattlesnake in town. The fragility of the land animal's place in the ecosystem was reflected by the population of the beaver, which was commercially depleted by overzealous trapping as early as the 1650s. With the exception of birds, wild animals played but a minor role in the New England economy, constituted a small part of the diet, and provided only a modest amount of recreation. By contrast, fish were basic to the economy and an important part of the diet; they provided ubiquitous recreation. Nor did the white settlers in the colonial period have any appreciable effect on the supply of fish, either along the coast or in the freshwater lakes and streams.[20]

## Eighteenth-Century Development in Sport

Fishing and hunting — as the Puritans did them — are classified by students of sport history as premodern sports in that they involve no spectators, rituals, or competitive rivalries and are based on ancient impulses related to survival. To some degree martial contests fall into the same category. English sports, which had already taken on many modern trappings, experienced transforming changes and developments in the Restoration period, after Charles II assumed the throne in 1660. By the beginning of the eighteenth century, organized ball sports with royal or noble patrons, paying crowds, paid players, betting entrepreneurs, recordkeeping, advertising, and prearranged regular schedules had emerged. Cricket, boxing, and horse racing drew festive crowds much as they do today. These events provided recreation for both spectators and participants. Track-and-field and swimming events with precise distances, weights, strokes, and rules replaced the heretofore informal martial contests. Sports heroes emerged: the boxer James Figg became a national celebrity in the early eighteenth century after winning all but one of three hundred publicly staged fights. English football and cudgel-fighting moved from irregular contests arising out of local challenges to regular events produced by promoters for profit. The vulgarity and violence of these events surpassed previous limits. One local noble at a cudgel fight put up a "fine broad gold laced hat to be cudgelled for with double stick; whoever breaks one head to have a shilling or more for each head he breaks." Scantily clad women, dwarfs, and men with wooden legs raced each other to provide diversions between the races for athletic men. Horse racing meets became boisterous affairs attended by much drinking and sexual promiscuity. English sport became a licentious, organized, violent, spectator-oriented circus by the end of the seventeenth century. By the latter part of the eighteenth century, the monarchy, established church, and leaders of polite society all felt constrained to use their authority, power, and moral suasion to check these excesses. Thus the period from the Restoration to the American Revolution stands out as the most raucous, ribald era of English sports history.[21]

To some extent the aggressive spirit of organized, competitive sports spread to the American South and to some other areas of English culture such as the developing society of Australia.[22] It did not, however, spread to New England. The very horror of the sporting specter in England confirmed the New Englanders' low opinion of ball and blood sports and spectator games. They redoubled their opposition to them and with only a few exceptions maintained the region's commitment to restrict these activities. Still, some changes and liberalization did occur.

Horse racing was the only organized spectator sport in eighteenth-century New England. Throughout the seventeenth century, militiamen had raced on horseback as part of their martial-arts competitions, but this was always done in the context of military preparedness and, of course, only on training days. More formal horse racing began in two areas of Rhode Island: urban Newport, which had New England's most cosmopolitan elite; and an area called the Narragansett country, which had a remarkably sophisticated gentry that patterned itself on the Virginia and South Carolina squirearchy. Both areas were atypical of New England. In the 1720s both began to provide horse racing not only to local residents but also to other New Englanders willing to travel to see organized, high-quality racing. By the 1730s promoters advertised meets weeks in advance, held dozens of races in one day, and hired professional riders, who wore special hats, boots, and the colors of their horse's owners. Much betting took place. The gentry from the town of South Kingston developed a special breed of horse, the Narragansett pacer, which became popular in the American South and the Caribbean as well as in Rhode Island.

Although less organized than in Rhode Island, horse racing began in Massachusetts in the same period. In the 1720s, Boston newspapers advertised races to be held a few miles outside the city. Massachusetts never officially outlawed horse racing, but did forbid it within four miles of any town center. By the 1760s horse races were held frequently at several sites in eastern Massachusetts adjacent to Boston and near some of the urban areas of Connecticut. No regular schedule of meets was arranged, but races were held frequently in those areas and advertised in advance. The festive crowds that gathered at these horse races behaved well and gave rise to no complaints of gross misconduct or rioting. By the eve of the Revolution betting took place everywhere men raced horses; although this was not officially sanctioned, neither was it prosecuted. In

New England, as in the American South, the most popular type of race was the quarter-race, which as the name suggests consisted of a quarter-mile dash. In contrast English races were usually several miles long.[23]

Ball sports made much less headway. Nine-pin bowling was the only game involving balls to be accorded even the slightest degree of legitimacy before the Revolution. Authorities did not usually punish bowlers in the eighteenth century, and some enterprising tavern-keepers promoted it to attract customers. It never became a commonplace activity, but neither did it shock most people. Bowling and other ball sports made their slow entry into New England society primarily through soldiers in the militia, mischievous adolescents, and the students at Harvard and Yale. Occasionally, commentators also made slighting references to sailors, young rowdies, or blacks playing ball games in the streets of port towns. During the Revolution, New Englanders encamped with soldiers from other colonies were more exposed to ball sports. The patriot troops outside Boston and Providence, lacking real bowls, used cannonballs for the sport, under the tutelage of visitors. With their neighboring comrades in arms, they also played more active ball games, including wicket, a form of cricket played with a long, shovel-shaped bat; shinny, a game like field hockey; fives, a game played by striking a leather ball with the hand; and a form of football close to modern American soccer. The hero-to-be Nathan Hale discovered that he loved football and was good at it. Similarly, at Harvard and Yale, where respectable young men also met visitors and ideas from other regions, ball games, particularly bowling and football, developed in the 1760s and 1770s. Thus, although ball sports did not become widely accepted or played in colonial New England, at the very end of the era they were on the verge of achieving legitimacy.[24]

Other recreational "sports of opportunity" developed late in the eighteenth century. Like ball sports, swimming for fun was primarily associated with rebellious adolescent boys or young men away from home with the military. Benjamin Franklin learned to swim as a teenager in Massachusetts and later amazed friends in England who did not expect a man of high social status to know how. Observers reported boys and sailors diving from ship riggings into Newport's harbor. But swimming did not constitute a commonplace or completely respectable sporting activity. Officers on bivouac with the militia worried about public nakedness—the troops customarily stripped off their clothes and jumped into the water nude—and about excessively boisterous play that gave offense to passersby. Officers and physicians also believed swimming in hot weather to be unhealthy; and, of course, naked troops frolicking in water were vulnerable to attack. George Washington, among others, tried to forbid it, but swimming proved too much fun to resist for troops deprived of many of life's pleasures. It became an accepted part of military life during the Revolution.[25]

The sports gaining marginal respectability during the Revolution joined wrestling, marksmanship, racing, fishing, hunting, and horse racing as part of an all-male experience. Sporting activity in colonial New England was limited for men, but the small amount that took place was also limited *to men*. Because of women's perceived delicate nature, society expected them to forgo unnecessary physical activity. Science and morality conspired to promote an ideal of womanly virtue that demanded modest, demure behavior and forbade anything that might be regarded as boisterous. In reality, of course, many women had to work hard; but strenuous activity could be justified only for necessity, not for enjoyment. Before the reform movements of the 1830s, no one seriously suggested that physical recreation for women could be morally acceptable or healthy. Most colonial New England women, for example, never went swimming in their lives. Society also discouraged them from foot racing, tree climbing, and other spontaneous activities. Nor were girl children or adolescents allowed a "tomboy" period before entering a more refined adulthood. In particular, social restrictions on exuberant play applied most to girls and women of high social status. Thus, the higher up the social structure girls and women were, the less likely they were to take part in physical exercise.[26]

The one exception came late in the colonial period. In the 1760s wealthy New Englanders of both sexes began to travel to mineral spas reputed to be effective for preventing and curing certain diseases. It was apparent from the beginning, however, that these outdoor baths were also being used for recreation. Elite Englishmen had long believed "the taking of the waters" to be healthy and relaxing. Puritans had believed this, too, but only a few New Englanders had the opportunity to go to mineral springs before the 1760s. Both Increase and Cotton Mather had tried a "noated" mineral bath in Lynne, Massachusetts, but they were exceptional. In September 1765, the *Connecticut Courant* announced that a spring of amazing curative powers had been discovered in northeastern Connecticut; hundreds of people flocked to Stafford Springs to bathe in its waters. New England's urban wealthy seemed primed to take advantage of these springs, probably because they knew of their popularity and allegedly beneficial effects in other colonies and in England. By 1766, a frenzy of interest had spread across southern New England, where the Connecticut springs were centrally located. Enterprising scientists and promoters quickly discovered other healthful mineral waters, and by the early 1770s a series of spas dotted the area.[27]

Patronized most heavily by the wealthy, who were willing and able to travel a day or two to get to one, spas also attracted nearby residents and other adventurous persons. Taverns near the various springs did a lively business in the warm weather; old ones expanded and new ones came into being primarily to accommodate the bathers. Mineral springs functioned as resorts, the first ones in New England's history. Both men and women patronized them, and although the purported reason for the experience was medical, everyone acknowledged that recreation played an equal role. Calling the bathing that took place "sport" or even "swimming" might be stretching the definition of either term. Usually the springs were not deep and did not permit much swimming beyond some slight paddling about. The waters were not hot springs, and bathers wore clothes that covered their entire bodies. Moreover, men and women bathed separately. So the practice of men and women swimming together at resorts began at the very end of the colonial period, permitted little real athletic activity, was defended theoretically as a medical treatment, and involved male-female interaction only in ancillary activities, not in the swimming itself.[28] The proverbial exception that proves the rule, spa activities furnished at best a minor opportunity for a small number of New England women to participate in sport. Though it is not usually thought of as a sport, dancing provided far more physical exercise to women than swimming did.

## Games and Gambling:
## Puritan Thought and New England Practice

When listing objections to a competitive sport, Puritans invariably included its propensity to promote gambling. Betting on the outcome of a contest was wrong, they believed—unequivocally wrong. Yet gambling, by itself, was not high on their list of sins and crimes. A relatively minor weakness in which many people indulged, gambling became a scourge only in association with more serious offenses such as wasting time, losing large sums of money, or neglecting duty. For example, although both cockfighting and horse racing were big betting sports, Puritans despised cockfighting for its unsavory promoters, bloodiness, and rowdy crowds, but only mildly disapproved of horse racing, which they did not link to the same social ills.

The first generation of Puritan colonists spent little time worrying about gambling in their communities. All five colonies—Plymouth, Massachusetts Bay, Connecticut, New Haven, and Rhode Island—passed laws against gaming, as they called gambling, but none dwelled on it. And for first infractions they imposed relatively light penalties, usually about twenty shillings, a substantial sum but less than the fine for allowing breaks in a fence or for disturbing the peace. Rhode Island's three-shilling fine for first offenders was little more than a nuisance. Moreover, each of the colonies aimed its antigaming laws primarily at those who gambled in taverns, where the dangers seemed more manifest. Alcohol, travelers, spare time, and gambling could combine to produce a potentially combustible mixture. Thus, tavern-keepers who permitted gambling received higher fines than the participants themselves and, of course, could easily have their licenses revoked.[29]

In practice as well as theory, gambling presented only minor problems during the early years of settlement. Constables brought few gambling cases before the magistrates. Compared to prosecutions for disorderly conduct, drunkenness, Sabbath-breaking, idleness, and swearing, gambling offenses were few. Those gambling cases that did come before a magistrate usually involved playing shuffleboard in a tavern. There were almost no other opportunities for betting: the usual subjects of gamblers in England—blood and ball sports—did not exist in New England.[30]

The colonies were being founded, however, just as another type of gambling activity was becoming prevalent in England. Playing cards originated in Asia in the first millennium—some scholars trace the game to the Chinese imperial court, others to India or Korea—but did not become known in western Europe until much later. The first set of cards historians can identify for certain appeared in 1392 at the court of Charles VI of France, for whom they were hand painted. Only gradually, however, did many Europeans become familiar with playing cards. In the fifteenth and sixteenth centuries they were associated primarily with the French nobility, but in the early seventeenth century cards became popular in England, and knowledge of them spread among all classes of Englishmen. By mid-century card games became the most commonplace type of gambling.[31]

As it did with several phenomena, the Restoration period carried recreational trends to excess. A country weary from a generation of religious disputes and civil war tried to repudiate its somber recent history by pursuing escapist pleasures. A veritable mania for cardplaying and other gambling swept England. Led by the "cavaliers" at the court of Charles II, many of whom had learned to love cards while in exile abroad, yeomen, apprentices, servants, elegant ladies at court—even some Puritans formerly known for abstemious behavior—joined in the craze. The future Queen Mary shocked her husband, William of Orange, when he discovered she played every day and willingly violated the Sabbath for a card game. The addiction of specific individuals and groups to card games became a favorite subject for satirists and social commentators. Charles Cotton's *The Complete Gamester* (1674) provided a detailed guide of rules and techniques for more than twenty card games.[32]

Not surprising, these developments in England fueled both fear and fascination among observers in New England. To some Puritan ministers looking on from the American side of the Atlantic, it looked as if the forces of impiety had triumphed over virtue in England and now threatened them. Increase and Cotton Mather both published sermons condemning cardplaying and gambling, as did several of their fellow ministers. In addition to the negative social consequences of gaming, the Mathers adduced two scriptural injunctions against it. When one played a game of chance, he or she implicitly asked God to intervene by silently invoking the Lord's name: "O, God, let me win," a gambler thought. This trivialized the Deity by requesting his intervention in petty, selfish matters, and it violated the Third Commandment by taking the Lord's name in vain.[33]

None of the Puritan governments passed new laws against gambling in the late seventeenth century, however; nor did they reissue and repeat old laws against it, as they often did to emphasize concern over a problem. On the positive side, cardplaying required skills that encouraged knowledge of arithmetic. Also, cards could be played without any wagering, did not use expensive equipment, were fun, and, in the final analysis, simply did not seem very threatening to good moral order if kept within bounds and out of taverns. Moreover, some officially sanctioned gambling of a sort had been present in New England from the beginning of settlement; proprietors often received land assignments by drawing lots for them. This precedent weakened the argument that gambling violated the Third Commandment.[34] Thus, to a degree that would surprise most casual students of Puritanism, cardplaying in New England became a commonplace, respectable activity in the early eighteenth century, a few decades after it took England by storm. Opposition to cardplaying, however, did not end completely. As late as 1756 a pamphlet published in Boston warned that cards would be the Devil's first choice "to teach our children how to wear out or stupify natural conscience."[35] But such dire warnings failed to carry the day and appeared quaintly anachronistic by the mid-eighteenth century.

Cardplaying proved especially popular with New England's lower classes, which had fewer opportunities than the elite for recreation, but it also appealed to people in all strata and occupations. In the 1730s several probate inventories of ministers' estates included playing cards; in the

1740s merchants advertised cards for sale in the Boston newspapers. Completely legal if not played for money, differing types of card games became associated with differing classes and groups of people.[36]

Whist was the most frequently played game in old and New England. Particularly popular with the upper classes in England, whist was so ubiquitous among the gentry and clergy that it became a staple of satirical literature used to lampoon them: "to cheat the thirsty moments, whist awhile," one wit advised a minister fighting boredom. People believed that whist required quiet concentration to devise strategy; hence its name: "whist" meant "silence." No one knows its origins for certain, but in England whist was first widely played in the 1640s. Its appeal to the elite rested somewhat on its snob appeal as a game reputedly for refined and intelligent players. *The Complete Gamester* provided a manual of rules for whist in 1674, and the first edition of *Hoyle's* guide to cards (1743) codified them for posterity. The third edition of *Hoyle's*, published at the end of the eighteenth century, contained rules for more than twenty games, but it devoted seventy-two of its two hundred pages to tips for whist players. Several varieties of whist developed, slam, and ruff and honours being the two best known.[37]

Whist appealed to the same constituency in New England as it did in England. Ministers, merchants, college students, and professionals embraced it as their game of choice. Women seldom played cards — the competition was thought to be inimicable to their nature — but elite women did often play whist, which seemed to be the exception to the rule. Card parties for several tables of players became popular in urbane social circles; these, invariably, were whist parties, at which both men and women played. Couples moved from table to table, playing several opposing teams in one evening.

In almost all ways whist was the ideal game for Puritan society: quiet, contemplative, and companionable, it required skills of logic and arithmetic; it could not be readily played in a rowdy atmosphere or under the influence of alcohol; and, unlike many games, whist needed no betting to make the competition exciting. In fact players seldom gambled on whist. Not likely to lead to other vices, whist met all the criteria for useful recreation. In the late eighteenth century, enthusiasts even developed a New England version of the game — "Boston whist."[38]

Of the twenty games whose rules *Hoyle's* outlined, four others — quadrille, all fours, cribbage, and piquet — were also widely played in New England. Each developed its own constituency. Quadrille, a game of four players — it was called ombre if played by three — was similar to but more elaborate than whist. A trump-and-trick game that used forty instead of fifty-two cards, quadrille lost popularity in the late eighteenth century because people regarded it as too complex and demanding. Not surprisingly, these same qualities recommended it to a small but loyal group of players.[39]

Two of the other three games, all fours and cribbage, were much less refined than whist or qaadrille, and the third, piquet, posed dangers in the eyes of conservative moralists because it alone among New England's popular card games was known to be conducive to gambling. *Hoyle's* called all fours, known variously as pitch, setback, or speculation, a "noisy round game requiring little skill." Popular with new cardplayers, servants, and young adults, it could be played easily in a lively atmosphere with many distractions. Cribbage enjoyed an even stronger reputation as a game for the lower classes. One of the few card games to originate in England, cribbage, invented in the early seventeenth century by the poet Sir John Suckling, was known in New England as a tavern game. Relatively simple and short, cribbage did require an ability to add quickly, which gave it some respectability and made it impossible to play for anyone who knew no arithmetic. Hoyle recommended cribbage as the best way to teach "young children in the science of calculation." By the middle of the eighteenth century, patrons played cribbage in most New England taverns; the antigaming laws were interpreted to make cardplaying in taverns illegal only if betting took place. "Friendly" games were acceptable.[40]

Neither whist, quadrille, all fours, nor cribbage enjoyed a reputation as a gambler's game. Piquet did. It also had other interesting qualities. A game of elaborate scoring that called for the subtlety, strategy, and memory needed for whist, piquet, like cribbage, required just two players at a time. Combining some of the attributes of modern rummy, such as melding, with some of the attributes of whist, such as trick taking, piquet, like quadrille, had a loyal but limited following. It had an unsavory reputation in New England and was perceived as the card game most likely to lead to vice. Its popularity was enhanced, however, by the fact that it required only two players.[41]

Nearly as informative as the card games played were the ones that were not. Quinze, a French game much like today's blackjack, was popular in England but not in New England. Pharo, lansquenet, and *rouge et noir* all routinely required betting and were games of sheer chance that involved no skills or strategy; virtually no one in colonial New England played them. Puritans disapproved of the game matrimony, the forerunner of modern pinochle, because they believed its terms mocked the institution of marriage. Thus, although card games enjoyed a great vogue and a reasonable measure of respectability, irreverent games or ones whose primary purpose was gambling were not tolerated.[42]

Nothing came close to matching the appeal of cards, but some other games did grow in popularity, particularly in the second half of the eighteenth century. Most of these had been frowned upon or prohibited by law in the seventeenth century; they achieved acceptability slowly in the face of grumbling but ineffectual opposition. In the first generation of settlement, most of the tavern-keepers fined for permitting gaming had been charged with allowing shuffleboard on their premises. Slide, as the popular game was called, gradually became part of the culture of nearly every taproom. By the middle of the eighteenth century no one seemed to think ill of it. Billiards went through much the same evolution in public opinion, but because billiards equipment was more costly and required more space, the game appeared only in larger and more urbane taverns. Backgammon became a popular game among gentlemen in the late colonial period. People viewed backgammon rather as they did whist, as a polite game of the elite; but unlike whist, backgammon had no women players. A variety of dice games became popular in Restoration England's taverns: among them inn and inn, passages, and hazzard (the forerunner of modern craps). None of these became even marginally acceptable either in or out of taverns in colonial New England. Reputedly sailors and servants gambled at dice and did occasionally play huzzle-cap, a game of pitching pennies against a wall, but these games remained furtive, a part of the subculture that functioned outside the bounds of respectability.[43]

The relative softness of Puritan opposition to gambling was reflected in the New England colonies' ambivalent attitude toward lotteries. English Puritans had made limited use of lotteries under controlled circumstances. William Ames, the Cambridge scholar who shaped much of the reform theology that New England Puritans brought with them, wrote that public (as opposed to private) lotteries "might haply be so ordered, that they might be lawful, namely if there were any need of a contribution to some pious use." As mentioned previously, New England's town founders often determined land assignments by drawing lots. Some mid-seventeenth-century merchants and taverns held lotteries without being prosecuted under the antigaming laws. As part of the movement to resist the perceived erosion of piety, however, ministers in the late seventeenth century unequivocally condemned lotteries as pure gambling — "scandalous games," Cotton Mather called them in 1693. A public lottery for a good cause, he wrote, with a uniquely knotted twist of logic, was worse than a private lottery held sheerly for gambling purposes, because the public one made the gaming table "a sacred thing" and elevated it to the level of a pulpit.[44]

Massachusetts, Connecticut, Rhode Island, and New Hampshire all passed laws in the eighteenth century prohibiting lotteries, but lotteries did not go away and no prosecutions took place under the laws. Public sentiment did not support the beliefs of the conservative magistrates on the matter. After unsuccessfully trying for a generation to eliminate lotteries, all four colony governments gave up and reverted to the philosophy of William Ames that public lotteries could be harnessed to promote good causes. Connecticut allowed companies of land speculators to distribute by lotteries all the lands of six new towns being settled in Litchfield County. Potential investors met in taverns, where they bid at auction for shares in the proposed town; after all shares were sold, each buyer "pitched" for his land assignments by drawing a lot. The Massachusetts government held a lottery in 1744 that raised £27,500 for military defense of the seacoast. This great financial success opened the floodgates to an outpouring of public lotteries. Connecticut raised £50,000 in 1747 to build new housing for Yale students. After this lotteries became accepted practice in Connecticut. The General Court authorized towns to hold them for a variety of civic purposes: laying out new streets in Hartford; clearing the Housatonic River of obstructions; building a lighthouse in New London; and so forth. Connecticut authorized at least one lottery per year but insisted on strict controls and accounting. The colony government established a rule that 85 percent of monies raised had to be paid out as prizes. Massachusetts and New Hampshire pursued similar lottery policies. Rhode Island, with a smaller population and fewer towns than the other colonies, became more active in the lottery business. In the 1760s, the Rhode Island General Court authorized three or four lotteries a year and occasionally allowed private citizens to hold them to recover financial losses from disasters such as shipwrecks or fires.[45]

In 1769, as part of its program to reorganize the empire, the British Parliament forbade lotteries in royal colonies, thus bringing a brief end to them in Massachusetts and New Hampshire but not in the charter colonies of Connecticut and Rhode Island. Ironically, England, a country reputed to be wallowing in hedonistic excess, ordered allegedly ascetic New England to stop publicly supported gambling. The prohibition was short-lived, however. During the Revolution all the colonies used lotteries frequently to raise money for troops, defense, provisions, and other civic needs. Buying lottery tickets became a sign of patriotism, much as buying war bonds would be in the twentieth century. In the late 1780s, cash-short Massachusetts held a huge land lottery of unprecedented proportions. Land for fifty town sites in present-day Maine, then an unsettled area of northern Massachusetts, was to be drawn for by lot from among 2,270 tickets authorized to be sold. Tickets cost £60 and every purchaser was guaranteed to win something ranging from the first prize of 21,760 acres (an entire town site) to 1,366 prizes of 160 acres each. The lottery ended up a financial failure in the eyes of the government: fewer than half the authorized tickets were sold. The £60 price was too high and the quality of land too low. Nevertheless, a frenzy of excitement gripped the entire New England region on October 12, 1787, the day of the draw.[46]

### Fishing and Whist

Lotteries and land; fishing and whist. Perhaps nothing captured the essence of the Puritan experience more accurately than the evolution of sport and gaming over two centuries of New England history. On the eve of colonization, England and Europe stocked a bulging storehouse of competitive activities for reformers to winnow as they transplanted Old World culture to new soil. Many of these activities engendered conduct anathema to Puritan values. English sports and games were often violent, noisy, destructive, wasteful, even cruel; they pitted man against man, divided communities, and were swathed in impiety. For a people intent on building a virtuous society, English sports and games provided stark examples of what not to do.

On the other hand, sport and gaming had much to offer a people who believed in the need for leisure and recreation. The Puritan settlers faced the task of setting New England on the path to virtue by separating the good from the bad. They did this in the world of sport and gaming with more confidence, less ambivalence, and greater consistency than they demonstrated in many other areas. By and large Puritans evaluated the goodness and badness of sports and games by historical and empirical criteria, not by scriptural or theological argument. Puritans despised boxing and bearbaiting because of their cruelty. They knew ball sports did not necessarily have to be wanton and destructive, but they also knew that historical evidence suggested they usually were. Fishing was more productive and less dangerous than hunting. Whist was more refined than cribbage, less likely than piquet to lead to gambling. Ideological considerations played a small role in deciding which sports and games to accept and which to reject. A practical tough-mindedness guided the process.

And the process was successful. New England's sports and games reflected the values Puritanism prized. Fishing and whist embodied virtues that John Winthrop, Samuel Sewall, and John Rowe could agree upon. Of course changes took place over the seventeenth and eighteenth centuries; these changes liberalized practice, and some conservatives thought the changes went too far. But the basic moderate, peaceful, companionable virtues that Puritans insisted be part of the culture they planted in the New World continued to suffuse the sports and games of the Revolutionary era. A consistent thread of wholesomeness ran through colonial New England's entire sport and gaming experience, and stood in stark contrast to the ripe excesses of Restoration and Georgian England.

# X

# The Fragmentation of Social Experience: Age, Gender, Location, and Social Class

It is a simple question often put to travelers abroad: "What do Americans do for fun?" But it does not usually prompt a simple answer. Another question—"Which Americans do you mean?"—is a likely response. Over 250 million people live in the present United States, and their recreational activities vary enormously. Much of the variety stems from personal preference: some people like to lie on the beach, some like to run marathons. But the variety also stems from opportunities dependent on age, gender, social class, and location. "What do kids do nowadays?" "Why do women have to work outside the home and still do most of the housework?" "How do the rich and famous live?" "Why do people move to suburbia?" These clichéd questions are often posed by the mass media. Despite their sophomoric quality, the questions presuppose a fundamental truth: personal vital statistics have a tremendous influence on behavior in all areas of life—including leisure and recreation.

"What did colonial New Englanders do for fun?" Although the New England colonies were relatively small and homogeneous compared to twentieth-century America, age, gender, location, and social class played conspicuous roles in providing and restricting opportunities for relaxation; and as

New England grew in size and social complexity so did the importance of these variables. Puritan communalism imposed a degree of uniformity on everyone's experience in the founding era. As religious intensity waned, the weakened communal fabric proved less effective at restraining secular forces unleashed by the rise of cities, the amassing of great wealth, the emergence of a class of poor people, and the development of an extensive network of retail services. Dissenters such as the Baptists and Quakers, the evangelical fragmentation spawned by the Great Awakening, and finally, the questioning spirit engendered by the American Revolution shattered any lingering pretense that an ideological consensus still existed in New England. Without such a consensus, the varied social characteristics were free to express themselves in a variety of behaviors. In the heterogeneous world of the eighteenth century, personal circumstances determined to a large extent how one had fun.

### The Young and The Old

"The child's toys and the old man's reasons are the fruits of two seasons," the poet William Blake wrote. His comment on the opposing ends of the life cycle had a particularly ironic application to seventeenth-century Puritanism. New England's religious theorists argued—in a vein directly contrary to Blake and to twentieth-century beliefs—that the very young and the very old were the two groups who should be most attentive to duty and least inclined to waste time on frivolous activities. The concepts of innocent childhood and of earned leisure during retirement were foreign to the Puritan mind. Children were not innocent spirits to be indulged; they were products of innate depravity, who must learn the lessons of life during infancy before their sinfulness hardened to become their essential character. At the other extreme, old people should be preparing for death and hence should be unusually virtuous. The old were expected to be wise and close to God as well as to death; hence, vice or undue levity was particularly offensive if found in them. By old age the passions should be tamed. Thus, the stages of leaving and arriving in the earthly world both had serious purposes in Puritan thought.[1]

Formal toys tell us much about how a society views childhood because they are manufactured by adults for children to use. Differing societies favor differing toys. In the late nineteenth and early twentieth centuries, for example, board games emphasizing money were popular. After World War II, parents bought military toys for boys and stylish dolls for girls. In the 1960s and 1970s space toys enjoyed a vogue. As far as anyone can tell, however, *no* toys for children were manufactured in seventeenth-century New England. Children, of course, will make toys out of their surroundings; but New England's adults did not provide them with any. This may seem astonishing, but it is consistent with Puritanism's somber view of childhood.[2]

Not only did children have no formal toys but, equally important, parents "must not make use of them as playthings," the English philosopher John Locke wrote in a treatise that captures the essence of what scholars call the Puritan-evangelical strain of child-rearing. By "humouring and cockering them when little," Locke argued, parents corrupted their children forever. "When children are too big to be dandled," he warned, parents then will have reason to complain that "the brats are untoward and perverse." Locke made famous, or infamous, what New England moralists had argued throughout the seventeenth century. The Puritan John Robinson's influential child-rearing manual of 1628 had put the matter directly: "[I]t is natural for parents tenderly to love all their children; yet it is wisdom to conceal their inordinate affections."[3]

Puritan rhetoric was remarkably consistent in the area of child-rearing; by virtually any standards, it advocated harsh, repressive training. Children were enjoined to love and fear their parents and their God. Yet in reality Puritans may not have differed dramatically in their treatment of children from other seventeenth-century Englishmen in the Home Isles or elsewhere in the colonies. The formal child-rearing treatises quoted by Puritans were written by religious leaders intent on reforming the world along biblical lines. In practice, women did more of the child-rearing than men did; Puritan diarists who reminisced about their childhood often referred to their mother's affection, softness, and tender love. Fathers were remembered as more harsh, more to be feared, but also more remote. Thus, mothers kept the love half of the injunction nearer to the child than the fear half. Fathers, too, often reflected a gap between theory and practice. Cotton Mather, for example, took the effort in his diary to collect his thoughts on child-rearing into a section he entitled, "Some Special Points Relating to the Education of My Children." Mather identified ten rules for raising properly trained children none of which mentioned tenderness, play, or leisure. If his dealings with his children had been governed strictly by his own rules, the relationship would have been joyless; it was not. Mather's diary is full of accounts of his children's play and of his playing with them. Mather also wrote about the depravity and wickedness found in all children, including his own. Yet he loved and doted on his children, marveling that they were "hearty and handsome," "lovely and lusty," and "comely." Puritan moralists feared precisely this contradiction between

Mather's language and actions. Despite being aware of the need for strictness, parents were inclined to soften their treatment of their children. Sermons warned people to resist the temptation to spoil children. And the word "spoil" expressed the expected consequences literally: early indulgence risked "spoiling" one's future life.[4]

The historian Philip Greven has identified two additional views of child-rearing that existed in the Protestant thought of the seventeenth century. Greven termed the first "a moderate model," in which love and fear were replaced by love and duty, and the second "a genteel model," which emphasized love and reverence for the child. The moderate model toned down the fierce authoritarian repression that men like Robinson recommended, but was essentially a softer version of the evangelical method. Moderate views characterized a minority of households in New England from the beginning of settlement onward and did provide an alternative emphasis if not an alternative system. The great theologian John Cotton, for example, sounded more moderate than many of his fellow ministers or than John Robinson. Children should "spend much time in pastime or play," Cotton wrote, because "their bodies are too weak to labour and their minds to study are too shallow." Other distinguished ministers advocated some degree of play but often in the give-with-one-hand-take-away-with-the-other rhetoric that reflected their serious misgivings or fears. Benjamin Wadsworth, the author of *The Well Ordered Family*, a treatise on domestic relations, agreed that "time for lawful recreation now and then, is not altogether to be denied . . . yet for such to do little or nothing else but play in the streets . . . is a great sin and shame."[5]

The genteel model of child-rearing began to emerge in New England at the end of the seventeenth century and tended to be espoused by affluent, educated, and socially eminent families. A much more indulgent method and a real alternative to the evangelical model, the genteel view downplayed the effects of original sin and innate depravity and emphasized instead the salutary effects of love on the development of a child's personality. Genteel parents believed that parents should not hide their love from their children but should instead continually show it by showering them with affection. The genteel model also unambiguously emphasized the importance of play for children. Indeed, as one moved on a continuum from the Puritan-evangelical to the moderate to the genteel models, the acceptance of play as an appropriate — even a productive — activity increased directly.

All three forms of child-rearing existed throughout the colonial period and survived into the nineteenth century, but the moderate and genteel views grew in popularity in the eighteenth century. No one can say with certainty when the repressive mentality of the evangelical model retreated into a minority position, but by the middle of the eighteenth century this was the case. Nothing summed up the harshness of approved child-rearing techniques in the seventeenth century better than *The New England Primer,* by which children of both sexes were taught to read and write. The twenty-six couplets it used to teach the letters of the alphabet are chilling. Nine of them deal with death—"the Cat doth play and after slay" or "Youth forward slips, death soonest nips"; others dealt with physical punishment—"the Idle fool is whipt at school" or "Job feels the rod yet blesses God"; and none could be regarded as endorsing play. In 1750, however, a rival to the revered *Primer* was published in Boston. The title of the new text speaks volumes: *The Child's New Plaything: Being a Spelling-Book Intending to Make the Learning to Read a Diversion Instead of a Task.* The authors taught the alphabet humorously through a drama based on a food treat. "A" was for "Apple-Pye"; "B bit it," "C cut it," and on in the same vein.[7]

What an extraordinary change. The appearance of a few formal toys also evinced this change. Virtually every boy had a spinning top by mid-century. No one would suggest that an alternative reader or a couple of toys meant that late colonial childhood became an idyllic time of fun and play.[8] Few organized recreational activities or games were designed specifically for children; those that were for the most part took place in urban areas among the children of the elite. Parents still expected submission, respect, and attentiveness to duty and chores from their children; they continued to dress them like miniature adults from the age of six onward. Yet the concept of modern childhood as a special time to play as well as to learn emerged over the course of the eighteenth century. At the end of the seventeenth century, children in the first decade of life were the persons most controlled by society; at the end of the eighteenth century, they were the persons most indulged.

The concept and experience of adolescence and youth similarly reflected a gap between theory and reality that narrowed in the eighteenth century. No period of adolescence—of appropriate youthful kicking up the heels—existed in formal Puritan ideology. Society placed adult demands upon children at early ages. Apprenticeships for boys and training in domestic skills for girls started between the ages of six and eight. Customarily both sexes were moved out of their homes and into another household for this training. Children over six who violated laws answered for their conduct in regularly constituted courts; no juvenile justice system existed. At age fourteen orphans could choose their own guardians; boys aged sixteen were required to serve in the militia.[9]

This burden of responsibilities, when coupled with the absence of any writing about the concept, has led some historians to suggest that adolescence did not exist in seventeenth-century Puritan culture. But it did—and the teens and early twenties were times of greater frivolity and more play than any other ages. Adult behavior for the youthful was the ideal; somewhat less than adult behavior was both the reality and the expectation. The reality of heightened play may be seen in a variety of sources. Court records show a bulge in prosecutions for idleness, carousing, sexual misconduct, and the like among young people. Travelers describe youthful social life as an exception to what was perceived as an otherwise dreary existence. And staid, morally upright adults often looked back with conscious horror—it is tempting to think, with subconscious pleasure—at the "infirmities, foolishness, and wickedness" of their youthful behavior. The large number of sermons directed against what was regarded as excessive and licentious play among young people, particularly young men, shows that although moralists never condoned this behavior, they accepted it as an inescapable fact that characterized the decade of life stretching from age thirteen or fourteen into the early to mid-twenties. In the eighteenth century, the notion of this special decade for leisure and recreation gained some legitimacy just as the concept of indulgent play for young children did among parents embracing the genteel method of child-rearing.[10]

Adults created no special recreational activities for youths in the seventeenth century; to do so would have amounted to a tacit endorsement of inappropriate behavior. Even in the eighteenth century, teenagers and young adults participated mainly in the same activities as other adults; young people merely pursued them more energetically.

Nor were any special recreational opportunities created for the elderly. Virtually all scholars agree that Puritan rhetoric extolled the virtues that came with age and demanded that the elderly be given respect and good physical care. Puritans honored the past, and of course they honored the makers of the past—the elderly. But both the ideological and material spheres of seventeenth-century New England provided impediments to anything remotely resembling a leisurely old age.[11]

In general Puritan morality exalted values associated with hard work, self-sacrifice, productivity, and piety. As the members of society closer to God than anyone else, the elderly had a "peculiar acquaintance with the Lord Jesus Christ" that came from a lifetime of worship and from a spiritual proximity as life on earth neared an end. Consequently, Puritans expected the elderly to personify the appropriate values and to set examples of worthiness for the rest of society. Retirement would have constituted an unthinkably bad example of idleness, as would any undue attention to leisure or recreation. Benjamin Colman's analysis of abuses of mirth targeted the young because they were most likely to offend. However, Colman saved his greatest contempt for the wicked elderly; the old seldom did abuse mirth, but when they did it was "more vile and horrid" because of the "abominable and pernicious example" it set. Cotton Mather at age twenty-six listed six virtues the aged should have in particular: sobriety, gravity, temperance, orthodoxy, charity, and patience. Mather did not even pay lip service to the concept of relaxation. As an old man he expressed views consistent with those of his youth. At age sixty-two, in his *Brief Essay on the Glory of Aged Piety* (Boston, 1726), Mather reiterated his earlier beliefs and cautioned others against "childish and frolicsome sort of carriage." The young "cannot reverence you unless your grave looks as well as your gray hairs demand it," he warned the fellow members of his generation.[12]

Thus, society enjoined the elderly to work hard, look serious, and act solemn. Old people also had heady responsibilities in a hierarchical society that turned to them for leadership and in a farming society where they usually owned the land—the means of production—until their deaths. Revered in rhetoric by their children and grandchildren, the elderly also inspired some hostility and envy in those who may have been forced to depend on them virtually until their own old age. In the early and middle years of the seventeenth century, men usually retained ownership of land resources until their death: children, forced to forgo independence, remained economically beholden to their elders. Beginning in the late seventeenth century and continuing over the eighteenth, a pattern developed of parents transferring some portion of land to children at earlier stages of life. But as long as they remained able, men shouldered heavy responsibilities for economic productivity.

Old women did not have the same control over daughters, nor did they have as many intergenerational economic responsibilities. New Englanders did not live in extended families consisting of several generations under the same roof. So old women ran their own domestic affairs, if they were able, but not those of their children. Old women were, of course, expected to be as grave, somber, and pious as old men were. Since old women tended to outlive their husbands, they often had to be supported by their children.[13]

Health problems created yet another impediment to leisure and recreation in old age. The gentle poet Anne Bradstreet, who took such delight in her family, friends, and life in North Andover, Massachusetts, found few pleasures in her old age, which she described in the following verse:

My almond-tree hairs doth flourish now
and back once straight, begins apace to bow
my grinders are few, my sight doth fail,
my skin is wrinkled and my cheeks are pale,
no more rejoice at music's pleasant noise
But I do awake at the cock's clanging voice.
I cannot scent savors of pleasant meat
nor savors find in what I drink or eat.
My hands and arms, once strong, have lost their might
I cannot labor nor can I fight.

Anne Bradstreet was luckier than most: she was lucid and ambulatory. In a world that made far greater physical demands on bodies than does our world today, and where medical care could do little to prevent or mitigate the problems of aging, the loss of strength, mobility, teeth, and general capacity was both more likely and more devastating than is the case today. Little could be done to ease pain. Words such as "decay," "infirmity," "deformity," and "weakness" were used constantly both by themselves and by others to describe the condition of the elderly. Revered by rhetoric, powerful in economics and politics, the elderly did not lead lives rich in possibilities for leisure and recreation.[14]

## Good Women, Sisters, and Shoppers

Early New England presented a more austere face to women than it did to men. Many of the activities that furnished men their greatest opportunities for leisure or recreation were barred to women: militia training, commercial sailing and fishing, political meetings, and sports. Women traveled less than men did; they received less education; and their daily routine usually kept them closer to their homes and exposed them less to the stimuli that the external workplace could provide. Moreover, Puritan religious and social thought combined to swathe women in a somber gauze designed both to protect them and to prevent boisterous expressions of joy, of levity, or of self. "Good women" appear uncommonly in Puritan documents—usually on three occasions: birth, marriage, and death. Only troublesome women such as Anne Hutchinson had enough impact to leave many footprints in the records.[15]

Always feared in Puritan theology as possible temptresses, women shouldered more of the burden of original sin. To contain the potential Eve that dwelt within them, women, even more than men, had to exemplify high moral standards. Historians who have compared Puritan views on women to those of Quakers and Anglicans are surprised by how much more the ideal Puritan woman was expected to suffer in silence—almost to the point of personifying perpetual sorrow—and to set an example of worthiness as a pure custodian of virtue. The Scriptures and biology united to promote this view. Puritan ministers often quoted from Genesis (3:16), which provided a grim description of women's lot: "Unto the women, He said, I will greatly increase the sorrows and thy conceptions. In sorrow shalt thy bring forth children."[16]

Men socialized with other men in the public activities associated with economic, political, and military life. In a parallel vein, women socialized much with other women, but in less visible and more private ways. Several historians have argued that in the nineteenth century American religion became feminized: women joined and attended church in greater numbers than men because church provided them with a social outlet that was not merely tolerated but actively encouraged. Although colonial New England men did not abandon the church to the degree that nineteenth-century American males did, the feminization of church membership began at least as early as the beginning of the eighteenth century and probably in the late seventeenth. "There are far more Godly women in the world than there are Godly men," Cotton Mather wrote in his 1691 tract on virtuous women. By 1735 approximately two-thirds of each congregation's church members were women, and in several congregations the proportion reached nearly three-fourths. A demographic imbalance in the overall sex ratios in society did not cause the imbalance in church membership. Women joined the church in greater numbers than men did because they wanted to and because they welcomed the opportunities church activities gave them to socialize. Women often met separately from men to discuss the Scriptures, sermons, and other moral matters. Anne Hutchinson's infamous meetings became notorious only because of their content: the practice of women meeting in these study groups was commonplace and eminently respectable. The church and church-related activities provided a convenient forum in which to socialize for both men and women; its importance was heightened for women because few other forums were open to them.[17]

Extending the modern concepts of "Momism" or "the bonds of sisterhood" into the colonial New England past creates a risk of ahistorical presentism; nevertheless, both phenomena seem to have been present in the seventeenth and eighteenth centuries. Puritan parents failed to contain their overt expressions of affection for their children as much as their moral leaders wanted them to. And if either of the parents weakened, it was likely to be the mother, the primary caregiver. Women often expressed the joy their children gave them. Massachusetts' two best-known women of the founding generation, Anne Hutchinson and Anne Bradstreet, found enduring, sustaining pleasure in the day-to-day raising of their children. Despite warnings to the contrary, children did become their mothers' playthings. A lonely eighteenth-century mother, Esther Edwards Burr, described the delight motherhood gave her: "In the morning Sally awakes me with her prattle. Like other birds as soon as she is awake to singing . . . the first thing after her eyes are open is to look for me and as soon as she sees me a very pleasant smile, her eyes sparkling like diamonds. She is very good company when I have no other."[18]

Burr also found pleasure in friendships with other women. Few women had her powers of expression—she referred to one friend as the "sister of my heart"—and fewer still so unabashedly articulated such love of female company. "My cousin left me to go home," Burr wrote to a woman friend. "It hurt me so to part with her for she is a clever creature. . . . I was very urgent with her to stay with me this winter as I was like to be alone, but her friends would not or could not spare her." Other women with a literary bent expressed similar sentiments in their diaries, letters, or travelogues; two of New England's most famous female writers, Sarah Kemble Knight of Boston and Sarah Osborn of Newport, were among these. Of necessity, a somewhat furtive quality characterized these testimonies to friendship, which bespoke the bonds of sisterhood. Women did not wish to be seen as subverting family values by ignoring men, but in reality they were doing just that. Out of a combination of patriarchal ideology, occupational specialization by gender, and fears over sexual misconduct, men created a world in which women were forced to spend much of their time with other women. Cloistered in domesticity to prevent contamination from outside influences, women took refuge and found pleasures within their segregation.[19]

Women also sought recreation in another thoroughly modern activity; shopping for or making clothes that they thought enhanced their appearance. New England men, too, suffered from this vanity, but women seemed especially vulnerable to concern with style and fashion. From the beginning of settlement, Puritan law tried to prevent excessive attention to personal appearance. A 1634 Massachusetts statute stipulated that "no person either man or woman shall hereafter make or buy any apparel, either woollen or silk, or linen with any lace on it, silver, gold or thread." It also forbade "slashed clothes [that is, clothing with unnecessary slits], cut-works, embroideries, or needlework cap . . . also all gold or silver girdles, hatbands, belts, ruffs, beaverhats." Similar laws were passed in Connecticut and New Haven and updated in all three colonies with added proscriptions over the next twenty years.[20]

The content and intent of these appearance laws should not be exaggerated. Puritans were not ascetics; they associated shapeless, color-less garments with the religious orders of the Catholic church. New Englanders wore many different types of fabrics that had a wide range of colors, russet being the most popular. Black, so associated in the popular mind with Puritanism, was worn primarily on formal occasions. Puritans wished to prevent undue attention being paid to clothes because they thought this bespoke vanity and unacceptable worldliness, and distracted people from more important matters: but they did not attach any special virtue to homely clothes. Puritans did dislike and try to prevent people from putting on airs about their dress; thus, Connecticut's primary law regulating appearance enjoined a "restraint of excess in apparel" by which people "exceeded their condition and rank" within society.[21]

A few cases did arise under the apparel laws but, by and large, the statutes existed to underscore an ideal rather than to provide a basis for frequent prosecutions. To an extent the laws were successful. Women of the first generation devoted little time to shopping or fashion. Yet Puritan pioneer women did not completely banish these matters from consider-ation in the first settlements. Nathaniel Hawthorne's saintly adulteress, Hester Prynne, allowed herself one vanity in embroidering her scarlet "A" with "fantastic flourishes of gold thread." In particular, some elite women chafed under the restrictions imposed by Puritan ideology and frontier isolation. Mary Downing, Governor John Winthrop's niece, who was living in Boston, wrote her father begging him to ask her mother to send some "lace . . . not out of any prodigal or proud mind," she hastened to add, "but only for some cross clothes which is the most allowable and commendable dressings here." Her mother, Downing was certain, "would have me wear dressings for which I do so long . . . whilst the elders [presumably including her uncle, the governor] with others intreated me to leave them off for they give great offense." Downing was no rebel living in Boston against her will but a pious young woman who nevertheless missed the fashions of London. Poor Governor Winthrop. His eldest

daughter, Mary Dudley, who lived in Ipswich, echoed her cousin's sentiments in a series of letters to friends back in England in which she also
lamented the absence of stylish clothes. An urbane woman, Winthrop's
daughter frankly disliked pioneer life and the restrictions Puritan laws
imposed on her dress.[22]

The two Winthrop women would have found fashions more congenial in a relatively short time. Although jewelry remained forbidden
throughout the seventeenth century, the ruffles, pleats, and flouncy skirts
worn in Restoration England began to appear on urbane New England
women in the 1670s. Ministers warned against these worldly trappings but
their own yielding to similar temptations undercut their censure.

New England's men adopted the fashions of England too. They
shaved their beards, cut their hair, and wore elaborate waistcoats. In the
1670s, figures no less pious and revered than Governor John Winthrop,
Jr., of Connecticut and Governor John Leverett of Massachusetts copied
the little mustache of the dandy, made popular by Charles II. At the turn
of the century many gentlemen—including ministers—started wearing
periwigs, those extraordinary cascading layers of shoulder-length curls
popular in England. Cotton Mather, who agonized over his own decision
to wear a wig, published a diatribe against excessive dressing of women,
*Ornaments for the Daughters of Zion* (Cambridge, 1692). "If a woman spends
more time in dressing than in praying or in working out her own salvation,
her dress is but the snare of her soul," Mather preached. His own weakness
in giving in to English fashion for men could not have strengthened his
arguments to the women in his congregation.[23]

Boston became a fashion center for women in the early eighteenth
century; styles and trends there were emulated in the provincial capitals
and county seats. The hoop petticoat—a fashion monument to frivolous
dress—became a symbol of the new New England woman. In 1714 the
hoop petticoat inspired a biting satire that mocked attempts to reinvigorate
the Puritan spirit of plain dress. The anonymous author demanded that
magistrates punish women wearing them because they "proved themselves
whores." The whipping of petticoat wearers would thus "suppress two
great sins at once." Other prevalent styles, the petticoat foe wrote, leave
women "almost naked" and instead of being "ashamed of their pride, they
are proud of their shame." One of humorist James Franklin's favorite
targets for satire was the styles of Boston's women. In a tongue-in-cheek
treatise on dyeing, Franklin provided a series of definitions of the messages
given off by various colors. It read much like a twentieth-century advertising manual for "power dressing." Women in love wore peach, forsaken

ones willow green, jealous ones lemon, defiant ones red, and so on. Franklin included over twenty colors and moods in his glossary. He also appended a poem that poked fun at the growing popularity of silk for women's clothes, which, according to him, was impoverishing fathers and husbands.[24]

By the 1730s the battle against excessive dressing was lost in Boston, and plain-dress advocates were fighting rearguard actions everywhere else in New England. Newspaper advertisements for goods and services, the development of extensive retail districts in provincial cities and secondary towns, and frequent references in personal correspondence all testify to the growth of a consumer culture for women centered around appearance. A local historian of Norwich, one of Connecticut's most urbane towns, described the silks, parasols, corsets, wigs, jewelry, makeup and powders, and peacock fans available to and sought out by the town's style-conscious women at mid-century. In Hartford, Mary Gabriel, "a French milliner from Paris," opened up shop, to the delight of her many customers. Earrings, bracelets, and necklaces turned up in numbers in the probate estates of women in the second half of the century. A mineral form of iron pyrite (which is still popular in the late twentieth century) — "marcasite," "marchasite," or "marquesett" as it was variously called—became a universally used ornament. It took a good polish and was put on shoes, buckles, hats, earrings, rings, and pins. Milliners used jewelry and other ornaments generously and advertised them as part of gowns, hats, and scarves. Adult women, youths, and even little girls began to wear ribbons, pompoms, plumes, rosettes, and artificial flowers in their hair. Probably the single most extravagant addition to a woman's personal appearance was the calash, an elaborate ornament used to dress hair with a garnish of silk and wool. The equivalent in attention getting and social status to the periwigs worn by men, the calash strained the sensibilities of even some of the more style-conscious urbanites.[25]

By the outbreak of the Revolution, a culture of style dominated New England with values directly opposed to those of the founding generation. The culture enshrined excess, drew particular attention to women, and was supremely impractical. People expended large sums of money and time on their wardrobes and looks. French notions set the standards. Women wore jewelry with all manner of dress, and sensuality replaced sobriety as the primary desired effect. Not surprisingly, this narcissistic extravagance horrified some New Englanders. During the Revolutionary years it was often cited as an example of the corruption and decay that brought God's wrath down upon the region and precipitated the terrible events of the imperial crisis. After the war ended, however, merchants again flooded New England's markets with women's clothes and fashions from England and Europe.[26]

Along with clothing fashions came a host of other consumer goods intended to appeal to New England's buying public. Most were unnecessary luxury items: pewter, rugs, artificial flowers, exotic wines, decorated horse harnesses. Silversmiths had been present in a few of the larger centers in the mid-seventeenth century primarily producing items for church services. In the eighteenth century, however, silversmiths branched out into general metalworking and increasingly did business as jewelers making cups, glasses, plates, flatware, and decorations, in addition to personal jewelry. The smiths worked in gold, brass, and copper as well as in silver. By the Revolution more than a hundred silversmiths had shops in Connecticut alone; the bulk of their work involved producing luxury goods for wealthy or prosperous individuals.[27]

### Periwigs and Piety

Although the wives of wealthy men led the fashion and shopping parade, their husbands often enthusiastically joined them. For fifty years, from the 1670s to the 1720s, periwigs fueled a heated debate in New England. Superficially a dispute over the appropriateness of a particular hairstyle, in reality the wig controversy served as a proxy for a battle between forces of piety and provincialism on one hand and secularism and internationalism on the other. In 1675, Hety Shepard, a devout fifteen-year-old living in rural Rhode Island, saw her first wig on a man—Elder Jones of her church. Shepard thought it one of the funniest and strangest things she had ever seen, yet she knew "it was greatly censured for encouraging worldly fashion." Several churches at the time held meetings to discuss and condemn the use of wigs. But, ironically, New England's clergy led the trend "to wig." Ministers were expected to act and look like the most eminent gentlemen of a community; inasmuch as wigs identified high social status in Restoration England, many New England ministers felt their position as gentlemen required one. Cotton Mather first wigged in 1691 and furiously lashed out at those "who preached against an innocent fashion, taken and used by the best of men." Another living symbol of piety, President Edward Holyoke of Harvard, kept a sparse diary that seldom mentioned his personal life; yet he recorded the purchase of several wigs with pride.[28]

Opposition to wigs, however, also came from within the church— usually from rural parishes and ministers. In the 1720s, long after most ministers wore them, Hugh Adams, a combative minister from Durham, New Hampshire, mounted a crusade against wigs, which he wanted to replace with the skullcaps worn by clerics of the founding generation. Worldly, vain, and above all, "Frenchified fashion," wigs were "frontier food" (scalps) unfit for decent men, according to Adams. He established a network of correspondents who soldiered alongside him in the campaign. They fought in vain. Adams warned in a rabid sermon that unless "the wigged ministers of our provinces shall repent of, or be discountenanced in the Babylonian garments of their anti-Christian locust-like head, bloodshed and destruction will befall New England." When a young minister died prematurely, Adams sanctimoniously preached that God had wrought his wrath on the "periwigged pastor."[29]

Small-town morality versus large-town urbanity lay at the heart of the wig fight and of a more general debate over the appropriateness of fancy clothes. Young ministers, invariably educated at either Harvard or Yale, often had a hard time fitting themselves into the mores of rural parishes. When the Coventry, Connecticut, parish fired Oliver Noble as its minister, he called on one of his mentors, John Ballantine of Westfield, Massachusetts, and told him that his troubles with the congregation started over his dress. His wig and "black velvet cape on a white great coat gave such a handle against him." Ballantine confessed that he, too, knew firsthand the intolerance of a small farming town. "Singularity in dress sometimes proves a snare to one that has a mind to be popular," he told his protégé. Nevertheless, Ballantine believed, "we should dare to be true though we expose ourselves to banter and ridicule." In other words, he counseled Noble not to pander to rustic demands but to continue to attire himself like an urbane gentleman.[30]

### Country Clowns and Urban Debauchees

The Congregational ministers of the eighteenth century felt the strain of urban-rural tensions more than any other group or class of New Englanders. They had strong attachments both to urbane worldliness and to rural piety. Without a doubt, location on the urban-rural continuum determined to a great extent opportunities for leisure and recreation. By the early eighteenth century New Englanders were acutely aware of differing urban and rural social structures; as the century progressed the differences became more pronounced.

In the 1970s and 1980s, historians analyzed the different political and economic roles of types of towns by applying an analytical tool developed by geographers—central place theory—to New England. According to this theory, mature societies have a hierarchy of communities that provide differing political and economic types of services at each level. New England's capital cities—for example, Boston, Massachusetts; Newport and Providence, Rhode Island; Portsmouth, New Hampshire; and Hartford and New Haven, Connecticut—all were primary political centers. Each county in the four colonies had a county seat in which important courts were held; these seats were secondary political centers. By the Revolution, Massachusetts had fourteen counties, Connecticut had eight, and New Hampshire and Rhode Island each had five. Although the thirty-two county seats contained substantial variations, all thirty-two exercised similar political functions. Beneath the county seats in the hierarchy were the towns themselves, which occupied a tertiary level. There were approximately 280 towns in Massachusetts, 90 in Connecticut, 140 in New Hampshire, and 30 in Rhode Island. These three ranks of political power existed in a ratio of 6 primary centers to 32 secondary ones to 550 tertiary ones.[31]

In central place analyses, economic importance is usually associated with political importance but not always in equal measure. In New England, for example, among the six capitals, only Boston and Newport maintained sizable direct trade with England and Europe. Hence, they were more important than the other capitals and had economic functions, particularly wholesale ones, that Hartford, New Haven, Providence, and Portsmouth did not have. And, of course, Boston had more economic power than Newport because of its larger population and greater volume of trade. Boston was the economic capital—"the Hub," it was called—of New England.

County seats exhibited even more variety in economic status than the capitals did. Some of them, such as Middletown and New London, Connecticut, equaled or surpassed Portsmouth in economic power and function. Others, in rural or remote areas such as Haverhill in Grafton County, New Hampshire, and South Kingstown in Washington County, Rhode Island, had little economic development other than farming and could not be considered secondary economic centers by any stretch of imagination. Similarly, some large towns that were neither capitals nor county seats—such as Norwich, Connecticut, or Newburyport, Massachusetts—had an economic importance exceeded only by Boston and Newport.

Although the definitions are less precise than the ones for political centrality, eighteenth-century New England towns can conveniently be grouped into four economic categories. In the first class are the two major cities of Boston and Newport. Into the second fall ten secondary economic centers: Portsmouth, New Hampshire; Salem, Springfield, and Newburyport, Massachusetts; Providence, Rhode Island; and Hartford, New Haven, Norwich, New London, and Middletown, Connecticut, all of which were heavily engaged in the coasting trade and served as distribution centers for surrounding regions. The third category includes forty tertiary market towns that provided retail and professional services and served as collection points for produce and other locally produced goods. In the fourth category are several hundred villages, small business centers consisting of a couple of general stores and a few taverns.

Aggregate population data are not always a reliable guide for differentiating between tertiary market towns and villages, since many of the latter were at the center of a town with a large physical area. Towns such as these would have a large population, but the people would be scattered across a rural countryside. Farmington, Connecticut, for example, had nearly six thousand residents in the 1774 census and was the sixth most populous town in New England, yet it had only a lightly developed business center. Most of its residents lived on farms dispersed over Farmington's two hundred square miles of land. Thus, despite Farmington's large population, its center is best described as a village.[32]

Classifying New England's towns by social function is even less precise than doing so by economic function. Both political and economic criteria come into play. Governmental activity—even that of a county seat—attracted visitors and activities; and greater economic development produced a more varied and cosmopolitan environment. A location on coastal water or adjacent to a larger center also affected a town's social structure, as did the presence of special institutions such as Harvard or Yale or the dominance of a particular economic activity such as fishing. Frontier towns exposed to invasion and danger; island towns dependent entirely on seagoing communications; the mountain towns of northern New Hampshire, cut off from the rest of New England by winter weather; and Western Connecticut and Massachusetts towns bordering on New York all had unusual circumstances that altered their residents' opportunities for leisure and recreation.

But the most basic distinction to be drawn is a general one between urban and rural New England. Boston anchored one end of a continuum that would have a tiny town landlocked in the White Mountains at the other. The rest of New England's communities were located along the line that stretched between these two points. Although urban-rural distinctions became pronounced in the early eighteenth century, they existed in every colony from the first settlements onward. By the 1650s Boston and Newport had become known not only as political and economic capitals but also as centers of earthly pleasure. "Lues Venerea," John Winthrop disparagingly called the spread of licentious behavior he witnessed in Boston in the 1640s. By the fourth quarter of the seventeenth century, scenes on Boston's public streets astonished a rural Rhode Island girl who had never seen such an "array of fashion and splendor . . . silken hoods, scarlet petticoats, bone lace, and silken scarves." A joke a Massachusetts farmer recorded in his diary in 1689 testified to the suspicion with which rural people regarded Boston. "A hectoring debauchee," according to the story line, met "an honest, ingenious countryman on the road." The Bostonian demanded to know some local news, to which the countryman replied tartly that he knew none. The Bostonian bellowed back: "I'll tell you some, the Devil is dead"—a rebuke to the farmer for his sanctimony. The farmer then delivered the punch line: "[I]f the Devil is dead, he has left many fatherless children in Boston."[33]

In the eighteenth century the gap between rural and urban culture widened. Cities and big towns grew more cosmopolitan; new farming towns were settled in areas more remote and farther from the coast than the farming towns of the seventeenth century had been. Country people often had good reason to be wary of their cousins from the city. Urbanites could treat rural visitors with disdain or outright meanness. Doctor Andrew Hamilton at mid-century described a trick called "hawling the fox" that Boston rowdies played upon "simple country clowns." Two or three strong men tied a fox to a stump and then ran a rope across a pond in such a way that it looked as if the rope was tied to the fox. In reality, the pranksters kept a tight grip on it. An accomplice on the other side would bet some unsuspecting newcomer that he could not beat the fox in a tug-of-war. When the victim allowed the rope to be tied around his waist "the sturdy fellows pull lustily for their friend the fox and haul poor pill-garlick while the water hisses and foams on each side of him as he ploughs the surface. I saw a poor country fellow treated in this manner."[34]

A young man from rural Rowley, Massachusetts, who visited Providence, Rhode Island, in the 1750s described its social structure and social life with a mixture of horror and admiration for its diversity and freedom. A "very growing and flourishing place," Providence had a population, the wide-eyed farmer thought, "immoral, licentious, and profane, and exceedingly famous for contempt of the Sabbath." Townspeople in Providence complained of rural visitors not understanding how to behave in a city.

Among the offenses committed, they brought their dogs everywhere with them. Providence residents, in turn, were astonished by the greater urbanity of Newport, in particular by the mansions, gardens, and wealth of the great merchants. Four wealthy Newport Loyalists placed under house arrest and exiled to the inland town of Glocester, Rhode Island, fascinated the "plain, quiet, inoffensive people" paid to board them. Conversely, the Newporters marveled at the simplicity of life in Glocester, a mere fifteen miles from Providence. In particular, the Loyalists found the rural people unsophisticated about food, they had never tasted radishes, were "regaled" by the urbane practice of "taking tea" in the afternoon, and ate such horrible things as "pouts or toad fish."[35]

### Gentlemen and Bundles of Wildfire

Historians of most urban centers in New England similarly describe these towns' abilities to astound visitors from the countryside. The lives of people at the two extremes of the urban social structure—the wealthy elite and the poor workmen, transients, and sailors—fascinated travelers from relatively homogeneous farming areas. Large towns offered special opportunities for the rich to indulge leisurely pursuits and for the footloose or dispossessed to misbehave.[36]

Nothing expressed this urbanity more than the social clubs created by like-minded gentlemen. Elite clubs had become popular in Restoration England and often were philanthropic as well as social in nature. Over twenty such clubs dedicated to promoting manners, morals, intellectual life, and good companionship existed in London in 1697. Cotton Mather, aware of these associations, wrote a pamphlet in 1703 advocating that similar societies be created in New England. Prominent and pious Bostonians started the first one in the region. Between 1703 and 1710 two dozen or so of these "engines of piety" spread to other large towns. After a brief flurry of success, however, the service and social clubs languished. By 1720 most had ceased to exist. Under Mather's prompting, they had channeled their efforts specifically toward preventing young men from getting into trouble. The proposed beneficiaries of these clubs did not rush to seize the opportunities offered; and the benefactors did not find the organizations sufficiently rewarding or much fun.

Another wave of social and service clubs began, however, as the first tide crested and then subsided. Organized in the second and third decades of the century by "significant gentlemen," these "societies for the suppression of disorder," as several of them were named, aimed at eliminating poverty and vice through charitable works. Ministers and the church played a role in these clubs, but the well-to-do members of the laity led the way. These clubs, combining "business acumen and religious virtue," were more general and more secular in their approach to philanthropy than their predecessors had been. They also originated in Boston, but spread throughout New England. Membership connoted liberality and gentility, which blunted criticisms raised in some quarters that the urban gentry had become corrupted by the pursuit of money. Self-consciously emulating the clubs of the London elite, these philanthropic societies helped ameliorate some of the urban problems that the Puritan village structure could no longer handle. The clubs also provided a convenient, secular, social forum and helped to specify class and role identities in the social structure.[37]

Pursuing a similar combined agenda of social life and service to community, the first meeting of Freemasons was convened in Boston on July 30, 1733. Eighteen Masons who had joined elsewhere organized the Boston chapter and were joined by eight new initiates. A second chapter begun in Portsmouth, New Hampshire, in 1736 was soon followed by others in New Haven, Hartford, Providence, and Newport. By 1776 forty chapters existed in Massachusetts, fifteen in Connecticut, five in New Hampshire, and three in Rhode Island. With two or three exceptions, the Masons confined their activities to the large towns. Boston alone had four separate chapters with over three hundred members. Most local lodges had more modest numbers averaging about fifty members drawn from the well-to-do or prosperous strata of society. Ostensibly existing to perform good works, much as did the societies to suppress disorders, the Masons were more explicitly social in practice. Unique among New England clubs because of their international organizational structure, the various chapters formed a social network to provide visiting members from one community with a ready welcome into the society of another.[38]

Boston contained a multitude of clubs by mid-century. During Dr. Alexander Hamilton's two-week visit in 1744, he attended meetings of three different ones. The Scot's Quarterly Society was composed of gentlemen of Scottish ancestry who met to enjoy each other's company and to perform charitable work; the Physical Club was a group of doctors and scientists who met to discuss theories and techniques of medical science; and a third club, whose name Hamilton did not record, met regularly to discuss philosophical issues. All these clubs met in taverns; as a Scot, a physician, and a gentleman, Hamilton was a welcome guest at all three meetings. At the Physical Club, he disagreed with the speaker, who "gave us a harangue upon a late book of surgery." Hamilton harangued the haranguer in a heated three-hour debate, to the delight of the other members.[39]

One of Boston's most famous special-interest clubs, the Marine Society, organized in 1752, admitted "such persons only, who now are or have been commanders of vessels." Also called the Fellowship Club, the society met the first Tuesday of every month at the Blockhouse Tavern for supper and an evening of convivial drinking. The club fined members for missing a meeting if they were in town, forbade any "gambling whatsoever" at the meetings, and did not allow "debates that may tend to disturb good order, peace, and friendship." Each member — 102 men joined in the 1750s and about thirty were added in each of the next several decades — took an oath to attend the others' funerals. Almost entirely a club to promote fellowship among sea captains, the Marine Society had one service aspect: dues were put into a fund called the Box, which was used at the discretion of the officers to aid the families of any member lost at sea. Thus, the Marine Society provided what amounted to a small amount of personal insurance for captains who died accidentally at sea.[40]

If a Bostonian belonged to one club, he probably belonged to others. John Rowe, the affable merchant, had memberships in the Posse, a group of friends who met for purely social reasons; the Wednesday Night Club, also social; the Fire Club, which was a private group of volunteers who provided each other with protection from fires; the Merchants' Club, a society much like a local chamber of commerce today; and the Charitable Society, a service club. Rowe was also an officer in the Masons and attended meetings of other clubs as a guest. A network of these associations existed in Boston that tied the elite together in an intricate web of social, service, fraternal, intellectual, and professional connections.

Clubs could be controversial. Samuel Adams hated the Sans Souci Club of Boston, formed during the 1780s. One of the first to admit women, the Sans Souci brought Boston's gentry together to play cards, dance, socialize, and, according to Adams, who considered the club an affront to the republican virtue generated by the Revolution, "to introduce new dissipations."[41]

Newport had New England's second most elaborate club system. Dr. Hamilton, who also visited there, found the Newport Philosophical Club pretentious and thought its members talked endlessly of "damned stuff of little consequence." Other people, however, such as Ezra Stiles, the scholarly Newport minister who later became president of Yale, found the Philosophical Club fascinating. Newport had a few unusual clubs that emanated from its history of religious dissent and toleration. In the 1740s, under the leadership of a remarkable person, Sarah Osborn, who followed in Anne Hutchinson's tradition of women's activism, a religious society for women organized and met once a month at Osborn's house to discuss religion and other moral matters. This was not terribly unusual; other towns had similar women's discussion groups. But by the 1760s several groups used Osborn's house as virtually a community center: the women's club continued; a club of black servants met there; and so also did a group of young men who met to discuss problems of youth and morality. In 1761, nine Jews formed Newport's most unusual social organization, the Club for Jews. The first of its kind in North America, the Club for Jews met every Wednesday to eat supper, drink wine, play cards, and in general socialize. Deliberately eschewing any purpose other than fellowship, the club fined members who discussed "synagogue affairs" or other serious matters.[42]

No other town could match Boston's or Newport's number or variety of clubs but by the middle of the eighteenth century most other large towns had several. Social-service clubs proliferated and Freemasonry, as we have seen, spread to approximately sixty towns by the Revolution. Even more numerous were fire clubs, which, although organized for a serious purpose, invariably played an active role in the social life of their members. Although many clubs were informal and left few or no records, hints of club activities in small towns in the pre-Revolutionary era reveal how widespread the movement for voluntary associations was becoming. A group of rural physicians formed a science club in remote Sharon, Connecticut, in 1767; merchants in nearby Salisbury, Connecticut, formed a merchants' association the following year; six young men formed the Social Club of Dedham in 1766, which was patterned on the elite clubs formed by the gentry in nearby Boston.[43]

Immediately after the Revolution, however, clubs grew rapidly in number, type, and size. And, more important, they spread to all sizes of towns and recruited their members as much from the middle classes as from the elite. Once a town had a population of approximately a thousand, as did over four-fifths of towns in Massachusetts, Connecticut, and Rhode Island in the 1780s, it seemed capable of sustaining several clubs. Literally hundreds of clubs were founded in the 1780s; they opened up social opportunities for all classes and regions of New England; and they began to blur some of the distinctions between urban and rural areas that had developed in the pre-Revolutionary eighteenth century. Certain kinds of clubs similarly blurred some class distinctions that had developed, but other kinds cemented class identity and made it more immediately visible.

Doctors, lawyers, and merchants continued to form clubs based on professional criteria, but so also did mechanics and several categories of tradesmen. Many more post-Revolutionary clubs included women. In particular, two popular new types of clubs, library and literary societies, had many women members. Some male clubs started women's auxiliaries—"female fragment societies." The growth of club society was one of the quietest yet most consequential changes occurring in New England's Revolutionary era. Clubs were a wonderful way for people to sample the knowledge of the world, escape daily routine, become more urbane, and enjoy more fully the pleasures of life and of their fellow citizens' company.[44]

Although club society expanded opportunities for New Englanders after the Revolution, other specialized groups that had provided exclusive social experiences to a few privileged people did not significantly widen their horizons and survived virtually intact into the early national period. Harvard and Yale, located respectively in Cambridge, Massachusetts, and New Haven, Connecticut, continued to exist in their own rarefied environment. Bright, hardworking young men, usually but not always from the elite, went to these colleges for the good education they provided. But students also had several years of a social whirl unavailable to any other group in New England. From the opening of Harvard in 1637 and Yale in 1702, students demonstrated a propensity to indulge in pranks, high jinks, and forbidden pleasures. John Winthrop took immense pride in Harvard's first commencement, but he expressed fear and loathing for the "fowl misbehavior, swearing, and ribaldry" practiced by some "young men of good hope."[45]

Smoking, excessive drinking, cardplaying, and hazing of freshmen were prevalent among Harvard undergraduates in the seventeenth century. Segregating thirty or forty young men between the ages of seventeen and twenty-one, even though they remained under close scrutiny by tutors some of whom lived with them, inevitably brought forth a degree of social rebellion. In the eighteenth century an increase in the number of students and a lessened sense of restraint in society as a whole combined to exacerbate the problem of student misbehavior. Yale grew more rapidly than Harvard, equaling Harvard's size by mid-century; by 1776 Yale enrolled 270 students, 100 more than Harvard. Both colleges allowed upperclassmen to force freshmen to run errands; both supplied a multitude of clubs for debating, literature, science, and so forth; and both had ritualistic games or contests such as wrestling matches or snowball fights between rival classes. As future leaders and as young men of privilege, college students at both schools were attractive to local girls and toyed with their affections. Occasionally a student was disciplined for indiscreet behavior with women. In the most serious scandal, six Harvard men were expelled and several others given lesser punishments for bringing a woman into the dormitory overnight. Students frequently gave derogatory names to unpopular tutors or professors. Thomas Graves of Harvard was known for "not having his name for naught"; students called Harvard's President Edward Holyoke "Guts" because of his toughness and excessive girth; the nickname for President Thomas Clapp of Yale, "Clapptrap," was understood by all to have a ribald sexual connotation.[46]

In the middle of the eighteenth century, the high-spiritedness of the undergraduates threatened to turn into outright rowdiness. Harvard experienced student unrest between 1766 and 1768 that degenerated into rioting on several occasions. After a student protest over bad food, the faculty touched off rioting when they attempted to punish a young man, Asa Dunbar, who parodied Scripture by holding his plate in front of a tutor and proclaiming: "Behold our butter stinkith and we cannot eat thereof." All but a few students deserted campus and returned home to protest Dunbar's suspension. The "Butter Rebellion" served as prelude to a major riot in 1768—again over punishment meted out to a student—in which one of the five tutors, Thomas Danforth (Old Horsehead), had his door smeared with manure; a vandal started a fire in a college building; and a student who testified against his classmates received a beating at the hands of fellow students. Yale, too, had its rebellions: battles between students and faculty broke out in 1755, 1761, and 1762. In 1766 Clapp lost control of the campus and the students rioted, ripping up floors, smashing windows, burning furniture and threatening tutors.[47]

Rioting, of course, is not necessarily a form of recreation. Some of what went on at the two campuses in the late colonial period should more properly be called criminality. The occasionally extreme behavior of the students, however, underscores the accuracy of Era Stiles's dry assessment when he succeeded Clapp as president of Yale and tried to calm the waters: "an hundred and fifty or one-hundred and eighty young gentlemen is a bundle of wildfire not easily controlled," he observed to some friends. And that is the crucial point to be made out of all the campus high jinks and rowdiness: New England's future leaders spent four years of their young adulthood living together in a situation that afforded them a special opportunity for a social life that other young men of the region did not have.[48]

After being graduated from college and leaving campus, Harvard and Yale men continued to have a special place in New England all their lives. Alumni wrote each other, exchanged visits, formed associations, and in general constituted elite networks of gentlemen—an informal Harvard Club and Yale Club for life. In 1740 Harvard had approximately 270 living graduates in the region; Yale had a hundred. By 1770 Harvard's exceeded three hundred and Yale's numbered nearly that many. Although the great majority of New England's ministers were Harvard or Yale graduates, fewer than half of the two schools' graduates became clergymen; the majority went into careers as merchants, physicians, lawyers, or gentlemen farmers. Thus, the Harvard and Yale clubs not only dominated the ministry but extended into every area of leadership.[49] Rhode Island College (Brown University), founded in Providence in 1764, remained small throughout the eighteenth century, but did establish a third nodule of college social life and another network of leaders.

The nearest parallel to the special experience of New England's college men was found at the other end of the social scale, among professional fishermen and sailors. "A wicked and drunken crew," Governor William Bradford called them in 1631. Nearly a century later Cotton Mather echoed these sentiments in more graphic language: "so poisoning, so polluting," he termed sailors; "filthy speaking, baudy speaking, unclean and obscene, they destroyed not just themselves but entire communities with their drunkenness, brawling and prostitution." Historians have tended to agree with Bradford and Mather. Ironically, since personal fishing was the ideal sport of Puritan New England, the world of the professional fisherman provided a stark contrast to godly society. Unsettled, loose, free of many of the restraints imposed by traditional community standards, fishermen often were a drunken, rowdy lot. And many young men chose a fishing career deliberately because it provided an alternative to a life of piety. "We are all three young men," a sixteen-year-old Gloucester, Massachusetts, youth wrote to two friends in 1666, "and can go when we will and come when we will" if they joined the fishing fleet. Some fishermen lived a Dr.-Jekyll-and-Mr.-Hyde life: law-abiding, respectful, religious at home; drunken, carousing, brawling when away. Without a doubt, dreadful behavior was much more prevalent in eighteenth-century fishing expeditions than in those of the seventeenth, but even during the founding years of the Puritan experiment, ministers and magistrates joined Governor Bradford in denouncing fishermen and other professional sailors. Several dozen coastal communities that were frequented by sailors became known for high rates of fornication, adultery, desertion of wives, and sodomy. Both criminal and divorce court cases were rife with testimony about the problems transient sailors caused in family life.[50]

## On The Road

Young men on shipboard became "bundles of wildfire" for much the same reasons as young men did at Harvard and Yale: they were away from home and in the company of others who were also. In general, travel of all kinds was liberating—and New Englanders traveled a great deal more than stereotypical views of static village peasant life would lead one to believe. Certain groups traveled more than others: lawyers, merchants, and the clergy, for example, did so in the course of business. Lawyers called on clients or traveled to argue cases in courts; merchants to buy or sell goods or arrange business deals; and ministers to attend ordinations, funerals, and the dedications of new parishes, as well as to be guest preachers. Wives frequently accompanied husbands. In particular, ministers' wives tended to travel with their husbands; they had a social-pastoral role to play that was somewhat akin to a professional obligation. Virtually all ministers' diaries record frequent travel—at least one overnight trip per month—and list what must at times have seemed to be an endless stream of visitors to their homes. Travelers often called at a minister's house, and to refuse hospitality to a person of equal social standing or to a young visitor with a letter of introduction would have been regarded as rude.[51]

The elite traveled more than the middle strata of society but everyone took advantage of opportunities to visit friends and view life elsewhere. Families attended weddings and funerals of out-of-town relatives; farmers brought produce to market towns, often accompanied by a family member or two; women traveled to attend daughters, sisters, or friends giving birth; college students visited each other during breaks from classes. Many people traveled for purely social reasons—just to see friends. New England seemed to be a region in motion. Travel broke the humdrum of daily life, cost little, and need not have posed any challenge to morality. People realized that opportunities for sin were increased when one was out of sight of the watchful eyes of family and neighbors, but they associated most temptations to sin with England, Europe, and other regions of the colonies, not with other parts of New England. Most travel—with the exception of military trips and sailing—took place within New England, and usually within fifty miles of home. Rural people may have been apprehensive about the moral environment of some New England cities, but they feared places like London, New York, and the West Indies as "temptations, full of Hell's factors." Young men and women were warned "not to frequent such places as are notorious and open seminaries of lewdness and debauchery." Boston's and Newport's problems seemed minor compared to the infamous cities of the corrupt world beyond New England.[52]

Travel, of course, had practical hazards as well as moral ones. Roads were dreadful throughout the entire colonial period—stony, muddy, and meandering. People frequently got lost. Isaac Norris, a Connecticut farmer and inveterate traveler, must have been among the worst navigators in the world: he often lost his way four or five times in a day. Yet he never tired of taking overnight trips. Horses went lame, the weather offered unpleasant surprises, ferries were late or suddenly canceled, and everyone complained about the quality and price of food and sleeping accommodations. Yet New Englanders voted with their feet to pursue the pleasures of the road and to see how green or brown the grass was in a nearby town or in an exciting city.[53]

Travel had another role to play in the history of leisure and recreation in New England. It lessened some of the distinctions and lowered some of the barriers raised by class and location. Often to their dismay, all classes mixed on the highway and in the tavern taproom, and on more equal terms, than they would have in their home communities. Travel also blurred urban-rural differences; visitors to the city may have been the butt of jokes, but they also saw and experienced things unavailable in their hometown. Travel offered a special opportunity for leisure and recreation; paradoxically, these special opportunities—unlike some—were available at some time to almost all New Englanders. Thus travel provided a measure of social democracy to a region increasingly stratified by other circumstances.

Section Six

# PURITANS, REVOLUTIONARIES, AND AMERICANS

# XI

# The Puritan Legacy:
# The National Inheritance

John Winthrop described the difference between natural and civil liberty to the Massachusetts General Court on July 3, 1645. "The first is common to man with beasts," Winthrop explained, and gives man the liberty to do "what he lists." "A liberty to evil as well as to good," natural liberty must be restrained by "all the ordinances of God." "If not, men grow more evil, and in time to be worse than brute beasts." Civil liberty, on the other hand, gave man the freedom to do "only that which is good, just, and honest. This liberty you are to stand for, with the hazard of your lives, if need be."[1]

The distinction between the liberty to be a "brute beast" and to do that which is "good, just and honest" had a particular relevance to the choice of appropriate leisure and recreational activities. "Snares to sin" tempted God's saints at every point in their pursuit of relaxation and pleasure. Although they knew the difficulty of the process, New England's first ministers and magistrates did not shrink from translating their general beliefs about the two types of liberty into specific advice and laws. They had the intellectual courage to try to define the brute beast rather than leave it a rhetorical abstraction. Their definition drew upon their reservoir of experience as Protestants, Englishmen, political reformers, intellectuals, communalists, pioneers, and New World residents.

The Puritans' critique of Roman and Anglican theology caused them to embrace many opinions at odds with prevalent ones in England and Europe. Their hatred of iconography, clerical celibacy, elaborate rituals, assurances of salvation through good works, and other tenets of Catholic dogma led Puritans to inescapable alterations in activities as varied as art, courtship and marriage, music, and religious meetings. Other aspects of the Puritans' way of life—their Sabbatarianism; their social vision of themselves as a covenanted people; their emphasis on education and literacy; their belief in the fusion of piety, work, and productivity into their calling—were as important as their theology was in shaping daily living patterns. New England's Puritans, however, were sociologists and historians as well as theologians and pietists. They rejected many activities primarily on empirical grounds: football because it was unruly and violent; tennis because of its association with the nobility and monasteries; certain types of card games because they lent themselves readily to gambling. And, finally, New England's Puritans were also Englishmen—Englishmen who shared many of their countrymen's loves, such as beer, feasting, and fishing, and their prejudices, such as disdain for things French or Italian.

All these elements were mixed in a specific physical setting that was relatively isolated from England and Europe. New England was indeed new—neighbors, needs, food, problems were often unfamiliar. For a time the entire region existed in a frontier, pioneer state. Thus, New World reality combined with the Protestant Reformation and English history to form the world of seventeenth-century New England. Unmistakably, it was a Puritan world. Dissenting persons and places notwithstanding, most of New England subscribed to the same ideal code of behavior. Neither Boston nor Newport dissented from the belief in sober mirth. The prescribed standards included all: ministers, merchants, farmers, sailors, the young, the old, men, women. No perfect equality of condition exists in any society, of course, but seventeenth-century New England rhetoric, law, and practice encouraged a high degree of conformity in the ways people pursued relaxation and pleasure. Compare Rhode Island, the most atypical part of the region, to Virginia or New York and its cultural affinity to the more orthodox Puritan colonies becomes apparent. A type of social democracy existed in seventeenth-century New England amidst frankly hierarchical principles based on piety, education, wealth, and gender. Everybody had to live *and play* according to much the same rules despite the fact that society was composed of the high and the low, the governors and the governed.

Few if any societies in western Christendom achieved or aspired to as great a degree of cohesion as Puritan New England did. In England and Europe a great gulf separated religious and other leaders from the peasantry of the countryside and the poor of the city. The bulk of the population had no daily contact with the clergy or with preaching. The morality of the English and Europeans was affected to a degree by the influence of the clergy, but that influence was indirect and remote. People in different layers of the class structure lived in separate and discrete strata of social experience.[2]

In seventeenth-century New England no similar gulf existed between the leaders and the rest of society. Religious and political leaders lived and worked among their townspeople and parishioners. Everyone knew ministers and magistrates. Moral messages were neither abstract nor remote, but part of everyday life. Church services were in English, not Latin; the Scriptures were in every home. No strata of the society were defined as dregs outside the moral community. And that is precisely what early New England aspired to be, and to a remarkable extent was: a moral community that bound people together in all the various activities of life—church, duty, civic enterprise, work, and, of course, play. Everyone and everything was included. William Bradford stated it simply but eloquently: "We came as the Lord's free people . . . to walk in *all* his ways."[3]

Puritan life was to be a totality, a society with no seams. The place for worship—the meetinghouse—could not be called a church because that would separate it from the rest of the material world, which would then be less sacred. To celebrate specific days as regular holidays was wrong because that separated them from the rest of the calendar, which would then be less holy. Work was a godly calling, not something separate from spiritual life. Puritans did not want separate spheres or separate rules for any activities. All were to take place in the same encompassing, interrelated world of piety.

Leisure and recreation posed a special threat to the ideal of a unity of experience. Puritans were acutely aware that much play historically occurred outside the normal bounds of society. English and European play often had its own physical space—a ball field, a chessboard, a tennis court. Play suspended the normal rules of life and substituted its own rules, which allowed violence, deception, destructive competition—even outright lying. Play mocked the community and its moral standards. And, most horrifying of all, formal play had its own rituals, which competed with social rituals for loyalty and time. Play had often given license to transgress society's values. Players might decline to accept moral responsibility for what they did because they were, after all, just playing. What they were doing was not real. Additionally, the play community did not always end when the activity was over. Participants brought back to regular society appreciations, feelings, and beliefs that adhered to other aspects of life.[4]

Puritans strove mightily to avoid allowing the world of leisure and recreation to separate from the rest of society. No separate physical space, no alternate rules, no suspension of reality, no rival ritual could be tolerated. Play had to be part of the totality of life. Leisure and recreation activities had to take place within the framework of the moral community; they had to be interwoven with Scripture, workplace, village, meeting-house, home, family, and all the other parts of godly life that collectively constituted the only acceptable ritual in New England. Play could become so attractive, so compelling, so seductive—so *enchanting* as an alternative ritual—that to allow any aspect of it to separate from the rest of society would inevitably break all the boundaries and break all the rules.

This, of course, did not happen. All the boundaries and rules were not destroyed. New England never broke through the walls of the moral community in a flash flood of licentiousness or liberalism. Nevertheless, Revolutionary New England looked very different from Puritan New England. A bustling world of variety replaced the pious community of saints. Nowhere was this as true as in the sphere of leisure and recreation. As a matter of normal course, activities took place that were theologically, morally, historically, and physically outside the perimeter circumscribing the Puritan ethos. Novels were the favorite reading fare; organs played hymns in Congregational churches; couples danced the night away; a pleasant date called for a goodnight kiss; premarital sex was too common-place to occasion more than raised eyebrows; people gathered for hours at the tavern; troops played ball on the village green; and the Sabbath no longer started at sundown on Saturday night but at sunrise on Sunday morning, after the revelry of the previous evening had run its course. All this would have been anathema to the founding generation. Even theater, the social activity that embodied all the forces Puritans thought evil— idleness, sensuality, homosexuality, deception, civic disorder, foreign li-centiousness—lay poised to make the leap to respectability. Town leaders laughed as Tom Brainless lampooned the established church; ministers took a flutter on lottery tickets; and virtuous women played the coquette to inspire patriotism in soldiers. Religious metaphors lost their primacy. Life was described as a contest or sport as often as it was called a pilgrimage or errand. None of this looked like the world of William Bradford, John Winthrop, or Roger Williams.[5]

It did not look much like the world of Increase or Cotton Mather, either. Those two middle-generation Puritans had seen the Revolutionary world of leisure and recreation coming, but they had been powerless to stop it. The changes that overtook New England at play—that breached the walls of one unified moral community—were not wrought primarily by people who defined themselves out of the Puritan value system; people from within the system liberalized it by extending the rhetorical commitment all Puritans had made to moderate, productive, appropriate leisure and recreation—to sober mirth. From the beginning, Puritans had known that snares to sin lay within their own belief in the need for leisure and recreation to refresh body and soul. Ministers and magistrates sensed intuitively what modern sociologists know from empirical analysis: play often subverts as well as reflects societal values.[6] Thus the fears, thus the ambivalence, thus the repeated attempts to hedge rhetorical support with practical restrictions. Almost everything in the play of Revolutionary New England grew incrementally out of Puritan values and prescribed codes of conduct. But incremental change accumulated to a stage where the new reality bore little resemblance to the original departure point. Out of sober mirth grew fancy frolics.

Many more opportunities existed to pursue leisure and recreation in Revolutionary New England than had existed in the seventeenth century. As important, a democracy of choice emerged to replace the democracy of inclusion. Several potent forces infused this democracy of choice with vitality: an increasingly heterogeneous economy; religious ferment and fragmentation; geographic mobility; and, of course, the assertive spirit of the American Revolution. The signs were everywhere in the second half of the eighteenth century of the creation of a multifaceted society where people felt competent and authorized to express their own values in selecting their leisure and recreation—to identify and seek out their own niche. Coercion gave way to voluntarism. Jews, sea captains, and servants formed social clubs; students at Harvard parodied Scripture at the dinner table; urban rowdies played tricks on country bumpkins; women created a feminine social milieu within the religious, domestic, cultural role allotted to them. People had a diverse menu from which to choose. Ironically, as choices increased, wealth, power, position, occupation, and location played more of a role in opening or restricting access to them. Choices in seventeenth-century New England had been limited by a prescribed code of conduct based on a relatively uniform set of religious, moral precepts; but they had not been limited much by an individual's personal attributes. By the late eighteenth century, people felt freer to pursue pleasure as they saw fit, unfettered by a narrowly defined matrix of thought; but they were more restrained by who they were, what they did for a living, and where they lived.

Revolutionary New Englanders still espoused a Christian, Protestant code of conduct. No one advocated letting the "brute beast" of natural liberty loose to roam at will. New Englanders continued to believe in the virtues of sobriety, fidelity, and neighborly decency.[7] But these generalities were closer to the concept of practical godliness that characterized the Anglican ideal of Virginia than to the intense piety that had characterized New England in the founding era. John and Samuel Adams, two somber patriots who did not approve of the way their fellow New Englanders played, seemed strangely out of touch with the social aspirations of the people they led—a couple of wallflowers feeling awkward at the dance. John Gardiner, the theater advocate from Boston, spoke more for the era when he told the General Assembly of Massachusetts that as much as he venerated the Puritan pioneers, "they were only men and like all other men were fallible—liable to frailties, to prejudices and to error."[8] By removing the Puritan founders from their position as divines and assigning them the role of venerable ancestors, Gardiner and the Revolutionary generation freed New England from the shackles of a tradition that paid obeisance to the founding generation as if their principles were scriptural. Hereafter, New England viewed its past as history, not theology.

Revolutionary New England, of course, did owe much to its Puritan past. Had the region been settled by Anglicans, Catholics, or Quakers it would have entered the nineteenth century under very different circumstances. A Puritan legacy gave and continues to give New England much of its special regional identity. The broad emphases of the Puritan ethos— the commitment to literacy and education, the fellowship engendered by gathering together, the plain style in art and language, the belief in hard work and enterprise—shaped New England's future in basic ways. This inheritance is reflected by the intellectual, physical, and political monuments we associate with nineteenth-century New England: the public school system, the flowering of literature, industrial success, the village green, the town meeting, and the elegant white Congregational churches.

Did this inheritance also include a residue of Puritan ambivalence about leisure and recreation that clung to New England culture throughout the boisterous eighteenth century? Of course it did. John and Samuel Adams were indeed out of touch with the prevailing social currents—they were living anachronisms—but the marrow of most New England souls carried traces of the same heritage that weighed so heavily on the two Revolutionary patriots. To deny this would be absurd: it would be to deny the theater debates of the 1790s, to deny the quiet of a New England Sunday morning, to deny the existence of other men and women like the Adamses—to deny the effect of history itself. Many New Englanders felt vaguely uneasy about their own and their neighbors' social lives.

To make too much of this residue of Puritan ambivalence about the pursuit of pleasure — to single it out and elevate it to a status as a primary determinant of American national character — is equally absurd. Puritanism's sense of mission and its belief in education have contributed far more to an American identity than has its struggle to come to grips with a workable definition of moderate leisure and recreation. Puritans held many of their views of pleasure in common with all Christians — including Catholics — although they would have been horrified at the thought of being lumped together in a category with the anti-Christs. They had even more in common with Protestants such as Baptists and Quakers, whom they also despised.

To put the matter simply, Puritans believed in a strict code of Christian morality that became considerably relaxed over the course of the colonial period. Some elements of the abstemious religious and secular thought that undergirded this code persisted into the nineteenth and twentieth centuries. It may be reasonable to argue that a vague American uneasiness with excessive pleasure-seeking has roots in the Puritan past, but, if so, it should be added that the unease has additional roots in most parts of Christendom and that Christians everywhere in the world are uncomfortable with immoderate social behavior. Beyond this general sense of Christian morality, decency, and restraint, however, it is difficult to attribute specific thoughts or practices concerning leisure and recreation to any leftovers from Puritan culture. We should stop looking for the ghosts of John Winthrop and Cotton Mather every time we see a prude or fanatic on the American landscape.

# Abbreviations Used in the Endnotes

AQ     *American Quarterly*

NEQ    *New England Quarterly*

WMQ   *William and Mary Quarterly*

PAAS  *Proceedings of the American Antiquarian Society*

EAL    *Early American Literature*

RIH    *Rhode Island History*

JSH    *Journal of Sport History*

CHSB  *Connecticut Historical Society Bulletin*

# Endnotes

## Introduction

1. For some general statements about the role of leisure and recreation in a society, see J. S. Hans, *The Play of the World* (Amherst, Mass.: University of Massachusetts Press, 1981); N. H. Cheek, Jr., and W. R. Burch, *The Social Organization of Leisure in Human Society* (New York: Harper and Row, 1976); and D. J. Tinsley, "A Theory of the Attributes, Benefits, and Causes of Leisure Experience," *Leisure Studies*, 8 (1986), 1-6. See also the most distinguished and influential history of play written: Johan Huizinga, *Homo Ludens: A Study of the Play Element in Culture* (Boston: Beacon Press, 1955), 4-20.

2. See the best-known general history of American leisure and recreation: Foster Rhea Dulles, *A History of Recreation: America Learns to Play*, 2nd ed. (New York: Meredith, 1965) especially the two chapters added in this edition: "The Changing Scene," 366-85, and "The New Leisure," 386-97. For the unusual emphasis placed on analyses of American play see Walter Podilchak, "Establishing the Fun in Leisure," *Leisure Studies*, 13 (1991), 124.

3. Some of the well-known commentators who described America's "desperate drive for leisure" are discussed in Daniel Bell, *The End of Ideology: On the Exhaustion of Political Ideas in the Fifties* (New York: Collier-MacMillan, 1962), 257-59. Americans "work easily, play hard," Bell argued. This is also implicitly argued in another scholarly analysis aimed at the mass market: John Kenneth Galbraith, *The Affluent Society* (Boston: Houghton Mifflin Co., 1958), 259-69 and passim.

4. For the quotation from *Le Monde* and for a wonderful statement of the association of Puritanism with an enduring prudery, see the recent editorial by Strobe Talbott in *Time*, "America Abroad: How Tout Le Monde Missed the Story." Talbott's essay features a graphic that shows eight Puritans questioning Professor Anita Hill on her morality and quotes extensively from the international press about the pernicious effect of Puritanism on modern-day American morality. See Talbott, "America Abroad," *Time*, Oct. 28, 1991, 15.

5. See, among others, the major revisionist histories of Puritanism by Perry Miller, *The New England Mind in the Seventeenth Century* (Cambridge, Mass.: Harvard University Press, 1939); Samuel Eliot Morison, *Builders of the Bay Colony* (Boston: Houghton Mifflin, 1930); and Edmund Morgan, *The Puritan Family: Religion and Domestic Relations in Seventeenth-Century New England* (New York: Harper and Row, 1966).

Many recent general interpretations of Puritanism disagree with important aspects of the Miller/Morison view but still agree with the conclusion that Puritans were not ascetic prudes. See, for example, the following diverse analyses: Sacvan Bercovitch, *The American Jeremiad* (Madison, Wisc.: University of Wisconsin Press, 1978); Francis Bremer, *The Puritan Experiment: New England Society from Bradford to Edwards* (New York: St. Martin's Press, 1976). See also the following recent discussions of Miller's work: Francis Butts, "Norman Fiering and the Revision of Perry Miller," *Canadian Review of American Studies*, 17 (1986), pp. 1-25; and Bruce Tucker, "Early American Intellectual History after Perry Miller," *Canadian Review of American Studies*, 13 (1982), 145-57.

6. Clifford Geertz, *The Interpretation of Cultures* (New York: Basic Books, 1973), chapter 13. See Ronald Walters, "Signs of the Times: Clifford Geertz and Historians," *Social Research*, 47 (1980), 551-52 for a critique of Geertz. "Thick descriptions," Walters argues, "can be too static unless they are accompanied with an analysis of general processes."

7. Huizinga, *Homo Ludens*, 1-3.

## Chapter I

1. For discussions of the humorous attacks on the Puritans by their contemporaries see John P. McWilliams, Jr., "Fictions of Merry Mount," *AQ*, 29 (1977), 3-30; Richard Drinnon, "The Maypole of Merry Mount: Thomas Morton and the Puritan Patriarchy," *Massachusetts Review*, 21 (1980), 382-410; Michael Zuckerman, "Pilgrims in the Wilderness: Community, Modernity, and the Maypole at Merry Mount," *NEQ*, 50 (1977), 255-77; C. R. Kropf, "Colonial Satire and the Law," *EAL*, 12 (1977-78), 234-38; Perry Miller, *The New England Mind: From Colony to Province* (Cambridge, Mass.: Harvard University Press, 1953), 333-35. For a convenient brief survey of more recent attacks on the Puritans by people such as Mencken see David Hall, ed., *Puritanism in Seventeenth-Century Massachusetts* (New York: Holt, Rinehart and Winston, 1968). See also Moses Coit Tyler, *A History of American Literature, 1607-1765*, 2 vols., (Williamstown, Mass.: Corner House, 1973; originally published 1873), 263-64.

2. The major literary works referred to here and their dates and places of first publication are: Nathaniel Hawthorne, *The Scarlet Letter* (Boston: Ticknor, Reed and Fields, 1850) and "The Maypole of Merry Mount," *Twice Told Tales* (Boston: Houghton Mifflin, 1850); Arthur Miller, *The Crucible* (New York: Viking, 1953); Robert Lowell, *Endecott and the Red Cross* (New York: Farrar, Straus, and Giroux, 1968); James Truslow Adams, *The Founding of New England* (Boston: Atlantic Monthly Press, 1921); Vernon Parrington, *Main Currents in American Thought*, vol. 1 (New York: Harcourt, Brace, and World, Inc., 1927).

3. Mark M. Hennelly, Jr., "*The Scarlet Letter*: A Play-Day for the Whole World?" *NEQ*, 61 (1988), 530-54; Drinnon, "The Maypole of Merry Mount," 384; Tyler, *A Literary History*, 264.

4. Samuel Eliot Morison, *Builders of the Bay Colony* (Boston: Houghton Mifflin, 1930); Perry Miller, *The New England Mind in the Seventeenth Century* (Cambridge, Mass.: Harvard University Press, 1939).

5. Michael McGiffert, "American Puritan Studies in the 1960s," *WMQ*, 27 (1970), 64.

6. Morison, *Builders of the Bay Colony*, 130, 131, 148.

7. Miller, *The New England Mind*, 35-41 and passim.

8. Moody quoted in Miller, ibid., 40-41.

9. Edmund Morgan, *The Puritan Family: Religion and Domestic Relations in Seventeenth-Century New England* (New York: Harper and Row, 1966), 16; Edmund Morgan, *The Puritan Dilemma: The Story of John Winthrop* (Boston: Little, Brown and Co., 1958); Edmund Morgan, *The Gentle Puritan: A Life of Ezra Stiles, 1727-1795* (Chapel Hill, N.C.,: University of North Carolina Press, 1962); Edmund Morgan, "The Puritans and Sex," *NEQ*, 15 (1942), 591-607.

10. Morison, *Builders of the Bay Colony*, 57, 217.

11. John Caughey, "The Ethnography of Everyday Life: Theories and Methods for American Culture Studies," *AQ*, 34 (1982), 222-25.

12. Rutman, "The Mirror of Puritan Authority," in George A. Billias, ed., *Law and Authority in Colonial Massachusetts* (Barre, Mass.: Barre Publishers, 1965), 115.

13. Kenneth Lockridge, *Settlement and Unsettlement in Early America: The Crisis of Political Legitimacy Before the Revolution* (New York: Cambridge University Press, 1981), passim.

14. The secondary literature criticizing and defending Miller and his generation of historians is vast. For a few important examples see McGiffert, "American Puritan Studies," 36-67; Andrew Delbanco, "The Puritan Errand Re-Viewed," *Journal of American Studies*, 18 (1984), 343-60; John C. Crowell, "Perry Miller as Historian: A Bibliography of Evaluations," *Bulletin of Bibliography and Magazine Notes*, 34 (1977), 77-85; Everett Emerson, "Perry Miller and the Historians: A Literary Scholar's Assessment," *History Teacher*, 14 (1981), 459-67; James Hoopes, "Art as History: Perry Miller's *New England Mind*," *AQ*, 34 (1982), 3-25; Francis Butts, "The Myth of Perry Miller," *American Historical Review*, 87 (1982), 665-94; Francis Butts, "Norman Fiering and the Revision of Perry Miller," *Canadian Review of American Studies*, 17 (1986), 1-25; George Marsden, "Perry Miller's Rehabilitation of the Puritans: A Critique," *Church History*, 39 (1970), 91-105; Sacvan Bercovitch, *The American Jeremiad* (Madison, Wisc.: University of Wisconsin Press, 1978). This large body of historiography is perceptively discussed in the most up-to-date analysis of it: David Hall, "On Common Ground: The Coherence of American Puritan Studies," *WMQ*, 44 (1987), 193-229. Hall believes that the sharpest part of the criticism of the intellectual historians has "run its course" and that the gap between social and intellectual historians is narrowing. Hall, "On Common Ground," 193-94.

15. Nicholas Noyes (1704), quoted in Kathleen Verduin, "'Our Cursed Natures': Sexuality and the Puritan Conscience," *NEQ*, 56 (1983), 222-24, 229-30. Zuckerman, "Pilgrims in the Wilderness," 266; and Ronald Bosco, "Lectures at the Pillory: The Early American Execution Sermon," *AQ*, 30 (1978), 157. Hooker and Danforth quoted in Zuckerman, "Pilgrims in the Wilderness," 266.

16. This paragraph is based on Philip F. Gura, *A Glimpse of Sion's Glory: Puritan Radicalism in New England*, 1620-1660 (Middletown, Ct.: Wesleyan University Press, 1984), 9-11, 49, 52-53, 82-85, and passim. See also Winston Solberg, *Redeem the Time: The Puritan Sabbath in Early America* (Cambridge, Mass.: Harvard University Press, 1977), 150-52.

17. Roger Thompson, *Sex in Middlesex: Popular Mores in a Massachusetts County, 1649-1699* (Amherst, Mass.: University of Massachusetts Press, 1986), 92-94.

18. John Robinson, "Of Children and Their Education" (originally published 1628), in Philip Greven, Jr., ed., *Child-Rearing Concepts, 1628-1861* (Itasca, Ill.: F. E. Peacock, 1973), 13, 14, 17; John Locke, "Some Thoughts Concerning Education" (originally published 1690), in Greven, ed., *Child-Rearing*, 18-41; Cotton Mather, "Some Special Points Relating to the Education of My Children" (originally published 1706), in Greven, ed., *Child-Rearing*, 41-43.

19. Ross Beales, "In Search of the Historical Child: Miniature Adulthood and Youth in Colonial New England," *AQ*, 27 (1975), 379-82; John Demos, *A Little Commonwealth: Family Life in Plymouth Colony* (New York: Oxford University Press, 1970), 127-70; John Demos, *Past, Present, and Personal: The Family and the Life Course in American History* (New York: Oxford University Press, 1986), 94-95; Emory Elliott, *Power and the Pulpit in Puritan New England* (Princeton, N.J.: Princeton University Press, 1975), 78-80; Thompson, *Sex in Middlesex*, 94-95.

20. This paragraph is based on Murray Murphy, "The Psychodynamics of Puritan Conversion," *AQ*, 31 (1979), 141-47.

21. Miller, *The New England Mind*, 61.

22. John Winthrop, *Winthrop's Journal: "History of New England, 1630-1649,"* 2 vols., ed. James Hosmer (New York: Barnes and Noble, 1908), vols. 1, 82, 115; vols. 2, 9, 18, 153; Increase Mather, *An Arrow Against Profane and Promiscuous Dancing, Drawn Out of the Quiver of the Scriptures* (Boston: Samuel Green, 1684), 6, 7.

23. Benjamin Colman, *The Government of Mirth* (Boston: B. Green, 1707).

24. Ibid., 1, 12, 18, 19.

25. Ibid., 19-20, 46-47.

26. Ibid., 46-47, 87, 89-120.

27. Cotton Mather, et al., *A Serious Address to Those Who Unnecessarily Frequent the Tavern, and Often Spend the Evening in Public Houses. By several ministers to Which is added, a private letter on the subject, by the Late Reverend Dr. Increase Mather* (Boston: A. Garrish, 1726), 10.

28. These letters are collected in Everett Emerson, *Letters from New England: The Massachusetts Bay Colony, 1629-1638* (Amherst, Mass.: University of Massachusetts Press, 1976).

29. Probably more than anyone else, Perry Miller has made historians aware of the function and nature of the jeremiad. See Miller, *The New England Mind*, 471-475. For recent analyses of the jeremiads see Sacvan Bercovitch, *The American Jeremiad* (Madison, Wisc.: University of Wisconsin Press, 1978), 3-30; Harry S. Stout, *The New England Soul: Preaching and Religious Culture in Colonial New England* (New York and Oxford: Oxford University Press, 1986), passim; and Peter Wagner, "American

Puritan Literature," *Canadian Journal of History of Sport and Physical Education,* 9 (1977), 62-75.

30. Michael Wigglesworth, *God's Controversy with New England* (Boston: B. Green, 1662).
31. See Wagner, "American Puritan Literature," 64-65 for a discussion of this collective warning.
32. Cotton Mather, *A Cloud of Witness Against Balls and Dances* (Boston: B. Green and J. Allen, 1700), 3-10; Cotton Mather, et al., *A Testimony Against Evil Customs Given by Several Ministers* (Boston: B. Green, 1719), passim.
33. Mather, *A Serious Address,* 2-30.
34. See Bruce C. Daniels, *The Connecticut Town: Growth and Development, 1635-1790* (Middletown, Ct.: Wesleyan University Press, 1977), chapters 2 and 6; and Bruce C. Daniels, *Dissent and Conformity on Narragansett Bay: The Colonial Rhode Island Town* (Middletown, Ct.: Wesleyan University Press, 1983), chapter 3, for analyses of this growth in two colonies.
35. Myron Wehtje, "The Ideal of Virtue in Post-Revolutionary Boston," *Historical Journal of Massachusetts,* 17 (1989), 67-68; Pauline Maier, *The Old Revolutionaries: Political Lives in the Age of Samuel Adams* (New York: Knopf, 1980), 31-39.

## Chapter II

1. Cotton is quoted in Louis Wright, "The Prestige of Learning in Early America," *PAAS,* 83, part 1 (1973), 24. Mather is quoted in David Cressy, *Coming Over: Migration and Communication Between England and New England in the Seventeenth Century* (Cambridge and New York: Cambridge University Press, 1987), 233.
2. David D. Hall, "Introduction: The Uses of Literacy in New England, 1600-1850," in William L. Joyce, *Printing and Society in Early America* (Worcester: American Antiquarian Society, 1983), 24; Kenneth Lockridge, *Literacy in Colonial New England,* (New York: W. W. Norton, 1974) 13-26; William J. Gilmore, "Elementary Literacy on the Eve of the Industrial Revolution: Trends in Rural New England, 1760-1830," *PAAS,* 92, part 1 (1982), 110-15; E. Jennifer Monaghan, "Literacy Instruction and Gender in Colonial New England," *AQ,* 40 (1988), 18; Linda Auwers,"Reading the Marks of the Past: Exploring Female Literacy in Colonial Windsor, Connecticut," *Historical Methods,* 15, (1980), 200.
3. Monaghan, "Literacy Instruction and Gender," 20-24; Gilmore, "Elementary Literacy," 110-11.
4. Cressy, *Coming Over,* 223-34 discusses at length the Puritans' commitment to maintaining their cultural ties with England. David D. Hall, "Literacy, Religion and the Plain Style," in Jonathan Fairbanks, ed., *New England Begins: The Seventeenth Century* (Boston: Museum of Fine Arts, 1982), vol. III, 102, emphasizes the literary quality of Puritan culture. For general discussions of education, legislation about education, and literacy, see James Axtell, *The School upon a Hill: Education and Society in Colonial New England* (New Haven: Yale University Press, 1974), especially 22-23; Bernard

Bailyn, *Education in the Formation of American Society* (Chapel Hill, N.C.: University of North Carolina Press, 1960), passim; and Lockridge, *Literacy in Colonial New England* especially 72-102.

5. Hall, "Literacy, Religion and the Plain Style," 102; Cressy, *Coming Over*, 233; James Gilreath, "American Book Distribution," *PAAS*, 95, part 2 (1985), 507; Worthington C. Ford, *The Boston Book Market, 1679-1700* (Boston: The Club of Odd Volumes, 1917), 25-26.

6. Gilreath, "American Book Distribution," 515-18; Elizabeth Carroll Reilly, "The Wages of Piety: The Boston Book Trade of Jeremy Condy," in William L. Joyce, ed., *Printing and Society in Early America* (Worcester: The American Antiquarian Society, 1983), 111-16, Stephen Botein, "The Anglo-American Book Trade Before 1776," in Joyce, ed., *Printing and Society*, 77-82.

7. Hall, "Literacy, Religion, and the Plain Style," 102, 110; Lynn Hains, "The Face of God: Puritan Iconography in Early American Poetry, Sermons, and Tombstone Carvings," *EAL*, 14 (1979), 15-47; Lillian Miller, "The Puritan Portrait: Its Function in Old and New England," in David Hall and David Grayson Allen, eds., *Seventeenth-Century New England* (Boston: The Colonial Society, 1984), 164; Barbara E. Lacey, "The World of Hannah Heaton: The Autobiography of an Eighteenth-Century Connecticut Farm Woman," *WMQ*, 45 (1988), 288.

8. Larzer Ziff, "Upon What Pretext? The Book and Literary History," *PAAS*, 95, part 2 (1985), 300-02; Hall, "On Native Ground: From the History of Printing to the History of the Book," *PAAS*, 98, part 2 (1988), 331-32; Hall, "The Uses of Literacy in New England, 1600-1850," in Joyce, ed., *Printing and Society*.

9. Hall, "Uses of Literacy," 21-23, discusses the custom of reading aloud. Diaries sometimes mention the practice. See, for example, Jeremiah E. Rankin, ed., *Esther Burr's Journal* (Washington, D.C.: Woodward and Lothrop, 1903), 48, 55; Anna Green Winslow, *Diary of Anna Green Winslow, A Boston School Girl of 1771*, ed. Alice Morse Earle (Boston and New York: Houghton Mifflin, 1891), 2; Monaghan, "Literary Instuction and Gender," 22-24

10. This paragraph is based on Ziff, "Upon What Pretext?" especially 300-02, and Phyllis Jones, "Biblical Rhetoric and the Pulpit Literature of Early New England," *EAL*, 11 (1976-77), 245-58.

11. Cotton Mather, *The Pure Nazarite. Advice to a Young Man, Concerning an Impiety and Impurity (Not easily to be spoken of) which many Young Men are to their Perpetual Sorrow, Too Easily Drawn Into* (Boston: T. Fleet for John Phillips, 1723), preface. *Onania, or the Heinous Sin of Self-Pollution, and all its Frightful Consequences in Both Sexes Considered* (Boston: John Phillips, 1724).

12. Hall, "Literacy, Religion and the Plain Style," 110-112, and "On Native Ground," 334-35; Ziff, "Upon What Pretext?" 303; and Dickson and Ann Tashjean, *Memorials for Children of Change: The Art of Early New England Stonecarving* (Middletown, Ct.: Wesleyan University Press, 1974), 37, all provide rich discussions of Puritan language.

13. Hall, "Literacy, Religion and the Plain Style," 104-105 and "Uses of Literacy," 33-38; Phyllis Jones, "Puritan's Progress: The Story of the Soul's Salvation in the Early New England Sermons," *EAL*, 15 (1950), 14-28,

14. The jeremiads are commented upon by most students of Puritan literature. See Perry Miller, *The New England Mind in the Seventeenth Century* (Cambridge, Mass.: Harvard University Press, 1939), chapter 16 and passim, for his pathbreaking analysis; Alan Heimert, *Religion and the American Mind: From the Great Awakening to the Revolution* (Cambridge, Mass.: Harvard University Press, 1966), 27, 31, 330-31, 424-35 for his discussion of the jeremiad in the eighteenth century; Sacvan Bercovitch, *The American Jeremiad* (Madison, Wisc.: University of Wisconsin Press, 1978), for a book-length treatment of the jeremiad in the colonial period and also in the post-Revolutionary era; and Philip F. Gura, "The Study of Colonial American Literature, 1966-1987: A Vade Mecum," *WMQ*, 45 (1988), 311-12, for an insightful discussion of recent writing on the jeremiad.

15. Gura, "The Study of Colonial American Literature," 311, Sacvan Bercovitch, "The Historiography of Johnson's Wonder-Working Providence," *Essex Institute Historical Collections*, 54 (1968), 138-61. For a collection of essays on the nature of the Puritans' use of typlogy see Sacvan Bercovitch, ed., *Typology and Early American Literature* (Amherst, Mass.: University of Massachusetts Press, 1972).

16. Alan B. Howard, "Art and History in Bradford's *Of Plymouth Plantation*," *WMQ*, 28 (1971), 237-38, 244-46.

17. William Bradford, *Of Plymouth Plantation*, ed. Harvey Wish (New York: Capricorn Books, 1962), 31; and quoted in Howard, "Art and History," 245.

18. For the general comments on Puritan Literature see the introduction in Wish, ed., *Of Plymouth Plantation*, 21-22; Louis B. Wright, *The Cultural History of the American Colonies, 1607-1763* (New York: Harper and Row, 1957), 160-62; and Ziff, "Upon What Pretext?" 297-315. For the specific remarks on *Magnalia Christi Americana*, see Ziff, "Upon What Pretext?" 303, and Sacvan Bercovitch, "New England Epic: Cotton Mather's *Magnalia Christi Americana*," *English Literary History*, 33 (1966), 337-45.

19. Wright, "The Prestige of Learning," 22-23; Hall, "Literacy, Religion and the Plain Style," 106-107.

20. Tashjean, *Memorials*, 39-48; Gura, "The Study of Colonial American Literature," 333; Emory Elliott, "The Development of the Puritan Funeral Sermon and Elegy, 1600-1750," *EAL*, 15 (1980), 151-64.

21. Daniel B. Shea, Jr., *Spiritual Autobiography in Early America* (Princeton, N.J.: Princeton University Press, 1968), x, xi, 133-34; Emory Elliott, *Power and the Pulpit in Puritan New England* (Princeton, N.J.: Princeton University Press, 1975), 8-9; Alden Vaughan and Edward Clark, eds., *Puritans Among the Indians: Accounts of Captivity and Redemption, 1676-1724* (Cambridge, Mass.: Harvard University Press, 1981), 4-5.

22. Gura, "The Study of Colonial American Literature," 324-25; Perry Miller, ed., *The American Puritans: Their Prose and Poetry* (New York: Doubleday, 1956), 265-66, 301-03.

23. William J. Scheick, "The Widower Narrator in Nathaniel Ward's *The Simple Cobbler of Aggawam in America*," *NEQ*, 47 (1974), 87-92; P. M. Zall, ed., *The Simple Cobbler of Aggawam in America* (Lincoln, Neb.: University of Nebraska Press, 1969), passim; Samuel Eliot Morison, *Builders of the Bay Colony* (Boston: Houghton Mifflin, 1930), 219, 234-40.

24. Morison, *Builders of the Bay Colony*, 234-40; J. A. Leo Lemay, *"New England's Annoyances:" America's First Folk Song* (Newark, Del.: University of Delaware Press, 1985), 68-70.

25. Lemay, *"New England's Annoyances,"* 1-21.

26. Jonathan Fairbanks, ed., *New England Begins, The Seventeenth Century* (Boston: Museum of Fine Arts, 1982, 3 vols.) vol. 2, xix; Miller, ed., *The American Puritans*, 282-301.

27. Miller, *The New England Mind*, 282; Ford, *The Boston Book Market*, 45-46.

28. Hall, "The Uses of Literacy," 24-37.

29. Roger Thompson, "'Holy Watchfulness' and Communal Conformism: The Function of Defamation in Early New England Communities," *NEQ*, 56 (1983), 514-17, 520-24; Margaret Spufford, *Small Books and Pleasant Histories: Popular Fiction and Its Readership in Seventeenth-Century England* (Athens, Ga.: University of Georgia Press, 1982), 15.

30. Vaughan and Clark, eds., *Puritans Among the Indians*, 3-21, 247-48, passim.

31. Daniel E. Williams, "'Behold a Tragic Scene Strangely Turned into a Theatre of Mercy': The Structure and Significance of Criminal Conversion Narratives in Early New England," *AQ*, 38 (1986), 828-43.

32. Perry Miller, *The New England Mind: From Colony to Province* (Cambridge, Mass.: Harvard University Press, (1953), 332, looks at the important role of this innocent-sounding satire.

33. *Hooped Petticoats, Arraigned and Condemned by the Light of Nature and Law of God* (Boston: James Franklin, 1722).

34. Miller, *From Colony to Province*, 336-37.

35. Ibid., 341-44, discusses this controversy at length.

36. Roger Wolcott, *The Poems of Roger Wolcott, 1725* (Boston: The Club of Odd Volumes, 1898). Henry Stiles, *The Histories and Genealogies of Ancient Windsor, Connecticut*, 2 vols. (Hartford: Case, Lockwood, and Brainard, 1891), vol. I, 89-90, comments on the local reception given to Wolcott's Work. Edwin T. Bowden, ed., *The Satiric Poems of John Trumbull: The Progress of Dullness and M'Fingal* (Austin, Tex.: University of Texas Press, 1962), 12-13.

37. Richard D. Brown, *Knowledge Is Power: The Diffusion of Information in Early America, 1700-1865* (New York and Oxford: Oxford University Press, 1989), 40; Allan R. Raymond, "To Reach Men's Minds: Almanacs and the American Revolution, 1760-1777," *NEQ*, 51 (1978), 370-75, 390-95; Robb Sagendorph, *America and Her Almanacs: Wit, Wisdom and Weather, 1639-1970* (Dublin, N.H.: Yankee, 1970), 30-66.

38. All these data are derived from Edward Connery Lathem, *Chronological Tables of American Newspapers, 1690-1820* (Barre, Mass.: 1972).

39. Brown, *Knowledge Is Power*, 37-38, 39, 79, 280; *Newport History*, I (1860-61), 230-232; Thomas Vernon, "The Diary of Thomas Vernon: A Loyalist," *Rhode Island Historical Tracts*, 3 (1881), 60; and J. A. Leo Lemay, *A Calendar of American Poetry in the Colonial Newspapers and Magazines and in the Major English Magazines Through 1765* (Worcester, Mass.: The American Antiquarian Society, 1972) xxiii-xxv.

40. Ziff, "Upon What Pretext?" 306-307; Hall, "Uses of Literacy," 39-40, 45-47; Winslow, *Diary of Anna Winslow*, 115-16.

41. Cotton Mather, *Winter Meditations. Directions How to Employ the Leisure of the Winter for the Glory of God* (Boston: Benjamin Harris, 1693), 13; Robert Winans, "Bibliography and the Cultural Historian: Notes on the Eighteenth-Century Novel," in Joyce, ed., *Printing and Society*, 174-85; Winans, "The Growth of a Novel-Reading Public in late Eighteenth-Century America," *EAL*, 9 (1975) 268-71; Brown, *Knowledge is Power*, 127-28; Laurel Ulrich Thatcher, "Vertuous Women Found: New England Ministerial Literature, 1668-1735," *AQ*, 28 (1976), 24-25; Gilreath, "American Book Distribution," 525.

42. Ziff, "Upon What Pretext?" 306; Janice Schimmelman, "Architectural Treatises and Building Handbooks Available in American Libraries and Bookstores Through 1800," *PAAS*, 95 (1985), 317-18.

43. Hall, "Uses of Literacy," 45-47; Brown, *Knowledge is Power*, 69-72; Norman S. Fiering, "The Transatlantic Republic of Letters: A Note on the Circulation of Learned Periodicals to Early Eighteenth-Century America," *WMQ*, 33 (1976), 642-43; David Lundberg and Henry F. May, "The Enlightenment Reader in America," *AQ*, 27 (1976), 266-71; Reilly, "The Wages of Piety," 119-21.

44. Goodrich is quoted in Hall, "Uses of Literacy," 21.

## Chapter III

1. Perry Scholes's seminal book, *The Puritans and Music in England and New England* (London: Oxford University Press, 1934) provided the first reexamination of Puritan attitudes toward music and opened lines of inquiry still being pursued. See Joyce Irwin, "The Theology of Regular Singing," *NEQ*, 51 (1978), 177-79; and Barbara Lambert, "Social Music, Musicians and Their Musical Instruments in and Around Colonial Boston," in Barbara Lambert, ed., *Music in Colonial Massachusetts, 1630-1820*, 2 vols. (Boston: The Colonial Society of Massachusetts, 1980, 1985), vol. 2, 411-12.

2. For a discussion of *The Bay Psalm Book* and John Cotton's attitudes, see Richard Crawford, "A Historian's Introduction to Early American Music," *PAAS*, 89 (1979), 264-65; Richard Crawford, "Massachusetts Musicians and the Core Repertory of Early American Psalmody," in Lambert, ed., *Music in Colonial Massachusetts*, vol. 2, 583-90; and Alice Morse Earle, *The Sabbath in Puritan New England* (New York: Charles Scribner's Sons, 1891), 145-46. For the practice of psalmody, see Crawford, "A Historian's Introduction," 277-79; and Irwin, "The Theology of Regular Singing," 176-77.

3. For a small sample of books that discuss early New England's difficulty in maintaining orthodoxy and conformity see Bruce C. Daniels, *Dissent and Conformity on Narragansett Bay: The Colonial Rhode Island Town* (Middletown, Ct.: Wesleyan University Press, 1983); Philip F. Gura, *A Glimpse of Sion's Glory: Puritan Radicalism in New England, 1620-1660* (Middletown, Ct.: Wesleyan University Press, 1984), and Paul Lucas, *Valley of Discord: Church and Society Along the Connecticut River, 1636-1725* (Hanover, N.H.: University Press of New England, 1976).

4. For a general discussion of this poor quality, see Irwin, "The Theology of Regular Singing," 179-81. Thomas Walter, *The Grounds and Rules of Musick Explained* (Boston: T. Green, 1721), 1-7. Franklin quoted in David P. McKay, "Cotton Mather's Unpublished Singing Sermon," *NEQ,* 48 (1975), 412-13.

5. Laurel L. Becker, "Ministers Versus Laymen: The Singing Controversy in Puritan New England, 1720-1740," *NEQ,* 55,(1982), 79-81.

6. This paragraph based substantially on Becker, "Ministers Versus Laymen," 79-89. See also Crawford, "A Historian's Introduction," 270-71; and Earle, *The Sabbath in Puritan New England,* 208-10.

7. Becker, "Ministers Versus Laymen," 85-86; Earle, *The Sabbath in Puritan New England,* 208-209.

8. John Ballantine, "Diary," in John Hoyt Lockwood, ed., *Westfield and Its Historic Influences, 1669-1919* (Westfield, Mass.: privately, 1922); Henry R. Stiles, *The Histories and Genealogies of Ancient Windsor, Connecticut,* 2 vols. (Hartford: Case, Lockwood, and Brainard, 1891), vol. 1, 604-06; Becker, "Ministers Versus Laymen," 93. Laurel Thatcher Ulrich, "Psalm-Tunes, Periwigs, and Bastards: Ministerial Authority in Early Eighteenth-Century Durham," *Historical New Hampshire,* 36 (1981), 259-62, provides several amusing accounts of these battles within congregations.

9. McKay, "Cotton Mather's Unpublished Singing Sermon," 422.

10. Lambert, "Social Music, Musicians, and Their Musical Instruments," 409-10; Barbara Owen, "Eighteenth-Century Organs and Organ Building in New England," in Lambert, ed., *Music in Colonial Massachusetts,* vol. 2, 660; Scholes, *The Puritans and Music,* introduction.

11. Lowell P. Beveridge, "Music in New England from John Cotton to Cotton Mather, 1640-1726," *Historical Magazine of the Protestant Episcopal Church,* 48 (1979), 145-52; Cynthia Adams Hoover, "Epilogue to Secular Music in Early Massachusetts," in Lambert, ed., *Music in Colonial Massachusetts,* vol. 2, 723-26.

12. Lambert, "Social Music, Musicians, and Their Musical Instruments," 416-17, 420-22.

13. Ibid., 442-43, 445, 460, 463, 476-77.

14. Walter's influential sermon in discussed at length in Irwin, "The Theology of Regular Singing," 184-86.

15. Owen, "Eighteenth-Century Organs," 656, 677-81; Hoover, "Epilogue to Sacred Music," 738-39; Sinclair Hitchings, "The Musical Pursuits of William Price and Thomas Johnson," in Lambert, ed., *Music in Colonial Massachusetts,* vol. 2, 631-32; Joyce Ellen Mangler, "Early Music in Rhode Island Churches: Music in the First

Congregational Church, Providence, 1770-1850," *RIH,* 17 (1958), 1-3; William Dinneen, "Early Music in Rhode Island Churches: Music in the First Baptist Church, Providence," *RIH,* 17 (1958), 33-38.

16. Earle, *The Sabbath,* 223. Mather especially feared the power of the organ to make Anglicanism more attractive. See Cotton Mather to John Stirling, May 17, 1714, in *Selected Letters of Cotton Mather,* compiled by Kenneth Silverman (Baton Rouge: Louisiana State University Press, 1971), 147-50. Samuel Sewall the Boston magistrate and famous diarist, was a self-confessed "Lover of Music to a fault," who despised the organ in worship but came to enjoy it in private. See T. B. Strandness, *Samuel Sewall: A Puritan Portrait* (East Lansing, Mich.: Michigan State University, 1967), 161-62; and Samuel Sewall, *The Diary of Samuel Sewall,* ed. M. Halsey Thomas, 2 vols. (New York: Farrar, Straus and Giroux, 1973), vol. 1, 602.

17. Hitchings, "The Musical Pursuits," 631-33; Owen, "Eighteenth-Century Organs," 681, 695.

18. Hoover, "Epilogue to Sacred Music," 738-39. Despite general acceptance, complaints were made against these schools. See William B. Weeden, *Economic and Social History of New England,* 2 vols. (New York: Hillary House, 1963; originally published 1890), vol. 2, 526. Samuel Sewall thought the schools were a good addition to Boston's social life. See Nov. 29, 1716, entry, *Diary of Samuel Sewall,* 838.

19. Hoover, "Epilogue to Sacred Music," 803-808; Hitchings, "The Musical Pursuits," 632-33 and Lambert, "Social Music, Musicians, and Their Musical Instruments," 437-42. Oscar G. Sonneck, *Early Concert-life in America 1731-1800* (Leipzig: Breitkopf and Hartel, 1907), appendix I, contains a list of New England concerts advertised in newspapers.

20. Crawford, "A Historian's Introduction," 272-74, 282-83; Raoul Francois Camus, "Military Music of Colonial Boston," in Lambert, ed., *Music in Colonial Massachusetts,* vol. 1, 84-85.

21. Mary Gosselink DeJong, "Both Pleasure and Profit: William Billings and the Use of Music," *WMQ,* 42 (1985), 105-109; David P. McKay and Richard Crawford, *William Billings of Boston: Eighteenth-Century Composer* (Princeton, N.J.; Princeton University Press, 1975), 37-39; and Steven Urkowitz and Bennet Lawrence, "Early American Vocal Music," *Journal of Popular Culture,* 12 (1978), 5-6. For a detailed account of the development of choirs and singing schools see Alan Buechner, "Yankee Singing Schools and the Golden Age of Choral Music in New England, 1760-1800" (Ph.D. diss.; Harvard University, 1960), passim.

22. See Ballantine, "Diary," 419; Urkowitz and Lawrence, "Early American Vocal Music," 5.

23. McKay and Crawford, *William Billings,* 24-25, 37; Urkowitz and Lawrence, "Early American Vocal Music," 7-9.

24. See McKay and Crawford, *William Billings,* 24-26, 37-38, for a technical analyses of the artistry. Adams quoted in David Warren Steel, "Sacred Music in Early Winchester," *CHSB,* 45 (1980), 36.

25. Urkowitz and Lawrence, "Early American Vocal Music," 7-9.

26. DeJong, "Both Pleasure and Profit," 104-107; McKay and Crawford, *William Billings*, ix, 82-83. See also Denise Boneau, "The Father of New England Music," *Humanities*, 8 (1987), 8-9.

27. Crawford, "Massachusetts Musicians," 593-99; Steel, "Sacred Music," 36; Urkowitz and Lawrence, "Early American Vocal Music," 6.

28. Camus, "Military Music," 92-103.

29. Ibid., 100-02.

30. Arthur F. Schrader, "Songs to Cultivate the Sensations of Freedom," in Lambert, ed., *Music in Colonial Massachusetts*, vol. 1, 106-11, 117, 121-25.

31. Hoover, "Epilogue to Secular Music," 771; Carleton Sprague Smith, "Broadsides and Their Music in Colonial America," in Lambert, ed., *Music in Colonial Massachusetts*, vol. 1, 157, 162, 202-203; Karl Kroeger, "Isaiah Thomas as a Music Publisher," *PAAS*, 86 (1976), 321-22; Irving Lowens, "Eighteenth-Century Massachusetts Songsters," in Lambert, ed., *Music in Colonial Massachusetts*, vol. 2, 547-49.

32. Lowens, "Eighteenth-Century Songsters," 557.

33. Steel, "Sacred Music," 33-39; Owen, "Eighteenth-Century Organs," 660-62; Earle, *The Sabbath*, 225.

34. Winton V. Solberg, *Redeem the Time: The Puritan Sabbath in Early America* (Cambridge, Mass.: Harvard University Press, 1977), 52-53.

35. See Edmund S. Morgan, "Puritan Hostility to the Theatre," *Proceedings of the American Philosophical Society*, 110 (1966), 340-47 for a general discussion of this subject and for a specific discussion of Prynne's arguments listed below. See also Solberg, *Redeem the Time*, 52-53.

36. B. W. Brown, "The Colonial Theatre in New England," *Newport Historical Society Bulletin*, 76 (1930), 6-9.

37. Ibid., 8-12.

38. Ibid., 20-25; Constance Sherman, "The Theatre in Rhode Island Before the Revolution," *RIH*, 17 (1958), 10-12. For the full terms of the bill and the conservative language of the preamble, see *Rhode Island Colonial Records*, 10 vols., ed. Joseph Bartlett (Providence: State of Rhode Island, 1856-65), vol. 6 (1762), 325-26.

39. Robert E. Moody, ed., "Boston's First Play," *Proceedings of the Massachusetts Historical Society*, 92 (1980), 118-19; Alice Morse Earle, *Stage Coach and Tavern Days* (New York: Macmillan, 1900); 200; Charles Warren, *Jacobin and Junto: Or Early American Politics as Viewed in the Diary of Dr. Nathaniel Ames* (Cambridge, Mass.: Harvard University Press, 1931), 26-27; Ebenezer Baldwin, "Diary," in *Yale College: A Sketch of Its History*, ed. William Kingsley (New York: Holt, 1879), 445.

40. Brown, "The Colonial Theatre," 26-27; Morgan, "Puritan Hostility to Theatre," 343; Isabella Bell to Catherine Livingstone, Nov. 25, 1785, Ridley Collection, Massachusetts Historical Society.

41. James Barriskill, "The Newburyport Theatre in the Eighteenth Century," *Essex Institute Historical Collections*, 91 (1955), 220, 222.

42. John Gardiner, *The Speech of John Gardiner, Esq. Delivered in The House of Representatives on Thursday the 26th of January 1792 on the Subject of The Report of The Committee Appointed*

*to Consider the Expediency of Repealing the Law Against Theatrical Exhibitions* (Boston: Joseph Bumstead Printer, 1792), 6, 7, 13, 48, 57, and passim.

43. See the discussion of theater's immense popularity in Katherine M. Doherty, "Playbills in the Massachusetts Historical Society of Amateur Theatricals, 1775-1921: A Preliminary Checklist," *Proceedings of the Massachusetts Historical Society,* 91 (1979), 101. See also Patricia Sankus, "Theatrical Entertainments and Other Amusements in Salem, Massachusetts, from the Colonial Period Through the Year 1830" (Ph.D. diss., Tufts University, 1981), chapter 2 and passim. For a fascinating discussion of explicit changes the Revolution wrought in American attitudes toward the arts and culture see Joseph J. Ellis, "Culture and Capitalism in Pre-Revolutionary America," *AQ,* 31 (1979), 169-73.

## Chapter IV

1. For the examples in this paragraph see Winton V. Solberg, *Redeem the Time: The Puritan Sabbath in Early America* (Cambridge, Mass.: Harvard University Press, 1977), 57, 113-14, 107-110, 153-54, 167, 169, 174-81. Solberg furnishes a rich, full discussion of Sabbatarianism in Protestant thought. See also Charles E. Hambrick-Stowe, *The Practice of Piety: Puritan Devotional Disciplines in Seventeenth-Century New England* (Chapel Hill, N.C.: University of North Carolina Press, 1982), 97 and passim, for a discussion of the practical aspects of Sabbatarianism.

2. Solberg, *Redeem the Time,* 57, 153-54, 295-97.

3. Alice Morse Earle, *The Sabbath in Puritan New England* (New York: Charles Scribner's Sons, 1889), 26-31, 33-35, 47, 51, 53-55, 113-14 provides charming descriptions of religious meetings. Earle's detail about meetings is accurate; her judgments, however, are far too romantic to be reliable. See also Hambrick-Stowe, *The Practice of Piety,* chapter 4.

4. The two phrases are found in Earle, *The Sabbath,* 57, 59.

5. See Bruce C. Daniels, *The Connecticut Town: Growth and Development, 1635-1790* (Middletown, Ct.: Wesleyan University Press, 1979), 140-46; and Douglas R. McManus, *Colonial New England: A Historical Geography* (New York, London, and Toronto: Oxford University Press, 1975), 41-66 for general descriptions of the process of dispersal.

6. Earle, *The Sabbath,* 104-111 describes these scenes as do many local histories. See for example, Charles H. S. Davis, *History of Wallingford, Connecticut* (Meriden, Ct.: privately by the author, 1870), 228-29; Elizabeth Schenck, *The History of Fairfield, Fairfield County Connecticut,* 2 vols. (New York, privately by the author, 1889), vol. 2, 59; Henry R. Stiles, *The Histories and Genealogies of Ancient Windsor, Connecticut* (Hartford: Case, Lockwood, and Brainard, 1890), 564, 597-98; and William Howard Wilcoxson, *History of Stratford, Connecticut, 1639-1939* (Stratford, Ct.: Stratford Tercentenary Commission, 1939), 228-29.

7. Daniels, *The Connecticut Town,* 168-69, and passim; Richard L. Bushman, *From Puritan to Yankee: Character and the Social Order in Connecticut, 1690-1765,* (Cambridge, Mass.: Harvard University Press, 1965), 54-72.

8.  Earle, *The Sabbath*, 104, 109-111; Davis, *Wallingford*, 228; Schenck, *Fairfield*, vol. 2, 59; Stiles, *Windsor*, 597; Wilcoxson, *Stratford*, 229; David D. Hall, *Worlds of Wonder, Days of Judgment: Popular Religious Beliefs in Early New England* (Cambridge, Mass.: Harvard University Press, 1990), 17.

9.  Solberg, *Redeem the Time*, 110-111, 150-51, 190-92, 265, 290-97; and Ola Winslow, *Meetinghouse Hill, 1630-1783* (New York: W. W. Norton, 1972), 172-96 describe these changes. See also T. B. Strandness, *Samuel Sewall: A Puritan Portrait* (East Lansing, Mich.: Michigan State University Press, 1968), 144-51.

10. Solberg, *Redeem the Time*, 150-51, 190-92, and passim; Winslow, *Meetinghouse Hill*, 172-96; Earle, *The Sabbath*, 93-101. Many accounts of Puritanism describe this process. See also Marian Card Donnelly, *The New England Meetinghouse of the Seventeenth Century* (Middletown, Ct.: Wesleyan University Press, 1968), 64-67. Local histories often mention these changes and debates. See Stiles, *Windsor*, 564; and Judge Sherman Adams and Henry R. Stiles, *The History of Ancient Wethersfield, Connecticut* (New York: The Grafton Press, 1904), 231-32. See also Kenneth Spencley, "The Rhetoric of Decay in New England Writing, 1665-1730" (Ph.D. diss. University of Illinois, 1967).

11. "The Sunday Law in Newport, 1739," *Newport Historical Magazine*, 1 (1880-1881), 251-53.

12. Jacob Bailey, "Diary," in *The Frontier Missionary*, ed. William S. Bartlett (Boston: Ide and Dutton, 1853), 4.

13. Harry S. Stout, *The New England Soul: Preaching and Religious Culture in Colonial New England* (New York and Oxford: Oxford University Press, 1986), 1-6. Stout's analysis of the role of the sermon is masterful and the finest treatment of the subject. See the earlier analysis by Perry Miller, *The New England Mind in the Seventeenth Century* (Cambridge, Mass.: Harvard University Press, 1939), 1-39; Emory Elliott, *Power and the Pulpit in Puritan New England* (Princeton, N.J.: Princeton University Press, 1975), 12-15; and Sacvan Bercovitch, *The American Jeremiad* (Madison, Wisc.: University of Wisconsin Press, 1978), passim.

14. Elizabeth Porter Phelps, "Diary," in *Under a Colonial Rooftree: Fireside Chronicles of Early New England*, ed. Arrias Huntington (Boston: Houghton Mifflin, 1891), 52. For a discussion of dissenting and evangelical performances, see Richard D. Brown, *Knowledge Is Power: The Diffusion of Information in Early America, 1700-1865* (New York and Oxford: Oxford University Press, 1989), 139; Harry S. Stout, "Religion, Communications, and the Ideological Origins of the American Revolution," *WMQ*, 34 (1977), 519-20; Alan Heimert, *Religion and the American Mind: From the Great Awakening to the Revolution* (Cambridge, Mass.: Harvard University Press, 1966), 221-36. Perry Miller, "The Rhetoric of Sensation," in *Errand Into the Wilderness* (Cambridge, Mass.: Harvard University Press, 1956), 167-75.

15. Stout, *The New England Soul*, 28-33; Hambrick-Stowe, *The Practice of Piety*, 94, 99-100, 133-34, 222-23; Elliott, *Power and the Pulpit*, 66, 89, 110, 120, and 146.

16. Stout, *The New England Soul*, 3-6; Elliott, *Power and the Pulpit*, 10-11; and, especially, Perry Miller, "The Marrow of Puritan Divinity," in *Errand Into the Wilderness*, 67-68, stress the role of preaching in Puritan society.

17. John Rowe, *Letters and Diary of John Rowe, Boston Merchant*, ed. Anne Cunningham (Boston: W. B. Clarke, 1903), 17-21.

18. For a discussion of the gathering of a church see, among others, Winslow, *Meeting-house Hill*, 39-42; Solberg, *Redeem the Time*, 128-34; Kenneth Lockridge, *A New England Town: The First Hundred Years* (New York: W. W. Norton, 1970), chapter 2.

19. Hambrick-Stowe, *The Practice of Piety*, 127-29 does a careful job of identifying with precision when these changes took place. Earle, *The Sabbath*, 82, 269-70, 273-79, contains a wealth of colorful detail and anecdotal material about ordinations.

20. Hambrick-Stowe, *The Practice of Piety*, 127-30; Earle, *The Sabbath*, 273-79; Alice Morse Earle, *Stage Coach and Tavern Days* (New York: Macmillan, 1900), 82.

21. Ebenezer Parkman, *The Diary of Ebenezer Parkman, 1703-1782*, ed. Francis G. Walett (Worcester, Mass.: American Antiquarian Society, 1974), 6-8.

22. "Town Meeting Minutes, Edgerton," Edgerton Town Hall, I (June, 1747), 190. Stiles, *Wethersfield*, 770-71; John Ballantine, "John Ballantine's Diary," in John Hoyt Lockwood, ed., *Westfield and Its Historic Influences, 1669-1919*, (Westfield, Mass.: privately by the author, 1922), 374-77; Joseph Green, *The Commonplace Book of Joseph Green*, ed. Samuel Morison, vol. 34, *Colonial Society of Massachusetts Publications* (Boston: Colonial Society of Mass., 1937-1942), 247. For the average length of tenure in office see Daniels, *The Connecticut Town*, 112-13; and Donald M. Scott, *From Office to Profession: The New England Ministry, 1750-1850* (Philadelphia: University of Pennsylvania Press, 1978), 4-6.

23. Earle, *The Sabbath*, 269-73, 276-79; Earle, *Stagecoach and Taverns*, 82; Ballantine, "Diary," 374-78; Stiles, *Wethersfield*, 766, 770-71.

24. See David E. Stannard, *The Puritan Way of Death: A Study in Religion, Culture, and Social Change* (New York: Oxford University Press, 1977), 45, 73-79; Dickram and Ann Tashjean, *Memorials for Children of Change: The Art of Early New England Stonecarving* (Middletown, Ct.: Wesleyan University Press, 1974), 20-22.

25. Stannard, *The Puritan Way of Death*, 75-79; Miller, "The Marrow of Puritan Divinity," 50-55, 92-98.

26. Stannard, *The Puritan Way of Death*, 98-107; Miller, *The New England Mind in the Seventeenth Century*, especially 3-34.

27. Stannard, *The Puritan Way of Death*, 73-77, 101-115; Tashjean, *Memorials for Children*, 20-27.

28. For a description of a typical funeral see Robert Blair St. George, "'Set Thine House in Order': The Domestication of the Yeomanry in Seventeenth-Century New England," in John Fairbanks, ed., *New England Begins: The Seventeenth Century*, 3 vols. (Boston: Museum of Fine Arts, 1982), vol. 2, 175. Edmund S. Morgan, *The Puritan Dilemma: The Story of John Winthrop* (Boston and Toronto: Little, Brown, 1958), 204.

29. Stannard, *The Puritan Way of Death*, 107-115; Tashjean, *Memorials for Children*, 28-33; St. George, "'Set Thine House in Order'," 175-76.

30. Stannard, *Puritan Way of Death*, 107-115.

31. Ibid.

32. Tashjean, *Memorials for Children*, 27-29.

33. *Newport Mercury* (Jan. 20, 1761), 1.

34. Rowe, *Diary,* 103, 128-29, 141.

35. Stannard, *The Puritan Way of Death,* 113-15; Tashjean, *Memorials for Children,* 22-27; St. George, "'Set Thine House in Order'," 175. See Parkman, *Diary,* 59 for a picture of the small-town funeral as a community event.

36. Solberg, *Redeem the Time,* 114-15; James H. Barnett, *The American Christmas: A Study in National Culture* (New York: Macmillan, 1954), 2-3; William Gilmore, "Elementary Literacy on the Eve of the Industrial Revolution: Trends in Rural New England, 1760-1830," *PAAS,* 92 (1982), 109; James P. Walsh, "Holy Time and Sacred Space in Puritan New England," *AQ,* 32 (1980), 79-80.

37. Barnett, *The American Christmas,* 3-7; Walsh, "Holy Time," 83-87; Ruth C. Page, "Celebrating Christmas in New Hampshire," *Historical New Hampshire,* 37 (1982), 121-24; Cotton Mather, *Winter Meditations. Directions How to Employ the Leisure of Winter for the Glory of God* (Boston: Benjamin Harris, 1693), 8.

38. Michael Zuckerman, "Pilgrims in the Wilderness: Community, Modernity, and the Maypole at Merry Mount," *NEQ,* 50 (1977), 272, describes Plymouth's first Christmas. See also William Bradford, *Of Plymouth Plantation,* ed. Harvey Wish (New York: Capricorn Books, 1962), 12-13.

39. Barnett, *The American Christmas,* 3-7; Gilmore, "Elementary Literacy," 109; Page, "Celebrating Christmas," 121-24; Walsh, "Holy Time," 83-87; Hety Shepard, "A Puritan Maiden's Diary," *New England Magazine,* 11 (1894-95), 20; Anna Green Winslow, *Diary of Anna Green Winslow, A Boston School Girl of 1771,* ed. Alice Morse Earle (Boston and New York: Houghton Mifflin, 1894), 11.

40. Solberg, *Redeem the Time,* 114-15; and Walsh, "Holy Time," 79-81, 84. See the descriptions of fasts at sea in Francis Higginson, "Letter to Friends in England," July 24, 1629, in *Letters from New England: The Massachusetts Bay Colony, 1629-1638,* ed. Everett Emerson (Amherst, Mass.: University of Massachusetts Press, 1976), 23-24.

41. One can find the acts requiring colony fasts in the records of each colony's general court.

42. J. Hammond Trumbull and Charles Hoadley, eds., *The Public Records of the Colony of Connecticut,* 15 vols. (Hartford, 1850-90), passim. The acts requiring fasts and thanskgivings are conveniently listed in the indexes to these volumes. Miller, *The New England Mind in the Seventeenth Century,* 21-33, discusses the pattern of fasts and thanksgivings. John Boyle, "Boyle's Journal of Occurrences in Boston," *New England Historical and Genealogical Register,* 84 (1930), 159; *Connecticut Courant,* March 30, 1767.

## Chapter V

1. See Samuel Eliot Morison, *Builders of the Bay Colony* (Boston: Houghton Mifflin, 1930), 130, 131; Henry R. Stiles, *The Histories and Genealogies of Ancient Windsor, Connecticut,* 2 vols. (Hartford: Case, Lockwood, and Brainard, 1890), 433-35; Alice Morse Earle, *The Sabbath in Puritan New England* (New York: Charles Scribner's

Sons, 1891), 8, for general discussions of house-raisings. See the following two diaries for descriptions of house-raisings in the 1690s and 1770s respectively: Thomas Minor, *The Diary of Thomas Minor, Stonington, Connecticut* (New London, Ct.: Press of the Day, 1899), entries for 1690s, unpaginated; and James Parker, "Extracts from the Diary of James Parker of Shirley, Massachusetts," *New England Historical and Genealogical Register,* 69 (1915), entries for 1770s, 117-21.

2. For the ceremonies see Morison, *Builders of the Bay Colony,* 131; Stiles, *Windsor,* vol. 1, 433; Earle, *The Sabbath,* 8. John Ballantine, "John Ballantine's Diary," in John Hoyt Lockwood, ed., *Westfield and Its Historic Influences, 1669-1919* (Westfield, Mass.: privately printed 1922), Feb. 19, 1761, Apr. 1, 1761, 385-95.

3. See a woodcutting described in Ebenezer Parkman, *The Diary of Ebenezer Parkman, 1703-1782,* ed. Francis G. Walett (Worcester, Mass.: The American Antiquarian Society, 1974), Dec. 11, 1750, 229.

4. Many scholars have discussed these agricultural practices. For the most sophisticated studies of the transfer of English custom to the colonies, see David Grayson Allen, *In English Ways: The Movement of Societies and the Transferral of English Local Law and Custom to Massachusetts Bay in the Seventeenth Century* (Chapel Hill, N.C.: University of North Carolina Press, 1981), 31-38, passim; Summer Chilton Powell, *Puritan Village: The Formation of a New England Town* (Middletown, Ct.: Wesleyan University Press, 1963), 1-14; Roy Akagi, *The Town Proprietors of the New England Colonies* (Philadelphia: University of Pennsylvania Press, 1924), 103-110.

5. Bruce C. Daniels, "Economic Development in Colonial and Revolutionary Connecticut: An Overview," *WMQ,* 37 (1980), 438-39; Thomas Lewis, Jr., "From Suffield to Saybrook: An Historical Geography of the Connecticut River Valley in Connecticut before 1800" (Ph.D. diss., Rutgers University, 1978), 124; Isabel S. Mitchell, *Roads and Road-Making in Colonial Connecticut,* Connecticut Tercentenary Series, 14 (New Haven: Connecticut Tercentenary Commission, 1933), 13-18. For the finest overall statement of communal economic patterns in a Puritan village, see Frank Thistlethwaite, *Dorset Pilgrims: The Story of Westcountry Pilgrims Who Went to New England in the Seventeenth Century* (London: Barrie and Jenkins, 1989), 150-55.

6. Charles Warren, *Jacobin and Junto: Or Early American Politics as Viewed in the Diary of Dr. Nathaniel Ames* (Cambridge, Mass.: Harvard University Press, 1931), 29.

7. Traditional—now regarded as old-fashioned—accounts of women's social activities in New England often discuss these bees. See for example, Catherine Fennelly, *Connecticut Women in the Revolutionary Era* (Chester, Ct.: Pequot Press, 1975), 37-46; William Weeden, *Economic and Social History of New England, 1620-1789,* 2 vols. (New York: Hillary House, 1963), vol. 2, 730-33.

8. Ezra Stiles, *The Literary Digest of Ezra Stiles,* 3 vols., ed. Franklin Bowditch Dexter (New York: Charles Scribner's Sons, 1901), vol. 1, 8-9.

9. Weeden, *Economic and Social History,* vol. 2, 731-33. For charming descriptions of berrying parties see Elizabeth Porter Phelps, "Diary," in Arrias Huntington, ed., *Under a Colonial Rooftree: Fireside Chronicles of Early New England* (Boston and New York: Houghton Mifflin, 1891), 27-28.

10. For the development of double standards of conduct, see especially Nancy F. Cott, "Divorce and the Changing Status of Women in Eighteenth-Century Massachusetts," *WMQ,* 33 (1976), 598-601; Mary Maples Dunn, "Saints and Sisters: Congregational and Quaker Women in the Early Colonial Period," *AQ,* 30 (1978), 584-90; Roger Thompson, *Sex in Middlesex: Popular Moves in a Massachusetts County, 1649-1699* (Amherst, Mass.: University of Massachusetts Press, 1986), 194-99.

11. Stewart L. Gates, "Disorder and Social Organization: The Militia in Connecticut Public Life, 1660-1860" (Ph.D. diss., University of Connecticut, 1975), 17, 75; Richard Marcus, "The Militia of Colonial Connecticut, 1639-1775: An Institutional Study" (Ph.D. diss., University of Colorado, 1965), 253-57; Frances Manwaring Caulkins, *A History of New London, Connecticut* (New London: privately by the author, 1895), 406-407.

12. For the concept of a "Christian soldier," see John Ferling, "The New England Soldier: A Study in Changing Perceptions," *AQ,* 33 (1981), 31; John Ferling, *A Wilderness of Miseries: War and Warriors in Early America* (Westport, Ct., and London: Greenwood Press, 1980), 93-126; William Howard Wilcoxson, *History of Stratford Connecticut, 1639-1939* (Stratford, Ct.: Stratford Tercentenary Commission, 1939), 282-85.

13. Sarah Kemble Knight, *The Journal of Madame Knight,* ed. Malcolm Frieberg (Boston: David R. Godine, 1972), Oct. 7, 1704, 20; Ferling, "The New England Soldier," 31-32; Wilcoxson, *History of Stratford,* 26; Cotton Mather, et al., *A Testimony Against Evil Customs Given by Several Ministers* (Boston: B. Green, 1719), 4-5.

14. Jabez Fitch, "The Diary of Jabez Fitch, Jr.," *Mayflower Descendant,* 2 parts (1899-1914), part 2, 43-49; L. Douglas Good, "Colonials at Play: Leisure in Newport, 1723," *RIH,* 33 (1974), 13; William Gregory, "A Scotchman's Journey in New England in 1771," *New England Magazine,* ed. Mary Powell, 12 (1895), 351; Samuel Pierce, "Diary," in *The History of the Town of Dorchester, Massachusetts* (Boston: E. Clapp, Jr., 1859), 360.

15. See Israel Litchfield, "Diary," in Wilford Litchfield, ed., *The Litchfield Family in America* (Southbridge, Mass.: privately by the editor, 1901), 325-26; Ferling, *A Wilderness of Miseries,* 118-19, passim.

16. Thomas Vernon, "The Diary of Thomas Vernon: A Loyalist," Rhode Island Historical Tracts, 3 (Providence: Providence Press, 1881), 77-78.

17. See Edward M. Cook, Jr., *The Fathers of the Towns: Leadership and Community Structure in Eighteenth-Century New England* (Baltimore and London: Johns Hopkins University Press, 1976), 1-10; Kenneth Lockridge, *A New England Town: The First Hundred Years* (New York: W. W. Norton, 1970), 37-46; Michael Zuckerman, *Peaceable Kingdoms: New England Towns in the Eighteenth Century* (New York: Knopf, 1970), 85-115, 172-76. Compare New England's elections to the raucous ones in Virginia described by Rhys Isaac, *The Transformation of Virginia, 1740-1790* (Chapel Hill, N.C.: University of North Carolina Press, 1982), 88-93, 110-14; Charles Sydnor, *Gentlemen Freeholders: Political Practices in Washington's Virginia* (Chapel Hill, N.C.: University of North Carolina Press, 1952), 21-34.

18. Bruce C. Daniels, "Connecticut's Villages Become Mature Towns: The Complexity of Local Institutions, 1676-1776," *WMQ,* 34 (1977), 93-100; Cook, *Fathers of the Towns,* chapter 1.

19. See Bruce C. Daniels, *The Connecticut Town: Growth and Development, 1635-1790* (Middletown, Ct.: Wesleyan University Press, 1979), 77-93; Bruce C. Daniels, *Dissent and Conformity on Narragansett Bay: The Colonial Rhode Island Town* (Middletown, Ct.: Wesleyan University Press, 1983), 98-101. See Vernon, "The Diary of Thomas Vernon," 77-78, for a description of formal dress.

20. Ronald A. Bosco, "Lectures at the Pillory: The Early American Execution Sermon," *AQ,* 30 (1978), 158-60; Edwin Powers, *Crime and Punishment in Early Massachusetts, 1620-1692: A Documentary History* (Boston: Beacon Press, 1966), 162-94.

21. Daniel E. Williams, "'Behold a Tragic Scene Strangely Changed into a Theatre of Mercy': The Structure and Significance of Criminal Conversion Narratives in Early New England," *AQ,* 37 (1986), 831-35; Good, "Colonials at Play," 14; Bosco, "Lectures at the Pillory," 158-70; Powers, *Crime and Punishment,* 252-80.

22. Bosco, "Lectures at the Pillory," 172-76; Williams, "'Behold a Tragic Scene,'" 827-31. Samuel Sewall notes executions throughout his diary: *The Diary of Samuel Sewall,* 2 vols., ed. M. Halsey Thomas (New York: Farrar, Straus and Giroux, 1973), vol. 1, 18, 22, 99, 100, 126, 153, 227, 292, 295, 310, 509.

23. Fitch, "The Diary of Jabez Fitch," part 1, 40-42; Sewall, *The Diary of Samuel Sewall,* vol. 1, 572; Anna Green Winslow, *Diary of Anna Green Winslow, A Boston School Girl of 1771,* ed. Alice Morse Earle (Boston and New York: Houghton Mifflin, 1894), 111; John Boyle, "Boyle's Journal of Occurrences in Boston," *New England Historical and Genealogical Register,* 84 (1930), 157.

24. Thompson, *Sex in Middlesex,* 89; Sewall, *The Diary of Samuel Sewall,* vol. 2, 627; Caulkins, *History of New London,* 482; Boyle, "Boyle's Journal," 266; James Barriskill, "The Newburyport Theatre in the Eighteenth Century," *Essex Institute Historical Collections,* 91 (1955), 214-15.

25. John Rowe, *Letters and Diary of John Rowe, Boston Merchant,* ed. Anne Rowe Cunningham (Boston: W. B. Clarke, 1903), 67-68.

26. Patricia Sankus, "Theatrical Entertainments and Other Amusements in Salem, Massachusetts from the Colonial Period Through the Year 1830" (Ph.D. diss., Tufts University, 1981), 8-10; Barriskill, "Newburyport Theatre," 214-215; Caulkins, *History of New London,* 481-82; Good, "Colonials at Play," 13-14; Boyle, "Boyle's Journal," 266.

27. For the king's birthday celebrations, see Raoul François Camus, "Military Music of Colonial Boston," in Barbara Lambert, ed., *Music in Colonial Massachusetts, 1630-1820,* 2 vols. (Boston: The Colonial Society of Massachusetts, 1980, 1985), vol. 1, 76. For the Havannah celebration, see Boyle, "Boyle's Journal," 159.

28. *Connecticut Courant,* March 30, 1766, describes the first Stamp Act party in Connecticut. Boyle, "Boyle's Journal," 259-60, 266, describes annual Stamp Act parties in Boston.

## Chapter VI

1. Joy Van Cleef and Kate Van Winkle Keller, "Selected American Country Dances and Their English Sources," in Barbara Lambert, ed., *Music in Colonial Massachusetts, 1630-1820,* 2 vols. (Boston: The Colonial Society of Massachusetts, 1980, 1985), vol. 1, 4-5.

2. Cleef and Keller, "Selected American Country Dances," 4-6, 10-12; Reet Howell, "Recreational Activities of Women in Colonial America," in Reet Howell, ed., *Her Story in Sport: A Historical Anthology of Women in Sports* (West Point, N.Y.: Leisure Press, 1982), 37-38, and Peter Wagner, "American Puritan Literature: A Neglected Field of Research in American Sport History," *Canadian Journal of History of Sport and Physical Education,* 8 (1977), 68-69. The Levett-Cotton exchange is quoted in Patricia Sankus, "Theatrical Entertainments and Other Amusements in Salem, Massachusetts from the Colonial Period Through the Year 1830" (Ph.D. diss., Tufts University, 1981), 3-4.

3. Increase Mather, *An Arrow Against Profane and Promiscuous Dancing, Drawn Out of the Quiver of the Scriptures* (Boston: Samuel Green, 1684). The opening of the schools is discussed by Cynthia Adams Hoover, "Epilogue to Secular Music in Early Massachusetts," in Lambert, ed., *Music in Colonial Massachusetts,* vol. 2, 735.

4. Mather, *An Arrow Against Dancing,* 2, 3, 6, 8, 21. Mather's sermon is often discussed in the literature on dance; see, for example, Cleef and Keller, "Selected American Country Dances," 6-8; and Wagner, "American Puritan Literature," 66-68.

5. Mather, *An Arrow Against Dancing,* 2, 3, 6, 8-12.

6. See Cleef and Keller, "Selected American Country Dances," 8,11, for the growth of dance under royal patronage. G. B. Warden, *Boston, 1689-1776* (Boston: Little Brown, 1970), 37-39, discusses Phips's relationship with the Mathers. For the impact of royalization on Boston's social life, see Carl Bridenbaugh, *Cities in the Wilderness: The First Century of Urban Life in America, 1625-1742* (London, Oxford, and New York: Oxford University Press, 1938), 250-51.

7. Cotton Mather, *A Cloud of Witness Against Balls and Dances* (Boston: B. Green and J. Allen, 1700), 2-4. Cleef and Keller, "Selected American Country Dances," 10-11, and Wagner, "American Puritan Literature," 66, both discuss Cotton Mather's tract.

8. Hoover, "Epilogue to Secular Music," 735, 746-47, discusses the growth of dance culture, as do Cleef and Keller, "Selected American Country Dances," 10-12, and James E. Morrison, *Early American Country Dances: Cotillions and Reels* (New York: Country Dance Society, 1978), 9-10. See also Sankus, "Theatrical Entertainments," 4-5.

9. Hoover, "Epilogue to Secular Music," 747; Bridenbaugh, *Cities in the Wilderness,* 276-77. For an account of a dancing school coming to a small town, see William Chauncey Fowler, *History of Durham, Connecticut, from the First Grant of Land in 1662 to 1866* (Durham, Ct.: By the Town of Durham, 1970), 22. For the contest over French dance masters see Jonathan Jackson to Joshua Brackett, Feb. 20, 1798, Putnam Collection, Massachusetts Historical Society.

10. See Hoover, "Epilogue to Secular Music," 746, 752, for the discussion of John and Samuel Adams's attitudes. See Spencer Mead, *Ye Historie of Ye Town of Greenwich* (Harrison, N.Y.: Harbor Hill Books, 1979), 48, for the incident in which the dance was broken up. John Griffith, *Etiquette for Dancemasters* (Northampton, Mass.: no publisher named, 1794).

11. Morrison, *Early American Country Dances*, 6-7; Hoover, "Epilogue to Secular Music," 746; Cleef and Keller, "Selected American Country Dances," 4-6.

12. Morrison, *Early American Country Dances*, 6-10, 64-66; Cleef and Keller, "Selected American Country Dances," 3-6, 8-12.

13. Morrison, *Early American Country Dances*, 46-53, and Cleef and Keller, "Selected American Country Dances," 73, both provide lists of popular local dances. See Kyms S. Rice, "Early American Taverns: For the Entertainment of Friends and Strangers," *Early American Life*, 14 (1983), 50, for a discussion of dance instruments. See also the critique of dance music in the travelogue of William Gregory, "A Scotchman's Journey in New England in 1771," *New England Magazine*, ed. Mary G. Powell, 12 (1895), 346, 351.

14. For material on these dances and attitudes toward them in New England, see Cleef and Keller, "Selected American Country Dances," 7-10; Hoover, "Epilogue to Secular Music," 746-48; and Morrison, *Early American Country Dances*, 10-12. For a revealing comparison of the role and types of dances in New England and in the South, see Rhys Isaac, *The Transformation of Virginia, 1740-1790* (Chapel Hill, N.C.: University of North Carolina Press, 1982), 80-87.

15. See accounts of dancing in three distinguished local histories of secondary centers: Frances Caulkins, *A History of Norwich, Connecticut* (Hartford: Case, Lockwood and Co., 1866), 322; Elizabeth Schenck, *The History of Fairfield*, 2 vols. (New York: Fairfield Historical Society, 1889), vol. 2, 102-103; and Fowler, *Durham*, 22. For the comments by the French visitor see J. P. Brissot De Warville, *New Travels in the United States of America, 1788*, ed. Durand Echeverria (Cambridge, Mass.: Harvard University Press, 1964), 118. Anna Green Winslow, *Diary of Anna Green Winslow, A Boston School Girl of 1771*, ed. Alice Morse Earle (Boston and New York: Houghton Mifflin, 1894), 6.

16. Hoover, "Epilogue to Secular Music," 744-52. John Rowe, *Letters and Diary of John Rowe, Boston Merchant*, ed. Anne Rowe Cunningham (Boston: W. B. Clarke, 1903), 34-36, provides a series of wonderful descriptions of Boston's balls. For the importance of dance in Portsmouth and in the Goddard family see Richard Crawford and David P. McKay, "Music in Manuscript: A Massachusetts Tune-Book of 1782," *PAAS*, 84 (1974), 46-47.

17. Rice, "Early American Taverns," 50. See also Gregory, "A Scotchman's Journey," 351.

18. For the best discussion of seventeenth-century weddings, see Edmund S. Morgan, *The Puritan Family* (New York: Harper and Row, 1966), 31-33. See also Francis J. Bremer, *The Puritan Experiment: New England Society from Bradford to Edwards* (New York: St. Martin's Press, 1976), 176-77. John Demos, *A Little Commonwealth: Family Life in Plymouth Colony* (New York: Oxford University Press, 1970), 162-63; Darrett

B. Rutman, *Winthrop's Boston: A Portrait of a Puritan Town, 1630-1649* (Chapel Hill, N.C.: University of North Carolina Press, 1965), 232-33.

19. Morgan, *Puritan Family*, 31-32. Joseph Green, "Commonplace Book," *Colonial Society of Massachusetts Publications*, ed. Samuel Morison, 34 (1937-1942), 250. Edmund S. Morgan, ed., *The Diary of Michael Wigglesworth* (New York: Harper and Row, 1946), 69, 74, 87; Samuel Sewall, *The Diary of Samuel Sewall*, 2 vols., ed. M. Halsey Thomas (New York: Farrar, Straus, and Giroux, 1973), vol. 2, 921, 933, 949, 1057; Cotton Mather, *The Diary of Cotton Mather*, 2 vols. (New York: Frederick Ungar, 1948), vol. 2, 97.

20. John Ballantine, "Diary," in John Hoyt Lockwood, ed., *Westfield and Its Historical Influences, 1669-1919* (Westfield, Mass.: privately printed, 1922), 378-80. Christian McBurney, "The South Kingstown Planters: Country Gentry in Colonial Rhode Island," *RIH*, 45 (1986), 89. Jacob Bailey, "Diary," in William S. Bartlet, ed., *The Frontier Missionary* (Boston: Ide and Dutton, 1853), 10-11.

21. Elihu Ashley, "Diary," in George Sheldon, ed., *A History of Deerfield, Massachusetts*, vol. 2 (Deerfield, Mass.: Press of A. E. Hall, 1896), 690. Elizabeth Porter Phelps, "Diary," in Arrias Huntington, ed., *Under a Colonial Rooftree: Fireside Chronicles of Early New England* (New York: Houghton Mifflin, 1891), 35. Judge Sherman Adams and Henry R. Stiles, *The History of Ancient Wethersfield, Connecticut* (New York: The Grafton Press, 1904), 338-39.

22. Sarah Kemble Knight, *The Journal of Madame Knight*, ed. Malcolm Frieberg (Boston: David R. Godine, 1972), 20; Ashley, "Diary," 610. The story of the hoax is in Henry R. Stiles, *The Histories and Genealogies of Ancient Windsor, Connecticut*, 2 vols. (Hartford: Case, Lockwood, and Brainard, 1891), vol. 2, 420.

23. Ballantine, "Diary," 435. John Boyle, "Boyle's Journal of Occurrences in Boston," *New England Historical and Genealogical Register*, 84 (1930), 265.

24. For an overall view of food in early Puritan society, see James W. Baker, "Seventeenth-Century English Yeoman Foodways at Plymouth Plantation," in Peter Benes, ed., *Foodways in the Northeast* (Boston: Boston University, 1982), 105-113. John Winthrop, *Winthrop's Journal: "History of New England, 1630-1649,"* 2 vols., ed. James Hosmer (New York: Barnes and Noble, 1908), vol. 1, 47, 49, 50, 69, 70, 71.

25. Baker, "Seventeenth-Century Foodways," 113; Daphne L. Derven, "Wholesome, Toothsome, and Diverse: Eighteenth-Century Foodways in Deerfield, Massachusetts," in Benes, ed., *Foodways*, 54-57; and Laurel Thatcher Ulrich, "It 'Went Away She Knew Not How': Food Theft and Domestic Conflict in Seventeenth-Century Essex County," in Benes, ed., *Foodways*, 98-101.

26. For the growth in sophistication in foods, see Sarah McMahon, "A Comfortable Existence: The Changing Composition of Diet in Rural New England, 1620-1840," *WMQ*, 42 (1985), 31, 50-51. See also Derven, "Wholesome, Toothsome, and Diverse," 55-57. The Portsmouth advertisements were called to my attention by Steven R. Pendery, "The Archeology of Urban Foodways in Portsmouth, New Hampshire," in Benes, ed., *Foodways*, 12-27.

27. Rowe, "Diary," 26-50.

28. Alice Morse Earle, *Stage Coach and Tavern Days* (New York: Macmillan, 1900), 89-91, discusses turtle frolics at great length, as does Carl Bridenbaugh, *Cities in Revolt: Urban Life in America, 1743-1776* (New York: Capricorn Books, 1955), 164-65. See also C. P. B. Jefferys, *Newport, 1639-1976: An Historical Sketch* (Newport: Newport Historical Society, 1976), 26. A riotous one is described by Solomon Drowne, "Dr. Solomon Drowne's Journal," *Newport Historical Magazine*, 1 (1880-1881), 67. The Holyokes' summer of turtle frolics is described in James Phillips, *Salem in The Eighteenth Century* (Boston and New York: Houghton Mifflin, 1937), 256.

29. "Providence Town Meeting Minutes" (June 1786), n.p., Providence City Hall.

30. The special status of tea and other drinks is discussed in Michael D. Coe and Sophie E. Coe, "Mid-Eighteenth-Century Food and Drink on the Massachustts Frontier," in Benes, ed., *Foodways*, 41-45. Phelps, "Diary," 90-92.

---

# Chapter VII

1. The authors of most general studies of Puritanism feel compelled to discuss sexuality at least in passing. Probably the most influential analysis remains the one by Edmund S. Morgan written a half century ago. See Morgan, "The Puritans and Sex," *NEQ*, 15 (1942), 591-607. Morgan's emphasis on the Puritans' ability to be frank and to enjoy sex has been recently challenged by several scholars, among them Michael Zuckerman, "Pilgrims in the Wilderness: Community, Modernity, and The Maypole at Merry Mount," *NEQ*, 50 (1977), 266-70; Kathleen Verduin, "Our Cursed Natures: Sexuality and the Puritan Conscience," *NEQ*, 56 (1983), 222-24, 229-30; and Ronald Bosco, "Lectures at the Pillory: The Early American Execution Sermon," *AQ*, 30 (1978), 157-58. Cotton is quoted in Edmund S. Morgan, *The Puritan Family: Family and Domestic Relations in Seventeenth-Century New England* (New York: Harper and Row, 1966), 29.

2. Bosco, "Lectures at the Pillory," 157-58; Perry Miller, *The New England Mind in the Seventeenth Century* (Cambridge, Mass.: Harvard University Press, 1939), 251-53; Murray Murphy, "The Psychodynamics of Puritan Conversion," *AQ*, 31 (1979), 146.

3. William Bradford, *Of Plymouth Plantation*, ed. Harvey Wish (New York: Capricorn Books, 1962), 197-98, 203.

4. Lilian Handlin, "Dissent in a Small Community," *NEQ*, 58 (1985), 194; Robert Roetger, "The Transformation of Sexual Morality in 'Puritan' New England: Evidence from New Haven Court Records, 1639-1698," *Canadian Review of American Studies*, 15 (1984), 243-50; Charles Hoadley, ed., *Records of the Colony and Plantation of New Haven, 1638 to 1649* (Hartford: Case, Tiffany, 1857), 62-73, 295-96. For general discussions of deviant sex in Puritan culture see Kai T. Erikson, *Wayward Puritans: A Study of the Sociology of Deviance* (New York: John Wiley and Sons, 1966).

5. Roger Thompson, *Sex in Middlesex: Popular Mores in a Massachusetts County, 1649-1699* (Amherst, Mass.: University of Massachusetts Press, 1986), 17-20, 36-37.

6. See Morgan, *The Puritan Family*, 45-55, and Thompson, *Sex in Middlesex*, for general discussions of marital contracts. Hety Shepard, letter, March 20, 1676, in "A Puritan

Maiden's Diary," *New England Magazine*, ed. Adeline Spicer, 11 (1894-95), 21-22. Wigglesworth's correspondence is discussed in Morgan, *Puritan Family*, 53-54. Wigglesworth's diary is filled with his unsuccessful attempts to subordinate his sexual and romantic attractions to an ascetic piety. Se Edmund S. Morgan, ed., *The Diary of Michael Wigglesworth*, 1653-1657 (New York: Harper and Row, 1965), 3, 6, 17, 25, 38, and passim.

7. Winthrop quoted in Morgan, *Puritan Family*, 85. Sarah Kemble Knight, *The Journal of Madame Knight*, ed. Malcolm Frieberg (Boston: David R. Godine, 1972), 18, 19; Ebenezer Parkman, *The Diary of Ebenezer Parkman, 1703-1782*, ed. Francis G. Walett (Worcester, Mass.: The American Antiquarian Society, 1974), 35; Roger Wolcott, *The Poems of Roger Wolcott* (Boston: The Club of Odd Volumes, 1898), 11-12.

8. See Emory Elliott, *Power and the Pulpit in Puritan New England* (Princeton, N.J.: Princeton University Press, 1975), 34-35, 73-74; and Daniel B. Shea, Jr., *Spiritual Autobiography in Early America* (Princeton, N.J.: Princeton University Press, 1968), 78, for analyses of guilt and sexuality in diaries. See Thompson, *Sex in Middlesex*, 67-68, 193-94, for evidence of an increase in premarital sex in the late seventeenth century.

9. Mather, *Addresses to Old Men, Young Men, and Little Children* (Boston: B. Green, 1690), 73; Mather, *The Pure Nazarite. Advice to a Young Man, Concerning an Impiety and Impurity (Not Easily to be Spoken of) Which Many Young Men are to their Perpetual Sorrow, Too Easily Drawn Into* (Boston: T. Fleet, 1723), 4, 6, 7, 8; Anonymous, *Onania or the Heinous Sin of Self Pollution and all its Frightful Consequences in both Sexes Considered* (Boston: Phillips, 1724), 15, 17-20.

10. *Reefer Madness: Tell Your Children* (1936) Distributed by New Line Cinema, New York.

11. Henry R. Stiles, *Bundling: Its Origins, Progress, and Decline in America* (Albany, N.Y.: Joel Munsell, 1865), 2, 3, 39. See also Dana Doten, *The Art of Bundling* (New York: Farrar and Rinehart, 1938), for a more titillating account.

12. Stiles, *Bundling*, 65-74; and B. A. Botkin, ed., *A Treasury of New England Folklore* (New York: Bonanza Books, 1967), 411-13.

13. Stiles, *Bundling*, 75-79; Botkin, ed., *New England Folklore*, 412.

14. Jonathan Edwards, "Temptation and Deliverance," *The Works of Jonathan Edwards, A. M., with an Essay on His Genius and Writings*, 2 vols., ed. Henry Rogers (London: F. Westby and A. H. Davis, 1834), vol. 1, 231.

15. Samuel Peters quoted in Stiles, *Bundling*, 53, 75-79. Andrew Burnaby, *Travels Through the Middle Settlements in North America* (New York: Augustus Kelly, 1970; originally published 1775), 141-42.

16. All three bundling ballads and others are reprinted in Stiles, *Bundling*, 81-87, 88-93, 93-99.

17. Douglas L. Good, "Colonials at Play: Leisure in Newport 1723," *RIH*, 33 (1974), 14-15.

18. Dr. Alexander Hamilton, *Gentleman's Progress: The Itinerarium of Dr. Alexander Hamilton, 1744*, ed. Carl Bridenbaugh (Westport, Ct.: Greenwood Press, 1973), 134-39.

19. See Bruce C. Daniels, *The Connecticut Town: Growth and Development, 1635-1790* (Middletown, Ct.: Wesleyan University Press), 115-16, for changes in meeting-house seating. See Henry Bronson, *The History of Waterbury, Connecticut* (Waterbury,

Ct.: Bronson Brothers, 1858), 228; and William Fowler, *History of Durham, Connecticut* (Durham, Ct.: Town of Durham, 1970), 22, for accounts of the growth in kissing. Edwards, "Temptation and Deliverance," 231.

20. Elihu Ashley, "Diary," in George Sheldon, *A History of Deerfield, Massachusetts,* 2 vols. (Deerfield, Mass.: Press of E. A. Hall, 1895, 1896), 686-91.

21. The following excerpts are from William Gregory, "A Scotchman's Journey in New England in 1771," *New England Magazine,* ed. Mary G. Powell, 12 (1895), 343-52.

22. Nathaniel Ames, "Diary," in Charles Warren, *Jacobin and Junto: Or Early American Politics as Viewed in the Diary of Dr. Nathaniel Ames* (Cambridge, Mass.: Harvard University Press, 1931), 3-14, 30-32.

23. John Boyle, "Boyle's Journal of Occurrences in Boston," *New England Historical and Genealogical Register,* 84 (1930), 158-59; Anna Green Winslow, *Diary of Anna Green Winslow, A Boston School Girl of 1771,* ed. Alice Morse Earle (Boston: Houghton Mifflin, 1894), 36-37; Esther Edwards Burr, *Esther Burr's Journal,* ed. Jeremiah E. Rankin (Washington, D.C.: Woodward and Lothrop, 1903), 138.

24. See two extraordinarily insightful discussions of the ideal woman and marriage: Jan Lewis, "The Republican Wife: Virtue and Seduction in the Early Republic," *WMQ,* 44 (1987), 695-98, 705; Laurel Thatcher Ulrich, "Vertuous Women Found: New England Ministerial Literature, 1668-1735," *AQ,* 28 (1976), 20-40.

25. Quoted in Lewis, "The Republican Wife," 705.

26. See Lewis, "The Republican Wife," 695-705; Ulrich, "Vertuous Women Found," 20-35; Nancy Cott, "Divorce and the Changing Status of Women in Eighteenth-Century Massachusetts," *WMQ,* 33 (1976), 598-602; Sheldon Cohen, "The Broken Bond: Divorce in Providence County, 1749-1809," *RIH,* 44 (1985), 67-75; Ellen K. Rothman, *Hands and Hearts: A History of Courtship in America* (New York: Harper and Row, 1984).

27. Susan Dion, "Women in the Boston Gazette, 1755-1775," *Historical Journal of Massachusetts,* 14 (1986), 90-91. The poem is in the *Connecticut Courant,* April 26, 1766, 3.

28. For changes in marital arrangements, see Daniel Scott Smith, "Parental Power and Marriage Patterns: An Analysis of Historical Trends in Hingham, Massachusetts," *Journal of Marriage and the Family,* 35 (1973), 425-27. For rates of premarital conception, see Thompson, *Sex in Middlesex,* 67-68; John Demos, "Families in Colonial Bristol, Rhode Island: An Exercise in Historical Demography," *WMQ,* 25 (1968), 56-57; Daniel Scott Smith and Michael Hindus, "Pre-Marital Pregnancy in America, 1640-1971: An Overview and Interpretation," *Journal of Interdisciplinary History,* 5 (1975), 537-45.

---

## Chapter VIII

1. For overall statements about English and Puritan attitudes toward alcohol see Mark Edward Lender and James Kirby Martin, *Drinking in America: A History* (New York: The Free Press, 1982), chapter 1; Carl Bridenbaugh, *Vexed and Troubled Englishmen* (London and New York: Oxford University Press, 1976), 148, 196-97, 363-66;

Samuel Eliot Morison, *Builders of the Bay Colony* (Boston: Houghton Mifflin, 1930), 130-48; Edmund Morgan, *The Puritan Family: Religion and Domestic Relations in Seventeenth-Century New England* (New York: Harper and Row, 1966), 16; Edwin Powers, *Crime and Punishment in Early Massachusetts, 1620-1692* (Boston: Beacon Press, 1966), 366-99; and Kym Rice, "Early American Taverns: For the Entertainment of Friends and Strangers," *EAL,* 14 (1983), 46-55.

For the role of alcohol and taverns in colonial America, see Alice Morse Earle, *Stage Coach and Tavern Days* (New York: Macmillan, 1900); Carl Bridenbaugh, *Cities in the Wilderness: The First Century of Urban Life, 1625-1742* (New York: Oxford University Press, 1938), 107-15, 265-74; 426-34, and passim; Louis Wright, *The Cultural Life of the American Colonies* (New York: Harper and Row, 1957), 248-49; Rice, "Early American Taverns," 46-55.

2. The Apostle Paul and Governor Bradford are quoted in Powers, *Crime and Punishment,* 369-71. John Pond to William Pond, March 15, 1630, in Everett Emerson, ed., *Letters from New England: The Massachusetts Bay Colony 1629-1638* (Amherst, Mass.: The University of Massachusetts Press, 1976), 65. For the importance of cider, beer, and fermented juices at meals, see Earle, *Stage Coach and Tavern Days,* 123-25 and Anna Winslow, *Diary of Anna Green Winslow, A Boston School Girl of 1771,* ed. Alice Morse Earle (Boston and New York: Houghton Mifflin, 1894), 101-02.

3. Richard S. Dunn, *Sugar and Slaves: The Rise of the Planter Class in the English West Indies, 1624-1713* (Chapel Hill, N.C.: University of North Carolina Press, 1972), 196-99; Rice, "Early American Taverns," 47-48; Daphne L. Derven, "Wholesome, Toothsome, and Diverse: Eighteenth-Century Foodways in Deerfield, Massachusetts," in Peter Benes, ed., *Foodways in the Northeast* (Boston: Boston University American and New England Studies Program, 1984), 49-50.

4. For the opening of Boston's first taverns, see Darrett B. Rutman, *Winthrop's Boston: A Portrait of a Puritan Town, 1630-1649* (Chapel Hill, N.C.: University of North Carolina Press, 1966), 37, 190-91. For other towns and the General Court laws, see Earle, *Stage Coach and Tavern Days,* 4-7.

5. William DeLoss Love, *The Colonial History of Hartford* (Hartford, Ct.: Connecticut Printers, 1935), 216-17. For the full text of the laws, see J. Hammond Trumbull and Charles Hoadley, eds., *The Public Records of the Colony of Connecticut,* 15 vols. (Hartford: Brown and Parsons, 1850-1890), vol. 1 (1644), 103; Charles Hoadley, ed., *Records of the Colony and Plantation of New Haven,,* 2 vols. (Hartford: Case, Tiffany, 1857), vol. 1 (1645), 166; and John Russell Bartlett, ed., *Records of the Colony of Rhode Island and Providence Plantations in New England,* 10 vols. (Providence: State of Rhode Island, 1856-1865), vol. 1 (1647), 185-86.

6. Earle, *Stage Coach and Tavern Days,* 4-5, 30; Rice, "Early American Taverns," 47.

7. For the details on the taverns on the Bay Path see Charles Banks, *The History of Martha's Vineyard, Dukes County Massachusetts,* 3 vols. (Edgertown, Mass.: Dukes County Historical Society, 1966), vol. 1, 461. For the taverns between New York and Boston, see Elizabeth Schenck, *The History of Fairfield, Fairfield County, Connecticut,* 2 vols. (New York: privately by the author, 1889, 1905), vol. 2, 429-430. And for the taverns in

western Massachusetts and Connecticut, see Albert E. Van Dusen, "The Trade of Revolutionary Connecticut" (Ph.D. diss., University of Pennsylvania, 1948), 48.

8. Daniel Vickers, "Work and Life on the Fishing Periphery of Essex County, Massachusetts, 1630-1675," in David D. Hall and David Grayson Allen, eds., *Seventeenth-Century New England* (Boston: The Colonial Society of Massachusetts, 1984), 113; Earle, *Stage Coach and Tavern Days*, 20-25; Douglas L. Good, "Colonials at Play: Leisure in Newport, 1723," *RIH*, 33 (1974), 9-10; Carl Bridenbaugh, *Cities in Revolt: Urban Life in America, 1743-1775*, 2nd ed. (New York: Capricorn Books, 1964), 157.

9. See the following for the number of taverns mentioned in this paragraph and the numbers listed in Table I: Bruce C. Daniels, *The Connecticut Town: Growth and Development, 1635-1790* (Middletown, Ct.: Wesleyan University Press, 1979), 194-95; James Montgomery Bailey, *History of Danbury, Connecticut, 1684-1896* (New York: Burr Printing House, 1896), 30, 173; Charles Henry Davis, *History of Wallingford, Connecticut from Its Settlement in 1670 to the Present Time* (Meriden, Ct.: By the Author, 1870), 409; Spencer Mead, *Ye Historie of Ye Town of Greenwich* (Harrison, N.Y.: Harbor Hill Books, 1979), 51; Henry R. Stiles, *The Histories and Genealogies of Ancient Windsor, Connecticut,* 2 vols. (Hartford: Case, Lockwood, and Brainard, 1891), vol. 1, 397; Edward Byers, *The Nation of Nantucket: Society and Politics in an Early American Commercial Center, 1660-1820* (Boston: Northeastern University Press, 1957), 150; Charles Banks, *History of York, Maine,* 3 vols. (Baltimore: Regional Publishing Co., 1967), vol. 2, 321-27; Daniel Lamson, *History of the Town of Weston, Massachusetts, 1630-1890* (Boston: Geo. H. Ells Co., 1913), 188-91; Charles Taylor, *History of Great Barrington, Massachusetts* (Great Barrington, Mass.: Clark W. Bryan and Co., 1882), 364-65; J. H. Temple, *History of North Brookfield, Massachusetts* (North Brookfield, Mass.: Town of North Brookfield, 1987), 266; Judge Sherman Adams and Henry R. Stiles, *The History of Ancient Wethersfield, Connecticut* (New York: The Grafton Press, 1904), 661; Charles S. Grant, *Democracy in the Connecticut Frontier Town of Kent* (New York: Columbia University Press, 1961), 36, 44; Michael Zuckerman, *Peaceable Kingdoms: New England Towns in the Eighteenth Century* (New York: Knopf, 1970), 174; Charles E. Clark, *The Eastern Frontier: The Settlement of Northern New England, 1610-1763* (New York: Knopf, 1970), 265, 345-46; Christopher Bickford, *Farmington in Connecticut* (Canaan, N. H.: The Farmington Historical Society, 1982), 207; Good, "Colonials at Play," 9; Litchfield County Historical Society, *A History of Litchfield County* (Philadelphia: privately printed, 1881), 183; William Willingham, "Windham, Connecticut: Profile of a Revolutionary Community, 1755-1818" (Ph.D. diss., Northwestern University 1972), 73; Ezra Stiles, *Extracts from The Itineraries and Other Miscellanies of Ezra Stiles*, ed. Franklin Bowditch Dexter (New Haven: Yale University Press, 1916), 367; Samuel Alvord, *A Historical Sketch of Bolton* (Bolton, Ct.: privately printed, 1920), 25; Bruce Stark, *Lyme, Connecticut: From Founding to Independence* (Old Lyme, Ct.: Lyme Bicentennial Commission, 1976), 52.

10. Earle, *Stage Coach and Tavern Days*, 20-25; Rice, "Early American Taverns," 46-55.

11. John Winthrop, *Winthrop's Journal: "History of New England, 1630-1649,"* 2 vols., ed. James Hosmer (New York: Barnes and Noble, 1908), vol. 1, 120; Adams and Stiles, *Ancient*

*Wethersfield*, 325; Powers, *Crime and Punishment*, 386-87; Earle, *Stage Coach and Tavern Days*, 8-9; Kai T. Erickson, *Wayward Puritans: A Study in the Sociology of Deviance* (New York, London, and Sydney; John Wiley and Sons, 1966), 174-75; Brenda D. McDonald, "Domestic Violence in Colonial Massachusetts," *Historical Journal of Massachusetts*, 14 (1986), 54-64; Roger Thompson, *Sex in Middlesex: Popular Mores in a Massachusetts County, 1649-1699* (Amherst, Mass.: University of Massachusetts Press, 1986), 88-91.

12. John Fiske, *The Notebooks of the Reverend John Fiske, 1644-1675*, ed. Robert Pope, *Colonial Society of Massachusetts*, 47 (1974), 93; Adams and Stiles, *Ancient Wethersfield*, 325; Powers, *Crime and Punishment*, 386.

13. Thompson, *Sex in Middlesex*, 85-91, 193-94; Powers, *Crime and Punishment*, 386; Vickers, "Work and Life on the Fishing Periphery," 113-14.

14. Increase Mather, *Wo to Drunkards* (Boston: Marmaduke Johnson, 1673); Increase Mather, *An Earnest Exhortation to the Inhabitants of New England to Harken to the Voice of God* . . . (Boston: John Foster, 1676). The extracts I quote are in Powers, *Crime and Punishment*, 615-18. Increase Mather, "A Notebook Kept by Increase Mather," *Massachusetts Historical Society Proceedings*, 2nd series, 13 (1899-1900), 397-411.

15. Benjamin Colman, *The Government and Improvement of Mirth, According to the Laws of Christianity, In Three Sermons* (Boston: B. Green, 1707); 48; Cotton Mather, et al., *A Serious Address to Those Who Unnecessarily Frequent The Tavern and Often Spend the Evening in Public Houses* (Boston: S. Garrish, 1726), 7, 17.

16. Powers, *Crime and Punishment*, 376-78, 385-87, 618, provides a detailed catalogue of provincial laws that concerned alcohol.

17. Clark, *The Eastern Frontier*, 265; Powers, *Crime and Punishment*, 392-95, 397.

18. Earle, *Stage Coach and Tavern Days*, 138-47, contains lists of typical tavern names.

19. Good, "Colonials at Play, 10-17; C. P. B. Jeffreys, *Newport, 1639-1976: An Historical Sketch* (Newport: Newport Historical Society, 1976), 16-18.

20. Bridenbaugh, *Cities in the Wilderness*, 271; Good, "Colonials at Play," 13-17; Jeffreys, *Newport*, 17-18.

21. Bridenbaugh, *Cities in the Wilderness,*, 112-13, 269-70, 433-34; Good, "Colonials at Play," 13-14; Jeffreys, *Newport*, 16-18. Dr Alexander Hamilton rated taverns in many parts of the colonies in his travel memoir of 1744: Newport's were among his favorite. Dr. Alexander Hamilton, *Gentleman's Progress: The Itinerarium of Dr. Alexander Hamilton, 1744*, ed. Carl Bridenbaugh (Westport, Ct.: Greenwood Press, 1973), 168-70.

22. Ebenezer Parkman, *The Diary of Ebenezer Parkman, 1703-1782*, ed. Francis G. Walett (Worcester, Mass.: American Antiquarian Society, 1974), 3, 75; John Ballantine, "The Diary of John Ballantine," in John Hoyt Lockwood, *Westfield and its Historic Influences, 1669-1919* (Westfield, Mass.: privately printed, 1922), 390.

23. Earle, *Stage Coach and Tavern Days*, 197-99; Rice, "Early American Taverns," 46-49; Bailey, *History of Danbury*, 16-18; Hamilton, *Gentleman's Progress*, 168-70; Sarah Kemble Knight, *The Journal of Madame Knight*, ed. Malcolm Frieberg (Boston: David R, Godine, 1972), 8; Susan Dion, "Women in the Boston Gazette, 1755-1775," *Historical Journal of Massachusetts*, 14 (1986), 92-93. William Gregory, "A Scotchman's Journey in New England in 1771," ed. Mary G. Powell, *New England Magazine*, 12 (1895), 349-50; Sheldon Cohen,

"Legal Change and Women in the American Revolution," a paper given to the Association for the Study of Connecticut History (New Haven, October 1988), passim. Earle, *Stage Coach and Tavern Days*, 25, counts the number of women tavern-keepers in early eighteenth-century Boston. For tavern licenses issued during the Revolutionary years see "Selectmen's Minutes, Boston," in *A Report of the Records Commission* (Boston: Rockwell and Churchill, 1894), 8, 9, 10, 11, 28, 29, 30, 31, 320, 321.

24. This paragraph and the next one are drawn from the delightful descriptions in Earle, *Stage Coach and Tavern Days*, 102-37, and also from Derven, "Eighteenth-Century Foodways," 49-50, and Sarah McMahon, "A Comfortable Existence: The Changing Composition of Diet in Rural New England, 1620-1840," *WMQ*, 42 (1985), 42-43.

25. Earle, *Stage Coach and Tavern Days*, 45, 52-53; 67, Rice, *Early American Taverns*, 48-50; Cynthia Adams Hoover, "Epilogue to Secular Music in Early Massachusetts," in Barbara Lambert, ed., *Music in Colonial Massachusetts, 1630-1820*, 2 vols. (Boston: The Colonial Society of Massachusetts, 1980, 1985), vol. 2, 754.

26. Rice, *Early American Taverns*, 48-49; Earle, *Stage Coach and Tavern Days*, 78-79; Knight, *Journal of Madame Knight*, 8; Gregory, "A Scotchman's Journey," 349.

27. Gregory, "A Scotchman's Journey," 347-50.

28. Ibid., 349-50. Earle, *Stage Coach and Tavern Days*, 12; Good, "Colonials at Play," 12; F. W. Fairholt, *Tobacco: Its History and Associations* (London: Chapman and Hall, 1859), 20, 43, 75-79, 85. Franklin's poem appeared in the *New England Courant* in 1721: it is quoted in Fairholt, *Tobacco*, 20. The minister Ebenezer Parkman often smoked when he socialized with other ministers in taverns. See Parkman, *Diary*, 4, 5, 22.

29. Knight, *Journal of Madame Knight*, 4, 5, 12, 17, 26.

30. Earle, *Stage Coach and Tavern Days*, 197-99, 203-204; Daniels, *The Connecticut Town*, 157-59; Grant, *Democracy in Kent*, 35, 36, 44; Richard D. Brown, *Knowledge Is Power: The Diffusion of Information in Early America, 1800-1865* (New York and Oxford: Oxford University Press, 1989), 40; David D. Hall, "Introduction: The Uses of Literacy in New England, 1600-1850," in William L. Joyce, ed., *Printing and Society in Early America* (Worcester: American Antiquarian Society, 1983), 37.

31. Hoover, "Secular Music," 754.

---

## Chapter IX

1. For some general discussions about sport as a key to societal concerns, see Peter Bailey, *Leisure and Class in Victorian England: Rational Recreation and the Contest for Control* (London: Methuen, 1987), introduction; Melvin L. Adelman, "Academicans and American Athletics: A Decade of Progress," *JSH*, 10 (1983), 86-90; Dennis Brailsford, "Religion and Sport in Eighteenth-Century England: For the Encouragement of Piety and Virtue, and for the Preventing or Punishing of Vice, Profaneness, and Immorality," *British Journal of Sports History*, 1 (1984), 141; Allen Guttmann, *From Ritual to Record: The Nature of Modern Sports* (New York: Columbia University Press, 1978), 58-59.

2. Thomas S. Henrichs, "Sport and Social Hierarchy in Medieval England," *JSH*, 9 (1982), 21-23; Richard D. Mandell, *Sport: A Cultural History* (New York: Columbia University Press, (1984), 113-14; Christopher Brooke, *From Alfred to Henry III, 871-1272* (New York: W. W. Norton, 1961), 241-44; George Holmes, *The Later Middle Ages, 1272-1485* (New York: W. W. Norton, 1962), 72-75.

3. Henrichs, "Sport and Social Hierarchy," 27-30; Guttmann, *From Ritual to Record*, 87; Brooke, *From Alfred to Henry III*, 221-23; Holmes, *The Later Middle Ages*, 136-48.

4. Mandell, *Sport*, 121-29, 132-33; Henrichs, "Sport and Social Hierarchy," 30-34; Guttmann, *From Ritual to Record*, 58-60; Brailsford, "Religion and Sport," 141-42.

5. Allen Guttmann, "English Sports Spectators: The Restoration to the Early Nineteenth Century," *JSH*, 12 (1985), 104-05; R. M. Wiles, "Crowd-Pleasing Spectacles in Eighteenth-Century England," *Journal of Popular Culture*, 1 (1987), 93-95.

6. Winton V. Solberg, *Redeem the Time: The Puritan Sabbath in Early America* (Cambridge, Mass.: Harvard University Press, 1977), 48-51, sums up these attitudes well. See also Brailsford, "Religion and Sport," 139-41; Guttmann, "English Sports Spectators," 103-05.

7. Henrichs, "Sport and Social Hierarchy," 21-31; Solberg, *Redeem the Time*, 70-77; Mandell, *Sport*, 120-21; Nancy Struna, "Puritans and Sport: The Irretrievable Tide of Change," *JSH*, 4 (1977), 6-7. The *Book of Sports* is reprinted in Samuel Gardiner, *The Constitutional Documents of the Puritan Revolution* (Oxford: Oxford University Press, 1906), 99-101.

8. For cultural historians' perception of Puritan hostility to sport, see John A. Lucas and Ronald Smith, *Saga of American Sport* (Philadelphia: Lea and Febiger, 1978), 7-8; Peter Wagner, "American Puritan Literature: A Neglected Field of Research in American Sport History," *Canadian Journal of History of Sport and Physical Education*, 8 (1977), 66; Wagner, "Puritan Attitudes Towards Physical Recreation in Seventeenth-Century New England," *JSH*, 3 (1976), 139-41; Ralph Gabriel, ed., *The Pageant of America* (New Haven, Ct.: Yale University Press, 1929), 2.

9. Lucas and Smith, *Saga of Sport*, 7-8; Samuel Eliot Morison, *Harvard College in the Seventeenth Century*, 2 vols. (Cambridge, Mass.: Harvard University Press, 1936), vol. 1, 116-23; William Bradford, *Of Plymouth Plantations*, ed. Harvey Wish (New York: Capricorn Books, 1962), 87; Edmund S. Morgan, *The Puritan Dilemma: The Story of John Winthrop* (Boston: Little, Brown, 1958), 8-12.

10. Peter N. Carroll, *Puritanism and the Wilderness: The Intellectual Significance of the New England Frontier, 1629-1700* (New York: Columbia University Press, 1969), 9-12; Roderick Nash, *Wilderness and the American Mind* (New Haven: Yale University Press, 1982), 23-28; George Williams, *Wilderness and Paradise in Christian Thought* (New York: Oxford University Press, 1962), passim; Douglas R. McManis, *Colonial New England: An Historical Geography* (New York, London, and Toronto: Oxford University Press, 1975), 36-38; Karen Ordahl Kupperman, *Settling with the Indians: The Meeting of English and Indian Cultures in America, 1580-1640* (Totowa, N.J.: Rowman and Littlefield, 1980), 43-47; John E. Ferling, *A Wilderness of Miseries: War and Warriors in Early America* (Westport, Ct.: Greenwood Press, 1980), 32-35. Perry

Miller makes the Puritan attempt to subdue the wilderness one of the important metaphors of his work. See Miller, *Errand into the Wilderness* (Cambridge, Mass.: Harvard University Press, 1956), chapter 1.

11. For descriptions of Puritan perception of the natives' physical strength, see Alden T. Vaughan, *New England Frontier: Puritans and Indians, 1620-1675* (Boston and Toronto: Little, Brown, 1965), 41-43. For descriptions of militia training and martial contests, see Ferling, *A Wilderness of Miseries*, 32-35; Richard H. Marcus, "The Militia of Colonial Connecticut, 1639-1775: An Institutional Study" (Ph.D. diss., University of Colorado, 1965), 253-57; and Stewart L. Gates, "Disorder and Social Organization: The Militia in Connecticut Public Life, 1660-1860" (Ph.D. diss., University of Connecticut, 1975), 17, 23, 75, 80. For Smith's and Trumbull's behavior see respectively, Judge Sherman Adams and Henry R. Stiles, *The History of Ancient Wethersfield, Connecticut* (New York: The Grafton Press, 1904), 154-55; and Henry Bronson, *The History of Waterbury, Connecticut* (Waterbury, Ct.: Bronson Brothers, 1858), 259-60.

12. Carroll, *Puritans and the Wilderness*, 9-10, Alden Vaughan, *American Genesis: Captain John Smith and the Founding of Virginia* (Boston and Toronto: Little, Brown, 1975), 98-97; McManis, *Colonial New England*, 37-38.

13. All the above are quoted in Carroll, *Puritans and the Wilderness*, 31, 48-52. For the importance of commercial fishing, see Bernard Bailyn, *New England Merchants in the Seventeenth Century* (Cambridge, Mass.: Harvard University Press, 1955), 82-83 and passim.

14. Thomas Minor, *The Diary of Thomas Minor, Stonington, Connecticut* (New London, Ct.: Press of the Day, 1899), 20, 21, 26; Samuel Sewall, *The Diary of Samuel Sewall*, ed., Harvey Wish (New York: Capricorn Books, 1967), 10; Morison, *Harvard College*, 117-18.

15. William Whitmore, ed., *The Colonial Laws of Massachusetts* (Boston: Massachusetts Historical Society, 1889), 37; Nathaniel B. Shortleff, ed., *Records of the Governor and Company of Massachusetts Bay in New England*, 5 vols. (Boston: 1853-54), vol. 4, part 2, 400, 450.

16. See Thomas Robert Davis, "Sport and Exercise in the Lives of Selected Colonial Americans: Massachusetts and Virginia, 1700-1775" (Ph.D. diss., University of Maryland, 1970), 46-49 for a discussion of colonial fishing. See also Jabez Fitch, "The Diary of Jabez Fitch, Jr.," *Mayflower Descendants* (1899-1914), 37-41; Israel Litchfield, "Diary," in Wilford J. Litchfield, *The Litchfield Family in America* (Southbridge, Mass.: W. J. Litchfield, 1901), 338-39; and Thomas Vernon, "The Diary of Thomas Vernon," *Rhode Island Historical Tracts*, 3 (Providence: Providence Press Co., 1881), 11-33. Ebenezer Parkman, *The Diary of Ebenezer Parkman, 1703-1782*, ed. Francis G. Walett (Worcester, Mass.: American Antiquarian Society, 1974), 81-87. "Record of Shad and Salmon Catch, Hartford, Connecticut, 1789-1796," Ms. Connecticut State Library, filed under Hartford manuscripts.

17. John Rowe, *Letters and Diary of John Rowe, Boston Merchant*, ed. Anne Rowe Cunningham (Boston: W. B. Clarke, 1903), 246-47.

18. Mandell, *Sport*, 112-13; Henrichs, "Sport and Social Hierarchy," 24-29; Morgan, *Puritan Dilemma*, 8-12.

19. Vaughan, *New England Frontier*, 108-109, discusses the lack of success New Englanders had at hunting. See Carroll, *Puritans and the Wilderness*, 192-93; and Ellen Larned, *History of Windham County, Connecticut*, 2 vols. (Chester, Ct.: The Pequot Press, 1976), vol. 1, 361-62 for accounts of hunting for pests and the bounties paid for them. For examples of people going out of their way to kill snakes, see Vernon, "The Diary of Thomas Vernon," 72, and William Gregory, "A Scotchman's Journey in New England in 1771," ed. Mary G. Powell, *New England Magazine*, 12 (1895), 351. Frances M. Caulkins, *A History of Norwich, Connecticut* (Hartford: Case, Lockwood, 1866), 299.

20. For discussions of accidents, see Lawrence Hammond, "Diary of Lawrence Hammond," *Massachusetts Historical Society Proceedings*, 2nd series, 7 (1891-1892), 147; and John Ballantine, "Diary," in John Hoyt Lockwood, *Westfield and Its Historical Influences, 1669-1919* (Westfield, Mass.: privately printed, 1922), 391, 399. John Winthrop spent one night lost in the woods; he recited psalms to himself. See Morgan, *The Puritan Dilemma*, 65, for the dangers of being lost. Caulkins, *History of Norwich*, 299; Larned, *Windham County*, vol. 1, 361-62; and Bailyn, *New England Merchants*, 54-55, 60, discuss the disappearance of game. The ubiquity of fishing and hunting among all types of New Englanders is discussed by William Weeden, *Economic and Social History of New England, 1620-1789*, 2 vols. (originally published, 1890; reprinted New York: Hillary House, 1963), vol. 1, 104-106, 125-39.

21. Mandell, *Sport*, 132-33; Guttman, *From Ritual to Record*, 58-60; Brailsford, "Religion and Sport," 141-43; Wiles, "Crowd-Pleasing Spectacles," 93-94.

22. See T. H. Breen, "Horses and Gentlemen: The Cultural Significance of Gambling Among the Gentry of Virginia," *WMQ*, 34 (1977), 239-56; Rhys Isaac, *The Transformation of Virginia, 1740-1790* (Chapel Hill, N.C.: University of North Carolina Press, 1982), 98-104; and Richard Waterhouse, "Popular Culture and Pastimes: The Transfer of Traditions" (ms. provided by Professor Waterhouse, University of Sydney), 1-15. For an interesting analysis of the transfer of English sport to New England and the South, see Nancy Struna, "The Cultural Significance of Sport in the Colonial Chesapeake and Massachusetts" (Ph.D. diss., University of Maryland, 1979), chapter 3 and passim.

23. Struna, "Puritans and Sport," 5-7; Struna, "The Cultural Significance of Sport," 168-70; Douglas Good, "Colonials at Play: Leisure in Newport, 1723," *RIH*, 33 (1974), 16-18; Christian McBurney, "The South Kingstown Planters: Country Gentry in Colonial Rhode Island," *RIH*, 45 (1986), 81-93; John M. Findlay, *People of Chance: Gambling in American Society from Jamestown to Las Vegas* (New York: Oxford University Press, 1986), 34; Bronson, *History of Waterbury*, 259; James Barriskill, "The Newburyport Theatre in the Eighteenth Century," *Essex Institute Historical Collections*, 91 (1955), 221-224.

24. Struna, "Puritans and Sport," 15-16; Struna, "The Cultural Significance of Sport," 165-68; Fitch, "Diary," 47; Bonnie S. Ledbetter, "Sports and Games of the American Revolution," *JSH*, 6 (1979), 29-35; Jonathan Scott Ware, "Students Versus the Puritan College: A Study of Conflict Between the Students and Authorities of Yale College, 1701-1795," *CHSB*, 40 (1975), 59.

25. Ledbetter, "Sports and Games," 35-36; Davis, "Sport and Exercise," 27-28; Good, "Colonials at Play," 16.

26. Roberta J. Park, "The Rise and Development of Women's Concern for the Physical Education of American Women, 1776-1885," in Reet Howell, ed., *Her Story in Sport: A Historical Anthology of Women in Sports* (West Point, N.Y.: Leisure Press, 1982), 44-47; Howell, "Recreational Activities of Women in Colonial America," in Howell, ed., *Her Story in Sport*, 40-42.

27. Carl Bridenbaugh, "Baths and Watering Places of Colonial America," *WMQ*, 3 (1946), 152-57; and Donald Yacovone, "A New England Bath: The Nation's First Resort at Stafford Springs," *CHSB*, 41 (1976), 2-4.

28. Bridenbaugh, "Baths and Watering Places," 154-58; and Yacovone, "A New England Bath," 4-10.

29. Massachusetts' gaming Laws are summarized in Edwin Powers, *Crime and Punishment in Early Massachusetts, 1620-1692: A Documentary History* (Boston: Beacon Press, 1966), 63-170; Plymouth's are summarized in George D. Langdon, Jr., *Pilgrim Colony: A History of New Plymouth, 1620-1691* (New Haven: Yale University Press, 1966), 207-209. J. Hammond Trumbull and Charles Hoadley, eds., *The Public Records of the Colony of Connecticut*, 15 vols. (Hartford: Case, Lockwood and Brainard, 1850-1890), vol. 1, 289, vol. 3, 202-203; Charles Hoadley, ed., *Records of the Colony and Jurisdiction of New Haven*, 2 vols. (New Haven: Case Tiffany, 1857; Case, Lockwood, 1858), vol. 2, 155; and Joseph Bartlett, ed., *Rhode Island Colonial Records*, 10 vols. (Providence: State of Rhode Island, 1856-1865), vol. 1, 185.

30. Powers, *Crime and Punishment*, 404-409.

31. Roger Tilley, *A History of Playing Cards* (New York: Clarkson N. Potter, 1973), 7-12, 22-23, 63, 73; Cyril Hartman, introduction to Charles Cotton, *The Complete Gamester or Instructions How To Play at Billiards, Trucks, Bowls, and Chess. Together with All Manner of Useful and Most Gentile Games Either on Cards or Dice* (originally published London: R. Cutler, 1674; reprinted London: George Routledge and Sons, 1930), xiii, xiv.

32. Hartman, "Introduction," ii-xvi; Tilley, *History of Playing Cards*, 63-73; Theophilus Lucas, *Memoirs of the Lives, Intrigues and Comical Adventures of the Most Famous Gamesters and Celebrated Sharpers in the Reigns of Charles II, James II, William II, and Queen Anne* (originally published London: John Brown, 1714; reprinted London: George Routledge and Sons, 1930), 18-27, passim; Henry Bohn, *Bohn's New Handbook of Games Enlarged and Improved by the Introductions of Several Games Almost Exclusively Known in the United States* (Philadelphia: Henry F. Anners, 1850), 2-3.

33. Cotton Mather, *Winter Meditations, Directions How to Employ the Leisure of the Winter for the Glory of God . . .* (Boston: Benjamin Harris, 1693); 10-11; Struna, "Puritans and Sport," 12-13; Catherine Hargrave, *A History of Playing Cards* (Boston and New York: Houghton Mifflin, 1930), 280-81; Findlay, *People of Chance*, 21.

34. See Roy Akagi, *The Town Proprietors of the New England Colonies* (Philadelphia: University of Pennsylvania Press, 1924), 107.

35. Anonymous, *A Letter to a Gentleman on the Sin and Danger of Playing Cards* (Boston: D. Fowler and Z. Fowle, 1755), 2.

36.  Hargrave, *History of Playing Cards*, 280-83; Findlay, *People of Chance*, 21-22.

37.  Bohn, *Bohn's New Handbook*, 2-4, 146-48; Edmund Hoyle, *Hoyle's Games* (London: Wynne and Scoley, 1804), 1-72.

38.  Hargrave, *History of Playing Cards*, 280-283; *Bohn's New Handbook*, 2-3, 146; Tilley, *History of Playing Cards*, 136; E. S. Taylor, *The History of Playing Cards* (Rutland, Vt.: Charles E. Tuttle, 1973), 506-507.

39.  Cotton, *The Complete Gamester*, 47-51; Bohn, *Bohn's New Handbook*, 225-44; and Hoyle, *Hoyle's Games*, 73-75. A group of Loyalists placed under house arrest in a small Rhode Island town played quadrille incessantly, to the amazement of their jailers. See Thomas Vernon, "The Diary of Thomas Vernon: A Loyalist," *Rhode Island Historical Tracts*, 3 (Providence: Providence Press, Co., 1881), 28-30.

40.  Hoyle, *Hoyle's Games*, 155; Hartman, *The Complete Gamester*, xiii; Taylor, *History of Playing Cards*, 506-507. Rhode Island actually repealed sections of the anti-gaming laws. See Bartlett, *R.I. Col. Recs.* (1753), 378.

41.  Tilley, *History of Playing Cards*, 136-137; Bohn, *Bohn's New Handbook*, 199-207; Cotton, *The Complete Gamester*, 68; Hoyle, *Hoyle's Games*, 106-129.

42.  Tilley, *History of Cards*, 137; Hoyle, *Hoyle's Games*, 106-129.

43.  Findlay, *People of Chance*, 21; Cotton, *The Complete Gamester*, 80-82; Myron Wehtje, "The Ideal of Virtue in Post-Revolutionary Boston," *Historical Journal of Massachusetts*, 17 (1989), 75-76. Dr. Robert Honeyman, a Scottish physician, visited New England in 1775 and played backgammon almost everywhere he went. It was obviously a passion of his. See Philip Padelford, ed., *Colonial Panorama, 1775: Dr. Robert Honeyman's Journal for March and April* (San Marino, Cal.: The Huntington Library, 1939), 46-59. Good, "Colonials at Play," 1, 7 describes huzzlecap.

44.  Ames quoted in John Exell, "The Lottery in Colonial America," *WMQ*, 5 (1948), 188. Mather, *Winter Meditations*, 10-11.

45.  For Connecticut's auctions and lotteries of town lands, see Charles Grant, *Democracy in the Connecticut Frontier Town of Kent* (New York: Columbia University Press, 1961), 18-20. Exell, "The Lottery in Colonial America," 187-88, discusses contracts in Massachusetts and New Hampshire. For Connecticut, see Trumbull and Hoadley, eds., *Conn. Col. Recs.*, vol. 9, 50, 279, 411, 468, 530, 624, and passim. For Rhode Island, see Bartlett, ed., *R.I. Col. Recs.*, vol. 6, 302, 316, 618, and passim.

46.  The great land lottery is described in William Welsh, "The Massachusetts Land Lottery of 1786-1787," *Historical Journal of Massachusetts*, 14 (1986), 104-109, 113.

---

## Chapter X

1.  Blake is quoted in Bernard Mergen, "Toys and American Culture: Objects as Hypotheses," *Journal of American Culture*," 3 (1980), 743. For an insightful general discussion of Puritan childhood see Emory Elliott, *Power and the Pulpit in Puritan New England* (Princeton, N.J.: Princeton University Press, 1975), 78-81. For a discussion of old age see John Demos, *Past, Present, and Personal: The Family and the Life Course in American History* (New

York and Oxford: Oxford University Press, 1986), 145-46; and David Hackett Fischer, *Growing Old in America* (New York: Oxford University Press, 1977), chapter 1.

2. Mergen, "Toys and American Culture," 746-50.
3. John Locke, "Some Thoughts Concerning Education" (originally published 1690), in Philip Greven, Jr., ed., *Child-Rearing Concepts, 1628-1681* (Itasca, Ill.: F. E. Peacock, 1973), 17-22; John Robinson, "Of Children and Their Education" (originally published 1628), in Greven, ed., *Child-Rearing Concepts*, 13-17.
4. Philip Greven, *The Protestant Temperament: Patterns of Child-rearing, Religious Experience, and the Self in Early America* (New York: Knopf, 1977), 21-32, discusses the relative roles of mothers and fathers in child-rearing. Cotton Mather, "Some Special Points Relating to the Education of My Children" (originally published: 1706), in Greven, ed., *Child-Rearing Concepts*, 41-43.
5. Greven, *Protestant Temperament*, 268-69. Cotton and Wadsworth are discussed in Edmund S. Morgan, *The Puritan Family: Religion and Domestic Relations in Seventeenth-Century New England* (Harper and Row, 1966), 66-67, 77.
6. Greven, *Protestant Temperament*, 269-74.
7. *New England Primer* (Boston: James Loring Co., 1820 ed.), 1-5. See Laurel Thatcher Ulrich, "It 'Went Away She Knew Not How': Food Theft and Domestic Conflict in Seventeenth-Century Essex County," in Peter Benes, ed., *Foodways in the Northeast* (Boston: Boston University American and New England Studies Program, 1984), 103-104.
8. Judge Sherman Adams and Henry Stiles, *The History of Wethersfield, Connecticut* (New York: The Grafton Press, 1904), 848 discusses eighteenth-century toys. See also Mergen, "Toys and American Culture," 743-51.
9. Demos, *Past, Present, and Personal*, 140-48; Morgan, *Puritan Family*, 66-68; and Oscar Handlin and Mary F. Handlin, *Facing Life: Youth and the Family in American History* (Boston and Toronto: Little, Brown, 1971), 26-53, passim, show the responsibilities thrust early upon children.
10. Ross Beales, "In Search of the Historical Child: Miniature Adulthood and Youth in Colonial New England," *A.Q.*, 27 (1975), 379-95 makes the best case for an adolescent culture. See also Roger Thompson, *Sex in Middlesex: Popular Mores in a Massachusetts County, 1649-1699* (Amherst, Mass.: University of Massachusetts Press, 1986), 88-89, 94-95, 155, passim; and Edmund S. Morgan, *The Puritan Dilemma: The Story of John Winthrop* (Boston: Little, Brown, 1958), 8-12. See Ebenezer Parkman, *The Diary of Ebenezer Parkman, 1703-1782*, ed. Francis G. Walett (Worcester, Mass.: American Antiquarian Society, 1974), 36-38, for the examples of references to youthful indiscretions.
11. Demos, *Past, Present, and Personal*, 143.
12. Ibid., 143-60; Fischer, *Growing Old in America*, 58-76; and Benjamin Colman, *The Government and Improvement of Mirth, According to the Laws of Christianity, in Three Sermons* (Boston: B. Green, 1707), 3. Cotton Mather, *Addresses To Old Men and Young Men and Little Children* (Boston: B. Green, 1690), and Mather, *Brief Essay*, are both quoted in Demos, *Past, Present, and Personal*, 157-60.

13. Philip Greven, Jr. *Four Generations: Population, Land, and Family in Colonial Andover, Massachusetts* (Ithaca, N.Y.: Cornell University Press, 1970), 270-76, passim, shows the power the elderly wielded through their control of land. For the political respect tendered the elderly throughout the colonial period, see Bruce C. Daniels, "Patrician Leadership and the American Revolution," chapter 6 in Daniels, *The Fragmentation of New England: Comparative Perspectives on Economic, Political, and Social Divisions in the Eighteenth Century* (Westport, Ct.: Greenwood Press, 1988), 95-114. For a general discussion of old age, see Fischer, *Growing Old in America*, chapter 1.

14. Bradstreet quoted in Demos, *Past, Present, and Personal*, 156-57, 178-79. See also Perry Miller, ed., *The American Puritans: Their Prose and Poetry* (Garden City, N.Y.: Doubleday, 1956), 265-82.

15. Mary Maples Dunn, "Saints and Sisters: Congregational and Quaker Women in the Early Colonial Period," *AQ*, 30 (1978), 584-601; and Laurel Thatcher Ulrich, "Vertuous Women Found: New England Ministerial Literature, 1668-1735," *AQ*, 28 (1976), 20-30.

16. Dunn, "Saints and Sisters," 584; Lyle Koehler, *A Search for Power: The 'Weaker Sex' in Seventeenth-Century New England* (Urbana, Ill., Chicago, London: University of Illinois Press, 1980), 21-23, 28-37; Roger Thompson, *Women in Stuart England and America* (London: Routledge and Kegan Paul, 1974), 30-40.

17. Mather is quoted in Richard Shiels, "The Feminization of American Congregationalism, 1730-1835," *AQ*, 33 (1981), 46-62. See also Barbara Welter, "The Feminization of American Religion, 1800-1860," in Mary Hartman and Lois Banner, eds., *Clio's Consciousness Raised* (New York: Harper and Row, 1973), 137-55; Nancy Cott, *The Bonds of Womanhood: 'Women's Sphere' in New England, 1780-1835* (New Haven: Yale University Press, 1977), 126-28; Ulrich, "Vertuous Women Found," 20-40; and Barbara E. Lacey, "The Bonds of Friendship: Sarah Osborn of Newport and the Reverend Joseph Fish of North Stonington, 1743-1779," *RIH*, 45 (1986), 134.

18. Koehler, *A Search for Power*, 56-59, describes Anne Hutchinson's relationship with her children. See Bradstreet's poetry and meditations in Miller, ed., *The American Puritans*, 270-81. Esther Burr, *Esther Burr's Journal*, ed. Jeremiah Rankin (Washington, D.C.: Woodward and Lothrop, 1903), 50-51.

19. Burr, *Esther Burr's Journal*, 53, 164; Lacey, "The Bonds of Friendship," 134.

20. These laws are quoted in Robert St. George, "Set Thine House in Order: The Domestication of the Yeomanry in Seventeenth-Century New England," in Jonathan L. Fairbanks, et al., *New England Begins: The Seventeenth Century*, 3 vols. (Boston: Museum of Fine Arts, 1982), vol. 2, 185; and in Alice Morse Earle, *Home Life in Colonial Days* (Boston: Houghton Mifflin, 1895), 282-83. J. Hammond Trumbull and Charles Hoadley, eds., *The Public Records of the Colony of Connecticut*, 15 vols. (Hartford: Case, Lockwood, 1850-1890), vol. 1, 64.

21. John Demos, *A Little Commonwealth: Family Life in Plymouth Colony* (New York: Oxford University Press, 1970), 52-55.

22. St. George, "Set Thine House in Order," 186; and Earle, *Home Life*, 283. Mary Downing to Emanuel Downing, *Collections of the Massachusetts Historical Society*, 1,

5th series (Boston: Massachusetts Historical Society, 1871), 81-82. Seven letters from Mary Dudley to Margaret Winthrop, *Collections of the Massachusetts Historical Society*, 1, 5th series, 69-72.

23. See "Portraits of Governors," *Rhode Island Historical Society Tracts*, 3 (Providence: Providence Press Club, 1882), 166-68. Cotton Mather, *Ornaments For the Daughters of Zion* (Cambridge, Mass.: B. Green, 1692), 70.

24. *Hoop Petticoats, Arraigned and Condemned By the Light of Nature and Laws of God* (Boston: James Franklin, 1722), 1-7. James Franklin, "Treatise on Dyeing and Coloring," *Colonial Society of Massachusetts Publications*, 10 (Boston: Colonial Society of Massachusetts, 1904-1906), 224-25.

25. Elizabeth Schenck, *The History of Fairfield, Fairfield County, Connecticut*, 2 vols. (New York: privately printed by the author, 1889, 1905), vol. 2, 393; Frances Caulkins, *A History of Norwich, Connecticut* (Hartford: Case, Lockwood, 1866), 335-36; William Deloss Love, *The Colonial History of Hartford* (originally published 1914: reprinted, Chester, Ct.: Pequot Press, 1974), 245-46; Roland Osterweiss, *Three Centuries of New Haven, 1635-1938* (New Haven: Yale University Press, 1953), 163; William B. Weeden, *Economic and Social History of New England, 1620-1789*, 2 vols. (originally published 1890: reprinted, New York: Hillary House, 1963), vol. 2, 695. Anna Green Winslow, *Diary of Anna Green Winslow, A Boston School Girl of 1771*, ed. Alice Morse Earle (Boston and New York: Houghton Mifflin, 1894), 102-103, shows the ubiquity of fashion concerns among young girls.

26. Myron Wehtje, "The Ideal of Virtue in Post-Revolutionary Boston," *Historical Journal of Massachusetts*, 17 (1989), 72-75.

27. Peter Bohan and Philip Hammerslough, *Early Connecticut Silver, 1700-1840* (Middletown, Ct.: Wesleyan University Press, 1970), 219-59.

28. Hety Shepard, "A Puritan Maiden's Diary," *New England Magazine*, ed. Adeline Slicer, 11 (1894-1895), 21; Laurel Thatcher Ulrich, "Psalm-tunes, Periwigs, and Bastards: Ministerial Authority in Early Eighteenth-Century Durham," *Historical New Hampshire*, 36 (1981), 264; Nicholas Noyes, "An Essay Against Periwigs," in John Demos, ed., *Remarkable Providences* (New York: George Braziller, 1972), 213-20; John Fiske, *The Notebooks of the Reverend John Fiske, 1644-1675*, ed. Robert Pope (Boston: Colonial Society of Massachusetts, 1974), 134-35; and Edward Holyoke, *The Holyoke Diaries*, ed. George Dow (Salem, Mass.: The Essex Institute, 1911), 2-4.

29. Ulrich, "Psalm-Tunes, Periwigs, and Ministerial Authority," 264-66.

30. John Ballantine, "The Diary of John Ballantine," in John Hoyt Lockwood, *Westfield and Its Historic Influences, 1669-1919* (Westfield, Mass.: privately printed by the author, 1922), 399.

31. See Brian Berry and William Garrison, "The Functional Bases of the Central Place Hierarchy," *Economic Geography*, 34 (1958), 149-54. The number of towns and their size and legal status can be found in most atlases or compendia of colonial population. For a convenient guide to towns, see Evarts B. Greene and Virginia Harrington, *American Population Before the Federal Census of 1790* (New York: Columbia University Press, 1922).

32. These paragraphs are summaries of work I have published elsewhere: Bruce Daniels, *The Connecticut Town: Growth and Development, 1635-1790* (Middletown, Ct.: Wesleyan University Press, 1979, especially chapters 2 and 6; *Dissent and Conformity on Narragansett Bay: The Colonial Rhode Island Town* (Middletown, Ct.: Wesleyan University Press, 1983), especially chapter 3; and "The Colonial Background of New England's Secondary Urban Centers," *Historical Journal of Massachusetts*, 14 (1986), 11-24.

33. Carl Bridenbaugh, *Cities in the Wilderness: The First Century of Urban Life in America, 1625-1742* (London, Oxford, and New York: Oxford University Press, 1938), 55-72, passim. Winthrop is quoted in Darrett B. Rutman, *Winthrop's Boston: A Portrait of a Puritan Town, 1630-1649* (Chapel Hill, N.C.: University of North Carolina Press, 1965), 242-43. Shepard, "A Puritan Maiden's Diary," 24. The joke is recorded in Lawrence Hammond, "Diary of Lawrence Hammond," *Massachusetts Historical Society Proceedings*, 2nd series, 7 (1891-1892), 147.

34. Dr. Alexander Hamilton, *Gentleman's Progress: The Itinerarium of Dr. Alexander Hamilton, 1744*, ed. Carl Bridenbaugh (Westport, Ct.: Greenwood Press, 1973), 135.

35. Providence Town Council Records (Oct. 1775), unpaginated, Providence City Hall. Jacob Bailey, "Diary of Jacob Bailey," in *The Frontier Missionary*, ed., William S. Bartlet, 2 vols. (Boston: Ide and Dutton, 1853), vol. 2, 17. Solomon Drowne, "Dr. Solomon Drowne's Journal," *Newport Historical Magazine*, 1 (1880-81), 68. Thomas Vernon, "The Diary of Thomas Vernon: A Loyalist," *Rhode Island Historical Tracts*, 3 (1881), 6-11, 15, 37.

36. Elizabeth Adams Rhoades, "The Furnishings of Portsmouth Houses, 1750-1775," *Historical New Hampshire*, 28 (1973), 1-18; Schenck, *Fairfield*, vol. 1, 144-45; Caulkins, *Norwich*, 325.

37. Virginia Bernhard, "Cotton Mather and the Doing of Good: A Puritan Gospel of Wealth," *NEQ,* 49 (1976), 229-35; and Christine Leigh Heyrman, "The Fashion Among More Superior People: Charity and Social Change in Provincial New England, 1700-1790," *AQ,* 34 (1982), 109-123.

38. Jacob Hugo Tatsch, *Freemasonry in the Thirteen Colonies* (New York: Macoy, 1929), 28-29, 38, 168-70, 172-74, 176-77, 192-95.

39. Hamilton, *Gentleman's Progress*, 133, 137, 144.

40. "Rules and Orders of the Fellowship Club," *Newport Historical Magazine*, 4 (1984), 163-78.

41. John Rowe, *Letters and Diary of John Rowe, Boston Merchant*, ed. Anne Rowe Cunningham (Boston: W. B. Clarke, 1903), 16-17, 35, 68-71. Wehtje, "The Ideal of Virtue," 76-77; and Charles Warren, "Samuel Adams and the Sans Souci Club in 1785," *Massachusetts Historical Society Proceedings*, 60 (1927), 318-20.

42. Hamilton, *Gentleman's Progress*, 151; Lacey, "The Bonds of Friendship," 131-32; David King, "A Club Formed by the Jews, 1761," *Newport Historical Magazine*, 4 (1884), 58-60.

43. Louis Kuslan, "Science, Technology, and Medicine in Eighteenth-Century Connecticut," *Connecticut Review*, 9 (1975), 36; Albert E. Van Dusen, *Connecticut* (New

York: Random House, 1961), 23; Charles Warren, *Jacobin and Junto: Or Early American Politics as Viewed in the Diary of Dr. Nathaniel Ames* (Cambridge, Mass.: Harvard University Press, 1931), 29.

44. Richard D. Brown, "The Emergence of Urban Society in Rural Massachusetts, 1760-1820," *Journal of American History*, 62 (1974), 33-59; Brown, *Knowledge Is Power: The Diffusion of Information in Early America, 1700-1865* (New York and Oxford: Oxford University Press, 1989), 120; Anne Farnum, "A Society of Societies: Associations and Voluntarism in Early Nineteenth-Century Salem," *Essex Institute Historical Collections*, 113 (1977), 181-82.

44. Farnum, "A Society of Societies," 181-90; Brown, "The Emergence of Urban Society," 35-42.

45. John Winthrop, *Winthrop's Journal: "History of New England, 1630-1649,"* ed. James Hosmer, 2 vols. (New York: Barnes and Noble, 1908), vol. 2, 84-85; Edward Taylor, *Diary*, ed, Francis Murphy (Springfield, Mass.: Connecticut Valley Historical Museum, 1964), 37.

46. Edmund S. Morgan, *The Gentle Puritan: A Life of Ezra Stiles, 1727-1795* (New Haven, Ct.: Yale University Press, 1965), 359; Louis L. Tucker, *Puritan Protagonist: President Thomas Clapp of Yale College* (Chapel Hill, N.C.: University of North Carolina Press, 1962), 18; Daniels, *The Fragmentation of New England*, 115-37; Sheldon Cohen, "The Turkish Tyranny," *NEQ*, 47 (1974), 564; Jonathan Scott Ware, "Students Versus the Puritan College: A Study of Conflict Between the Students and Authorities of Yale College, 1701-1795," *Connecticut Historical Society Bulletin*, 40 (1975), 48-52; Warren, *Diary of Ames*, 115-16; Taylor, *Diary*, 37; Ballantine, *Diary*, 414.

47. Cohen, "Turkish Tyranny," 565-68; Ware, "Students Versus the Puritan College," 50-52, 54; Theodore Chase, "Harvard Student Disorders in 1770," *NEQ*, 61 (1988), 28-29.

48. Ware, "Students Versus the College," 54.

49. Brown, *Knowledge Is Power*, 298; Daniels, *The Fragmentation of New England*, 116-35.

50. Mather and Bradford are quoted in Perry Miller, *The New England Mind: From Colony to Province* (Cambridge, Mass.: Harvard University Press, 1953), 330-31. Much of this paragraph is based on Daniel Vickers, "Work and Life on the Fishing Periphery of Essex County, Massachusetts, 1630-1675," in David D. Hall and David Grayson Allen, eds., *Seventeenth-Century New England: A Conference Held by The Colonial Society of Massachusetts* (Boston: The Colonial Society of Massachusetts, 1984), 83-87. See the two types of behavior in Benjamin Bangs, "Diary," in *History and Genealogy of the Bangs Family in America*, compiled by Dean Dudley (Montrose, Mass.: privately printed by the compiler, 1896), 4-6.

51. Brown, *Knowledge Is Power*, 104-105, 115. See, for example, Parkman, *Diary*, passim; Ballantine, *Diary*, passim; and Walter Powell, "The Daily Transactions of a Westfield Pastor, 1726-1740," *Historical Journal of Massachusetts*, 14 (1986), 146-54.

52. Brown, *Knowledge Is Power*, 136-37. Ebenezer Pemberton, *Advice to a Son: A Sermon Preached at the Request of a Gentleman in New England, Upon His Son's Going to Europe* (Boston: B. Green, 1705), 21.

53. Isaac Norris, "Journey to Rhode Island," *Pennsylvania Magazine of History and Biography*, 85 (1961), 414-15; Bailey, *Diary*, 15-20; Sarah Kemble Knight, *The Journal of Madame Knight*, ed. Malcolm Frieberg (Boston: David R. Godine, 1972), Boston: 24-26; and Parkman, *Diary*, 2-3. For the problems encountered, see Thomas Minor, *The Diary of Thomas Minor, Stonington, Connecticut* (New London, Ct.: Press of the Day, 1899), 20-27.

---

## Chapter XI

1. Winthrop's address is reprinted in Roy Harvey Pearce, ed., *Colonial American Writing* (New York: Holt, Rinehart, and Winston, 1963), 50-51.
2. See T. H. Breen and Stephen Foster, "The Puritans' Greatest Achievement: A Study of Social Cohesion in Seventeenth-Century Massachusetts," *Journal of American History*, 60 (1973), 5-7, and David D. Hall, *Worlds of Wonder, Days of Judgment: Popular Religious Belief in Early New England* (Cambridge, Mass.: Harvard University Press, 1990), 3-11.
3. Bradford quoted in Hall, *Worlds of Wonder*, 239.
4. The historical and sociological literature that supports this analysis of play as alternative ritual is vast. See, among others, Roger D. Abrahams, "Play in the Face of Death: Transgression and Inversion in a West Indian Wake," in *The Many Faces of Play*, Kendall Blanchard, ed. (Champaign, Ill.: Human Kinetics Publishers, 1986); Norman Denzin, "The Paradoxes of Play," in *The Paradoxes of Play*, John Loy, ed. (West Point, N.Y.: Leisure Press, 1982), 14-15; Johan Huizinga, *Homo Ludens: A Study of the Play Element in Culture* (Boston: Beacon Press, 1955), 12-15, 25; Lynn Hunt, ed., *The New Cultural History*, (Berkeley, Los Angeles, and London: University of California Press, 1989), 12-13; and Aletta Biersack, "Local Knowledge, Local History: Geertz and Beyond," in *The New Cultural History*, Hunt, ed. 72-75.
5. Control of the metaphors in society is essential to sustain a religious or cultural mentalité. See Roger Chartier, *Cultural History: Between Practices and Representations* (Ithaca, N.Y., and London: Cornell University Press, 1988), 97; Victor Turner, *Drama, Fields and Metaphors: Symbolic Action in Human Society* (Ithaca, N.Y., and London: Cornell University Press), 25-27; Ann Marie Guilmette, "Play as Metacommunicative Frames of Action," in *The Paradoxes of Play*, Loy, ed., 10-11; and Helen B. Schwartzman, "Play and Metaphor," in *The Paradoxes of Play*, Loy, ed. 26-27.
6. For play as a subversive force, see Abrahams, "Play in the Face of Death," 29-32; Denzin, "The Paradoxes of Play," 14; and Huizinga, *Homo Ludens*, 49-50.
7. Edmund Morgan, "The Puritan Ethic and the American Revolution," *WMQ*, 24 (1967), 3-43, discusses the general residue of Puritanism in the era of the Revolution.
8. John Gardiner, *The Speech of John Gardiner, Esq. Delivered in The House of Representatives on Thursday the 26th of January 1792 on the Subject of The Committee Appointed to Consider the Expediency of Repealing the Law Against Theatrical Exhibitions* (Boston: Joseph Bumstead Printer, 1792), vii, 6, 7.

# Index

Adams, Hugh, 199
Adams, James Truslow, 4
Adams, John, 23, 63-64, 113, 116, 122, 159, 220
Adams, Samuel, 23, 113, 122, 205, 220
alcohol,
consumption of, 5, 8, 142-43
fears of, 117
types of, 142-43, 154-55
almanacs, 44-46
ambivalence,
among historians, 5-11
tensions caused by, 15-20
within preaching, xii-xiii, 11-13
American Company, 68-70
Ames, Nathaniel, 70, 95, 137
Ames, William, 181
Anglicanism, 22, 30, 58, 63, 66, 79, 81-82, 85, 89, 112, 115, 118, 166, 168, 193, 215, 220
antinomianism, 12-13, 80
asceticism, 3-6, 9, 23, 195, 221
Ashley, Elihu, 119, 135
Australia, 173

Bailey, Jacob, 118-119
Ballantine, John, 55-56, 94, 118, 120, 153, 199
Baptists, 12, 22, 79, 81, 89, 186, 221

barn and house raisings, 94-95
"Bay Path," 145
The Bay Psalm Book, 52-54
Billings, William, 63-64
The Singing Master's Assistant, 64
Boas, Franz, 9
Boston,
booksellers of, 29, 121
clubs in, 204-206
fashions in, 196-97
influence of, 29, 90, 94, 112, 196-97, 203-204
taverns in, 143, 145-147
urbanity of, 6, 29, 81, 90, 94, 112-114, 116, 132, 173, 202
Boston Post Road, 145
Bradford, William, 20, 33-34, 89, 101, 126-27, 142, 167, 209, 217
Of Plymouth Plantation, 20, 126-27, 142
Bradstreet, Anne, 5, 12, 36, 192, 194
Brattle, Thomas, 59-60
bundling, 131-33
Burnaby, Andrew, 132
Burr, Esther Edwards, 137, 194
"The Butter Rebellion," 208

Calvin, John, 27, 52-53, 85
Cambridge, Mass., 28, 38, 143
Canary Islands, 155

Catholicism
    Puritan views of, 11, 33, 52-53,
        55, 77, 85, 87, 88-89, 104, 166,
        195, 215, 220-21
    theology of, 85, 88-89, 215-16
Charles I, king of England, 21, 166
Charles II, king of England, 172,
    177, 196
child-rearing,
    adolescence, 189-90
    affects on development, 14-16,
        186-89
    psychological views of, 13-14,
        187-90
    repressive attitudes of, 13,
        186-88
Clapp, Thomas, 208
Clark, John, 12
clubs (social), 152, 170, 203-207
Coles, Robert, 146, 148
Colman, Benjamin, *The Government
    and Improvement of Mirth,* 17-20,
    191
concerts, 61-63
Condy, Jeremy, 29
Connecticut,
    as different from other colonies,
        10, 22, 89, 91, 99, 118, 182,
        204
    holidays in, 79, 81, 84, 89, 91
    music and theater in, 63, 65, 70
    taverns in, 143, 150
    *see also names of individual cities
        and towns*
Cotton, Charles, *The Complete
    Gamester,* 178-79
Cotton, John, 14, 16, 17, 27, 53,
    110-125, 188
criminality, xii, 100-102, 126-30,
    146-51, 176-77, 209

Cromwell, Oliver, 109
courtship, 139-40
Coventry, Ct., 199

dance,
    opposition to, 109-115
    popularity of, 112-117
    schools of, 112-113
    types of, 113-115, 117
Danforth, Thomas, 208
Dedham, Mass., 118, 137
Diggers, 12
Dominion of New England, 118
Downing, Mary, 195
drunkenness, 141, 147-51, 157; *see
    also* criminality
Dudley, Mary, 196
Dudley, Thomas, 169
Dunbar, Asa, 208
Durham, N.H., 199

Edwards, Jonathan, 132-33, 135
Eliot, John, 28, 34
England,
    alcohol consumption in,
        142-43
    eighteenth-century society,
        148, 203, 210
    Elizabethan culture and
        literature, 27, 30, 66, 131
    literacy in, 14, 27-29, 48
    religious dissent in, 12-13, 89
    Restoration period of, 21,
        177, 184
    sports in, 163-66, 169-70,
        172-73, 175
    theater in, 66-68

Farmington, Ct., 146
fashions in dress, 194-99

fishing,
    commercial, 168, 170, 209-210
    sport, 169-70, 183
Fiske, John, 148
food,
    class structure of, 121-22
    enjoyment of, 120-21
    types of, 121-23
France,
    French cultural influences, 98,
        100, 113, 115, 177, 197
    Puritan views of, 86, 98
Franklin, Benjamin, 174
Franklin, James, 31, 42-43,
    196-97
funerals, 85-88

gambling,
    cardplaying, 177-81
    lotteries, 181-83
    in taverns, 176-77
Gardiner, John, 71, 220
Geertz, Clifford, xiii
*Geneva Bible*, 30, 52-53
geography, affect on social struc-
    ture, 10, 20, 29, 216-17
Glocester, R.I., 99
Gloucester, Mass., 209
Goddard family, 116
Gorton, Samuel, 12
Granger, Thomas, 126
Graves, Thomas, 208
Greenfield, Mass., 119
Gregory, William, 135-37, 156-58
Greven, Philip, 188
Griffith, John, 113
Guy Fawkes Day, 103-105

Hadley, Mass., 123-24
Hallam, William, 68-69

Hamilton, Dr. Andrew, 134, 154,
    204-205
Hancock, John, 122
Hartford, Ct., 105, 112, 114, 143,
    146, 197
Harvard College, 28, 48, 70, 118,
    137, 169, 174, 199, 207-210
Hawthorne, Nathaniel, *The Scarlet
    Letter*, 4, 6, 195
Hogg, Thomas, 126
holidays,
    Christmas, 89-90
    days of thanks, 90-91
    Easter, 44
    fasts, 88-91
    St. Valentine's, 44
    theology of, 88
Holyoke, Edward, 44, 123, 198,
    208
Hooker, Thomas, 12
*Hoyle's* guide to cards, 179-80
Huizinga, Johan, xiii
humor, 32-33
Hutchinson, Anne, 11, 193-94
Hutchinson, Thomas, 122

Indians, 98-104, 150
Irving, Washington, *History of New
    York*, 131

Jamaica, 143, 157
James I, king of England, 21, 79, 166
Jeremiad, 21-24, 33
Johnson, Edward,
    *History of New England*, 37
    *New England Annoyances*, 38

King Philip's War, 91, 98
Knight, Sarah Kemble, 98, 129, 156,
    158, 194

Leeward Islands, 143
Levett, Richard, 110
literacy,
    commitment to, 28, 48-49
    compared to England and
        Europe, 27-29, 48
    reading aloud, 31
    reading parties, 31
    reading schools, 28
    women and, 47
literature,
    almanacs, 44-46
    ballads, 40
    bestsellers, 40
    captivity tales, 40-41
    children's stories, 46
    confessional tales, 42
    diaries, 32-35
    elegies, 35
    guidebooks, 34-35, 47
    histories, 34-35
    horror tales, 41
    novels, 46, 48
    poetry, 37-39
    satire, 42
    schoolbooks, 39-40
    sermons, 31
    spiritual autobiographies, 36
Locke, John, 187
Lockridge, Kenneth, 10
London, England, 151, 203, 210

Malinowski, Bronislaw, 9
marriage, 127-28, 138-40
Maryland, 134
Marblehead, Mass., 104, 145
Masons (Freemasons), 87-88, 204
Massachusetts,
    as different from other colonies,
        10, 22, 69-70, 99, 182, 204

elections in, 99-100
holidays in, 79, 80-81, 84, 89, 91
music and theater in, 63, 65,
    69-70
taverns in, 143, 150
see also names of individual cities
    and towns
Mather, Cotton, 21-22, 34, 56, 59,
    65, 87, 89, 118, 129-30, 149-50,
    169, 181, 187, 218, 221
    Brief Essay on the Glory of Aged
        Piety, 191
    Cloud of Witness Against Balls and
        Dances, 112-113
    Magnalia Christi Americana, 34
    The Pure Nazarite, 31, 130
    A Serious Address To Those Who
        Unnecessarily Frequent the
        Tavern, 149-50
Mather, Increase, 14, 17, 21-22, 27,
    37, 110-112, 218
    An Arrow Against Profane and
        Promiscuous Dancing, 110-112
    Wo to Drunkards, 149
Mather, Richard, 36, 169
Mayflower, 142
McCarthyism, 4
meetinghouses, 77-79, 93
Mencken, H. L., 3-4
militia training days, 97-99
Miller, Arthur, 4
Miller, Perry, The New England Mind
    in the Seventeenth Century, 5-8,
    11-12, 39
Milton, John, 109, 138
Moody, Joshua, 7
Morgan, Edmund, 8-9
Morgan, James, 101
Morison, Samuel Eliot, Builders of
    the Bay Colony, 5-6, 8-9

Music,
  Americanization of, 62-63
  in American Revolution, 64-65
  ballads, 65
  church reform, 53-56
  concerts, 61-63
  golden age of, 58-66
  instruments in, 56-58
  military and, 64-65
  organs, 59-60
  psalmody, 52-36
  publishers of, 65
  singing schools, 61-63
  songbooks, 66

Newburyport, Mass., 104, 113
*New England Courant,* 42-43, 55
*New England Primer,* 14, 28, 189
New Hampshire,
  as different from other colonies,
    22, 70, 99-100
  elections, 10, 99
  theater in, 10, 70
  *see also names of individual cities
    and towns*
*New Hampshire Gazette,* 122
New Haven, Ct., 75, 91, 112, 115,
  126, 135, 137, 143-44
New London, Ct., 101, 104, 169
Newport, R.I., 69, 79, 94, 101, 104,
  112, 123, 136-37, 151-54, 205-06,
  174, 203, 203-206
newspapers, 45-47, 122-23, 173
New York City, 3, 70, 145, 210,
  216, 221
Norwich, Ct., 112, 171, 197
Noyes, Nicholas, 11

Ocuish, Hannah, 101
old age, 190-92

*Onania,* 130
ordinations, 82-85
original sin, 7, 12, 125
Osborn, Sarah, 194, 206
Otis, James, 122

Parkman, Ebenezer, 84, 129, 153, 169
parties,
  berrying, 97
  cornhuskings, 95-96
  dinner, 120-22
  oysterbakes, 123
  quilting, sewing, spinning bees,
    96-97
  teas, 123-24
  turtle frolics, 122
  wedding receptions, 117-120
Peters, Samuel, 3, 132
Phelps, Elizabeth, 123
Philadelphia, 145
"plain style," 31-32
play,
  democracy of, 216-17
  theory of, xi-xiii
Playford, John, *The English Dance
  Master,* 113
Plymouth, Mass., 89, 91, 100, 104,
  126, 151, 167
Portsmouth, N.H., 113-14, 116
Portugal, 143, 155
Providence, R.I., 112, 114, 123, 136,
  202-203
Prynne, Hester, 4-6, 195
Prynne, William,
  *Histriomastix,* 67
  views of theater, 67-69
publishing, 28-29

Quakers, 12, 22, 79, 81, 89, 186,
  193, 221

Ranters, 12

Rhode Island,
as different from other colonies,
10, 13, 22-23, 36, 60, 69, 79,
99, 118, 132, 144, 150, 173,
177, 182, 216
elections in, 99
music and theater in, 69
Sabbath in, 79-80
taverns in, 150
*see also names of individual cities
and towns*

Rhode Island College (Brown
University), 209

Robinson, John, 14, 187-88

Rogers, Esther, 101

Rowe, John, 81-82, 87, 122, 124,
169-70, 205

Rowley, Mass., 118, 202

Rutman, Darrett, "The Mirror of
Puritan Authority," 9-10

Sabbatarianism, 68, 75-76, 78-80,
88, 167, 177

Sabbath houses, 78

Salem, Mass., 104, 110, 123, 143,
145, 158

Seekers, 12

sermons, xii, 80-82, 129-30

Sewall, Samuel, 118, 169

sexuality,
bundling, 131-33
Catholics and, 11-12
crimes of, 126-28, 138-40
discussions of, 13, 128, 137
enjoyment of, 8-9, 125,
133-40
fear of, 11, 125
flirting, 134-38, 140
kissing, 75, 128, 134, 137, 140
masturbation, 129-31
theater and, 68

Shepard, Hety, 198

Shepard, Thomas, 12, 14
"Theses Sabbaticae," 76

Sheriot, Henri, 110

Smith, Henry, 168

Smith, Polly, 120

smoking, 157-58, 207

social history, 9-10

Sons of Liberty, 105

South Carolina, 173

Spencer, George, 126

sport,
ball sports, 164-66, 174-75,
blood sports, 165-67
in England, 163-65, 169-70,
172-73, 175
fishing, 164, 166, 170-172
horse racing, 173-74
hunting, 164, 166-70, 172
swimming, 174-76

Stafford Spring, Ct., 175

Stamp Act, 105

Stiles, Ezra, 8, 205, 208

taverns,
alehouse culture, 151-58
control of, 141-45
eating in, 155-57
number of, 147
role of, 143-46, 158-59
sleeping in, 146
women in, 153-54, 156-58

theater,
English background to, 66-68
Puritan opposition to, 67-71

Thomas, Isaiah, 65

towns,
changes in, 23, 82

distinctions among, 49, 81-82, 94, 116, 200-203
government of, 100, 200-201
population of, 22
types of, 124, 200-201, 206-207
urban functions of, 23, 45, 82, 112-113, 116, 197, 203-204
travel, 210-211
Trumbull, John, *The Progress of Dullness,* 43-44
Tyler, Moses Coit, 3,4
typology, 33-34

Victorian culture, xii
Virginia, 3, 22, 69, 163, 216

Wadsworth, Benjamin, *The Well Ordered Family,* 188
Walter, Thomas, 54, 58-59
Walton, Izaak, *The Compleat Angler,* 171
Ward, Nathaniel, *The Simple Cobbler of Aggawan,* 36-38, 43, 48
wedding receptions, 117-120
Weld, Thomas, 12
Wendle, Thomas, *New England's First Fruits,* 37
Westfield, Mass., 118
Wethersfield, Ct., 119, 143, 168
Wheelwright, Benjamin, 12
whist, 179-81, 183
Wigglesworth, Michael, 75, 118, 128
*The Day of Doom,* 38-40
*God's Controversy with New England,* 39
Willard, Samuel, 7
William and Mary, king and queen of England, 177-78
Williams, Roger, 11-12, 218
Windsor, Ct., 119, 143

Winslow, Anna, 90-102, 116, 137
Winthrop, Fitz-John, 128
Winthrop, John, 8, 16-17, 20, 35, 86, 101, 120-21, 142, 146, 167, 195-96, 207, 215, 221
Winthrop, John, Jr., 196
Winthrop, Margaret, 86
Wolcott, Roger, 43, 129
women,
character of, 137-40, 175, 179
church membership, 193-94
as consumers, 194-98
as mothers, 194
theology of, 192-94
Worcester, Mass., 65

Yale College, 8, 48, 70, 174, 199, 205, 207-209